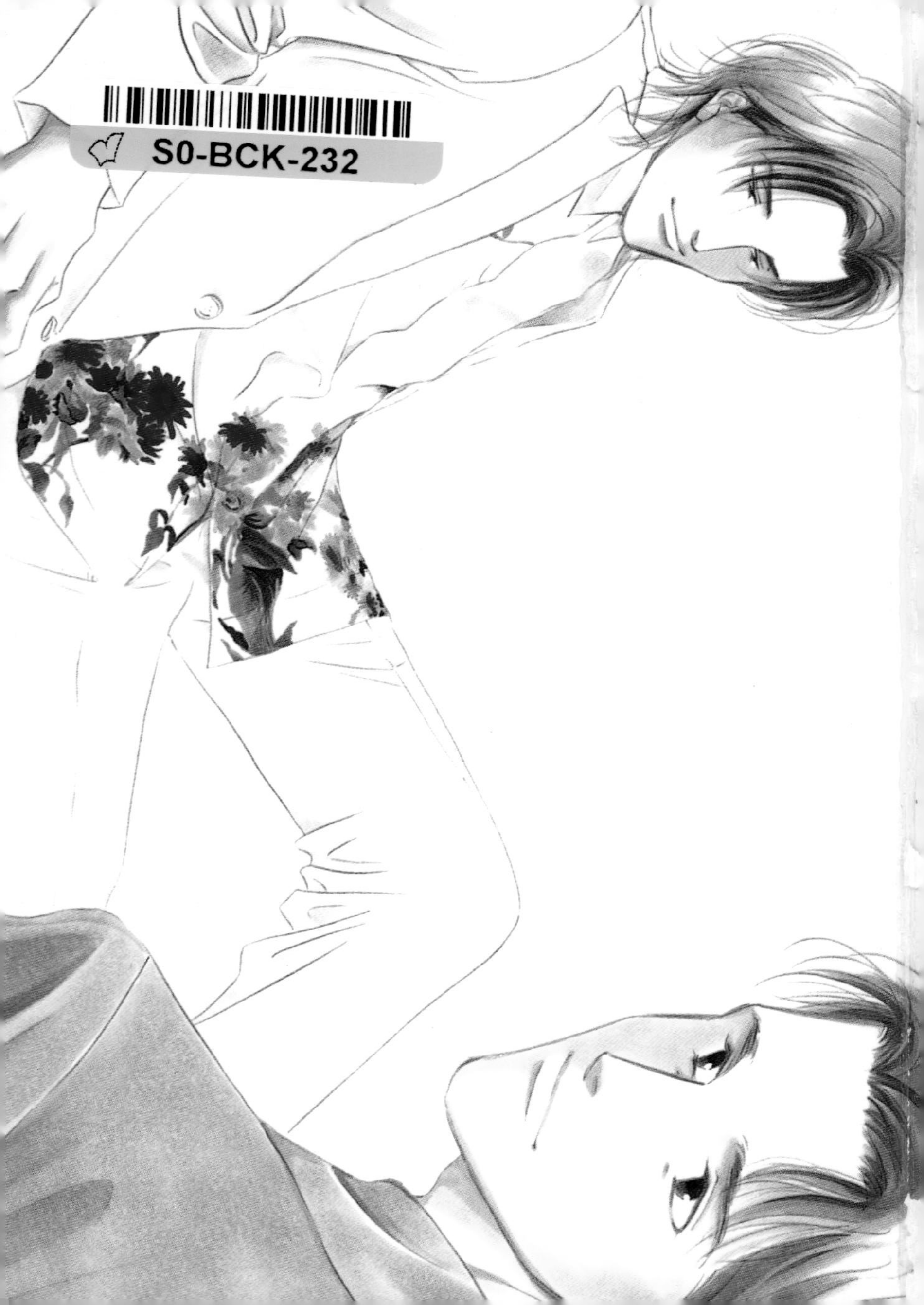

Ichigenme... 2
The First Class is Civil Law

Translation / Andrew Marshall
Editing / W. Johns
Lettering / Peter Wong
Graphic Design / W. Johns/Daryl Kuxhouse

801 Media, Inc.
www.801media.com
contact@801media.com

ISBN-10: 1-934129-02-X
ISBN-13: 978-1-934129-02-9
First edition printed July 2007

10 9 8 7 6 5 4 3 2 1

Printed in China

1限めはやる気の民法

ICHIGENME 2 ②

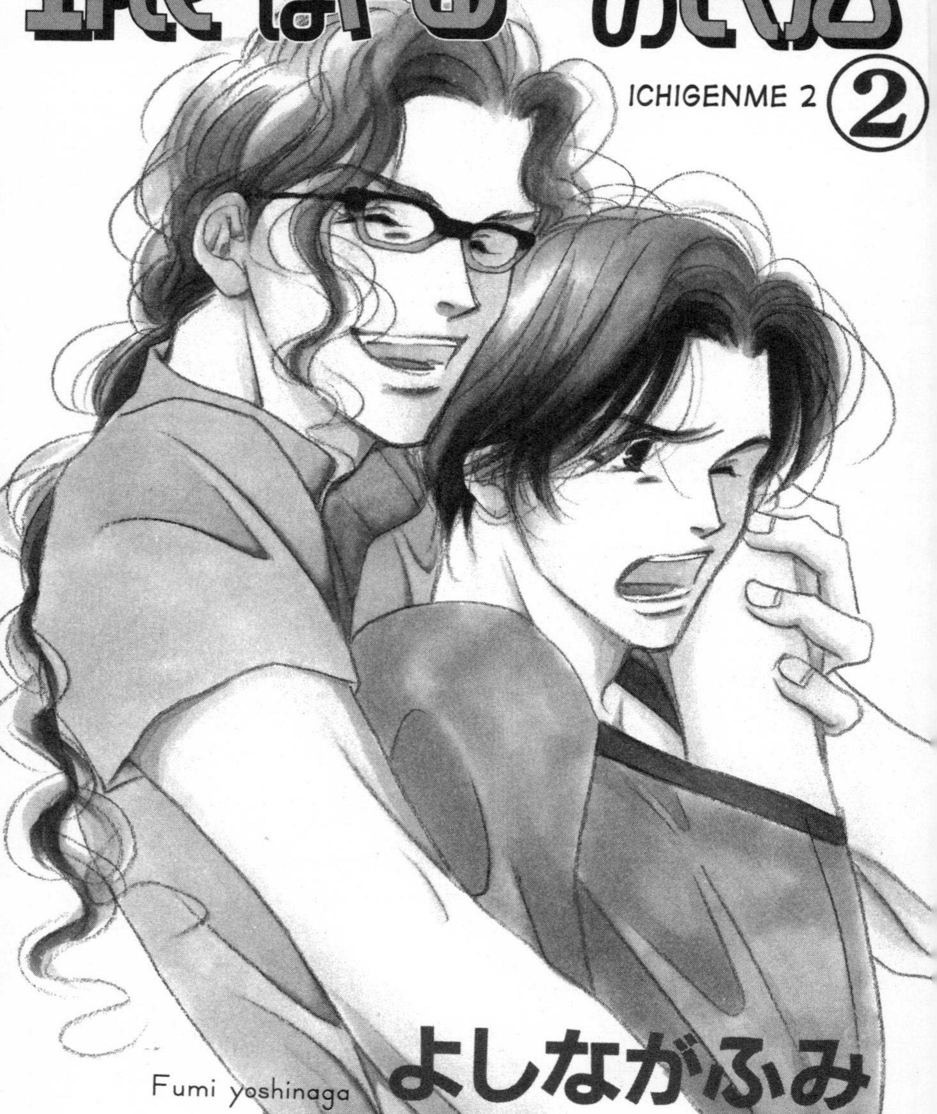

Fumi yoshinaga よしながふみ

ICHIGENME 2

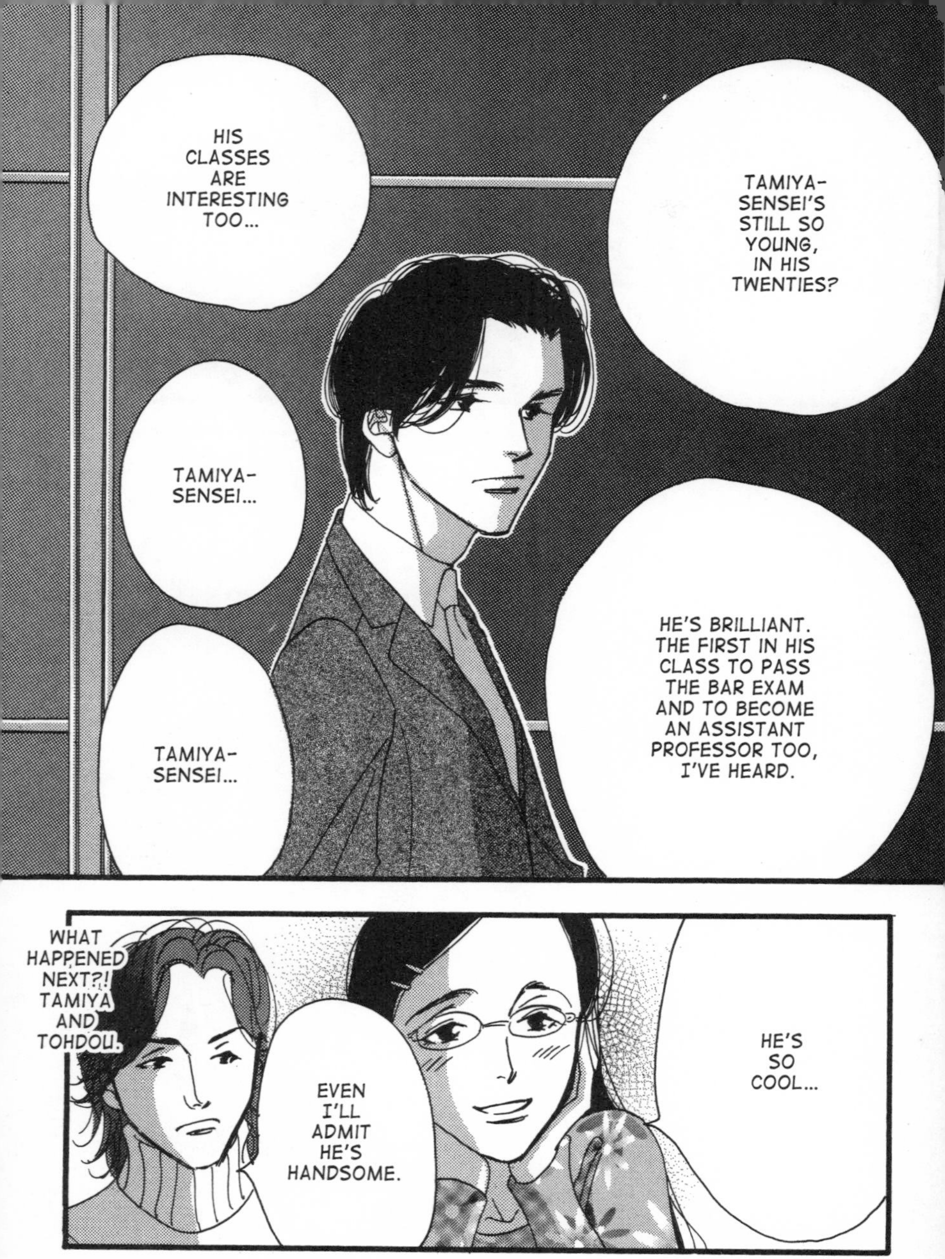
TAMIYA-SENSEI'S STILL SO YOUNG, IN HIS TWENTIES?
HIS CLASSES ARE INTERESTING TOO...
HE'S BRILLIANT. THE FIRST IN HIS CLASS TO PASS THE BAR EXAM AND TO BECOME AN ASSISTANT PROFESSOR TOO, I'VE HEARD.
TAMIYA-SENSEI...
TAMIYA-SENSEI...
HE'S SO COOL...
EVEN I'LL ADMIT HE'S HANDSOME.
WHAT HAPPENED NEXT?! TAMIYA AND TOHDOU.

HIS TESTS ARE SUPPOSED TO BE KILLERS THOUGH, SEMPAI, ARE YOU STILL TAKING IT?
WELL, THAT IS THE PROBLEM...

WHAT HAPPENED NEXT?! TAMIYA AND TOHDOU.

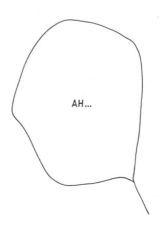

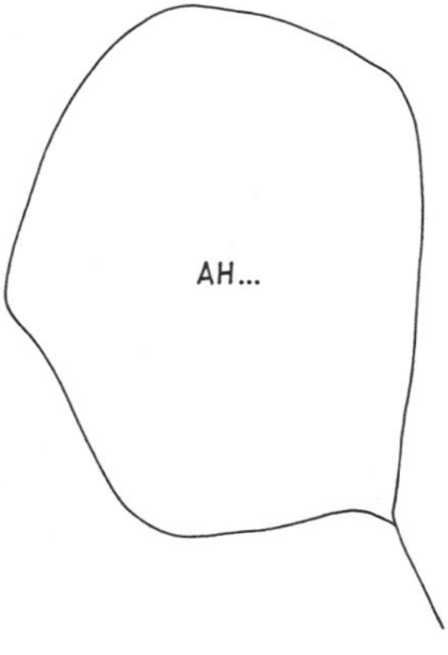

AH...

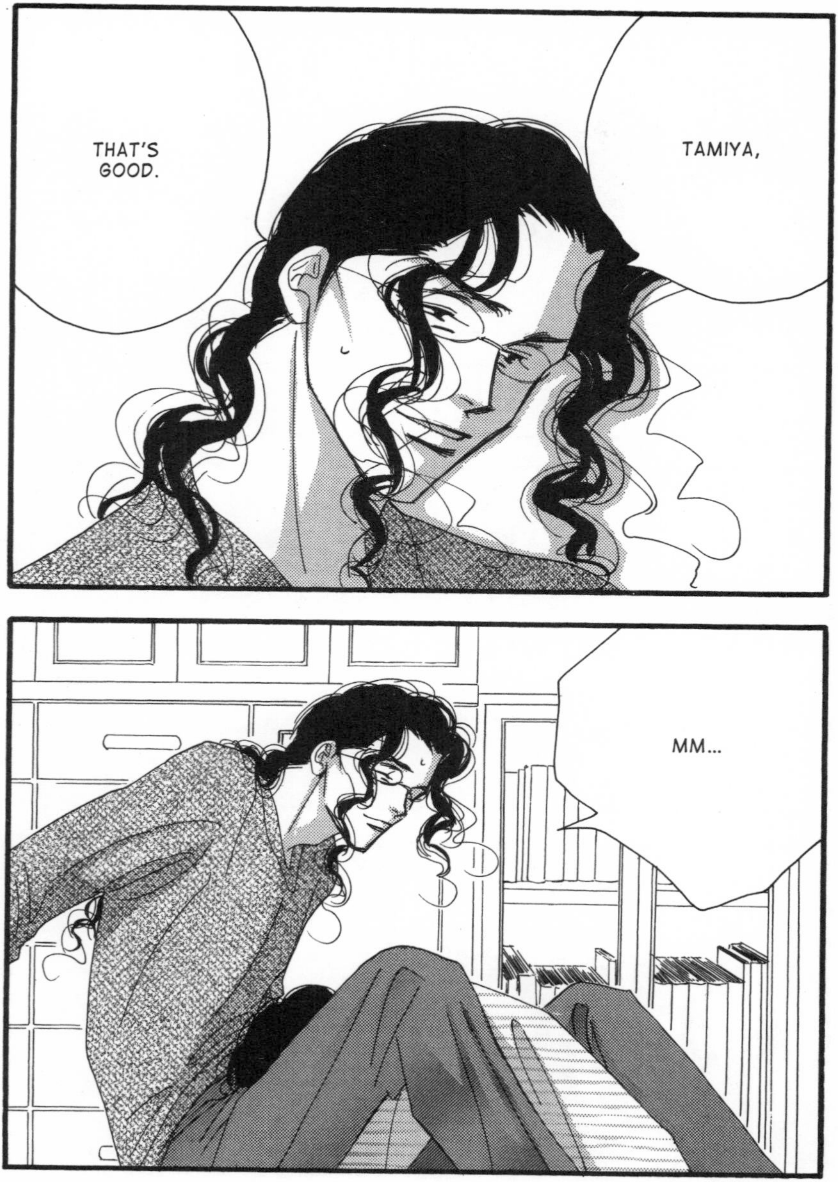
TAMIYA,
THAT'S GOOD.
MM...

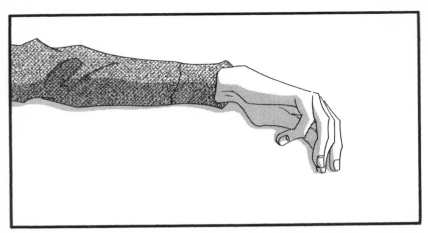

LET'S
SWITCH.

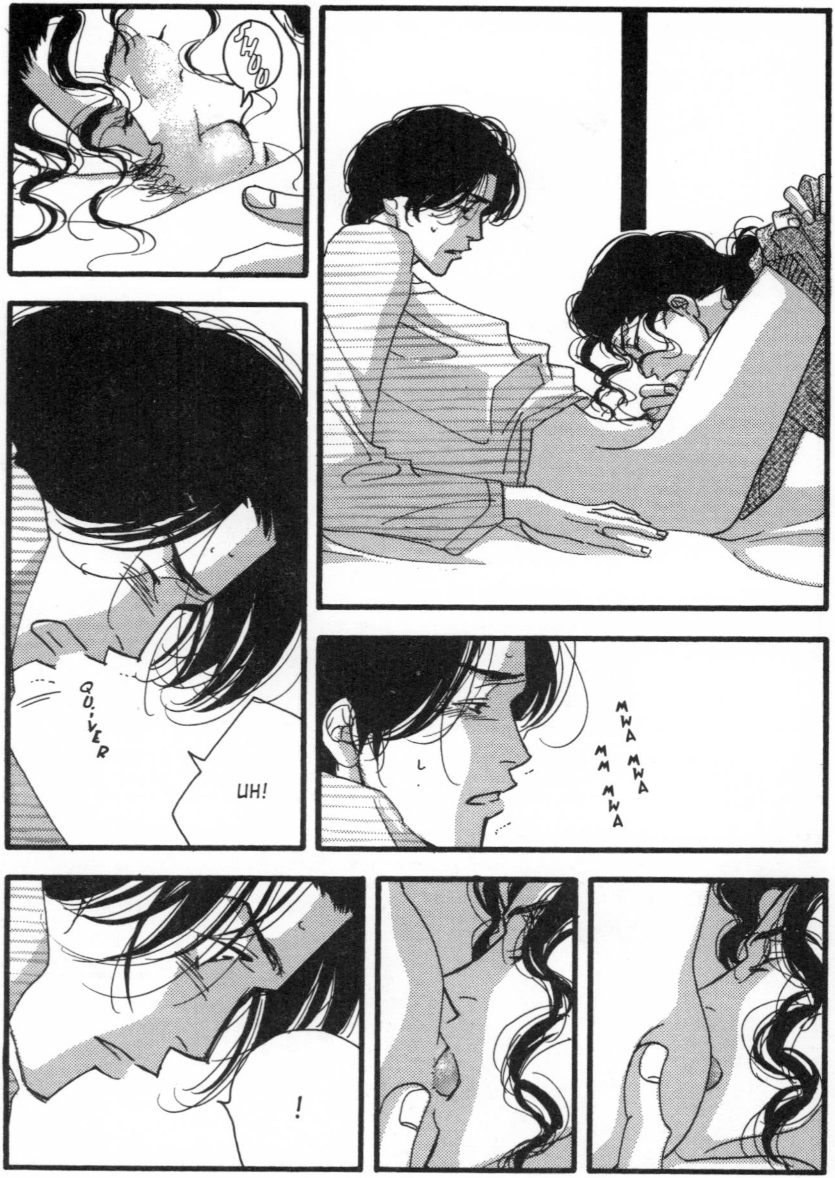
MWA MWA
MM MWA
SHUU
QUIVER
UH!
!

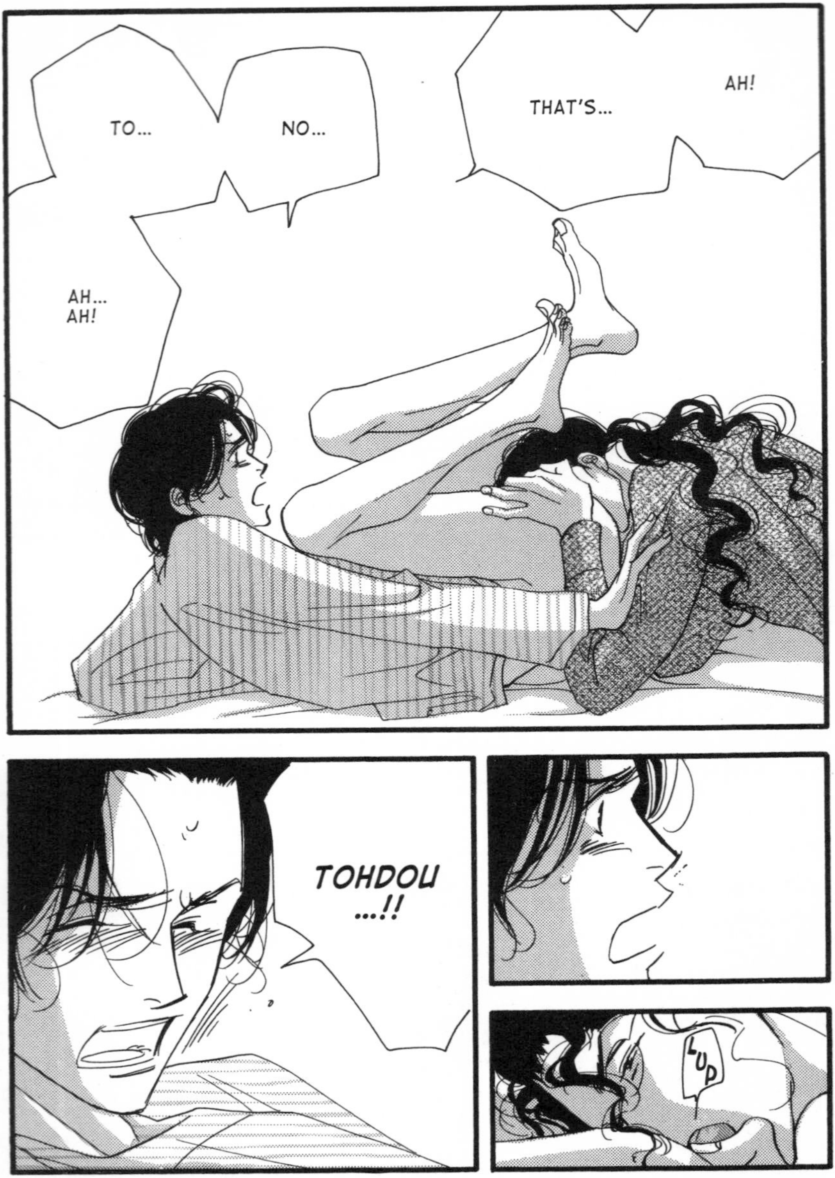
AH!
THAT'S...
NO...
TO...
AH...
AH!
LUP
TOHDOU
...!!

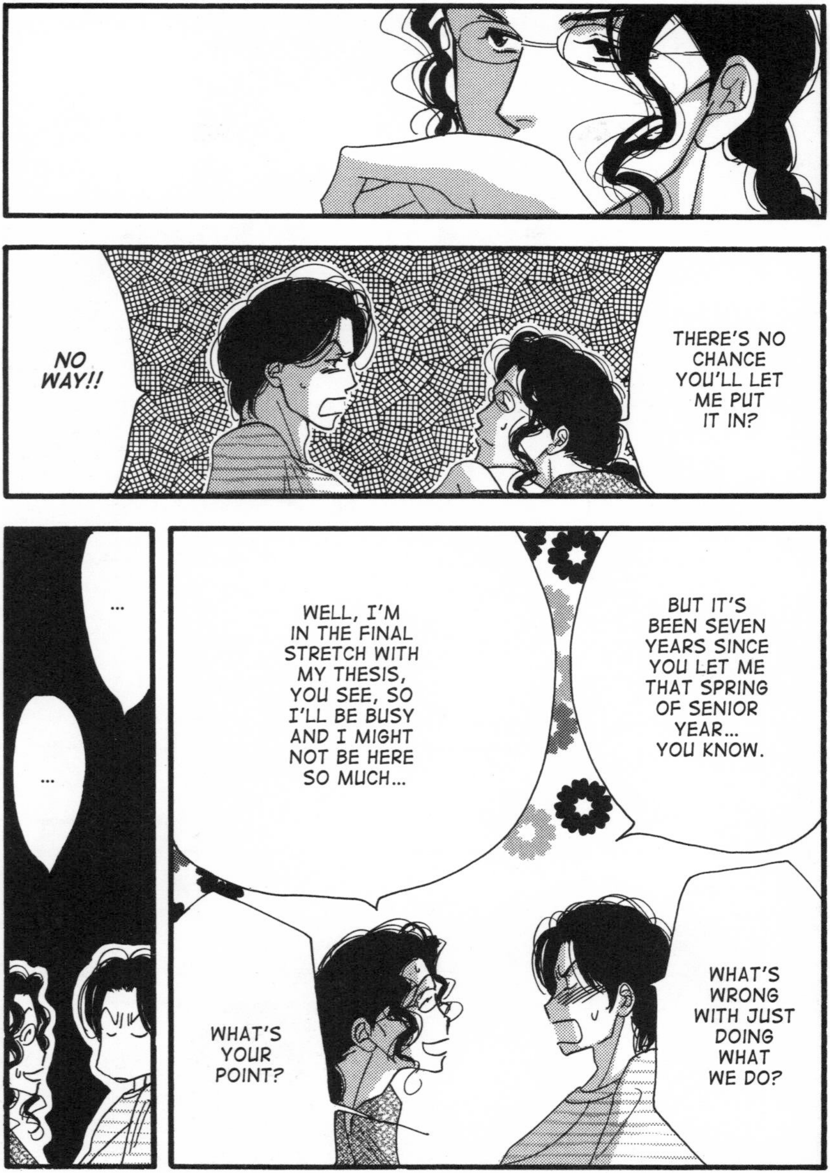
THERE'S NO CHANCE YOU'LL LET ME PUT IT IN?
NO WAY!!
BUT IT'S BEEN SEVEN YEARS SINCE YOU LET ME THAT SPRING OF SENIOR YEAR... YOU KNOW.
WELL, I'M IN THE FINAL STRETCH WITH MY THESIS, YOU SEE, SO I'LL BE BUSY AND I MIGHT NOT BE HERE SO MUCH...
WHAT'S WRONG WITH JUST DOING WHAT WE DO?
WHAT'S YOUR POINT?
...
...

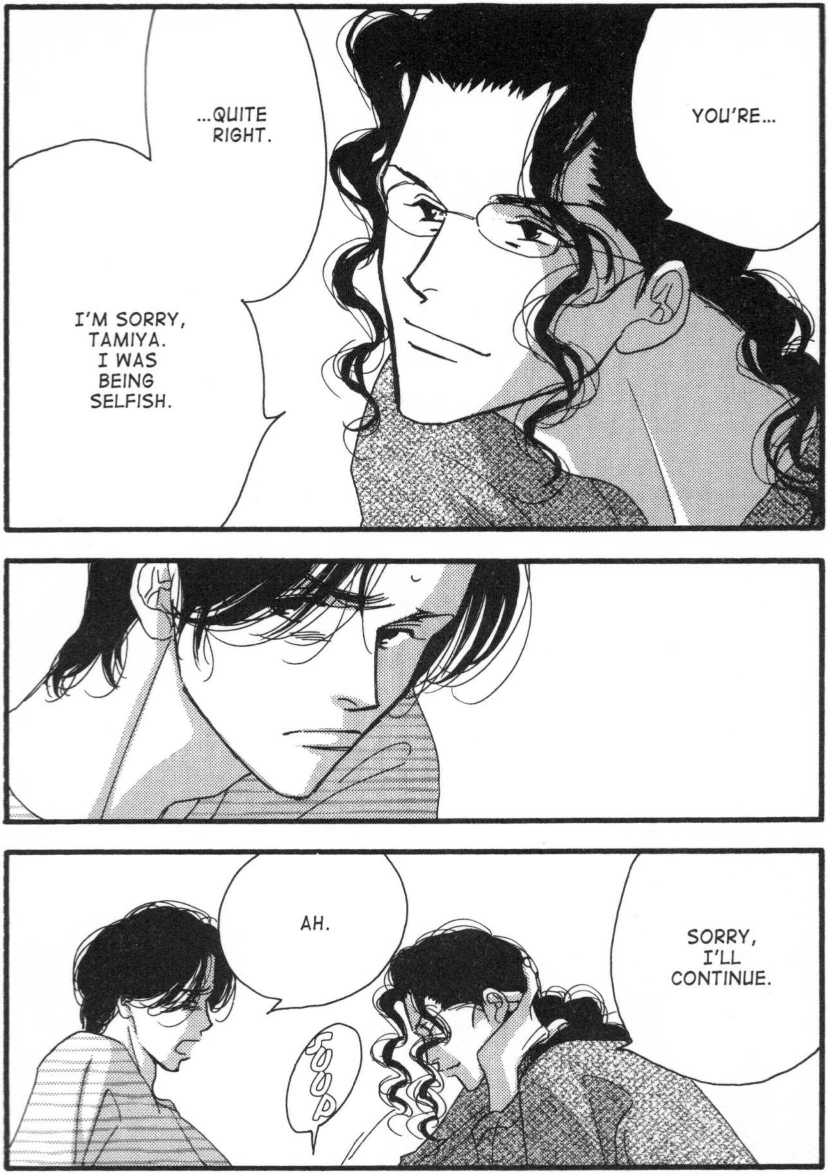
YOU'RE...
...QUITE RIGHT.
I'M SORRY, TAMIYA. I WAS BEING SELFISH.
SORRY, I'LL CONTINUE.
AH.
SOUP

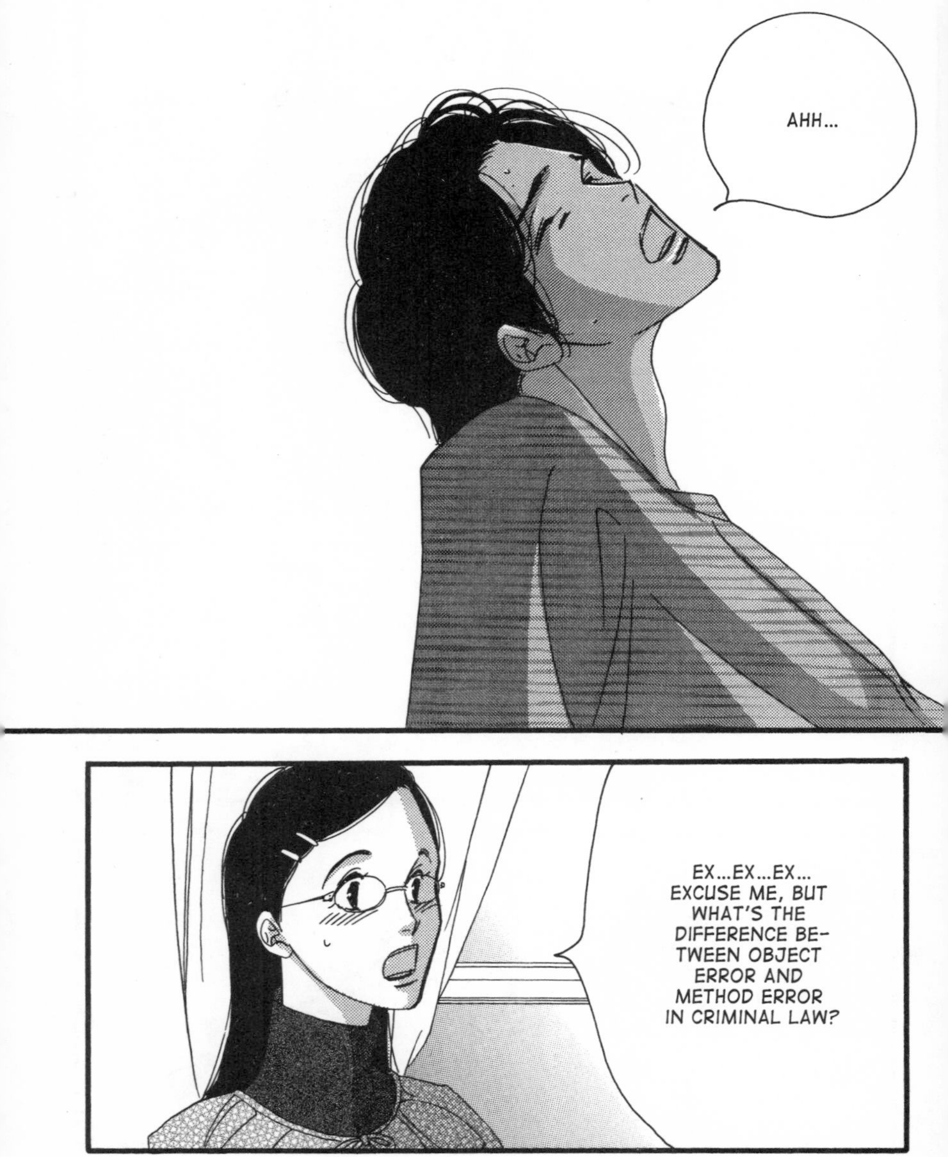
AHH...
EX...EX...EX... EXCUSE ME, BUT WHAT'S THE DIFFERENCE BE-TWEEN OBJECT ERROR AND METHOD ERROR IN CRIMINAL LAW?

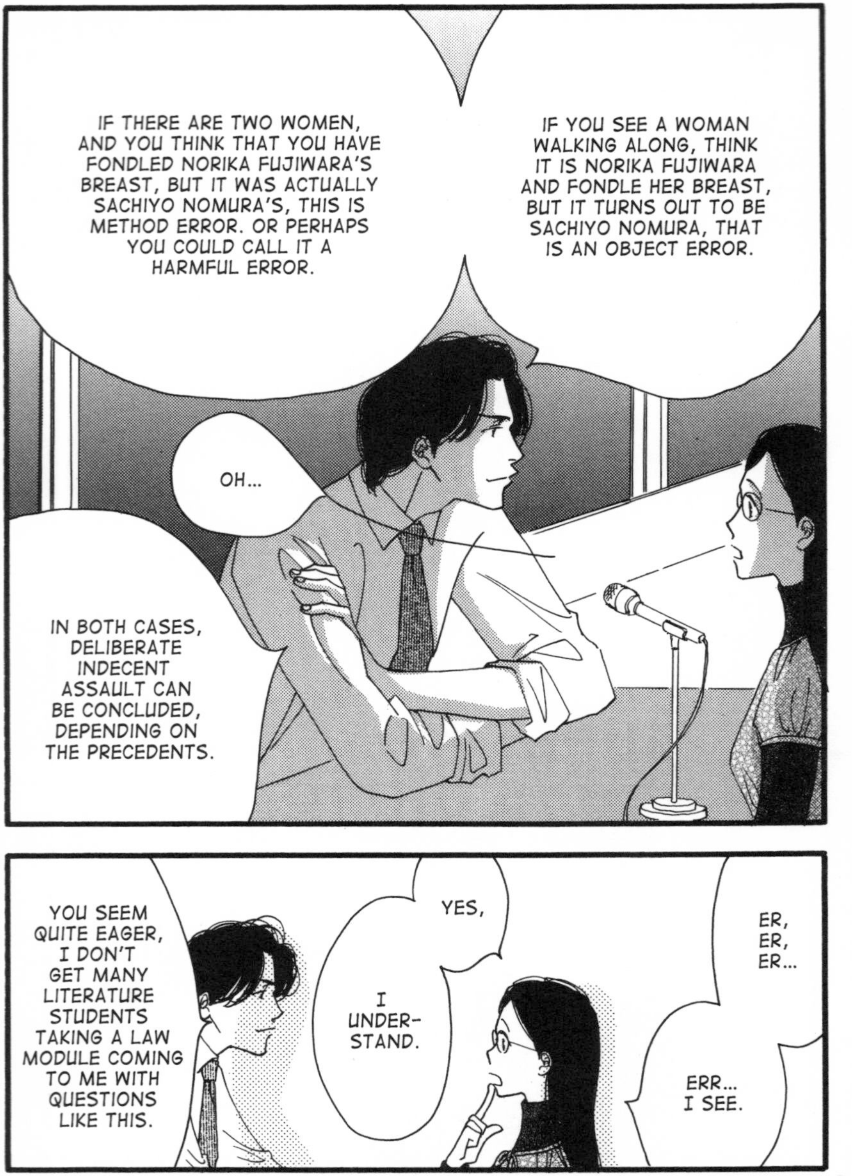
IF YOU SEE A WOMAN WALKING ALONG, THINK IT IS NORIKA FUJIWARA AND FONDLE HER BREAST, BUT IT TURNS OUT TO BE SACHIYO NOMURA, THAT IS AN OBJECT ERROR.
IF THERE ARE TWO WOMEN, AND YOU THINK THAT YOU HAVE FONDLED NORIKA FUJIWARA'S BREAST, BUT IT WAS ACTUALLY SACHIYO NOMURA'S, THIS IS METHOD ERROR. OR PERHAPS YOU COULD CALL IT A HARMFUL ERROR.
OH...
IN BOTH CASES, DELIBERATE INDECENT ASSAULT CAN BE CONCLUDED, DEPENDING ON THE PRECEDENTS.
ER, ER, ER...
ERR... I SEE.
YES,
I UNDER-STAND.
YOU SEEM QUITE EAGER, I DON'T GET MANY LITERATURE STUDENTS TAKING A LAW MODULE COMING TO ME WITH QUESTIONS LIKE THIS.

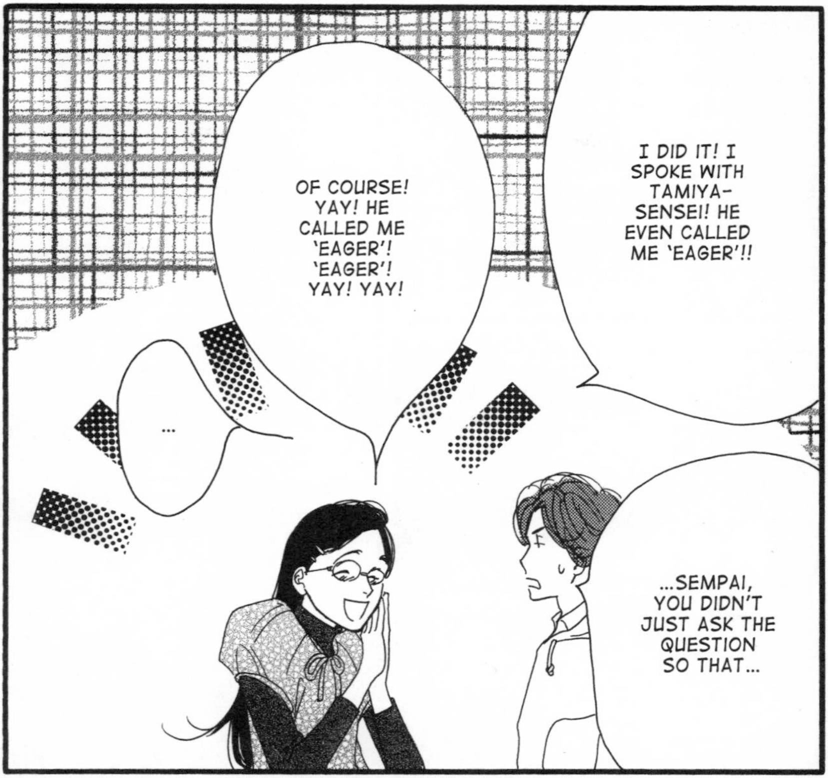
I DID IT! I SPOKE WITH TAMIYA-SENSEI! HE EVEN CALLED ME 'EAGER'!!
OF COURSE! YAY! HE CALLED ME 'EAGER'! 'EAGER'! YAY! YAY!
...SEMPAI, YOU DIDN'T JUST ASK THE QUESTION SO THAT...
...

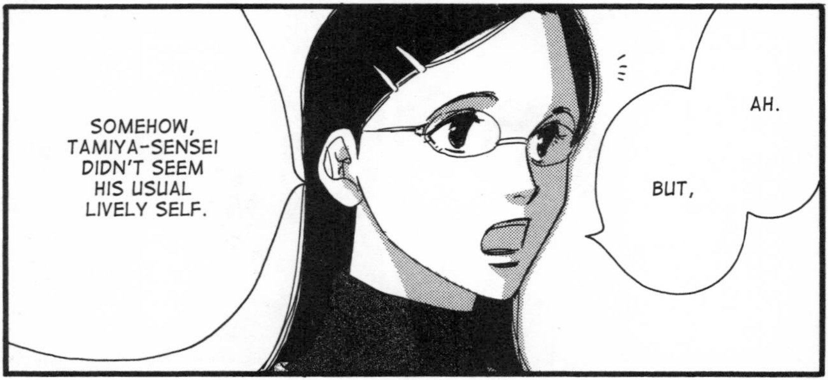
AH.
BUT,
SOMEHOW, TAMIYA-SENSEI DIDN'T SEEM HIS USUAL LIVELY SELF.

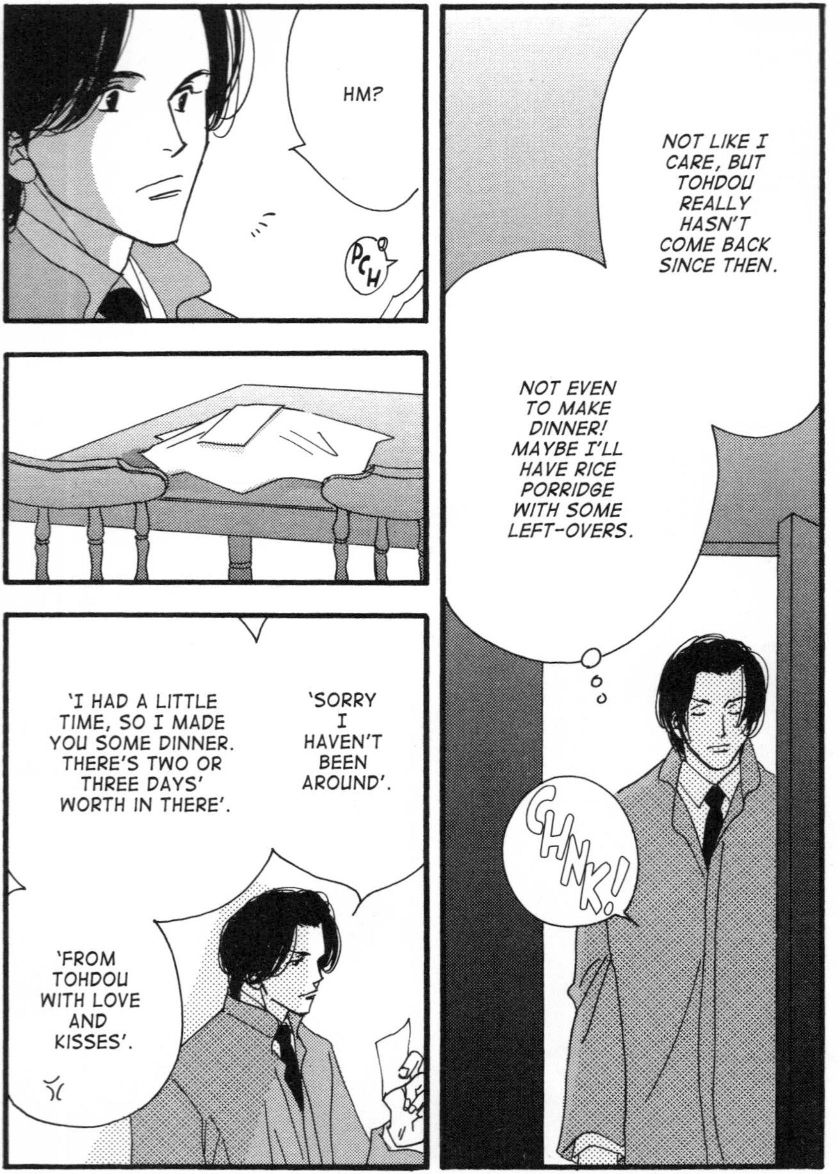
NOT LIKE I CARE, BUT TOHDOU REALLY HASN'T COME BACK SINCE THEN.
NOT EVEN TO MAKE DINNER! MAYBE I'LL HAVE RICE PORRIDGE WITH SOME LEFT-OVERS.
CHNK!
HM?
PCH
'SORRY I HAVEN'T BEEN AROUND'.
'I HAD A LITTLE TIME, SO I MADE YOU SOME DINNER. THERE'S TWO OR THREE DAYS' WORTH IN THERE'.
'FROM TOHDOU WITH LOVE AND KISSES'.

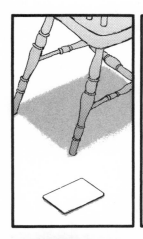

OH, BOILED ALFONSINO, SPINACH OMELET AND NAMEKO OROSHI.

ALL MY FAVORITES, HE'S TRYING TO GET ON MY GOOD SIDE...HUH?

BSSH

...

TOHDOU'S LIBRARY CARD. HE CAN'T GET IN THERE WITHOUT IT...

I GUESS I'VE GOT NO CHOICE...

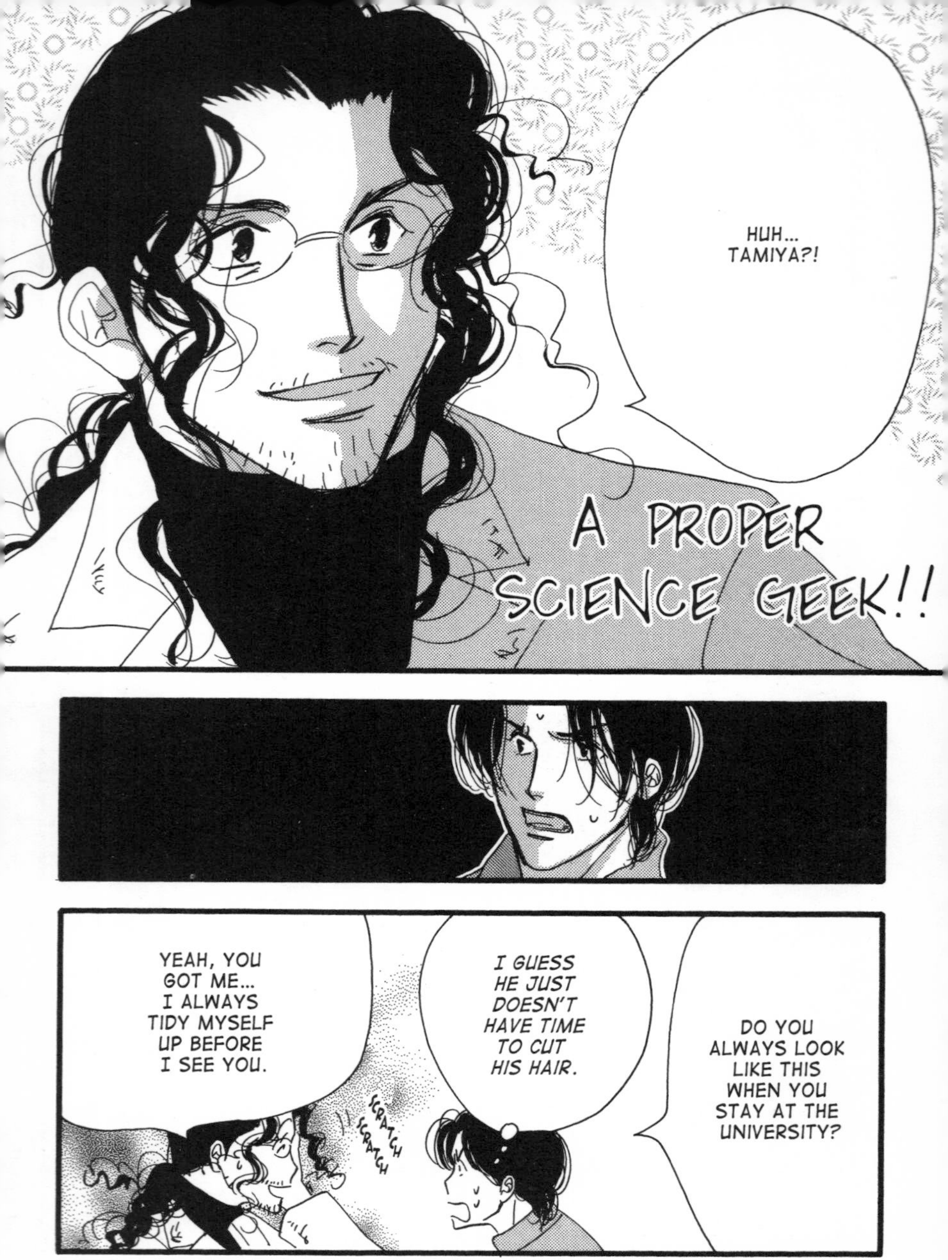
HUH... TAMIYA?!
A PROPER SCIENCE GEEK!!
DO YOU ALWAYS LOOK LIKE THIS WHEN YOU STAY AT THE UNIVERSITY?
I GUESS HE JUST DOESN'T HAVE TIME TO CUT HIS HAIR.
YEAH, YOU GOT ME... I ALWAYS TIDY MYSELF UP BEFORE I SEE YOU.
SCRATCH SCRATCH

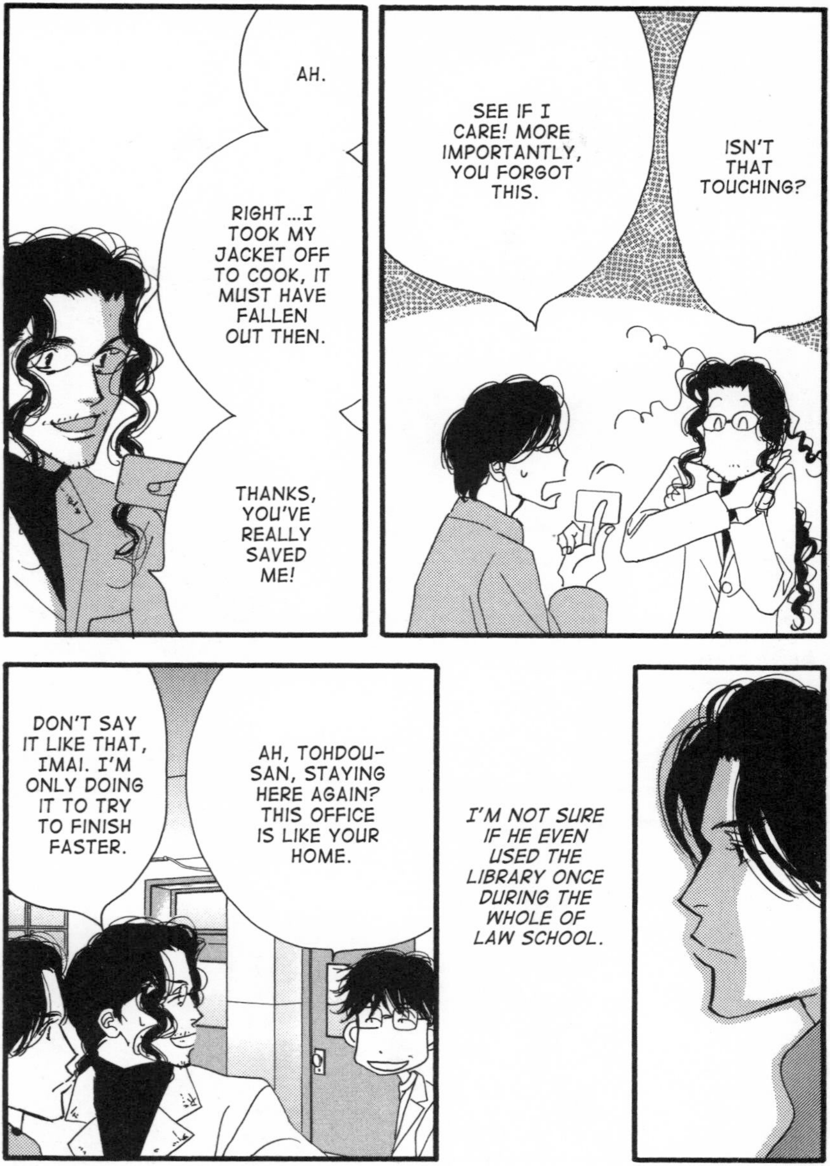
ISN'T THAT TOUCHING?
SEE IF I CARE! MORE IMPORTANTLY, YOU FORGOT THIS.
AH.
RIGHT...I TOOK MY JACKET OFF TO COOK, IT MUST HAVE FALLEN OUT THEN.
THANKS, YOU'VE REALLY SAVED ME!
I'M NOT SURE IF HE EVEN USED THE LIBRARY ONCE DURING THE WHOLE OF LAW SCHOOL.
AH, TOHDOU-SAN, STAYING HERE AGAIN? THIS OFFICE IS LIKE YOUR HOME.
DON'T SAY IT LIKE THAT, IMAI. I'M ONLY DOING IT TO TRY TO FINISH FASTER.

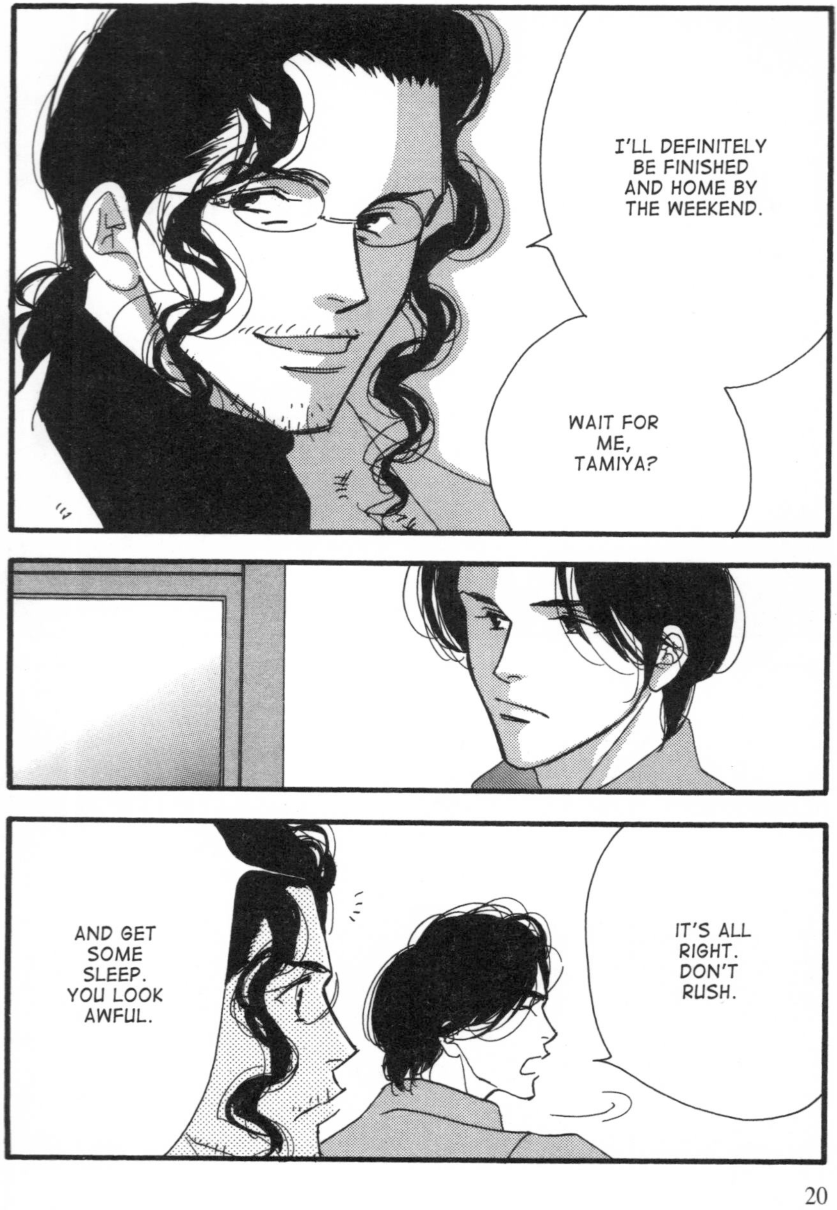
I'LL DEFINITELY BE FINISHED AND HOME BY THE WEEKEND.
WAIT FOR ME, TAMIYA?
IT'S ALL RIGHT. DON'T RUSH.
AND GET SOME SLEEP. YOU LOOK AWFUL.

SEE YOU.
AT LEAST MAKE IT BETTER THAN YOUR UNIVERSITY DISSERTATION.
YEP!!
THANKS, TAMIYA, I'LL DO MY BEST!!
GAH.
BUT WHY ARE THERE SO MANY LIGHTS ON HERE? IT'S NEARLY 10PM.
EXCUSE ME...

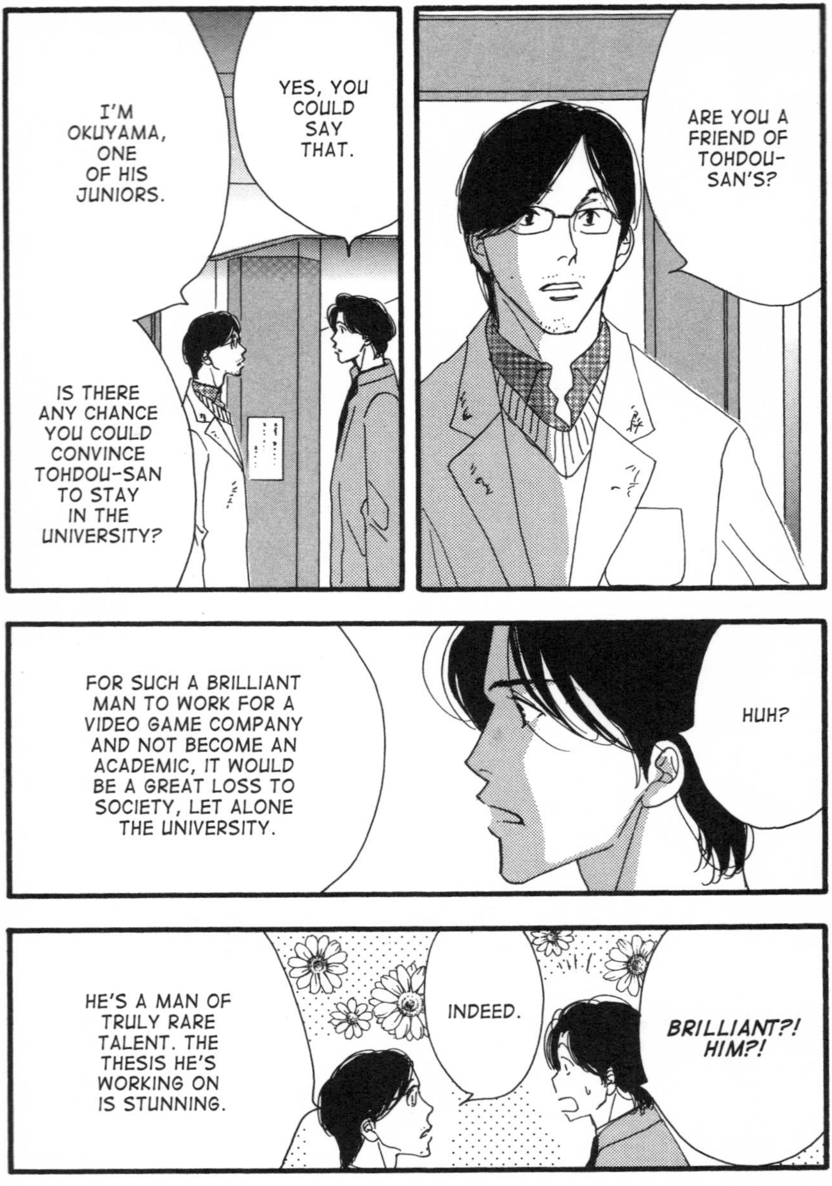
ARE YOU A FRIEND OF TOHDOU-SAN'S?
YES, YOU COULD SAY THAT.
I'M OKUYAMA, ONE OF HIS JUNIORS.
IS THERE ANY CHANCE YOU COULD CONVINCE TOHDOU-SAN TO STAY IN THE UNIVERSITY?
HUH?
FOR SUCH A BRILLIANT MAN TO WORK FOR A VIDEO GAME COMPANY AND NOT BECOME AN ACADEMIC, IT WOULD BE A GREAT LOSS TO SOCIETY, LET ALONE THE UNIVERSITY.
BRILLIANT?! HIM?!
INDEED.
HE'S A MAN OF TRULY RARE TALENT. THE THESIS HE'S WORKING ON IS STUNNING.

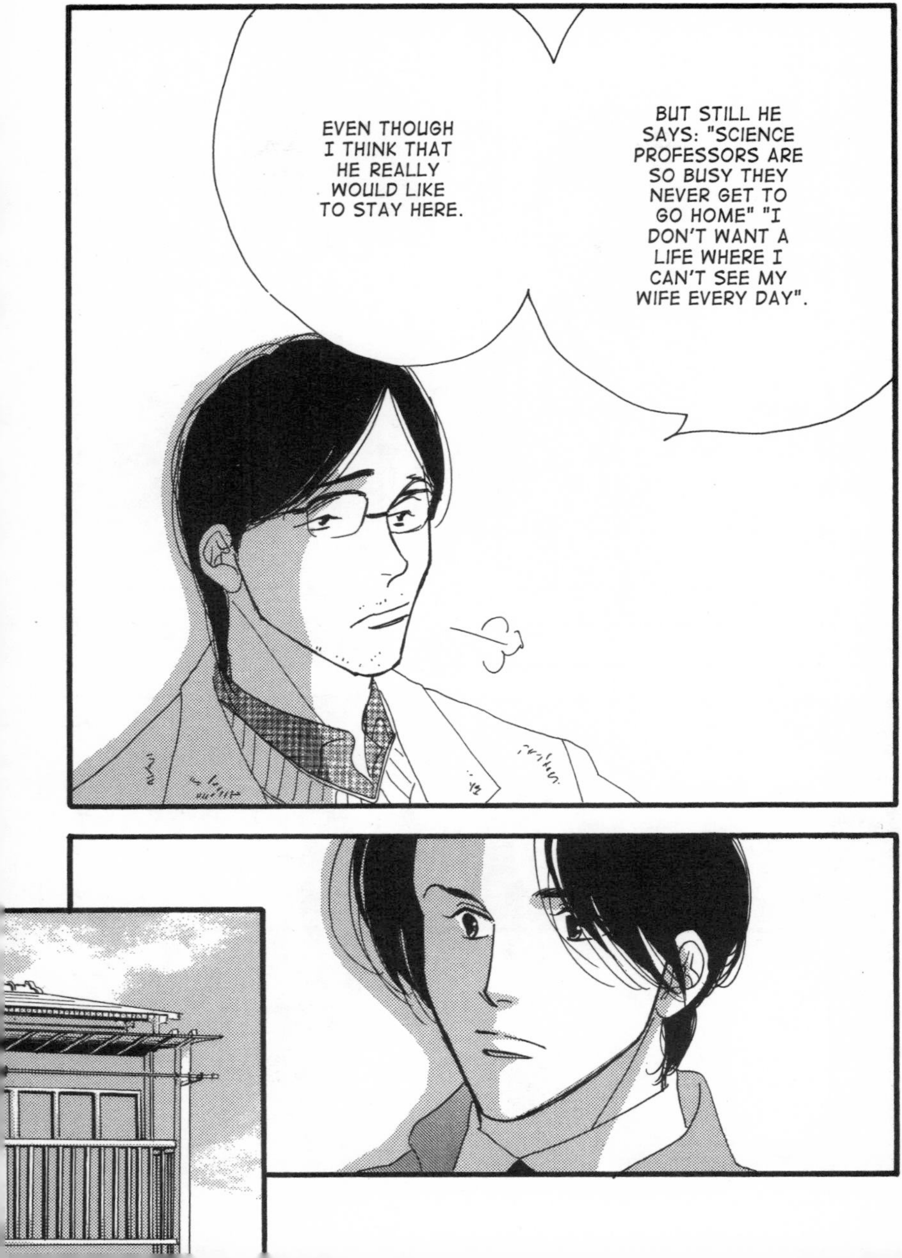
EVEN THOUGH I THINK THAT HE REALLY WOULD LIKE TO STAY HERE.
BUT STILL HE SAYS: "SCIENCE PROFESSORS ARE SO BUSY THEY NEVER GET TO GO HOME" "I DON'T WANT A LIFE WHERE I CAN'T SEE MY WIFE EVERY DAY".

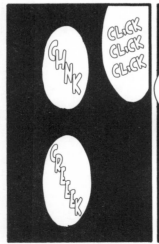

CHHNK

CLICK
CLICK
CLICK

CREEEK

CLANG

CLANG

CLANG

CLANG

CLANK!

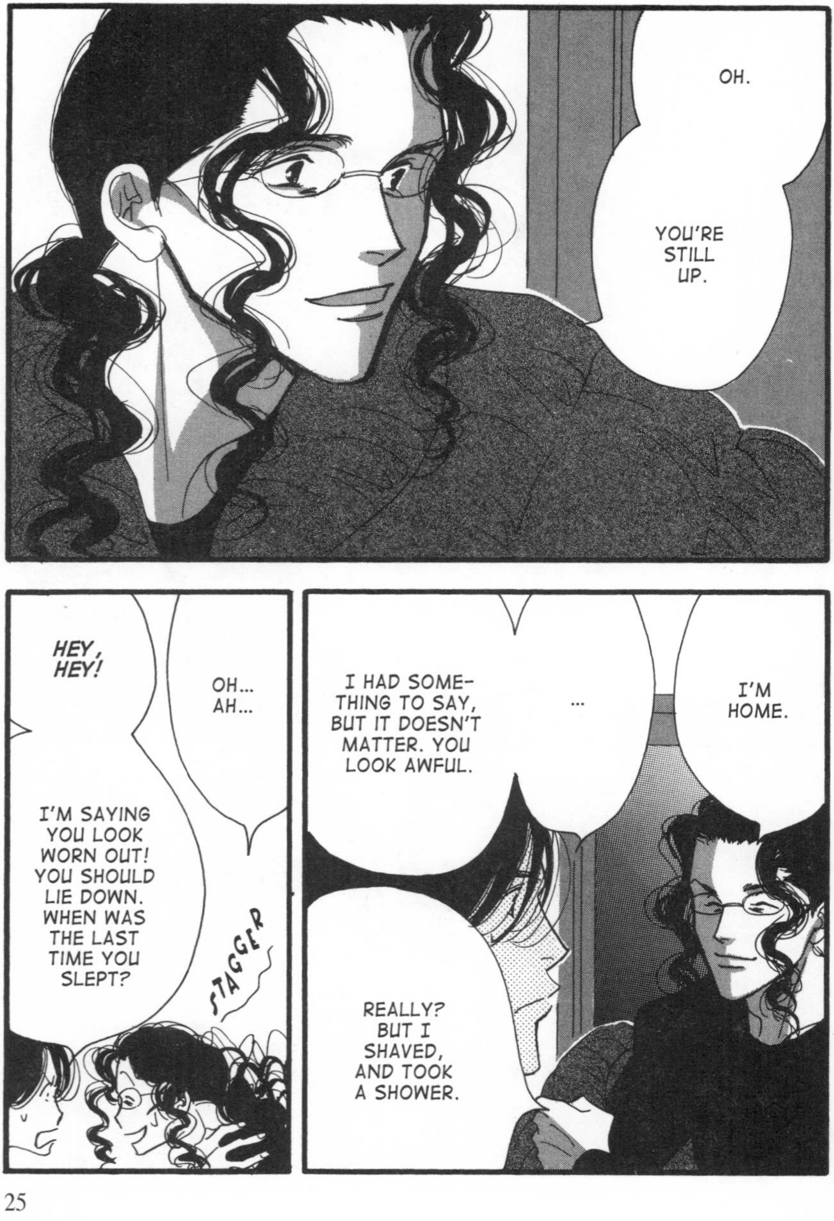
OH.
YOU'RE STILL UP.
I'M HOME.
...
I HAD SOME-THING TO SAY, BUT IT DOESN'T MATTER. YOU LOOK AWFUL.
REALLY? BUT I SHAVED, AND TOOK A SHOWER.
OH... AH...
HEY, HEY!
I'M SAYING YOU LOOK WORN OUT! YOU SHOULD LIE DOWN. WHEN WAS THE LAST TIME YOU SLEPT?
STAGGER

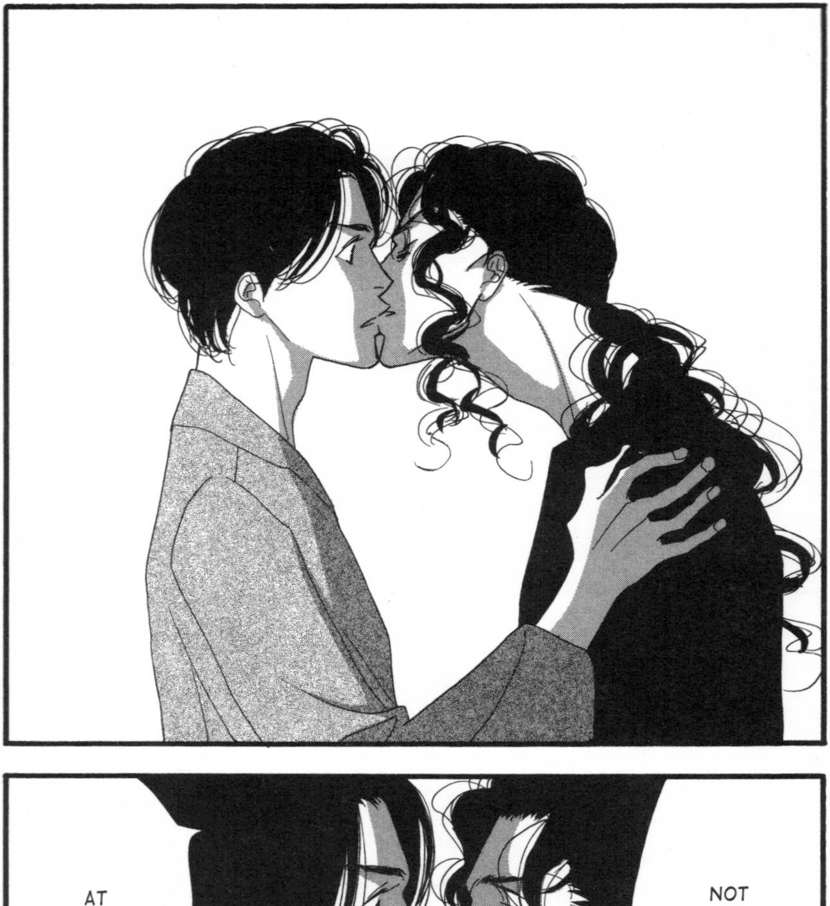

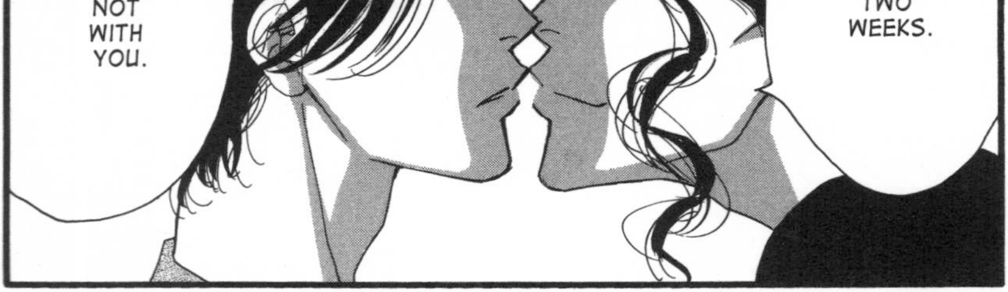
NOT IN TWO WEEKS.
AT LEAST, NOT WITH YOU.

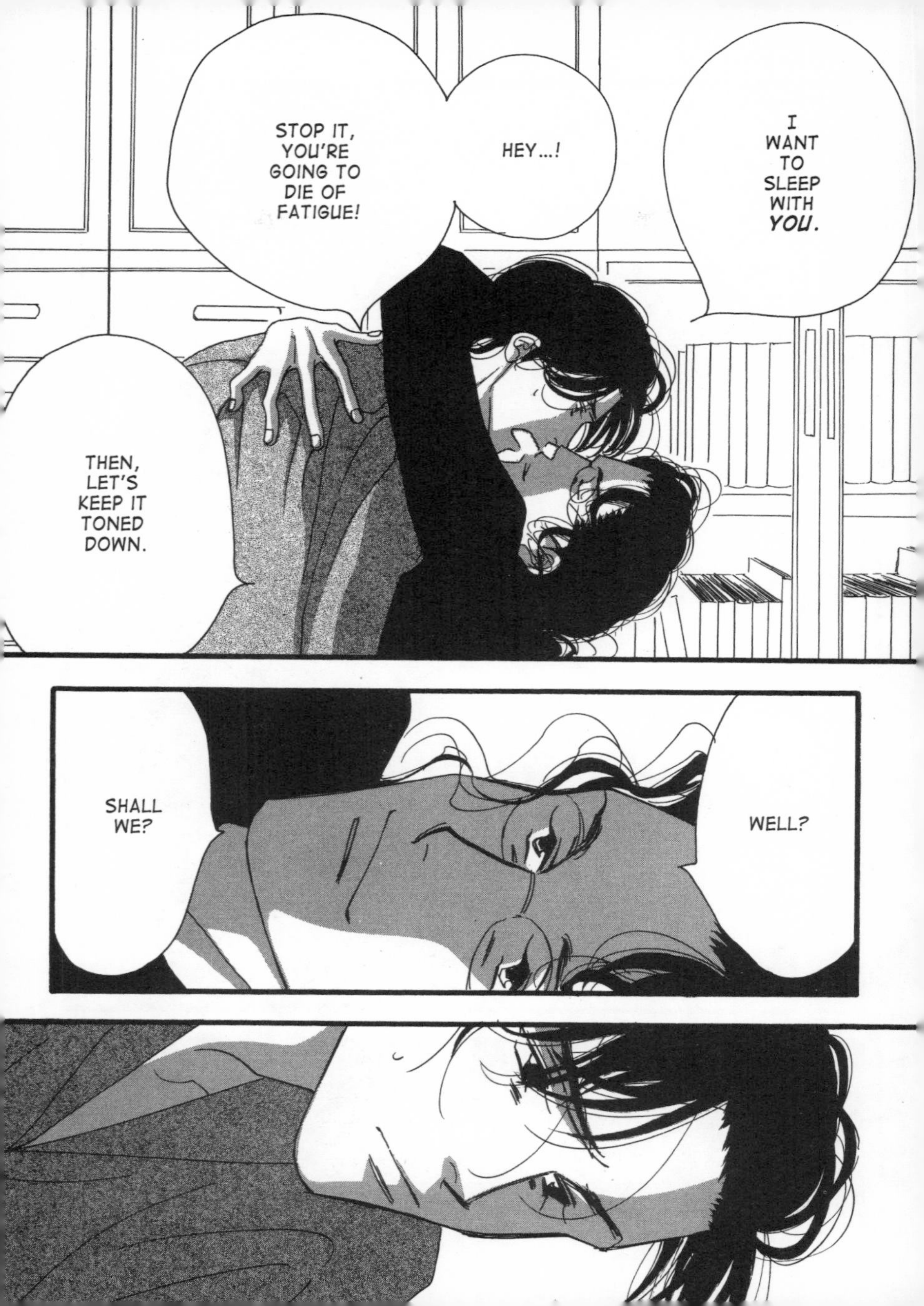
I WANT TO SLEEP WITH *YOU*.
HEY...!
STOP IT, YOU'RE GOING TO DIE OF FATIGUE!
THEN, LET'S KEEP IT TONED DOWN.
WELL?
SHALL WE?

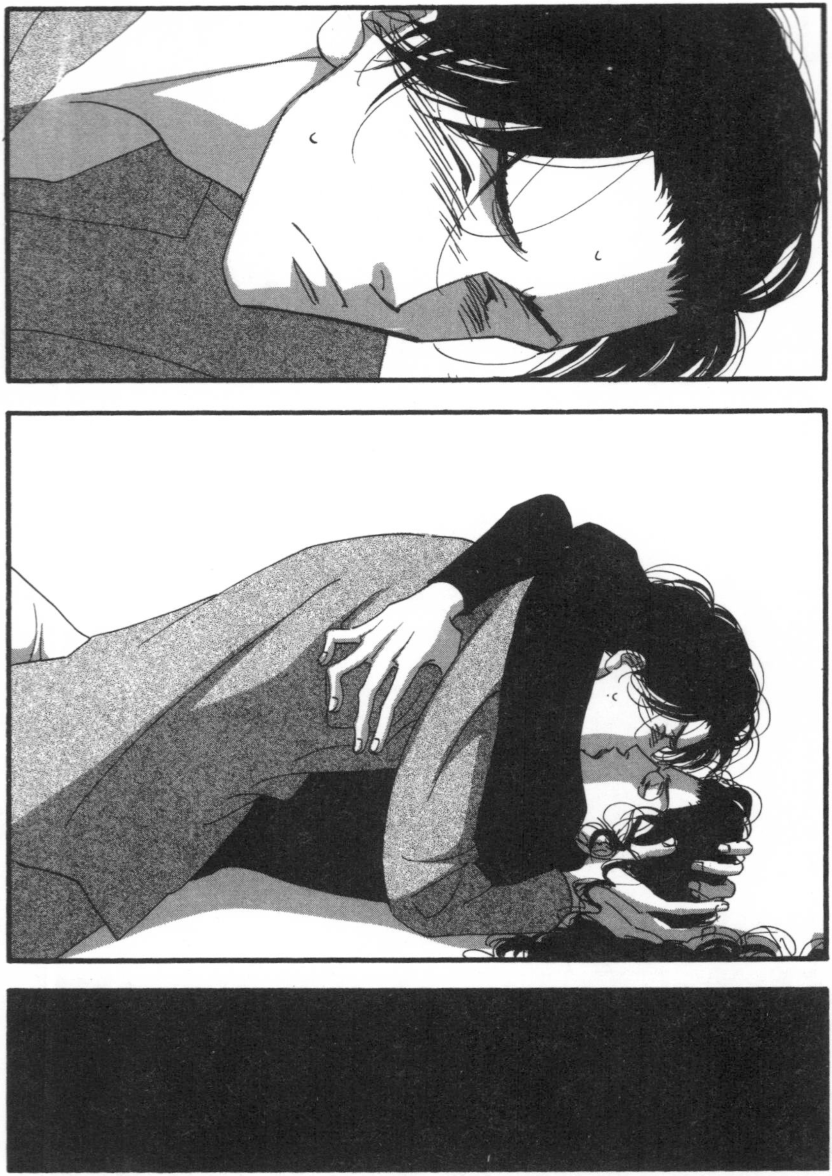

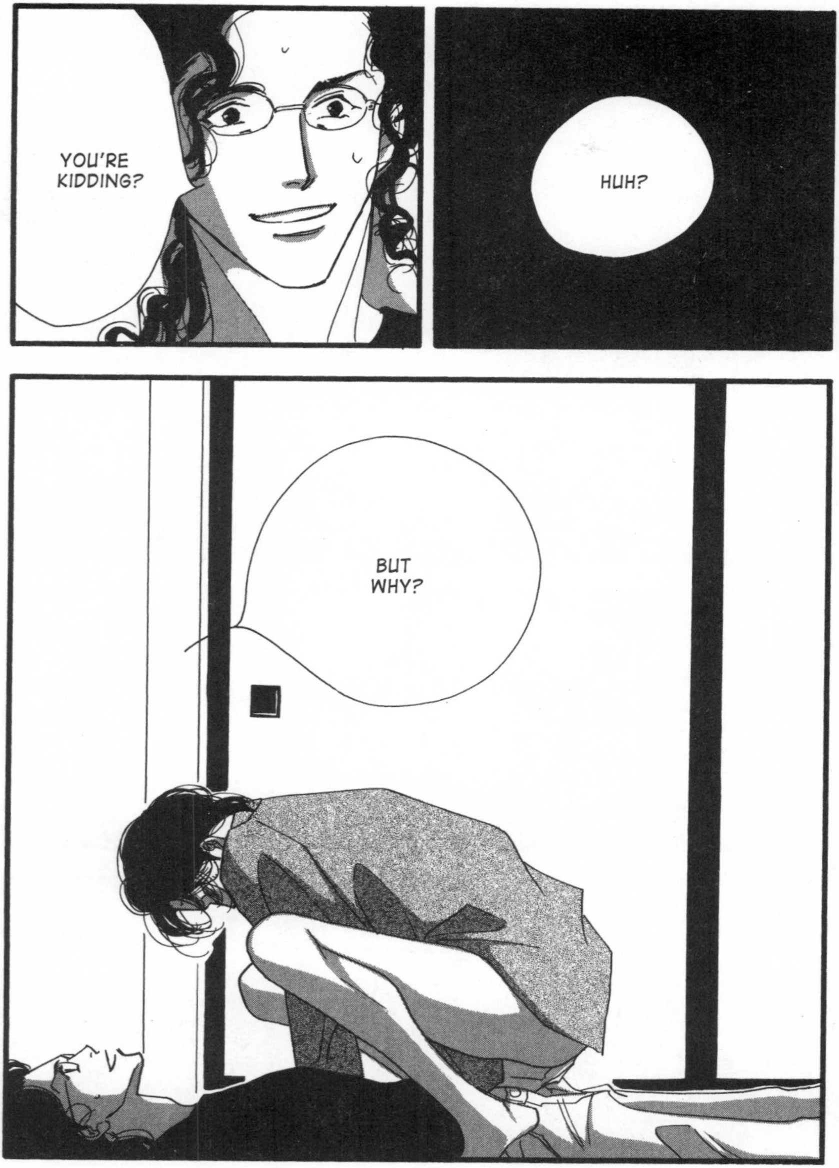
HUH?
YOU'RE KIDDING?
BUT WHY?

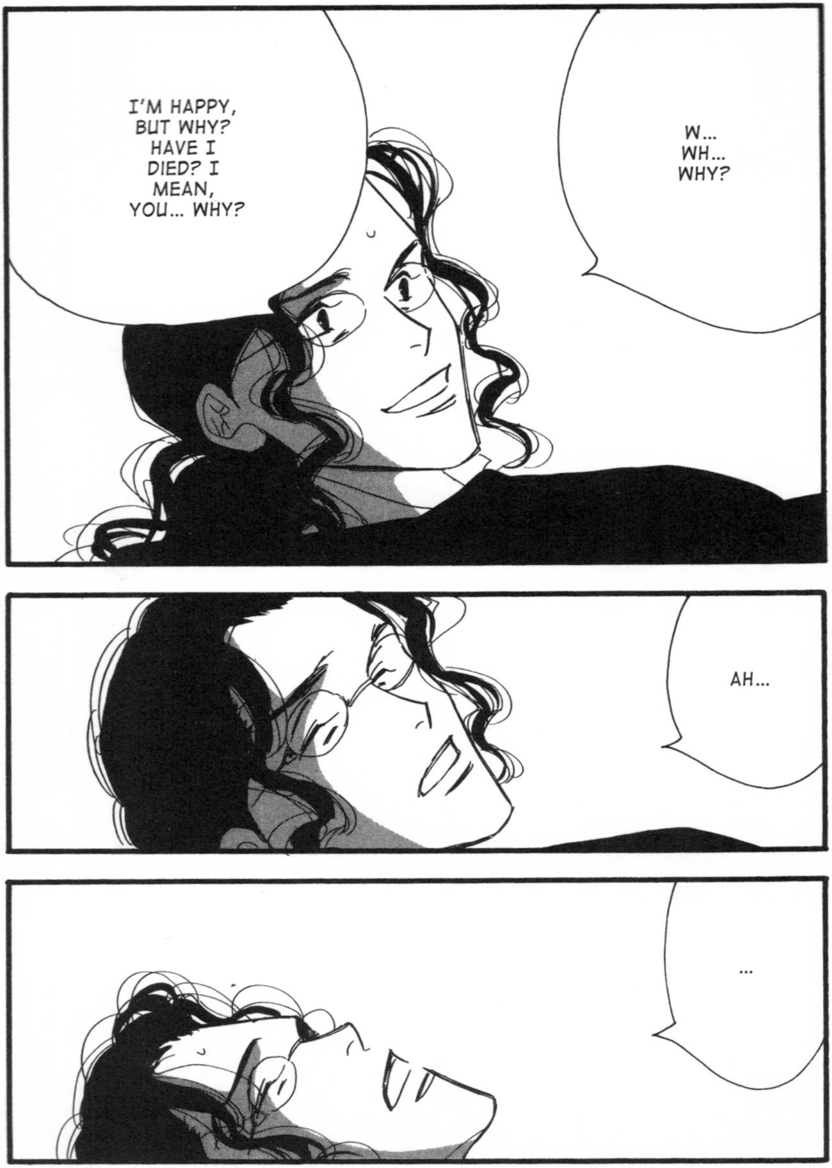
W... WH... WHY?
I'M HAPPY, BUT WHY? HAVE I DIED? I MEAN, YOU... WHY?
AH...
...

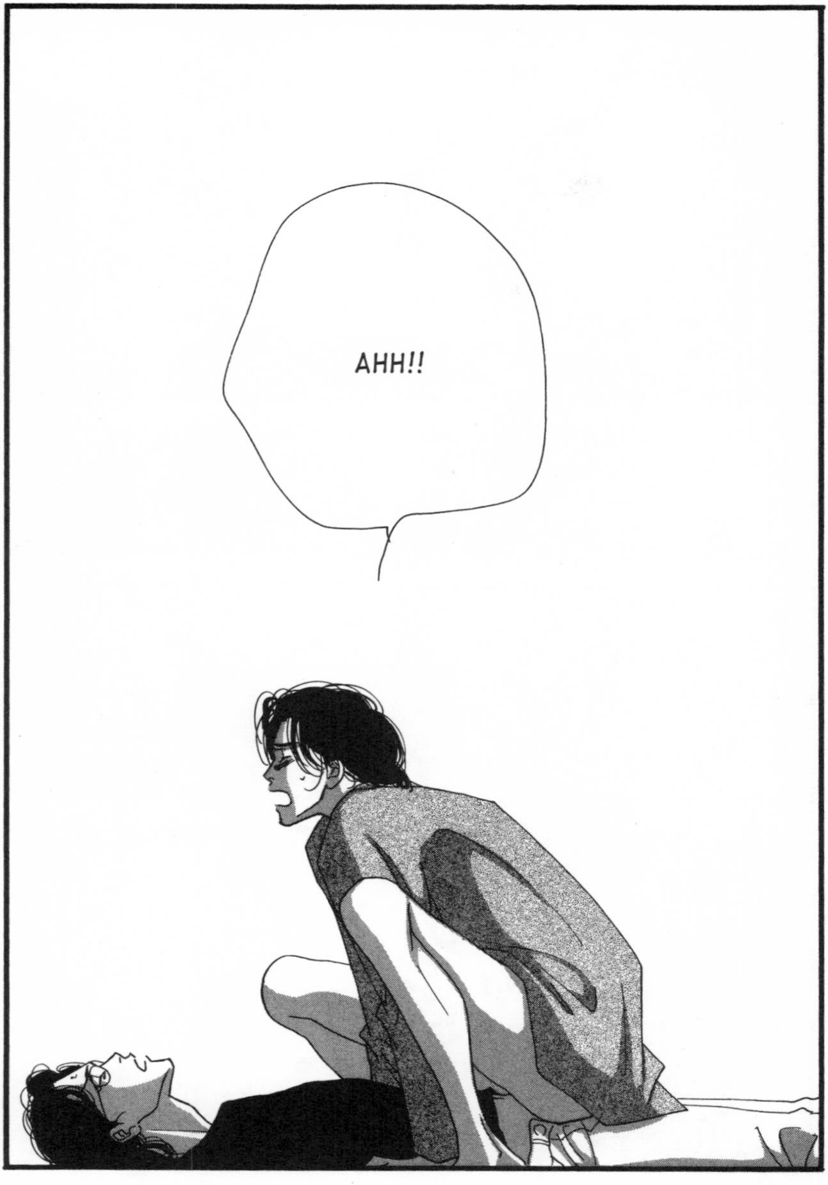
AHH!!

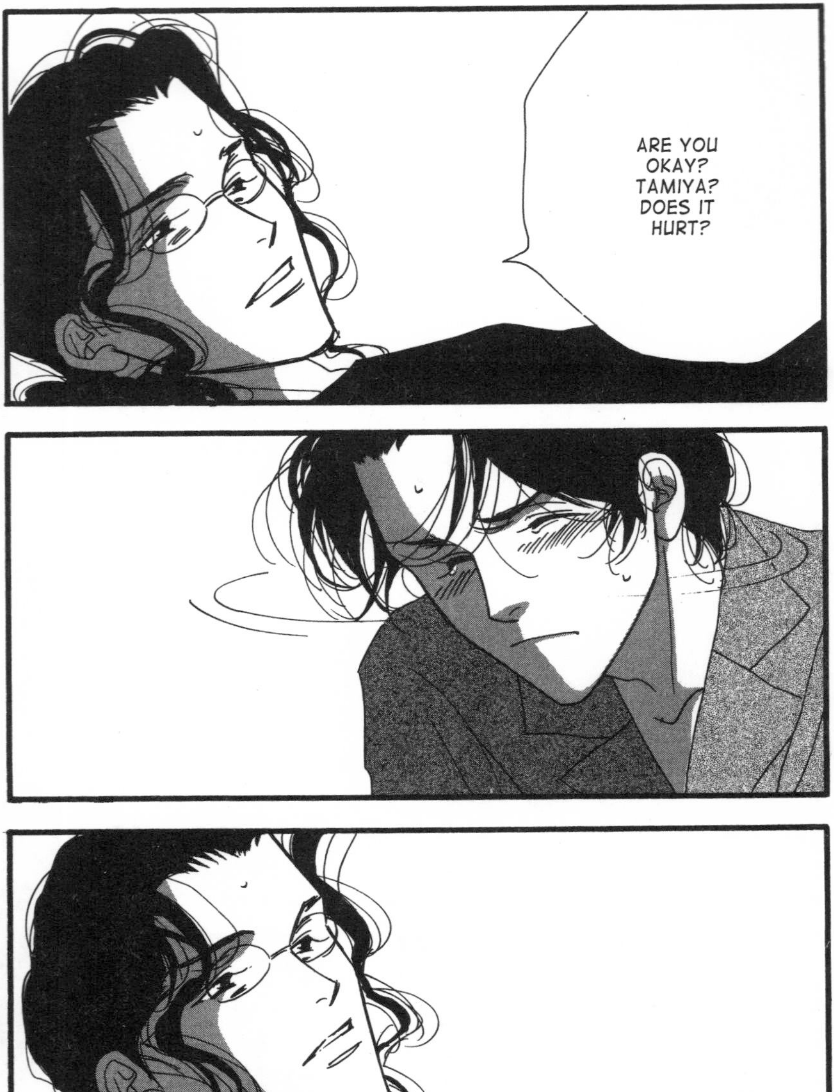
ARE YOU OKAY? TAMIYA? DOES IT HURT?

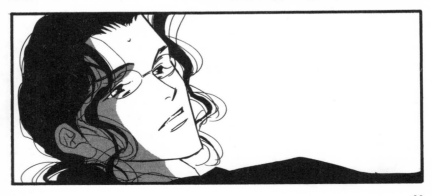

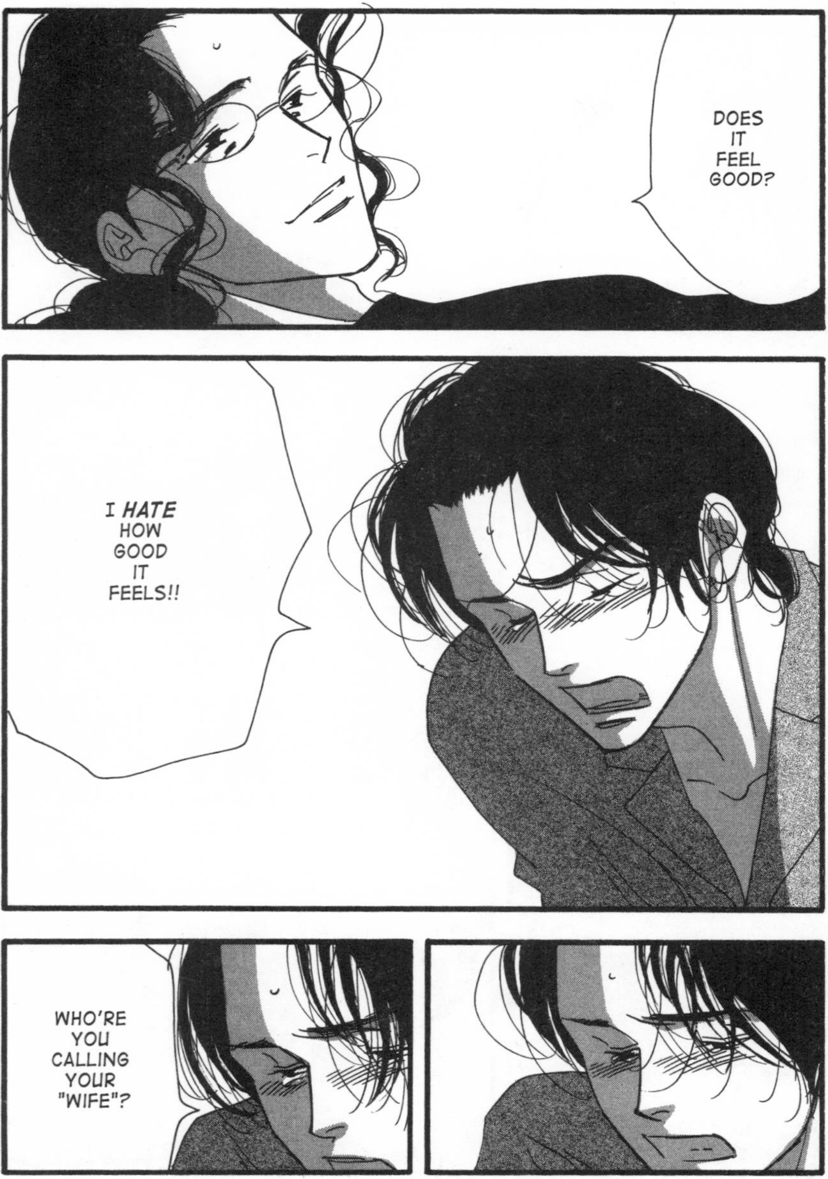
DOES IT FEEL GOOD?
I *HATE* HOW GOOD IT FEELS!!
WHO'RE YOU CALLING YOUR "WIFE"?

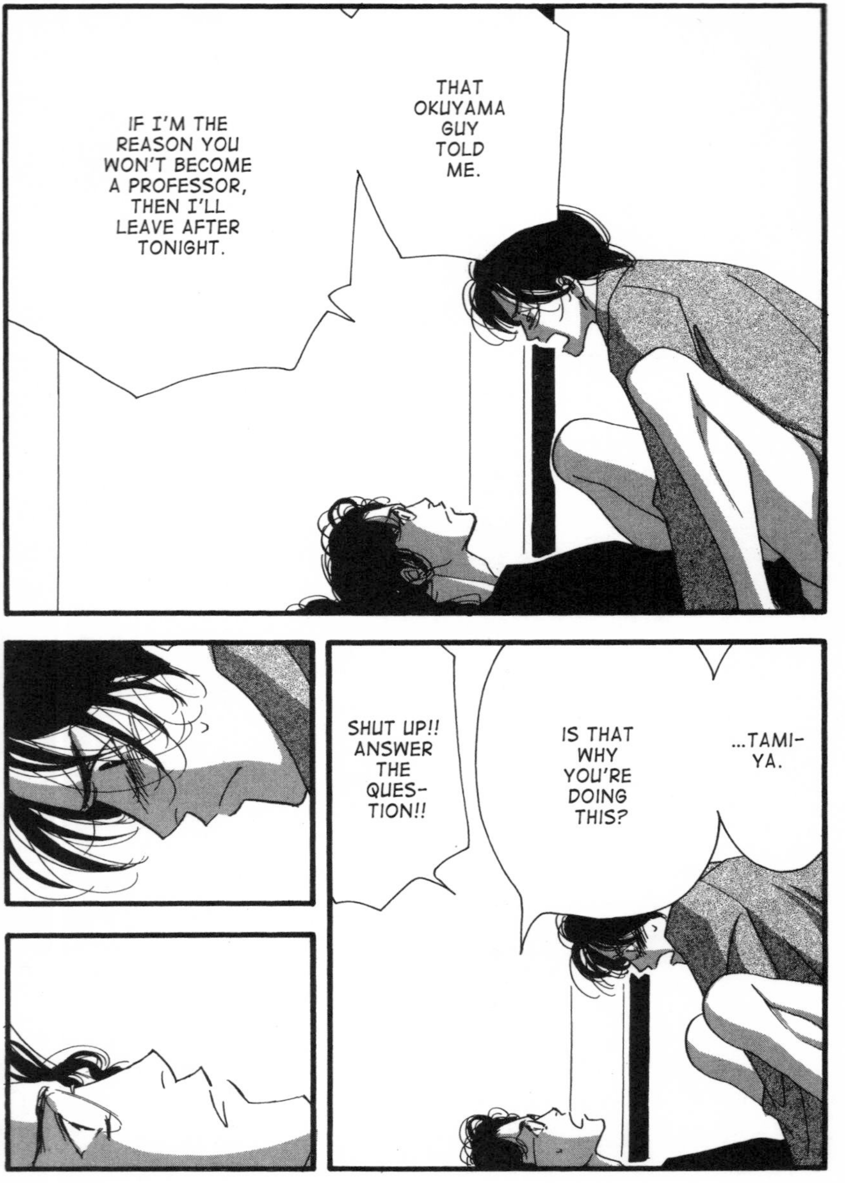
THAT OKUYAMA GUY TOLD ME.
IF I'M THE REASON YOU WON'T BECOME A PROFESSOR, THEN I'LL LEAVE AFTER TONIGHT.
...TAMI-YA.
IS THAT WHY YOU'RE DOING THIS?
SHUT UP!! ANSWER THE QUES-TION!!

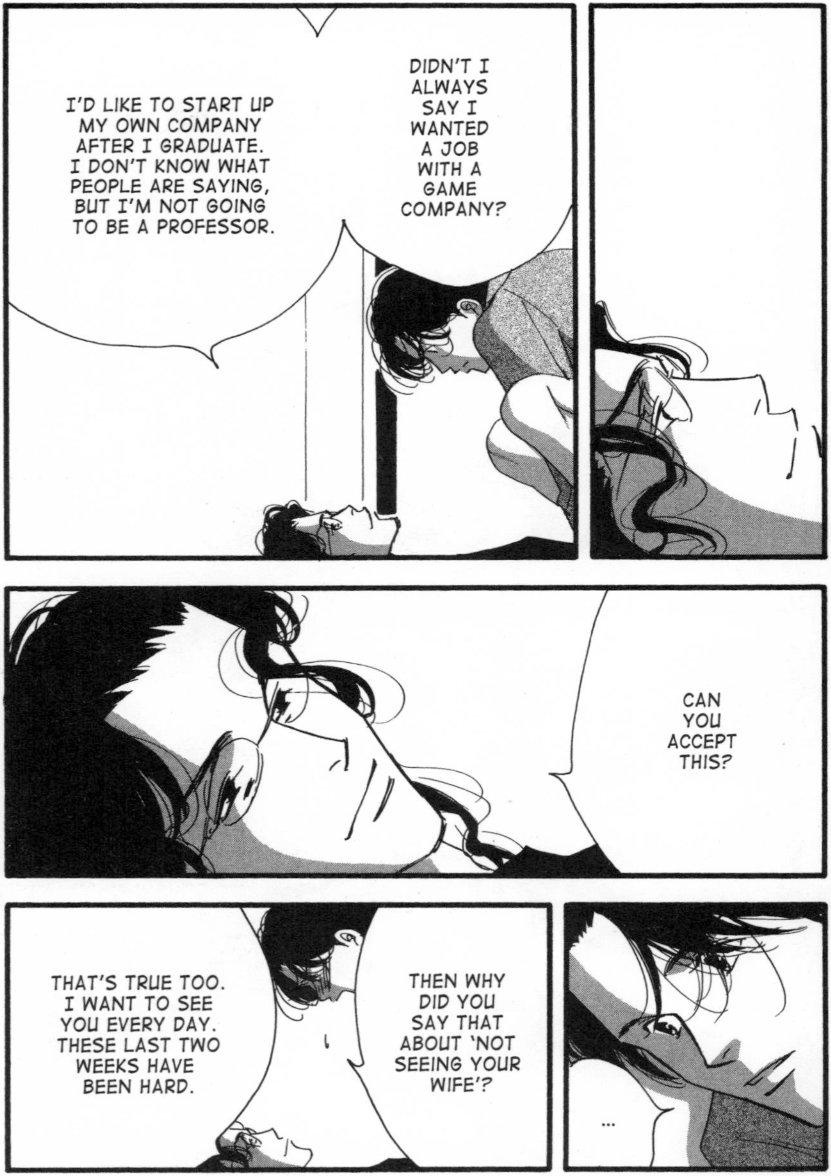
DIDN'T I ALWAYS SAY I WANTED A JOB WITH A GAME COMPANY?
I'D LIKE TO START UP MY OWN COMPANY AFTER I GRADUATE. I DON'T KNOW WHAT PEOPLE ARE SAYING, BUT I'M NOT GOING TO BE A PROFESSOR.
CAN YOU ACCEPT THIS?
...
THEN WHY DID YOU SAY THAT ABOUT 'NOT SEEING YOUR WIFE'?
THAT'S TRUE TOO. I WANT TO SEE YOU EVERY DAY. THESE LAST TWO WEEKS HAVE BEEN HARD.

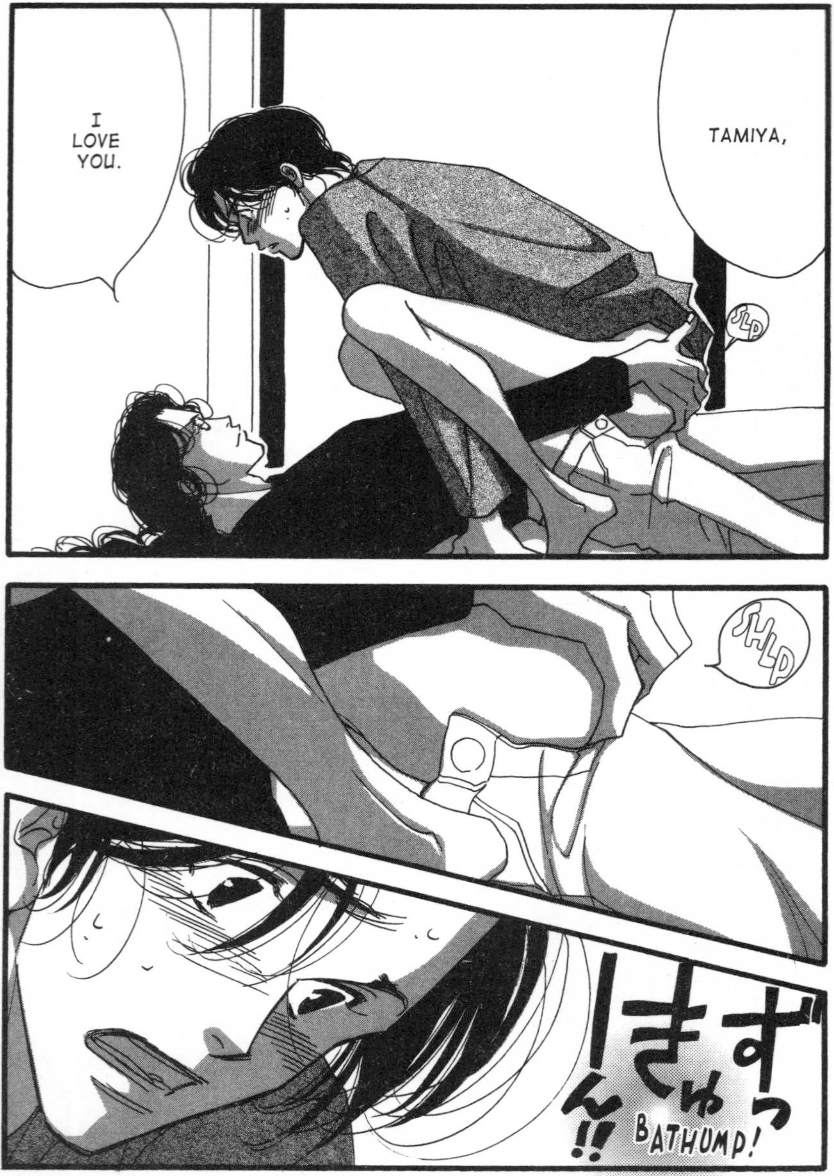

TAMIYA,
I LOVE YOU.
SLP
SHLP
ずっきゅん!!
BATHUMP!

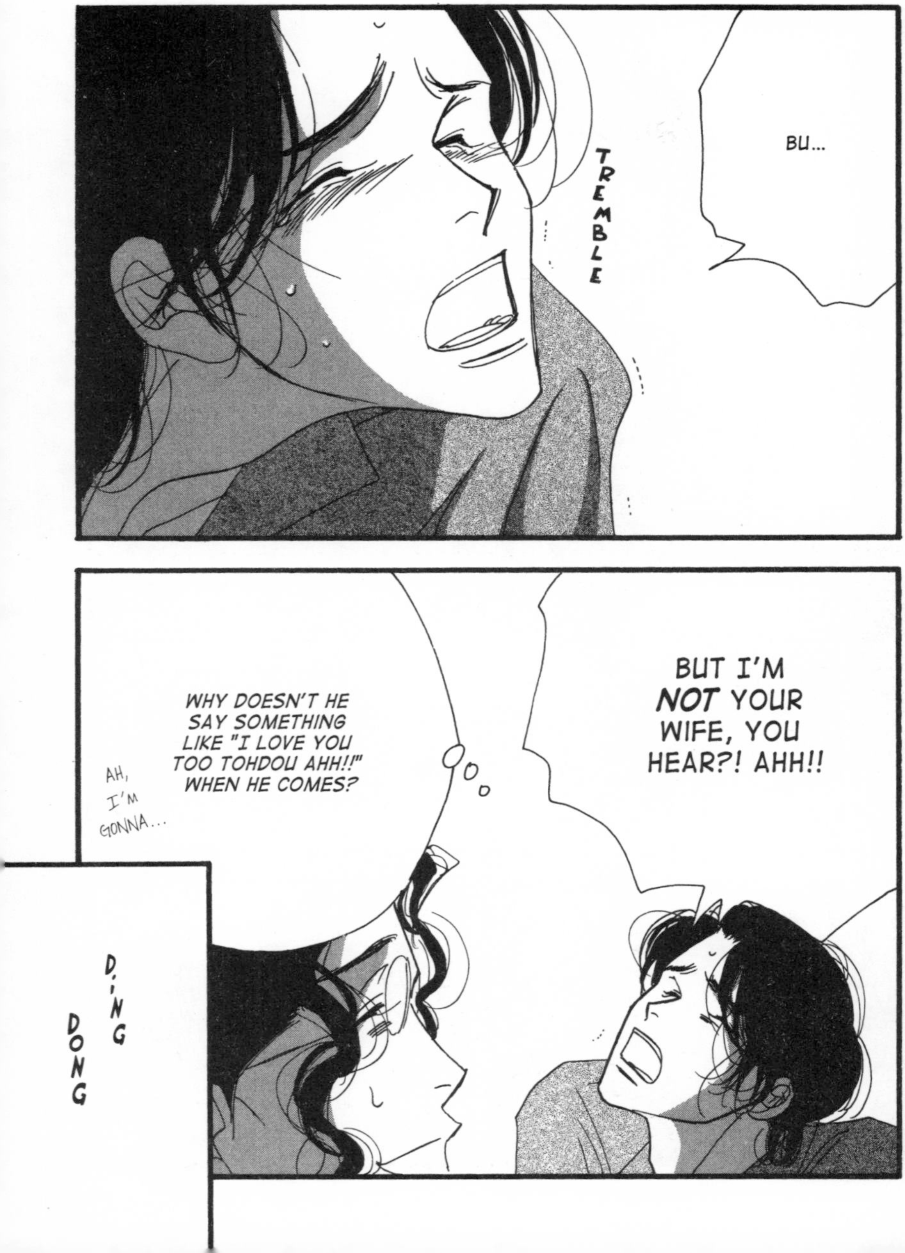
BU...
TREMBLE
BUT I'M **NOT** YOUR WIFE, YOU HEAR?! AHH!!
WHY DOESN'T HE SAY SOMETHING LIKE "I LOVE YOU TOO TOHDOU AHH!!" WHEN HE COMES?
AH, I'M GONNA...
DING DONG

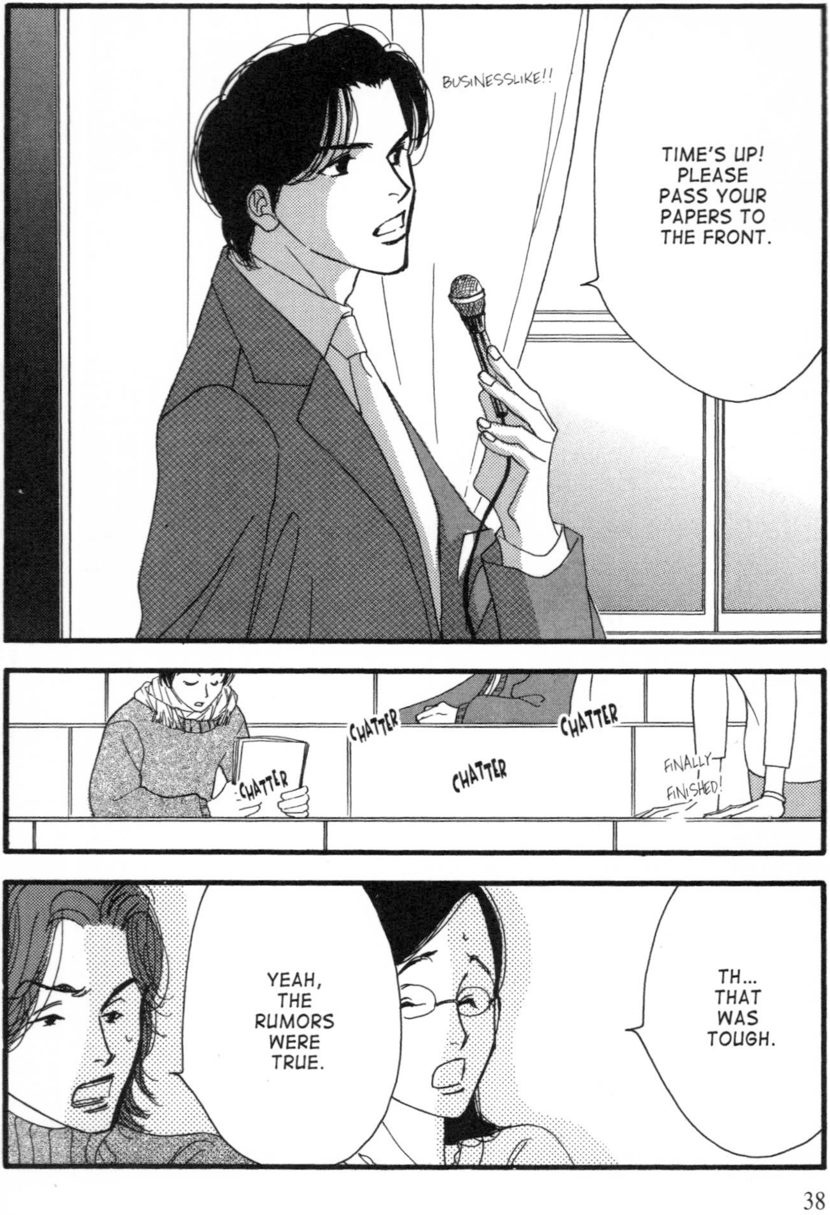
TIME'S UP! PLEASE PASS YOUR PAPERS TO THE FRONT.
BUSINESSLIKE!!
FINALLY FINISHED!
CHATTER
CHATTER
CHATTER
CHATTER
TH... THAT WAS TOUGH.
YEAH, THE RUMORS WERE TRUE.

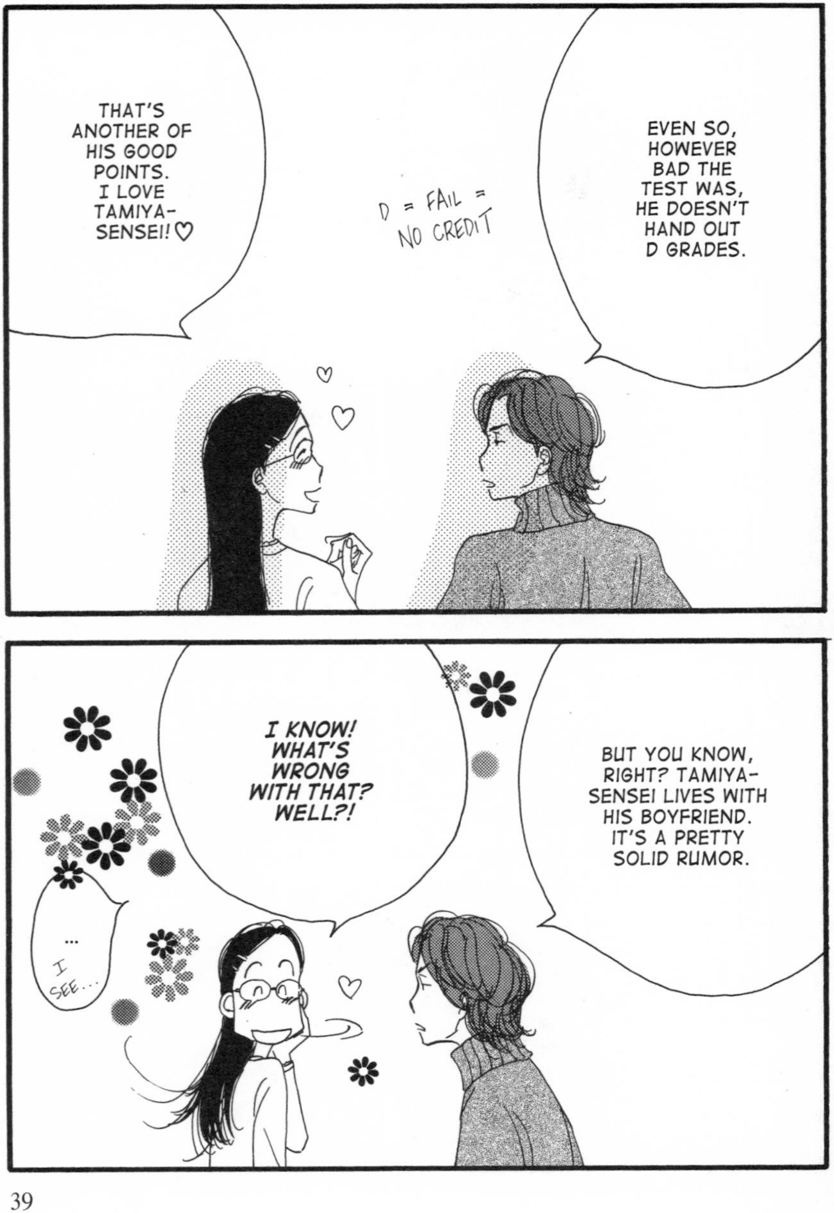
EVEN SO, HOWEVER BAD THE TEST WAS, HE DOESN'T HAND OUT D GRADES.
D = FAIL = NO CREDIT
THAT'S ANOTHER OF HIS GOOD POINTS. I LOVE TAMIYA-SENSEI! ♡
BUT YOU KNOW, RIGHT? TAMIYA-SENSEI LIVES WITH HIS BOYFRIEND. IT'S A PRETTY SOLID RUMOR.
I KNOW! WHAT'S WRONG WITH THAT? WELL?!
... I SEE...

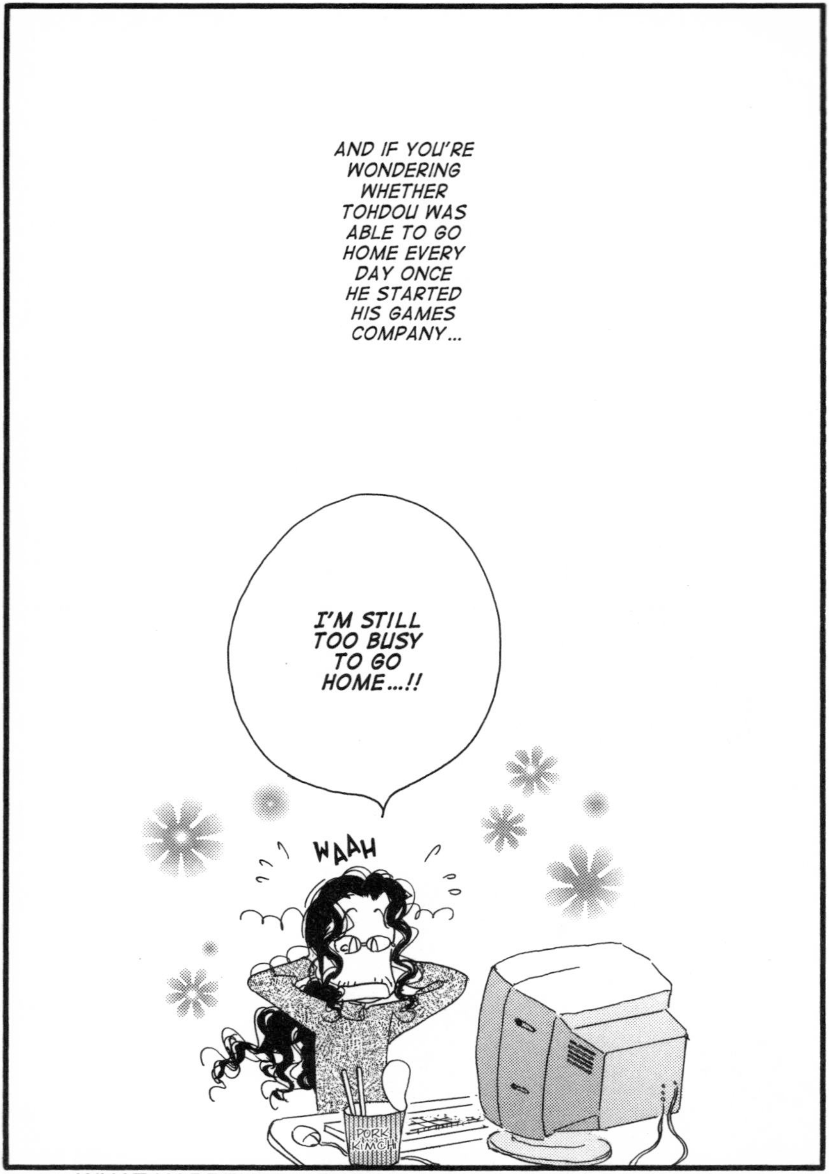
AND IF YOU'RE WONDERING WHETHER TOHDOU WAS ABLE TO GO HOME EVERY DAY ONCE HE STARTED HIS GAMES COMPANY...
I'M STILL TOO BUSY TO GO HOME...!!
WAAH
PORK KIMCHI

WHAT HAPPENED NEXT?! TOHDOU AND TAMIYA / END

TOHDOU'S RAISON D'ETRE.

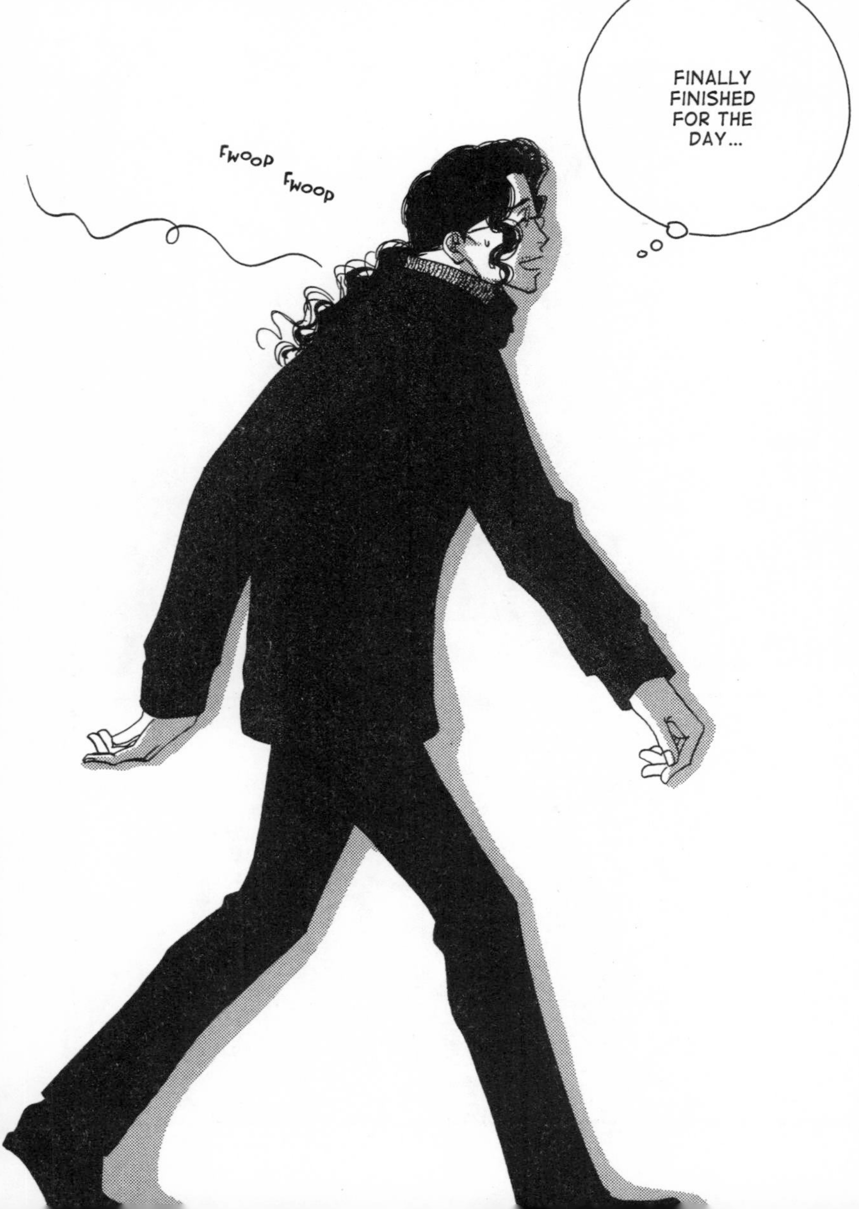
FINALLY FINISHED FOR THE DAY...
FWOOP FWOOP

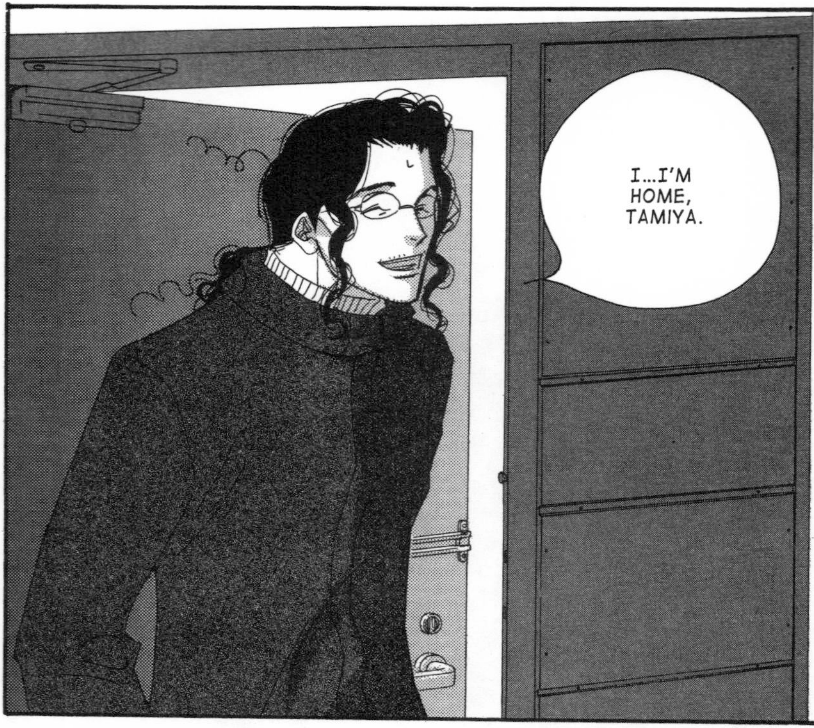
I...I'M HOME, TAMIYA.
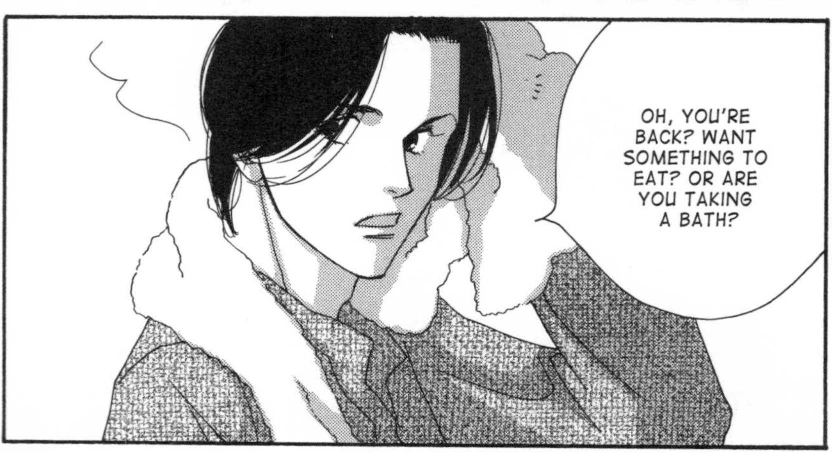
OH, YOU'RE BACK? WANT SOMETHING TO EAT? OR ARE YOU TAKING A BATH?

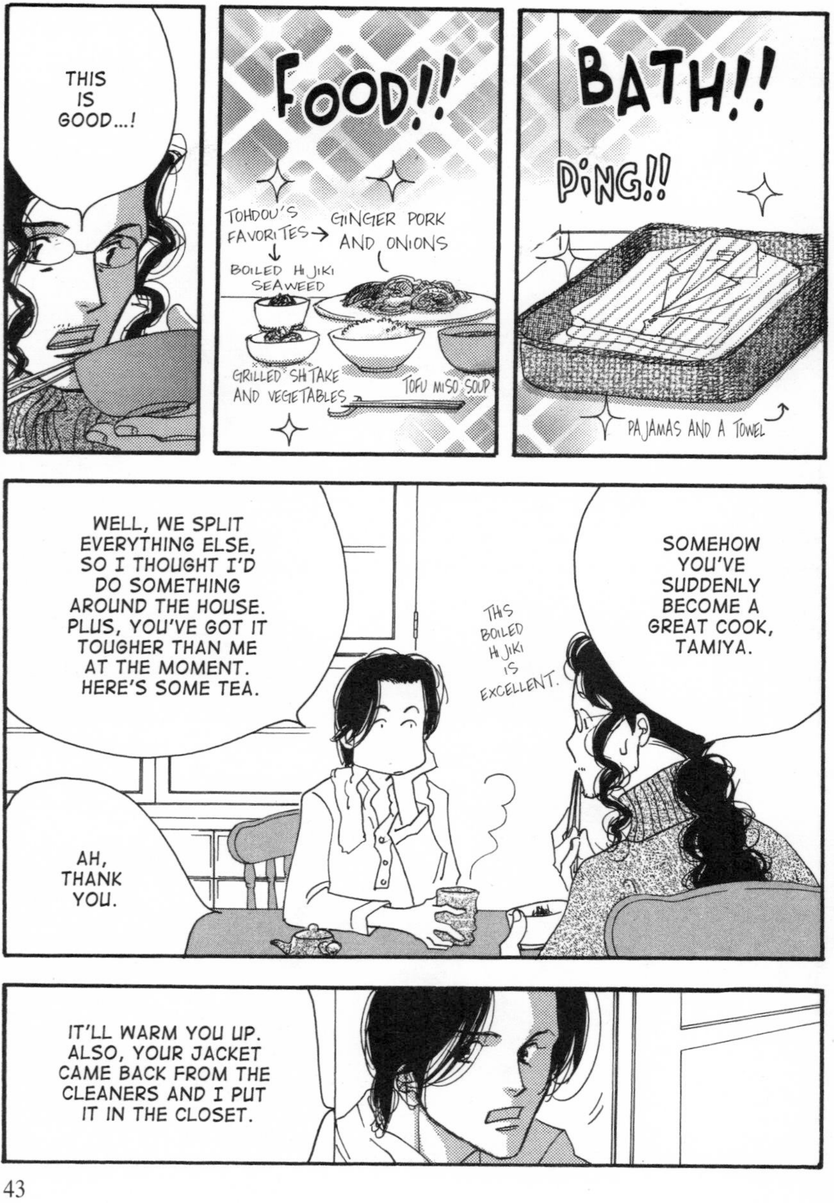
BATH!!
PING!!
PAJAMAS AND A TOWEL
FOOD!!
TOHDOU'S FAVORITES
GINGER PORK AND ONIONS
BOILED HIJIKI SEAWEED
GRILLED SHITAKE AND VEGETABLES
TOFU MISO SOUP
THIS IS GOOD...!
SOMEHOW YOU'VE SUDDENLY BECOME A GREAT COOK, TAMIYA.
THIS BOILED HIJIKI IS EXCELLENT.
WELL, WE SPLIT EVERYTHING ELSE, SO I THOUGHT I'D DO SOMETHING AROUND THE HOUSE. PLUS, YOU'VE GOT IT TOUGHER THAN ME AT THE MOMENT. HERE'S SOME TEA.
AH, THANK YOU.
IT'LL WARM YOU UP. ALSO, YOUR JACKET CAME BACK FROM THE CLEANERS AND I PUT IT IN THE CLOSET.

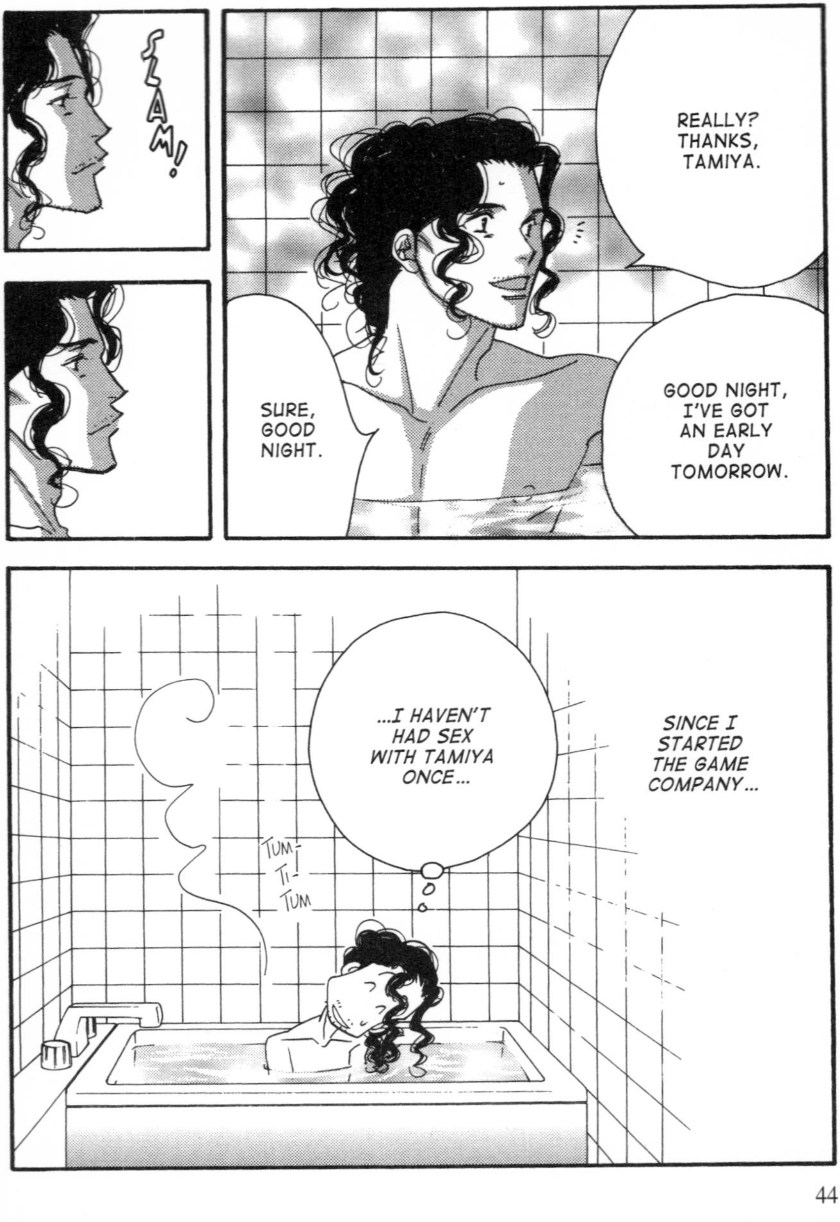
REALLY? THANKS, TAMIYA.
GOOD NIGHT, I'VE GOT AN EARLY DAY TOMORROW.
SURE, GOOD NIGHT.
SLAM!
SINCE I STARTED THE GAME COMPANY...
...I HAVEN'T HAD SEX WITH TAMIYA ONCE...
TUM-TI-TUM

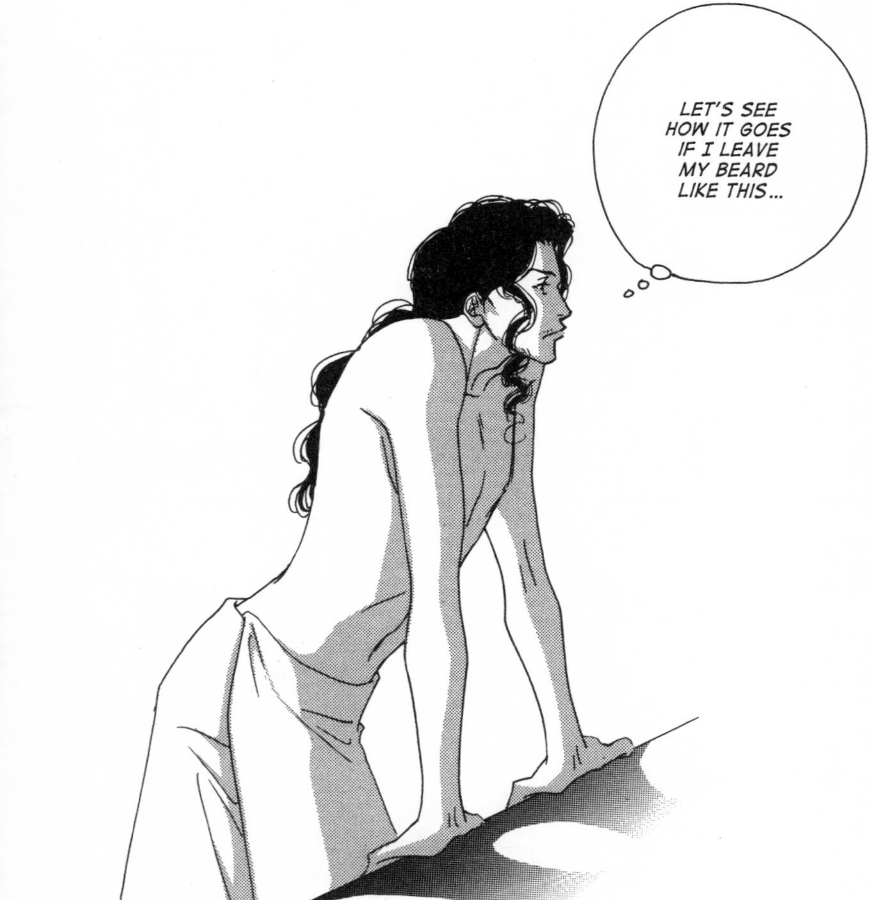
LET'S SEE HOW IT GOES IF I LEAVE MY BEARD LIKE THIS...

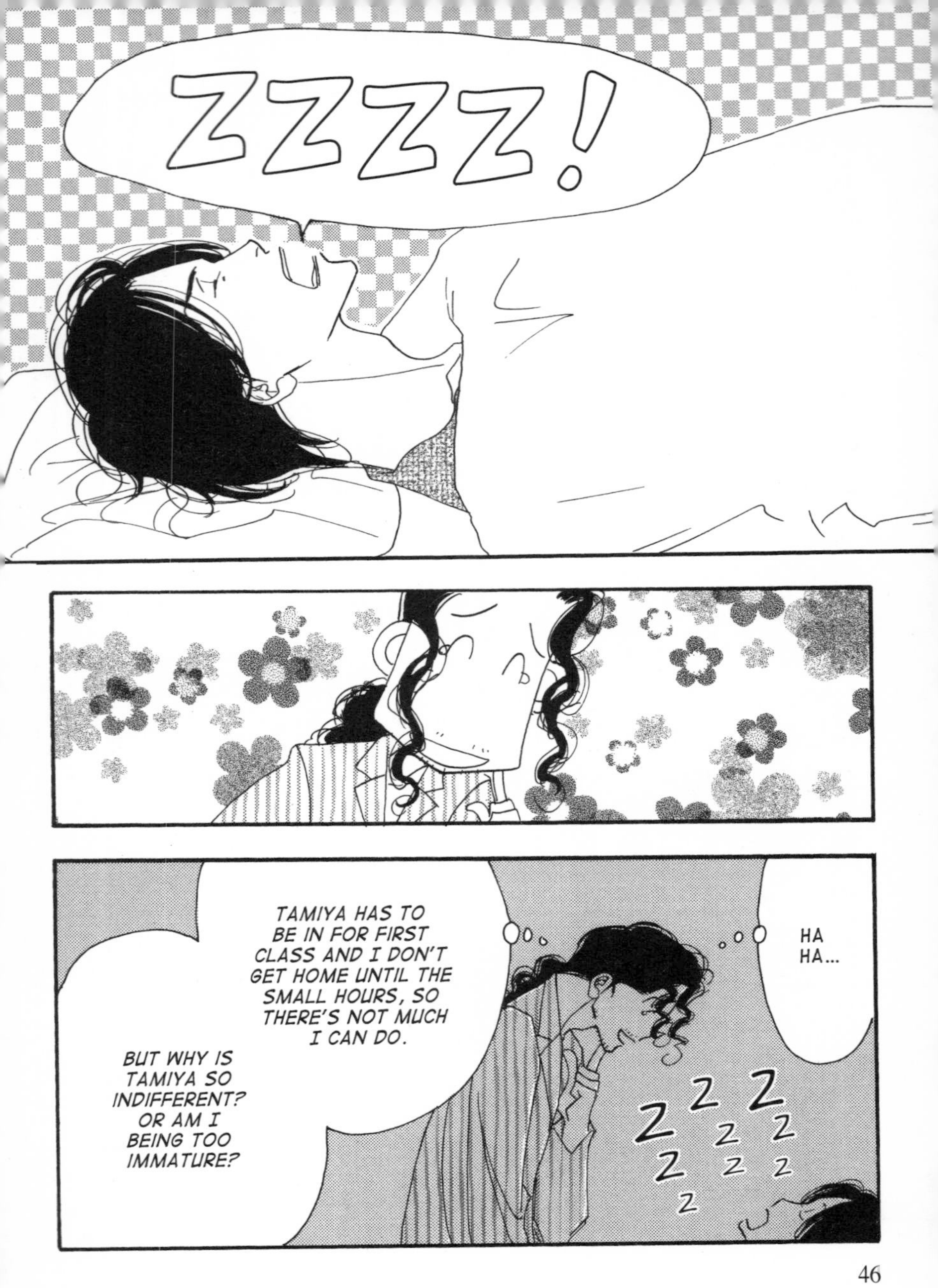
ZZZZ!
HA HA...
TAMIYA HAS TO BE IN FOR FIRST CLASS AND I DON'T GET HOME UNTIL THE SMALL HOURS, SO THERE'S NOT MUCH I CAN DO.
BUT WHY IS TAMIYA SO INDIFFERENT? OR AM I BEING TOO IMMATURE?
Z Z Z Z Z Z Z Z Z Z Z

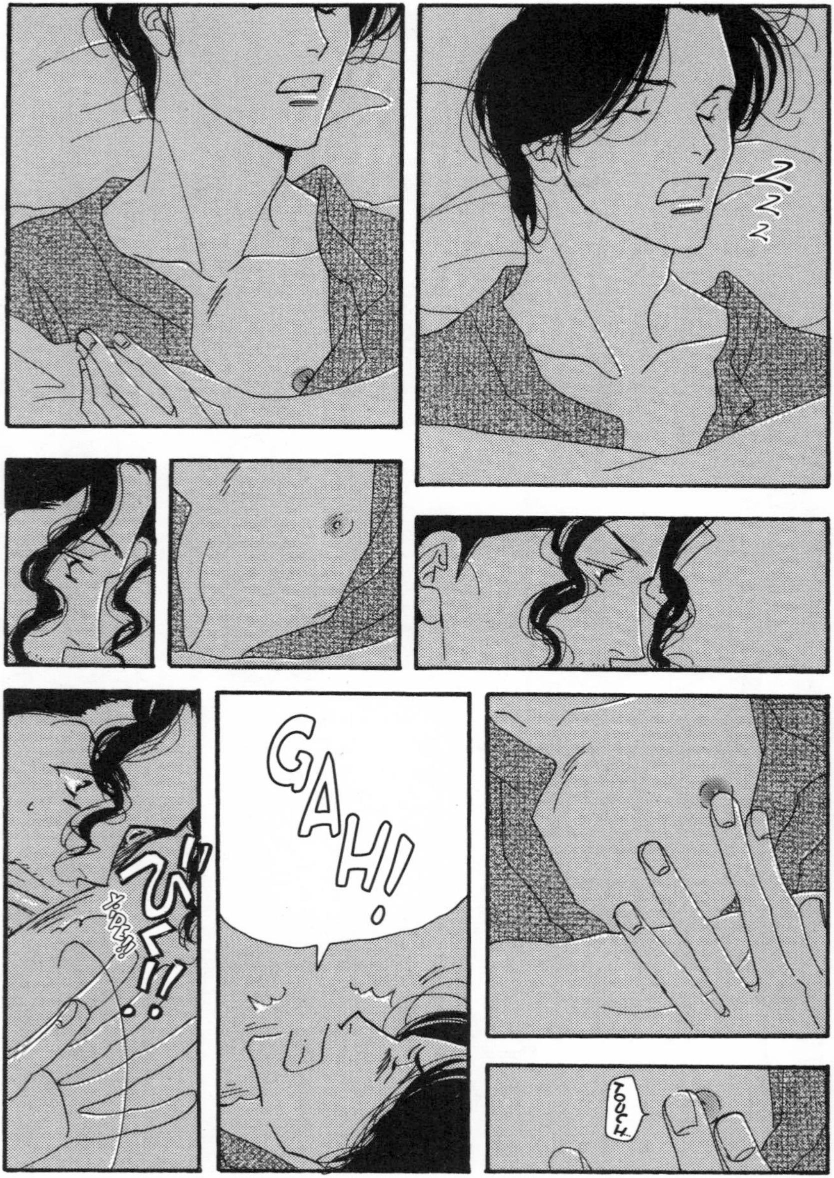
ZZZ
TOUCH...
GAH!
YIPE!!

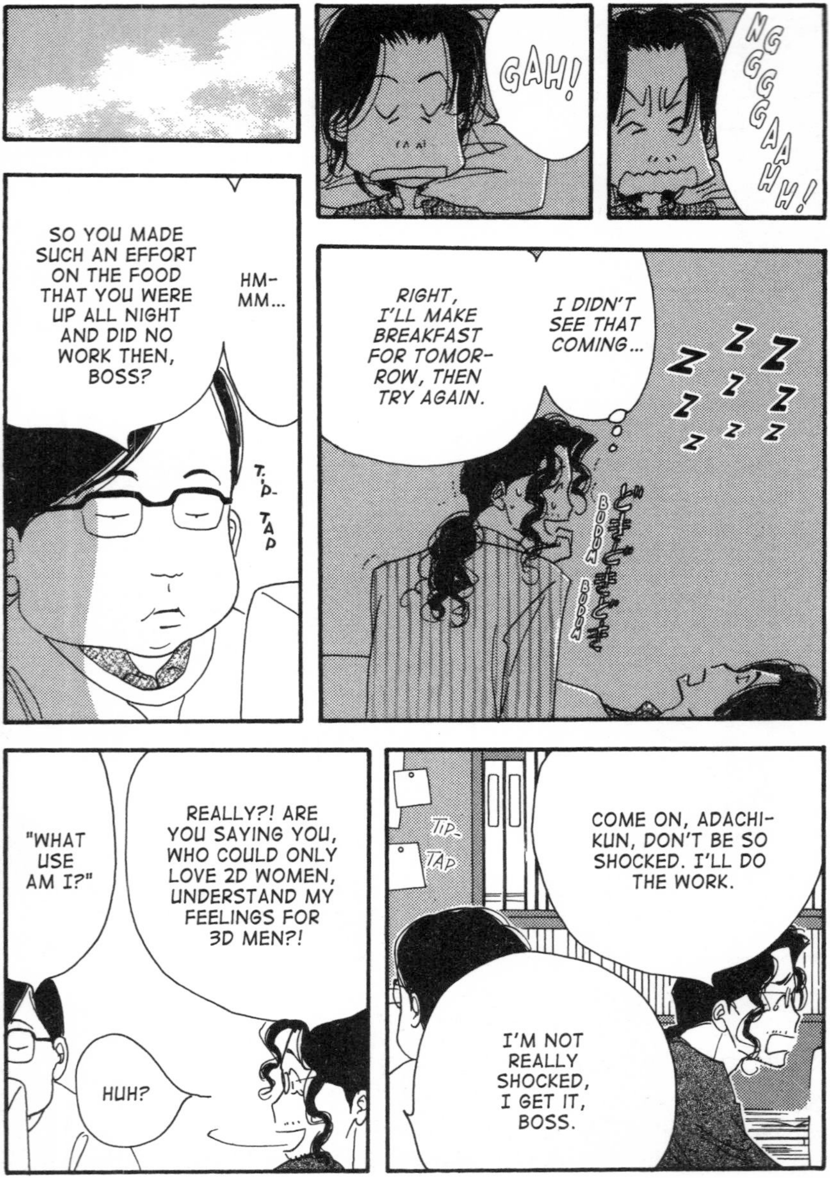
NGGGAAHH!
GAH!
I DIDN'T SEE THAT COMING...
RIGHT, I'LL MAKE BREAKFAST FOR TOMORROW, THEN TRY AGAIN.
ZZZZZZZZZ
BUDUM BUDUM
HM-MM...
SO YOU MADE SUCH AN EFFORT ON THE FOOD THAT YOU WERE UP ALL NIGHT AND DID NO WORK THEN, BOSS?
TIP-TAP
COME ON, ADACHI-KUN, DON'T BE SO SHOCKED. I'LL DO THE WORK.
TIP-TAP
I'M NOT REALLY SHOCKED, I GET IT, BOSS.
REALLY?! ARE YOU SAYING YOU, WHO COULD ONLY LOVE 2D WOMEN, UNDERSTAND MY FEELINGS FOR 3D MEN?!
"WHAT USE AM I?"
HUH?

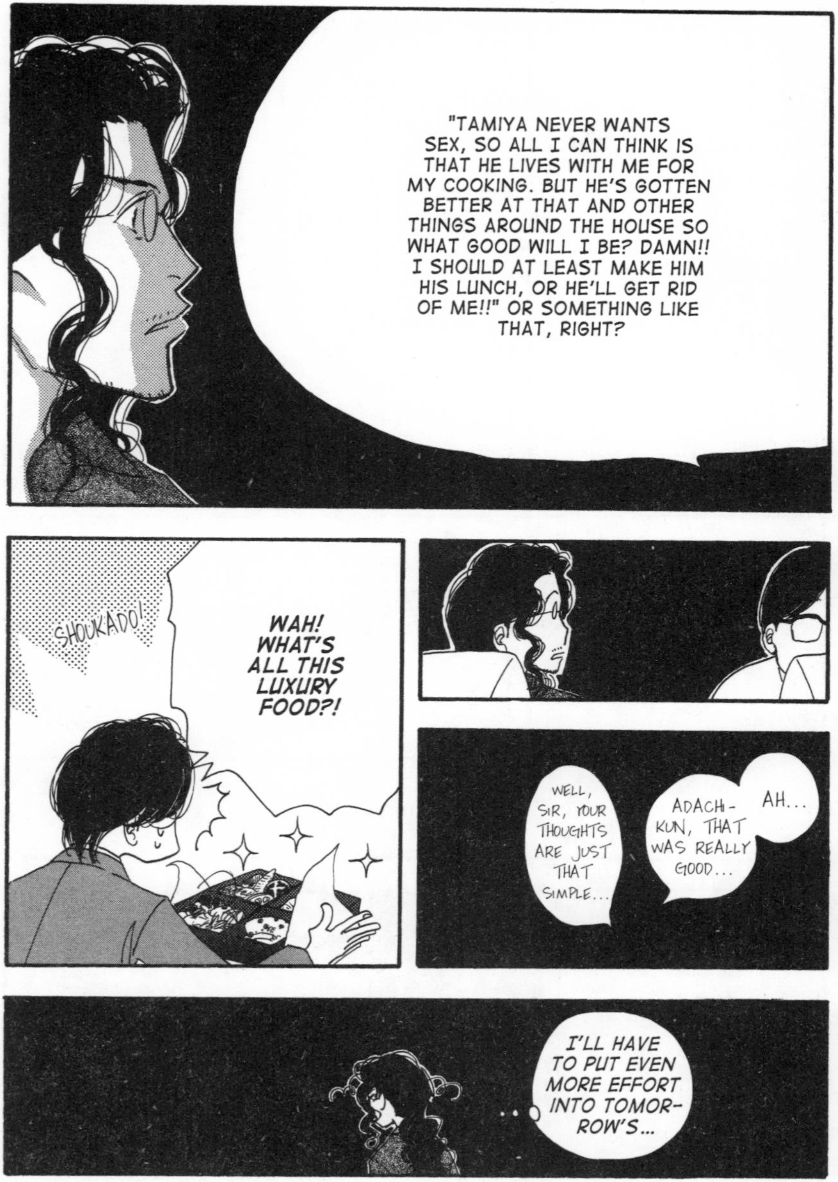
"TAMIYA NEVER WANTS SEX, SO ALL I CAN THINK IS THAT HE LIVES WITH ME FOR MY COOKING. BUT HE'S GOTTEN BETTER AT THAT AND OTHER THINGS AROUND THE HOUSE SO WHAT GOOD WILL I BE? DAMN!! I SHOULD AT LEAST MAKE HIM HIS LUNCH, OR HE'LL GET RID OF ME!!" OR SOMETHING LIKE THAT, RIGHT?
AH...
ADACHI-KUN, THAT WAS REALLY GOOD...
WELL, SIR, YOUR THOUGHTS ARE JUST THAT SIMPLE...
WAH! WHAT'S ALL THIS LUXURY FOOD?!
SHOUKADO!
I'LL HAVE TO PUT EVEN MORE EFFORT INTO TOMORROW'S...

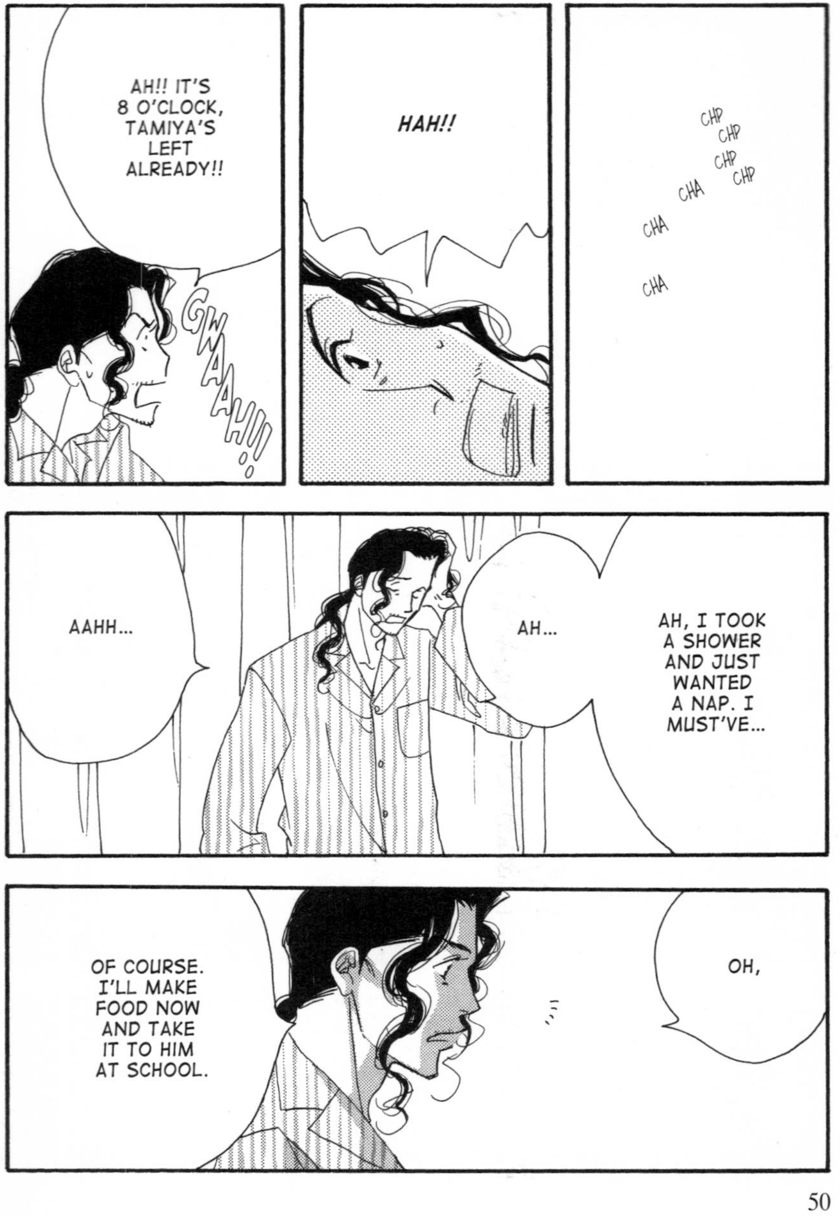
CHP CHP CHP CHP
CHA CHA CHA
HAH!!
AH!! IT'S 8 O'CLOCK, TAMIYA'S LEFT ALREADY!!
GWAAAH!!
AH, I TOOK A SHOWER AND JUST WANTED A NAP. I MUST'VE...
AH...
AAHH...
OH,
OF COURSE. I'LL MAKE FOOD NOW AND TAKE IT TO HIM AT SCHOOL.

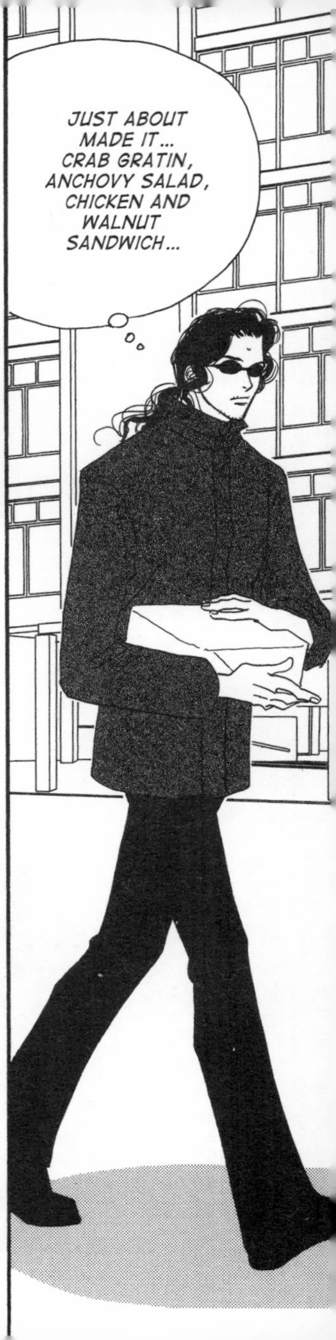
JUST ABOUT MADE IT... CRAB GRATIN, ANCHOVY SALAD, CHICKEN AND WALNUT SANDWICH...
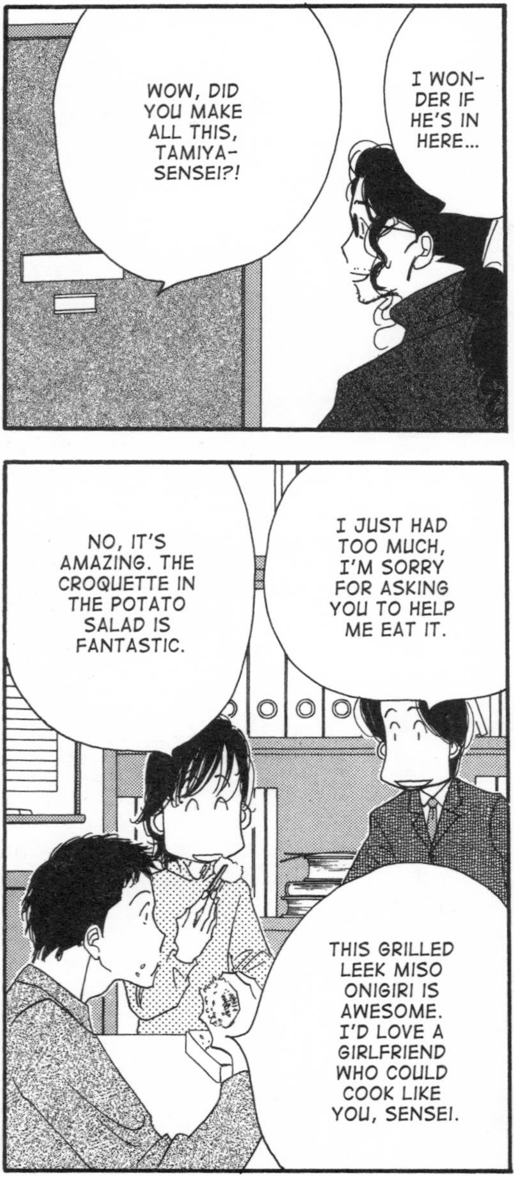
I WON-DER IF HE'S IN HERE...
WOW, DID YOU MAKE ALL THIS, TAMIYA-SENSEI?!
I JUST HAD TOO MUCH, I'M SORRY FOR ASKING YOU TO HELP ME EAT IT.
NO, IT'S AMAZING. THE CROQUETTE IN THE POTATO SALAD IS FANTASTIC.
THIS GRILLED LEEK MISO ONIGIRI IS AWESOME. I'D LOVE A GIRLFRIEND WHO COULD COOK LIKE YOU, SENSEI.

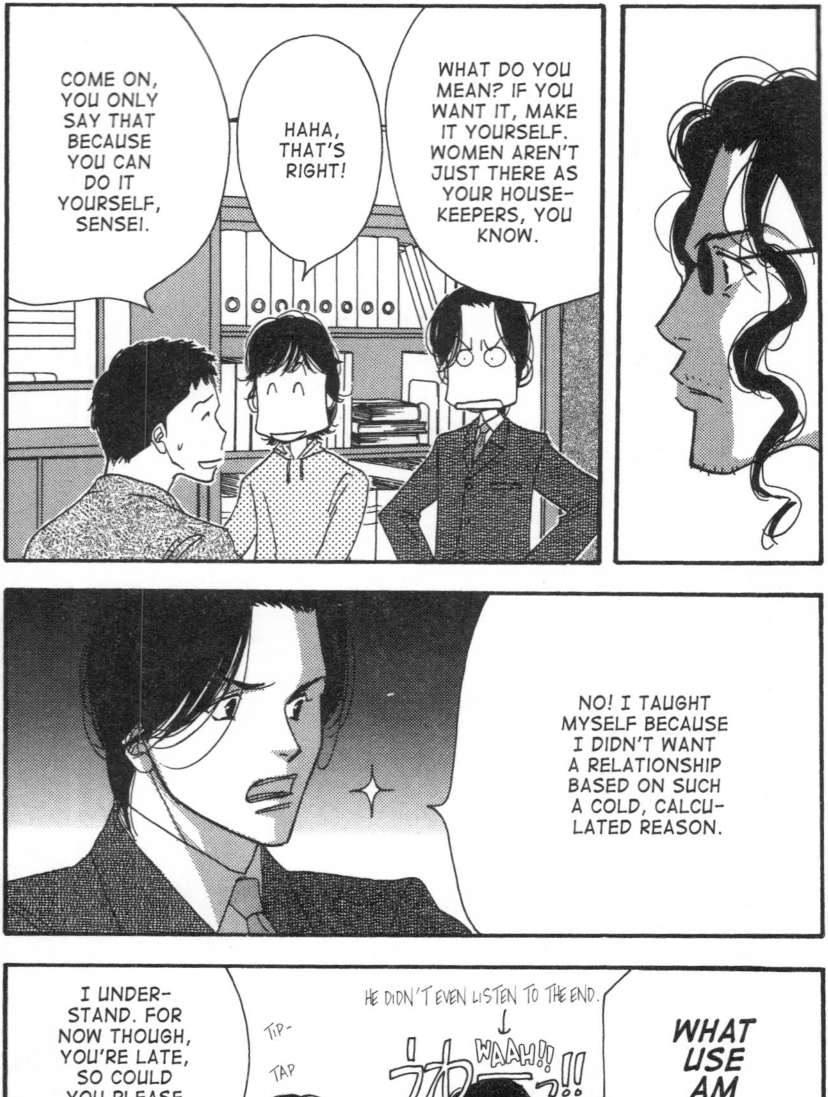
WHAT DO YOU MEAN? IF YOU WANT IT, MAKE IT YOURSELF. WOMEN AREN'T JUST THERE AS YOUR HOUSE-KEEPERS, YOU KNOW.
HAHA, THAT'S RIGHT!
COME ON, YOU ONLY SAY THAT BECAUSE YOU CAN DO IT YOURSELF, SENSEI.
NO! I TAUGHT MYSELF BECAUSE I DIDN'T WANT A RELATIONSHIP BASED ON SUCH A COLD, CALCU-LATED REASON.
WHAT USE AM I!!
HE DIDN'T EVEN LISTEN TO THE END.
WAAH!!
うわーっ!!
TIP-
TAP
I UNDER-STAND. FOR NOW THOUGH, YOU'RE LATE, SO COULD YOU PLEASE DO SOME WORK SIR?

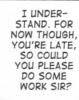

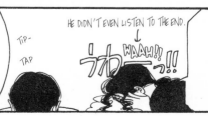

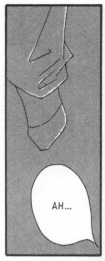

AH...

TAMIYA MUST BE ASLEEP.

CREE

AH, IT'S PAST 1:30...

MM...

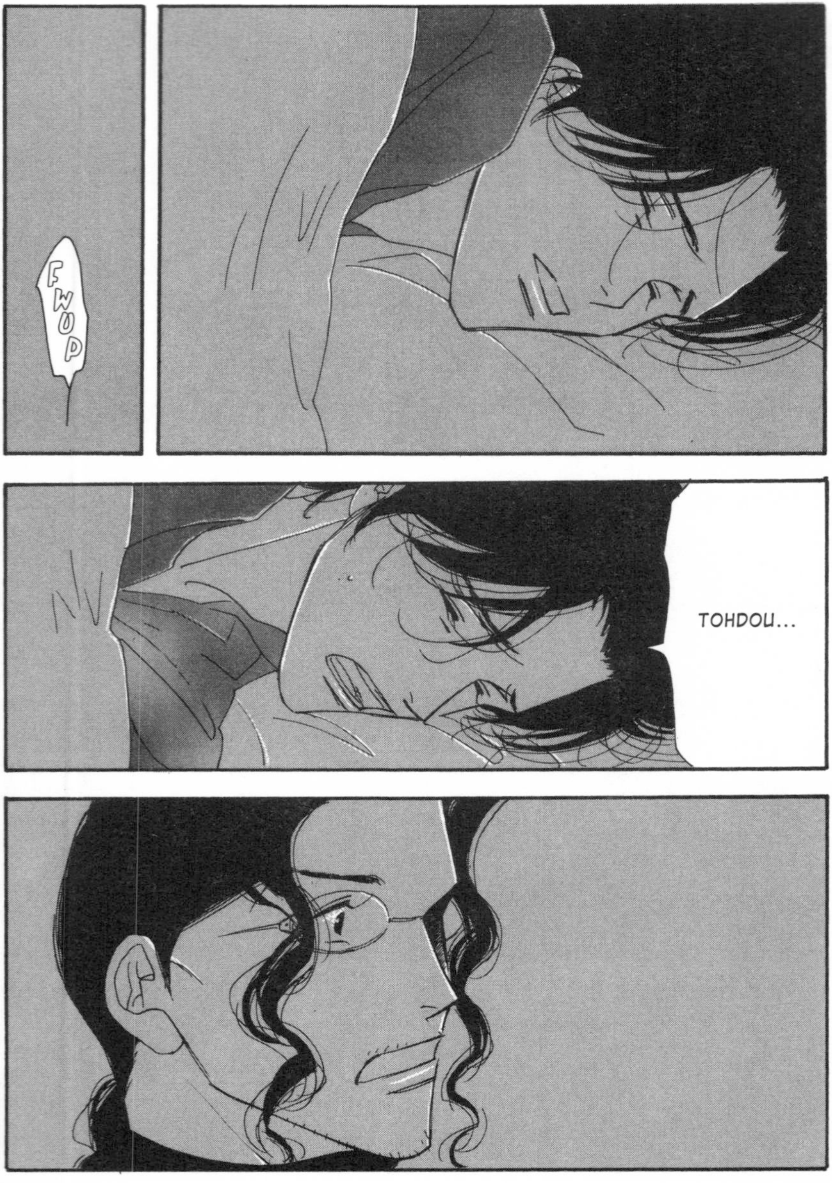
FWUP
TOHDOU...

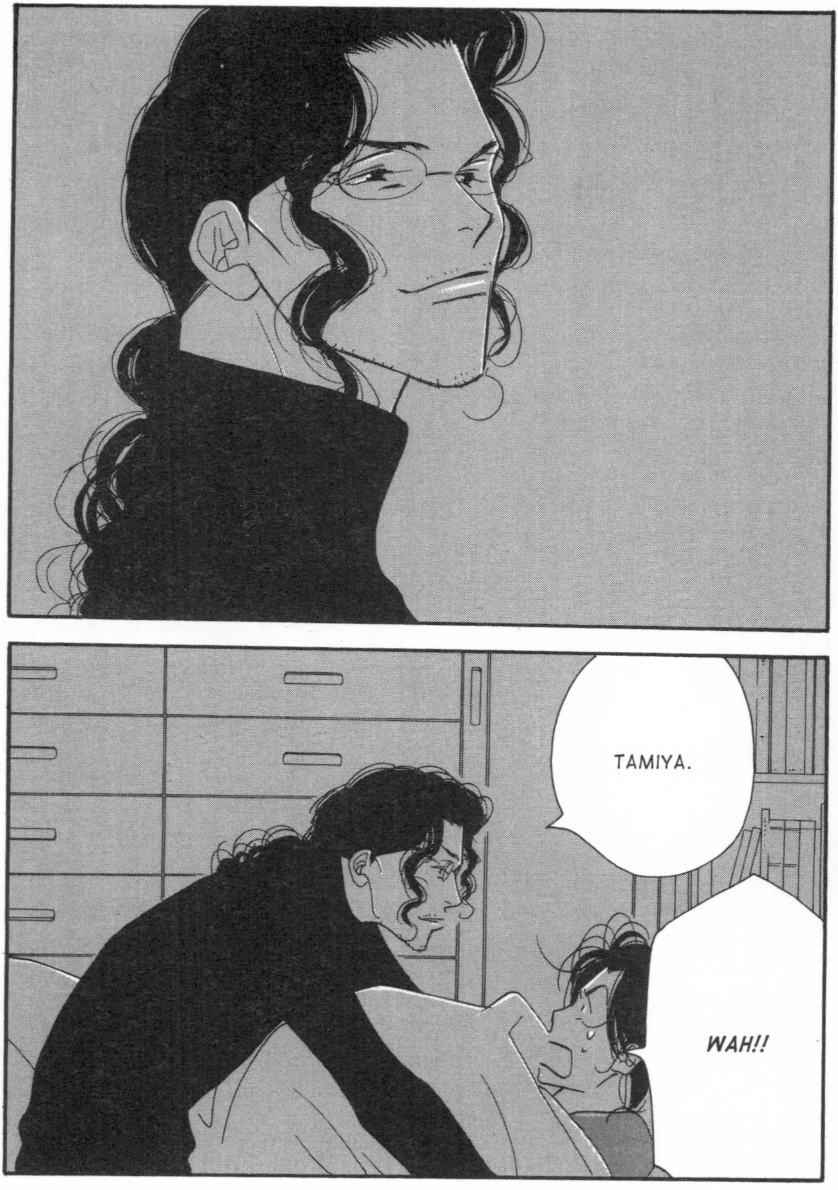
TAMIYA.
WAH!!

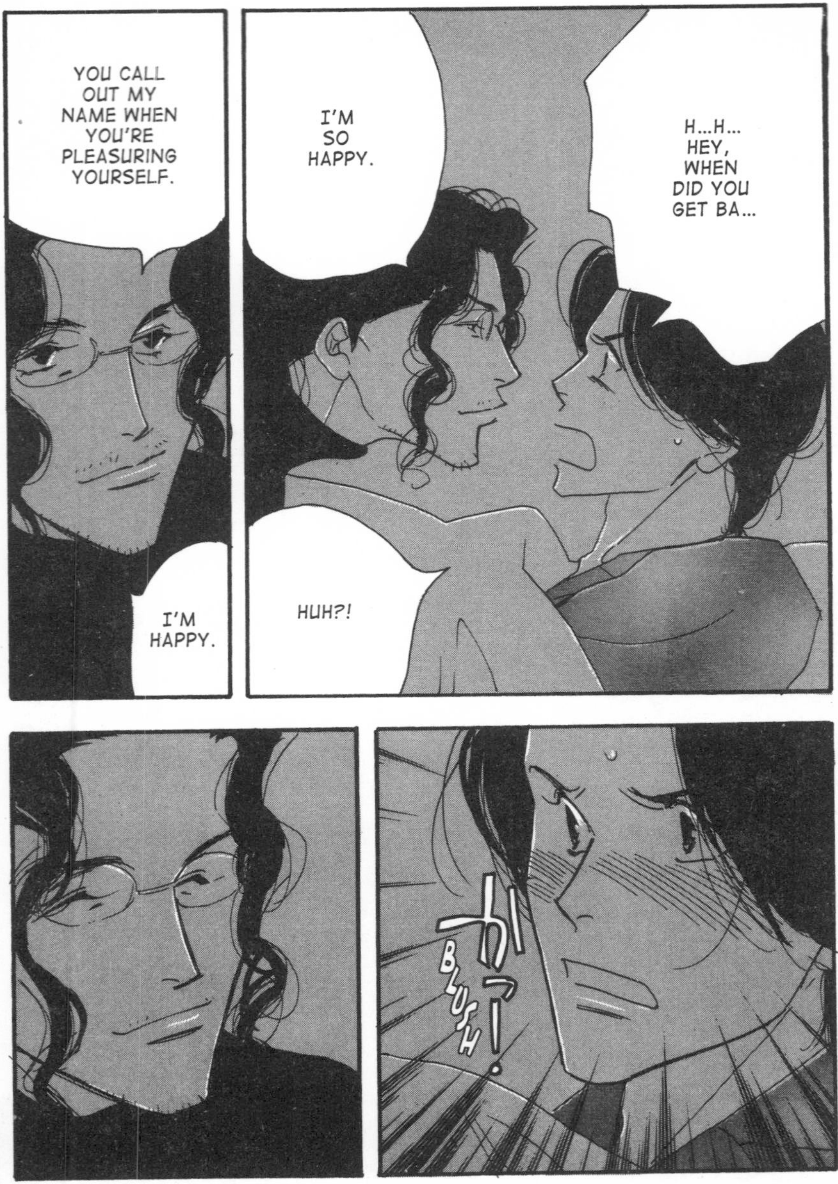
H...H... HEY, WHEN DID YOU GET BA...
I'M SO HAPPY.
HUH?!
YOU CALL OUT MY NAME WHEN YOU'RE PLEASURING YOURSELF.
I'M HAPPY.
BLUSH

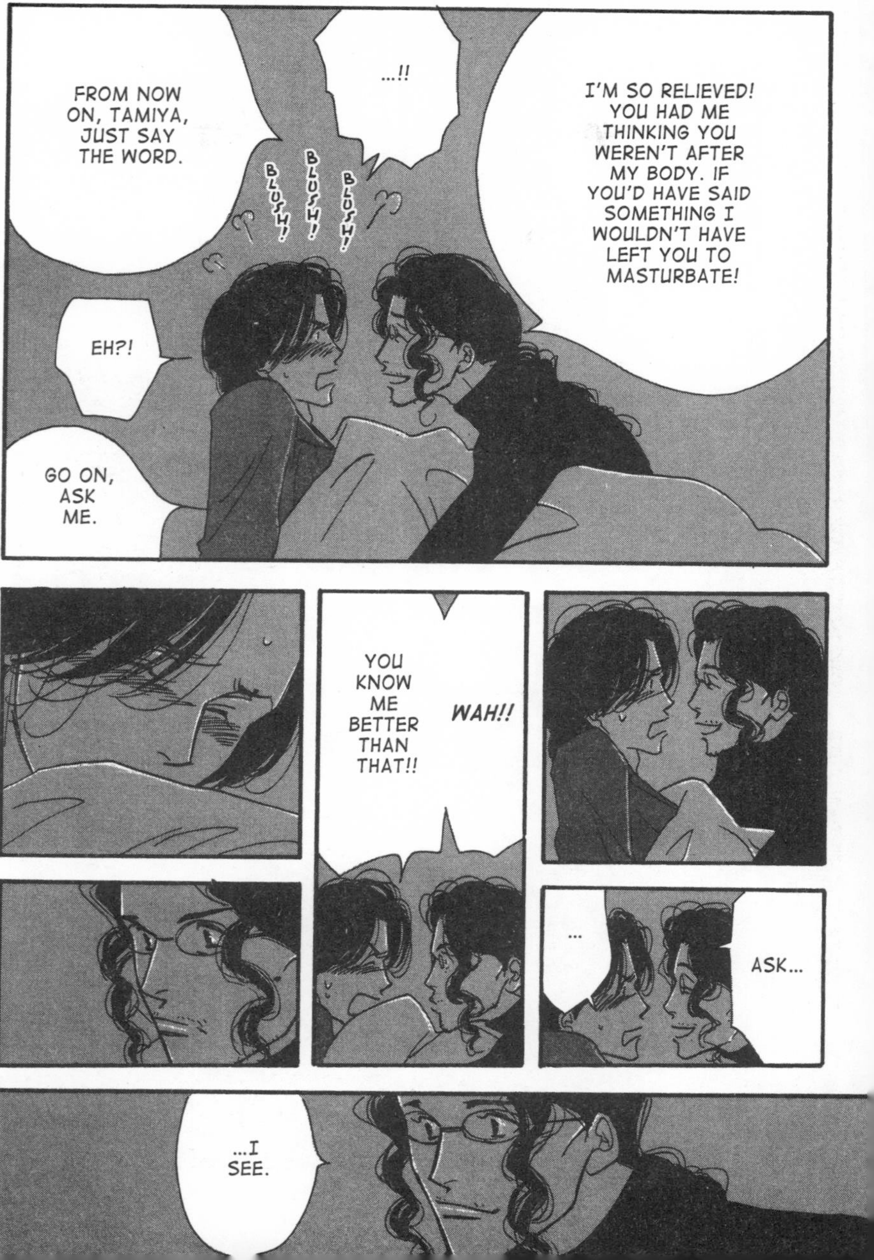
I'M SO RELIEVED! YOU HAD ME THINKING YOU WEREN'T AFTER MY BODY. IF YOU'D HAVE SAID SOMETHING I WOULDN'T HAVE LEFT YOU TO MASTURBATE!
...!!
FROM NOW ON, TAMIYA, JUST SAY THE WORD.
BLUSH! BLUSH! BLUSH!
EH?!
GO ON, ASK ME.
ASK...
...
WAH!!
YOU KNOW ME BETTER THAN THAT!!
...I SEE.

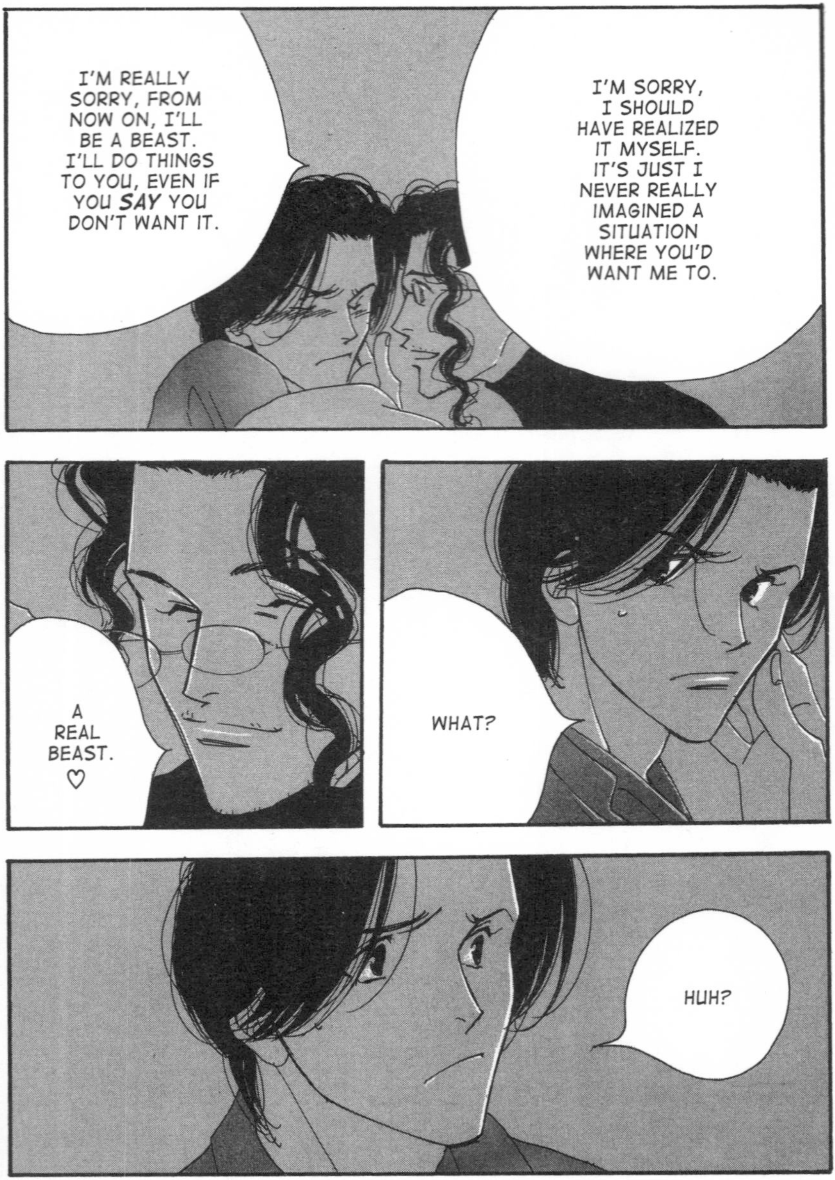
I'M SORRY, I SHOULD HAVE REALIZED IT MYSELF. IT'S JUST I NEVER REALLY IMAGINED A SITUATION WHERE YOU'D WANT ME TO.
I'M REALLY SORRY, FROM NOW ON, I'LL BE A BEAST. I'LL DO THINGS TO YOU, EVEN IF YOU *SAY* YOU DON'T WANT IT.
WHAT?
A REAL BEAST. ♡
HUH?

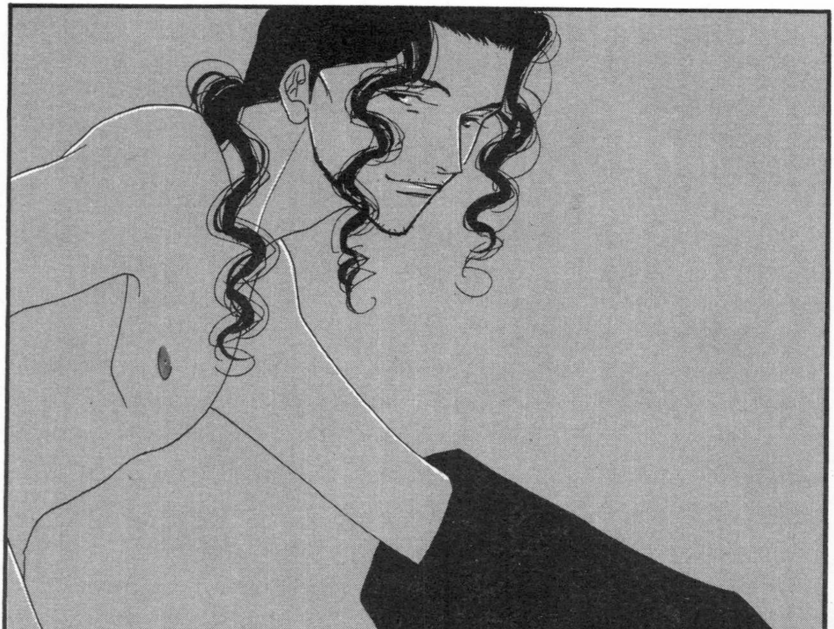

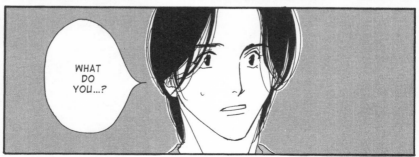

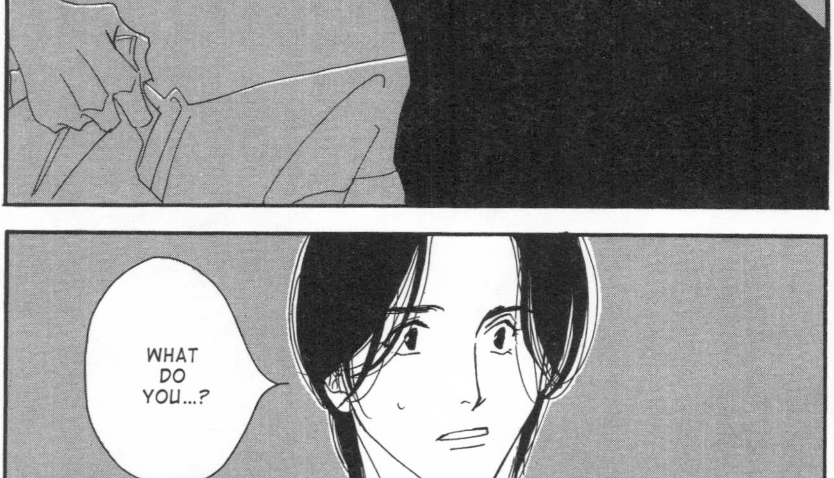
WHAT DO YOU...?

UHH!

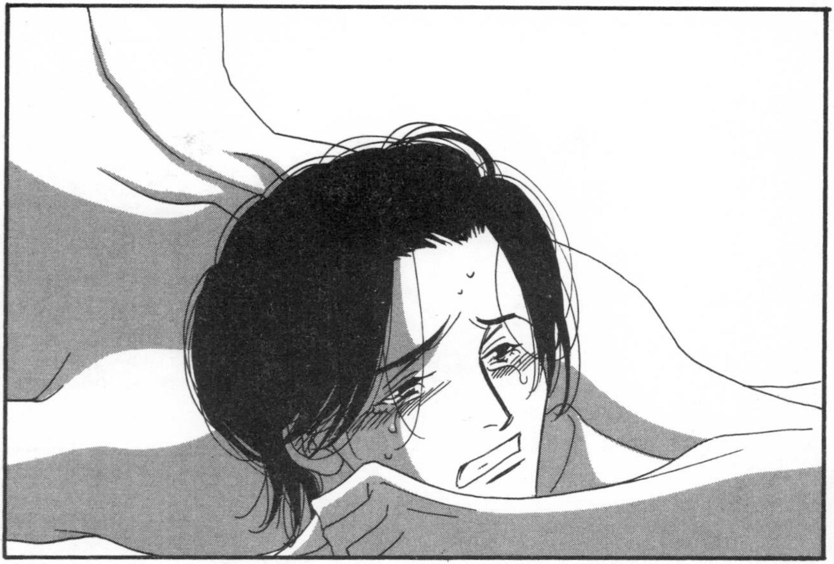

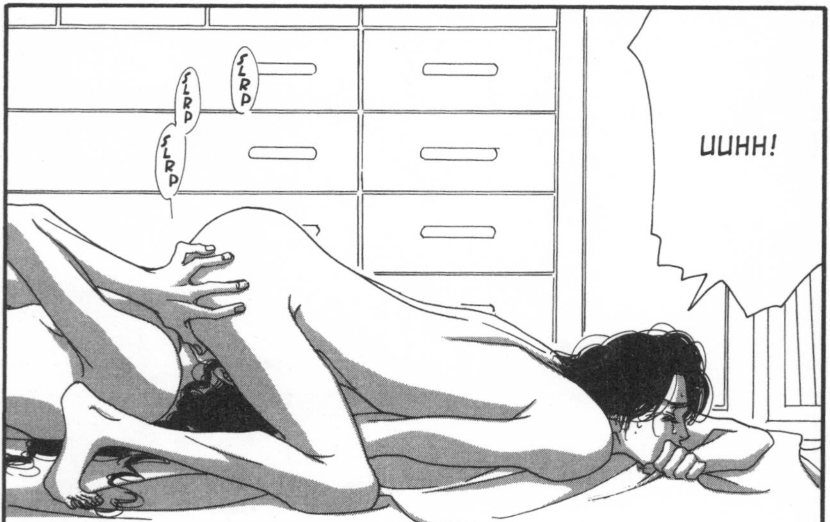
UUHH!
SLRP
SLRP
SLRP

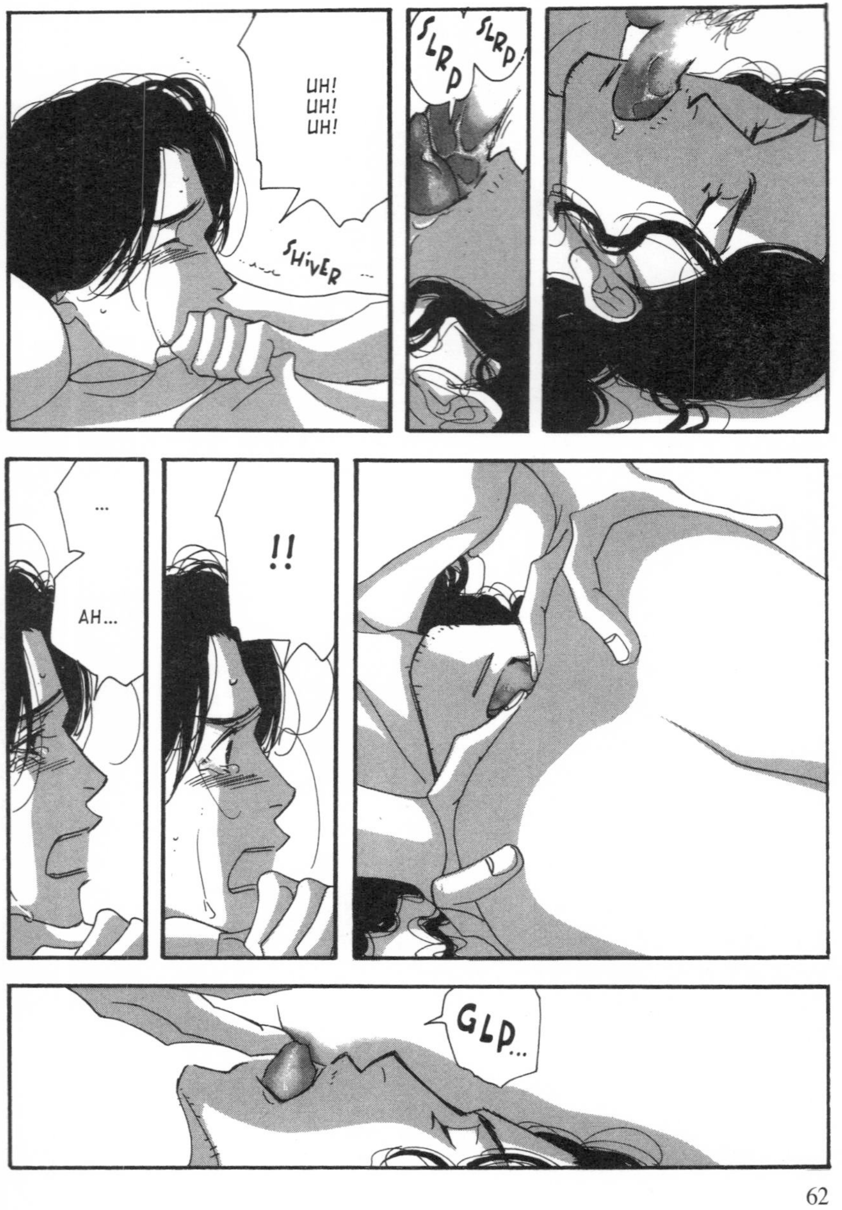
SLRP
SLRP
UH! UH! UH!
SHIVER
!!
...
AH...
GLP...

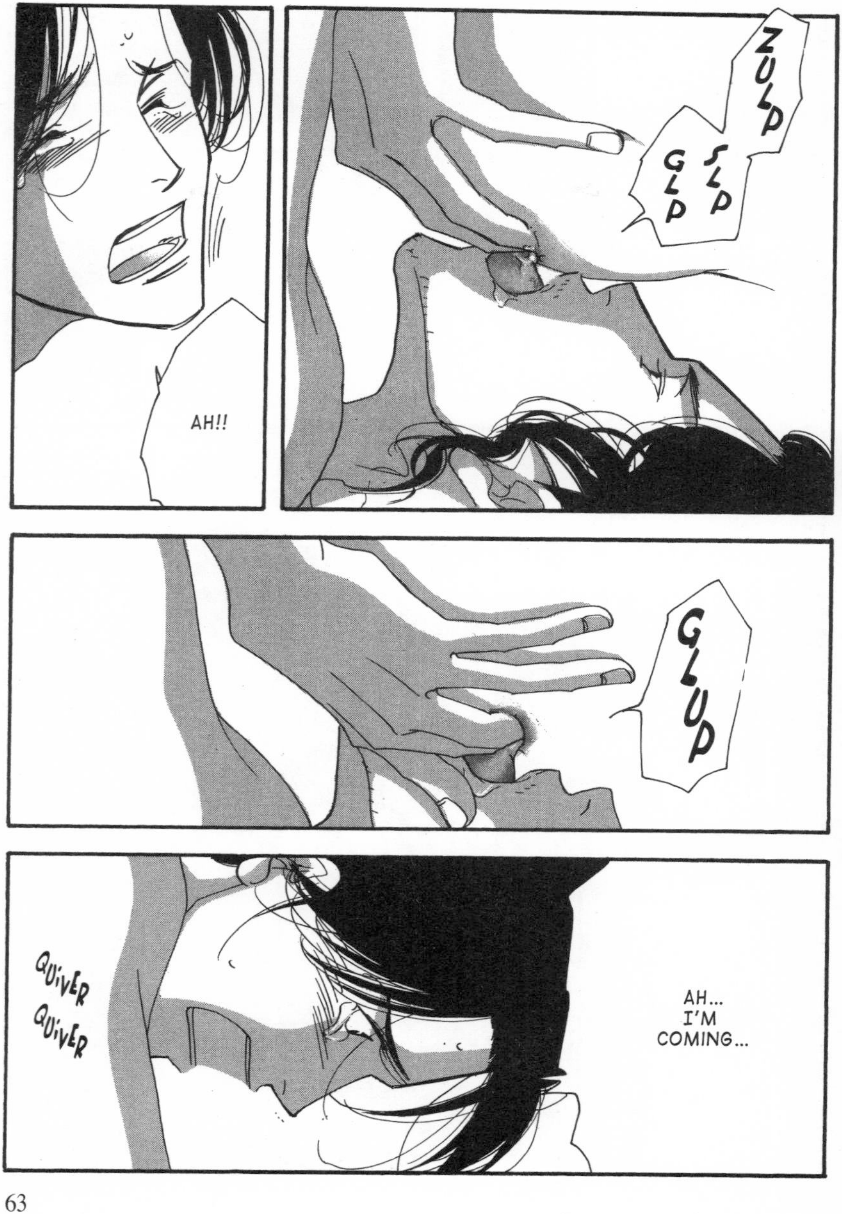
ZULP
SLP
GLP
AH!!
GLUP
AH... I'M COMING...
QUIVER
QUIVER

AH!!

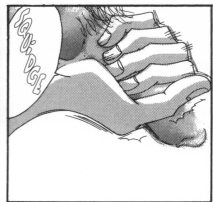

SGUIDGE

NOPE,
NOT
YET...

N...
NO
WAY...
TO...

EH?
AH...
AH...

SLRP
LICK

BO-DUM!

WAH!!

SHMP

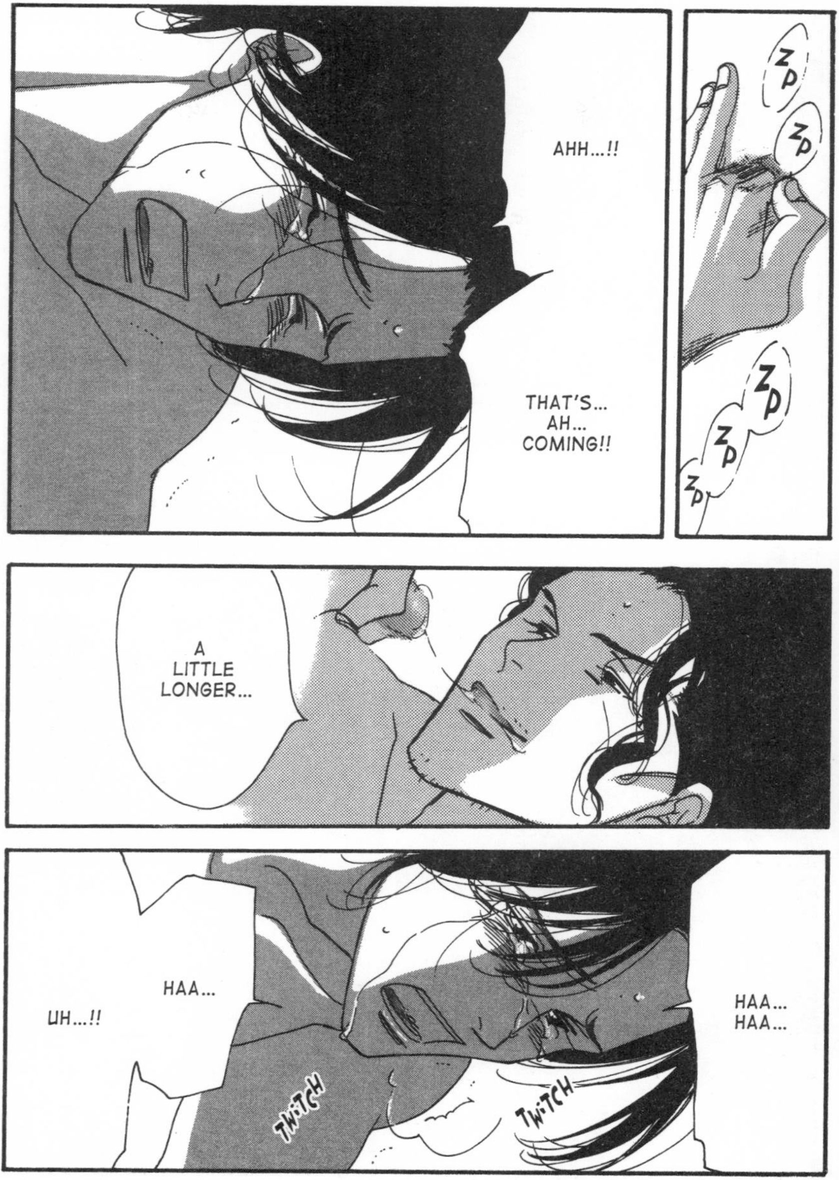
ZP
ZP
ZP
ZP
ZP
AHH...!!
THAT'S... AH... COMING!!
A LITTLE LONGER...
HAA... HAA...
TWITCH
TWITCH
HAA...
UH...!!

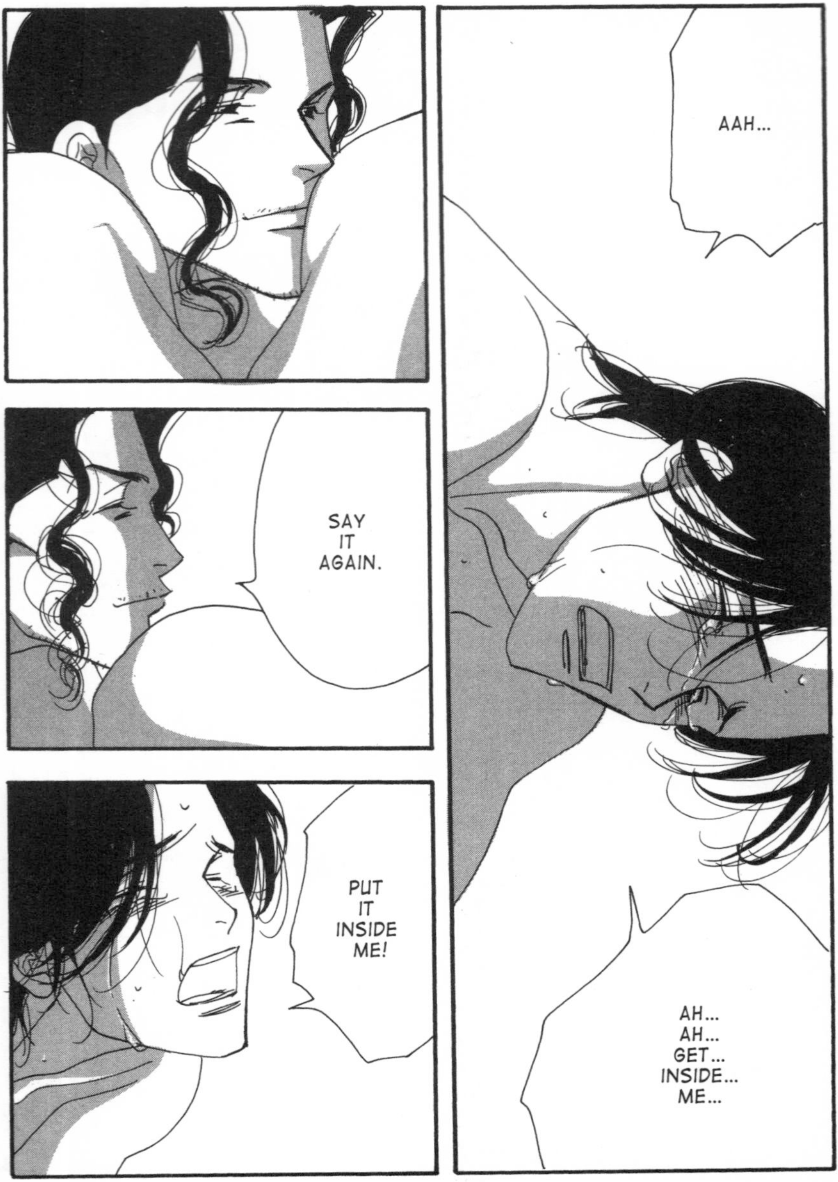
AAH...
AH... AH... GET... INSIDE... ME...
SAY IT AGAIN.
PUT IT INSIDE ME!

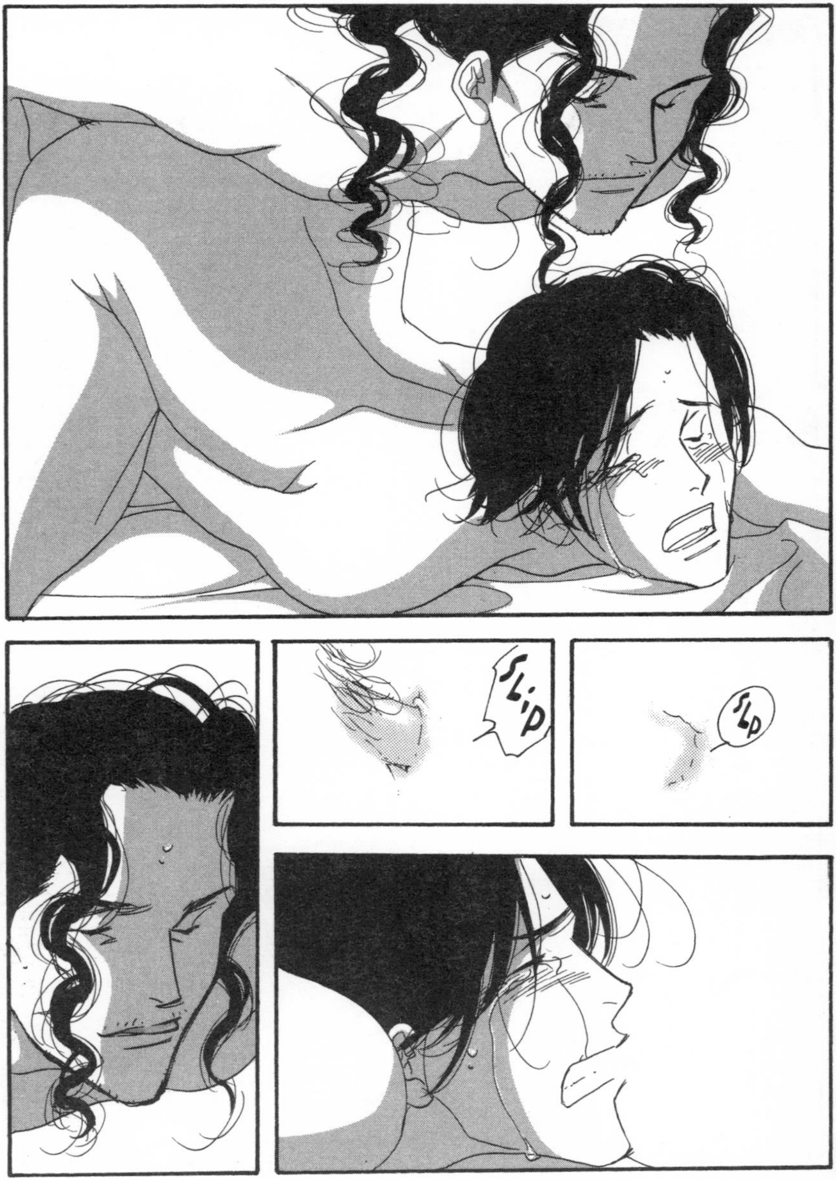
SLP
SLiP

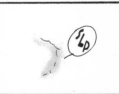

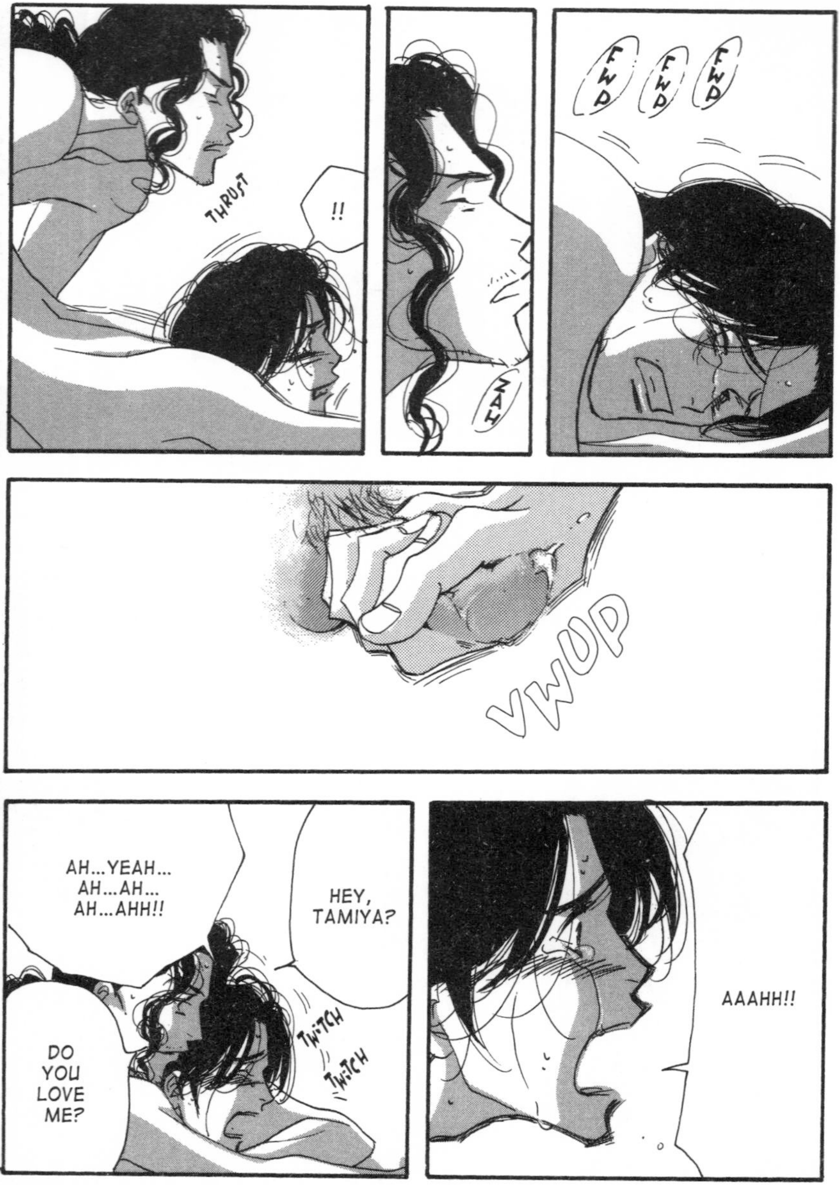
FWP FWP FWP
ZAH
THRUST
!!
VWUP
AAAHH!!
HEY, TAMIYA?
AH...YEAH... AH...AH... AH...AHH!!
TWITCH TWITCH
DO YOU LOVE ME?

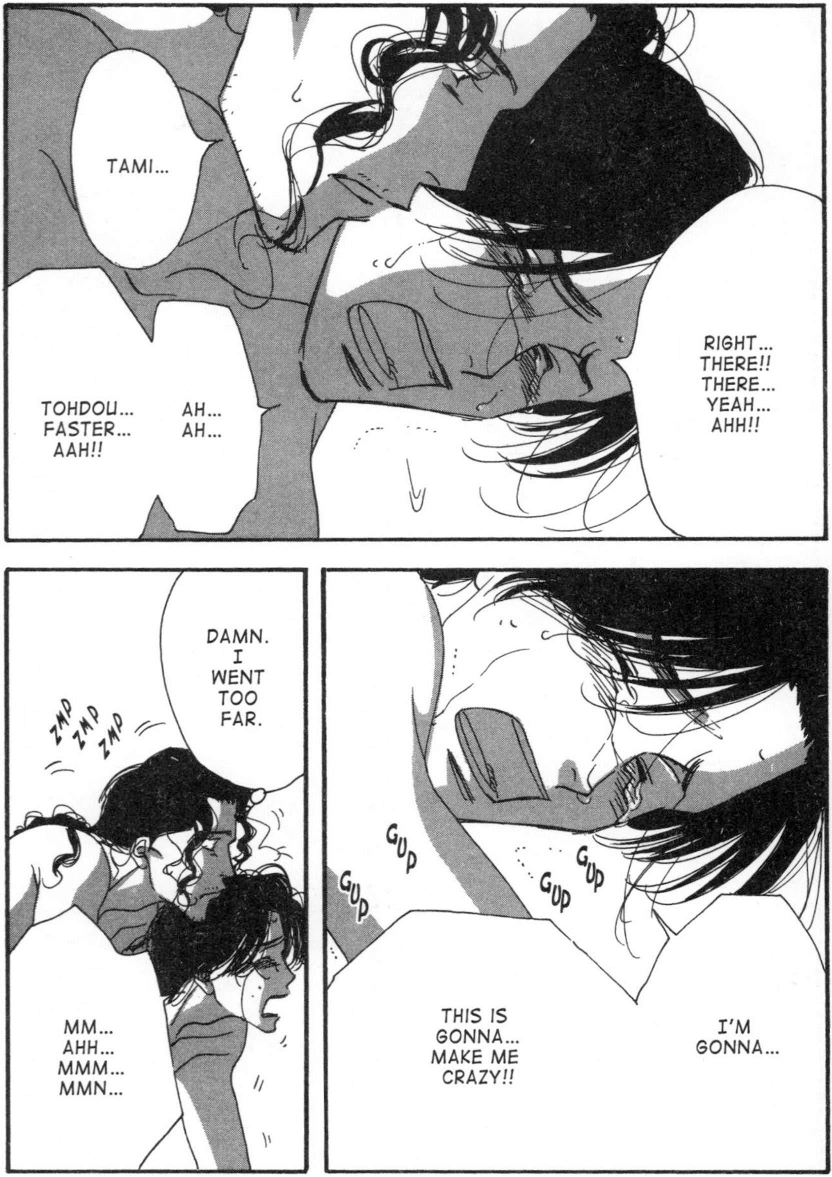
TAMI...
RIGHT... THERE!! THERE... YEAH... AHH!!
AH... AH...
TOHDOU... FASTER... AAH!!
GUP GUP GUP GUP
I'M GONNA...
THIS IS GONNA... MAKE ME CRAZY!!
DAMN. I WENT TOO FAR.
ZMP ZMP ZMP
MM... AHH... MMM... MMN...

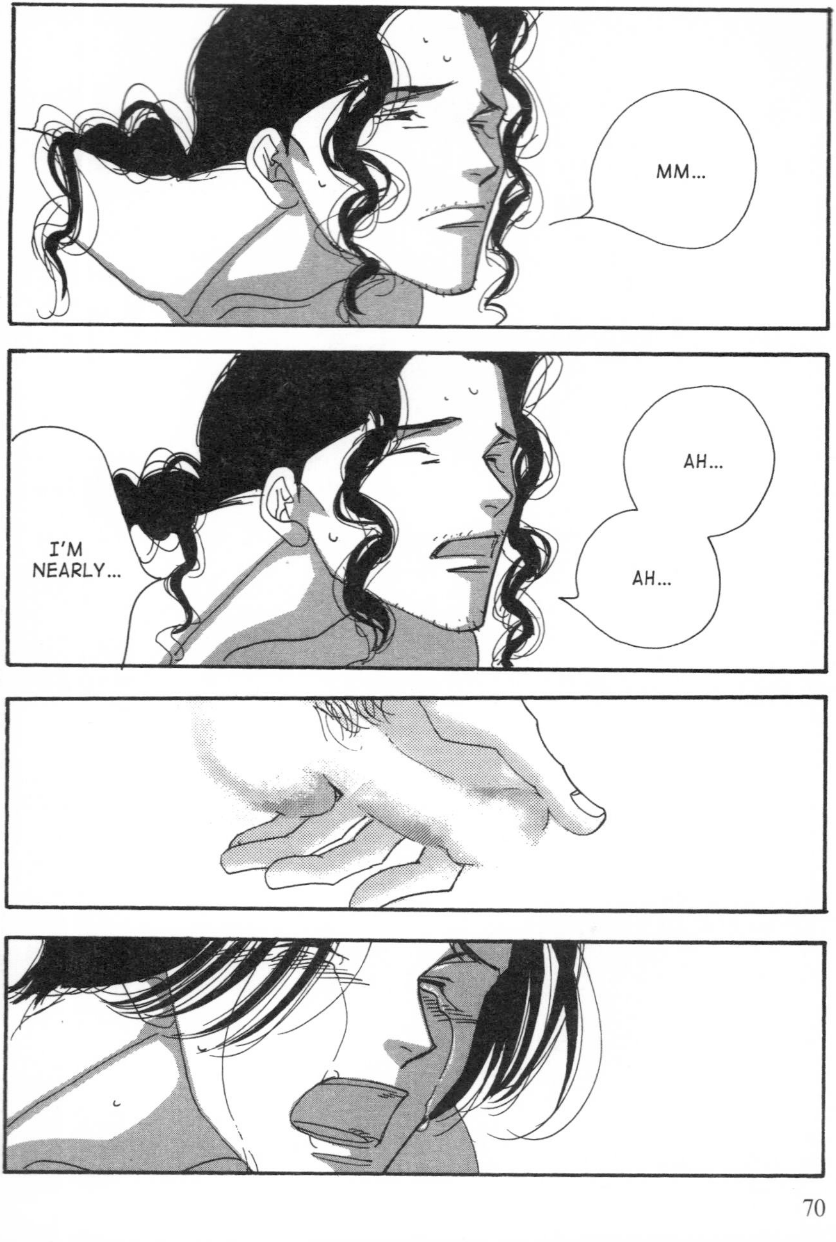
MM...
AH... AH...
I'M NEARLY...

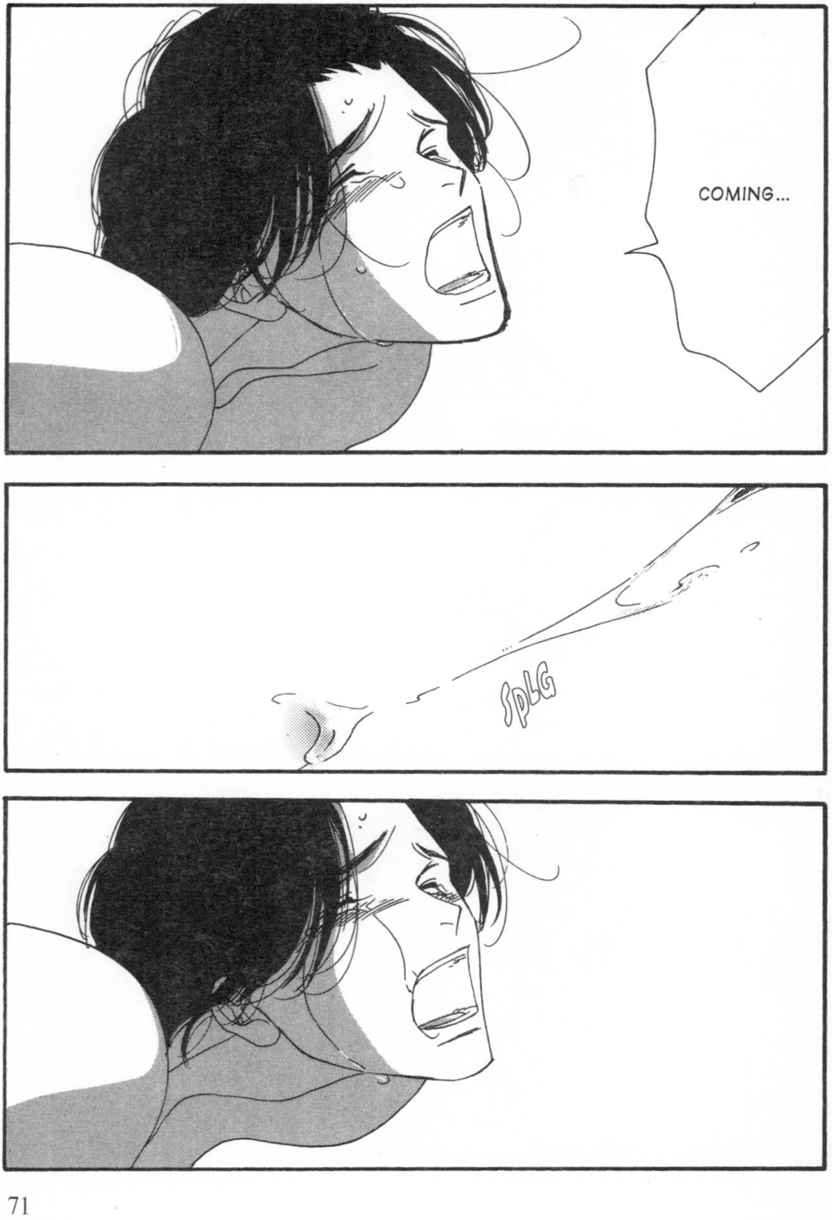
COMING...
SpLG

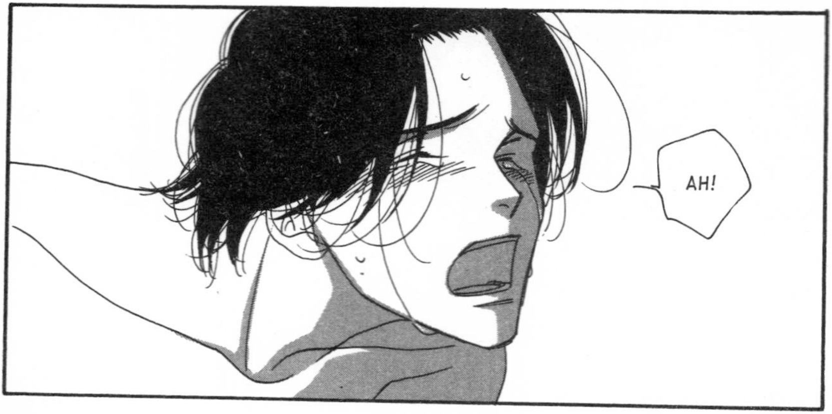
AH!

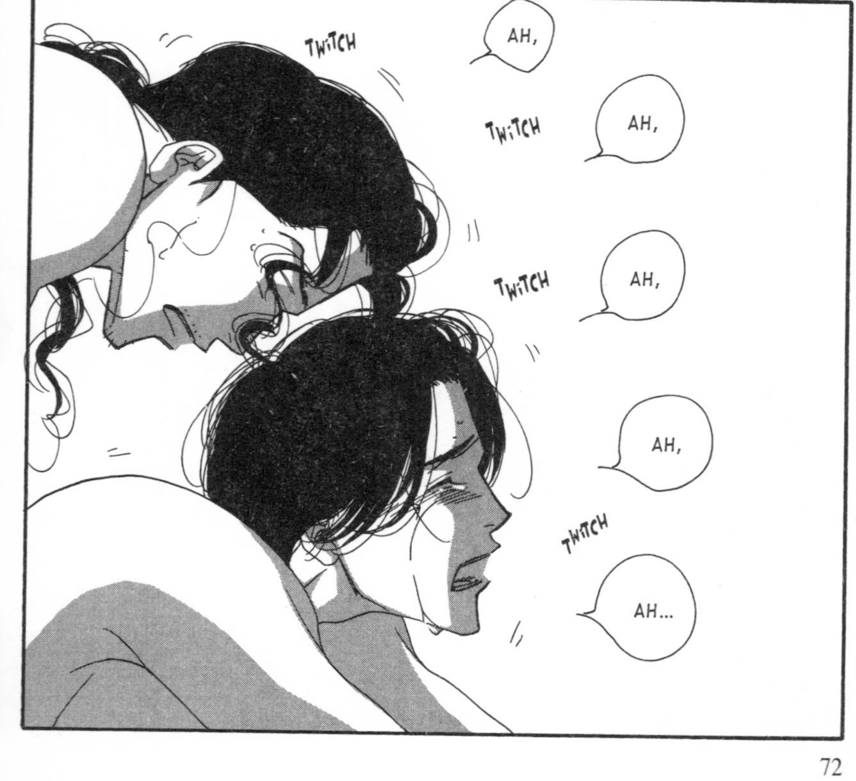
AH,
TWITCH
AH,
TWITCH
AH,
TWITCH
AH,
TWITCH
AH...

HAAH...

HAAH...

HMM?

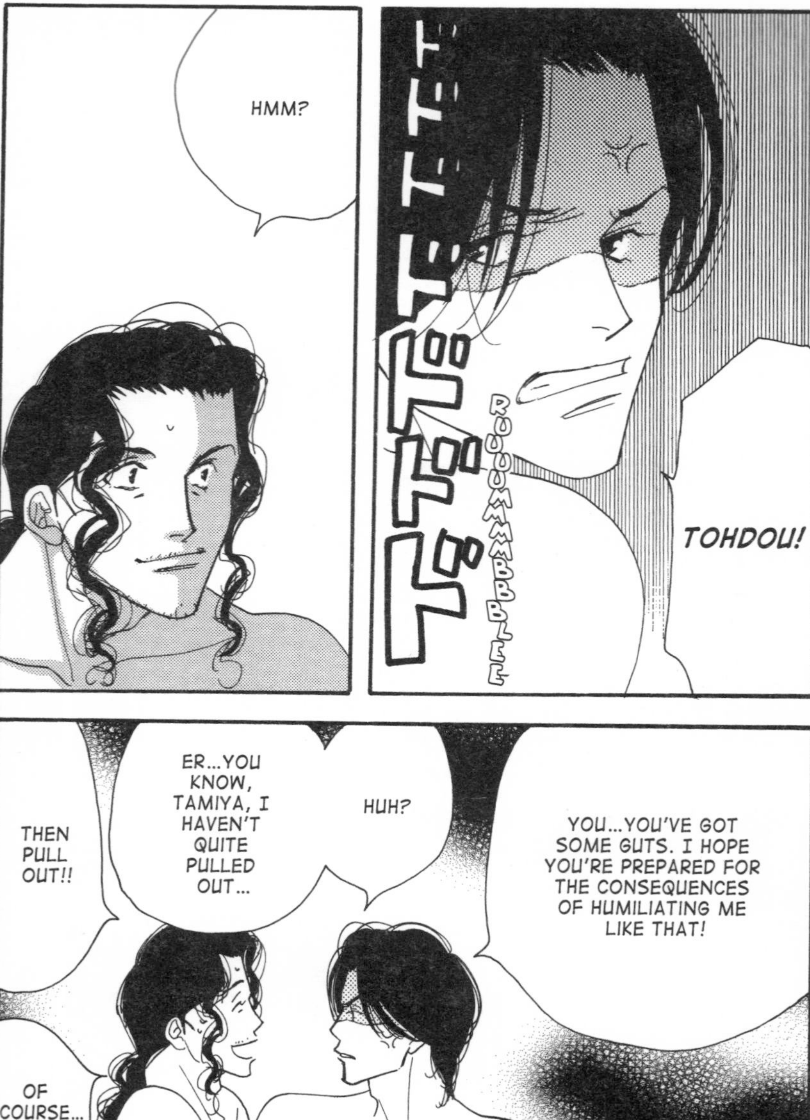
TOHDOU!
RUUUMMMBBBLEE
HMM?
YOU...YOU'VE GOT SOME GUTS. I HOPE YOU'RE PREPARED FOR THE CONSEQUENCES OF HUMILIATING ME LIKE THAT!
HUH?
ER...YOU KNOW, TAMIYA, I HAVEN'T QUITE PULLED OUT...
THEN PULL OUT!!
OF COURSE...

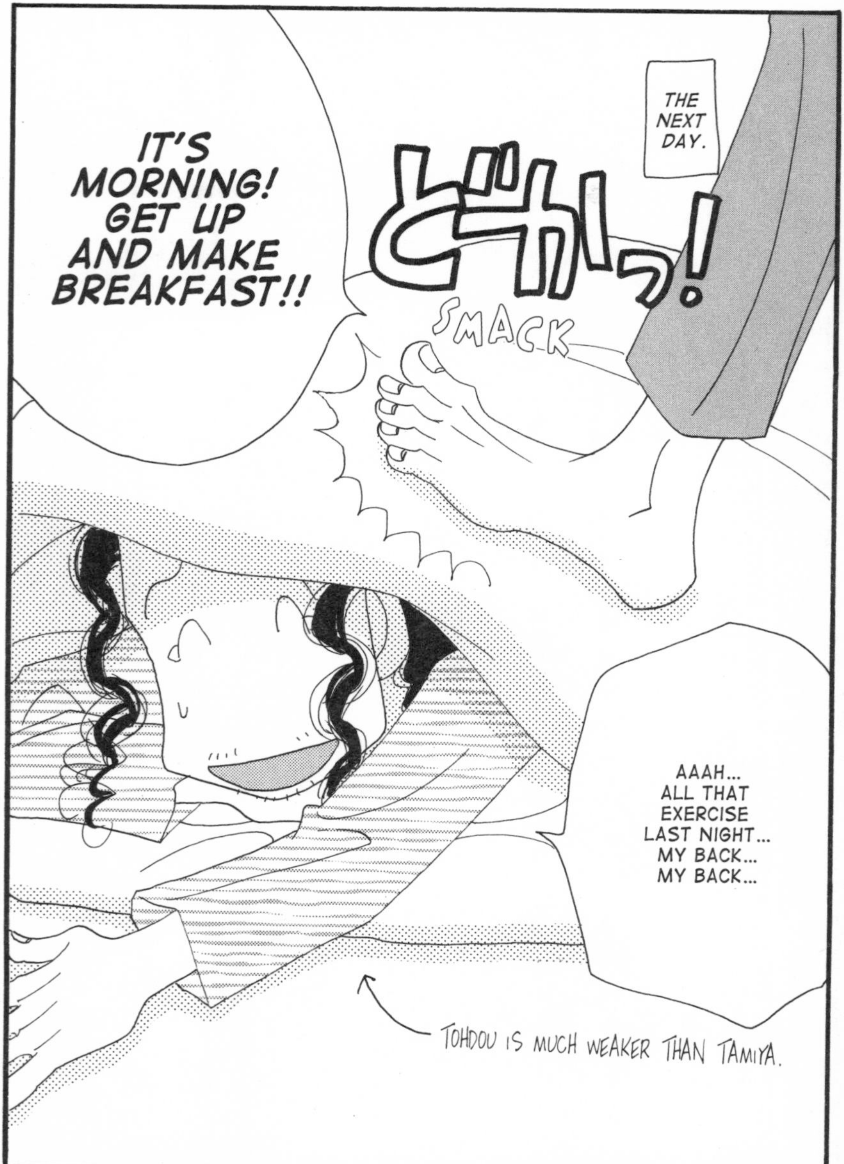
THE NEXT DAY.
どかっ!
SMACK
IT'S MORNING! GET UP AND MAKE BREAKFAST!!
AAAH... ALL THAT EXERCISE LAST NIGHT... MY BACK... MY BACK...
TOHDOU IS MUCH WEAKER THAN TAMIYA.

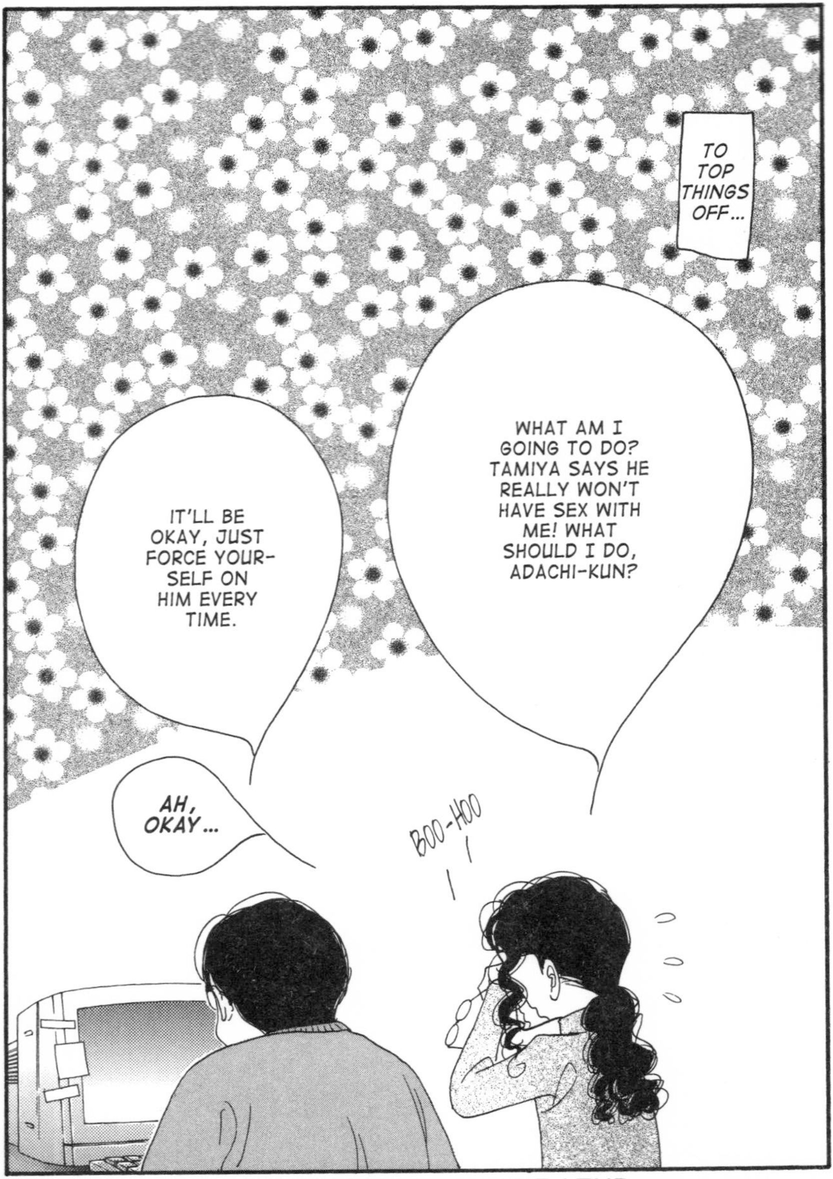
TO TOP THINGS OFF...
WHAT AM I GOING TO DO? TAMIYA SAYS HE REALLY WON'T HAVE SEX WITH ME! WHAT SHOULD I DO, ADACHI-KUN?
IT'LL BE OKAY, JUST FORCE YOUR-SELF ON HIM EVERY TIME.
BOO-HOO
AH, OKAY...

TOHDOU'S RAISON D'ETRE / END

IN THE WAKE
OF THE KING
OF SUPER-EASY
ZEMIS, SABUROU
TATSUMOTO,
THE NEW ZEMI
TO TAKE THE
THRONE IN TEINOU
UNIVERSITY LAW
SCHOOL IS...

WELL, IT'S NOT LIKE HE DIED, THOUGH...

CAN PROFESSORS LOVE THEIR STUDENTS?

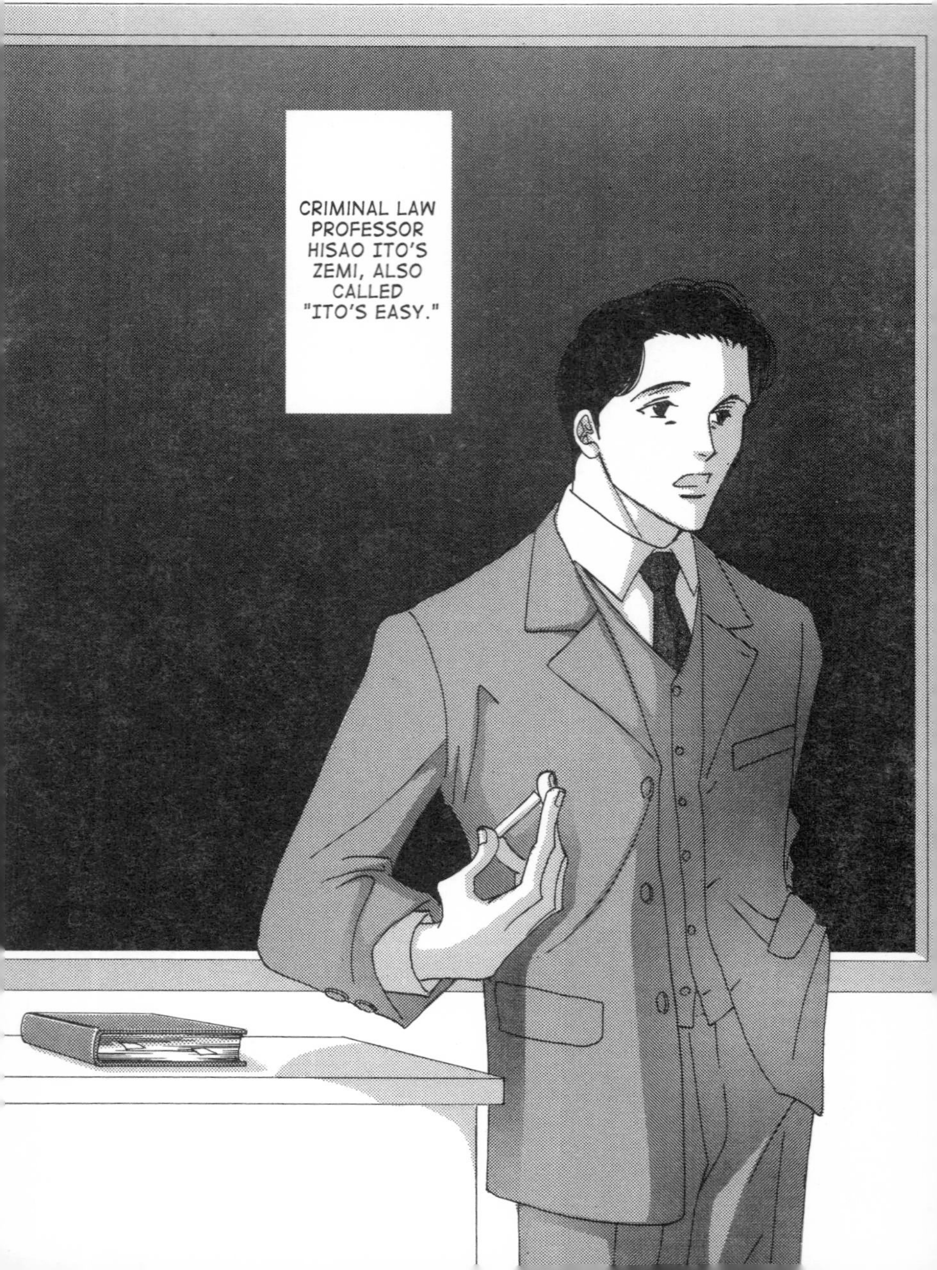
CRIMINAL LAW PROFESSOR HISAO ITO'S ZEMI, ALSO CALLED "ITO'S EASY."

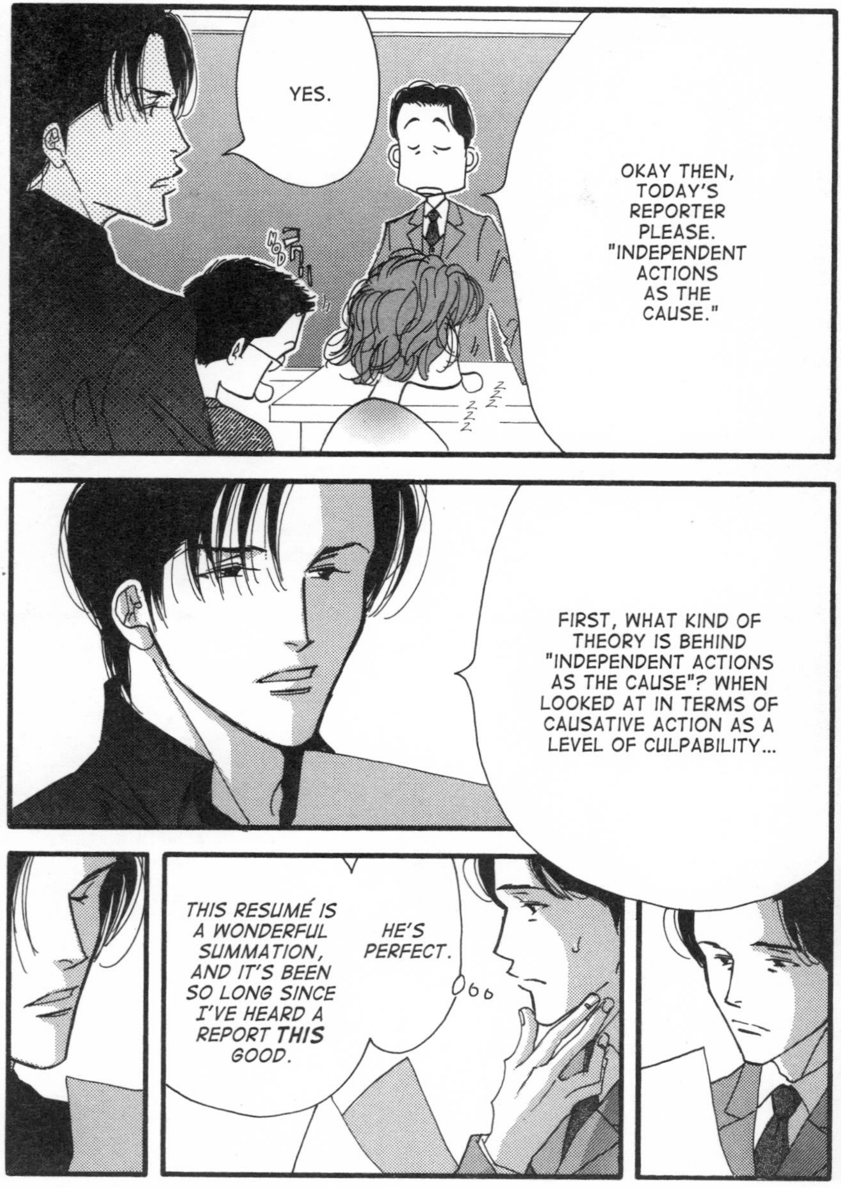
OKAY THEN, TODAY'S REPORTER PLEASE. "INDEPENDENT ACTIONS AS THE CAUSE."
YES.
NOD
FIRST, WHAT KIND OF THEORY IS BEHIND "INDEPENDENT ACTIONS AS THE CAUSE"? WHEN LOOKED AT IN TERMS OF CAUSATIVE ACTION AS A LEVEL OF CULPABILITY...
HE'S PERFECT.
THIS RESUMÉ IS A WONDERFUL SUMMATION, AND IT'S BEEN SO LONG SINCE I'VE HEARD A REPORT **THIS** *GOOD.*

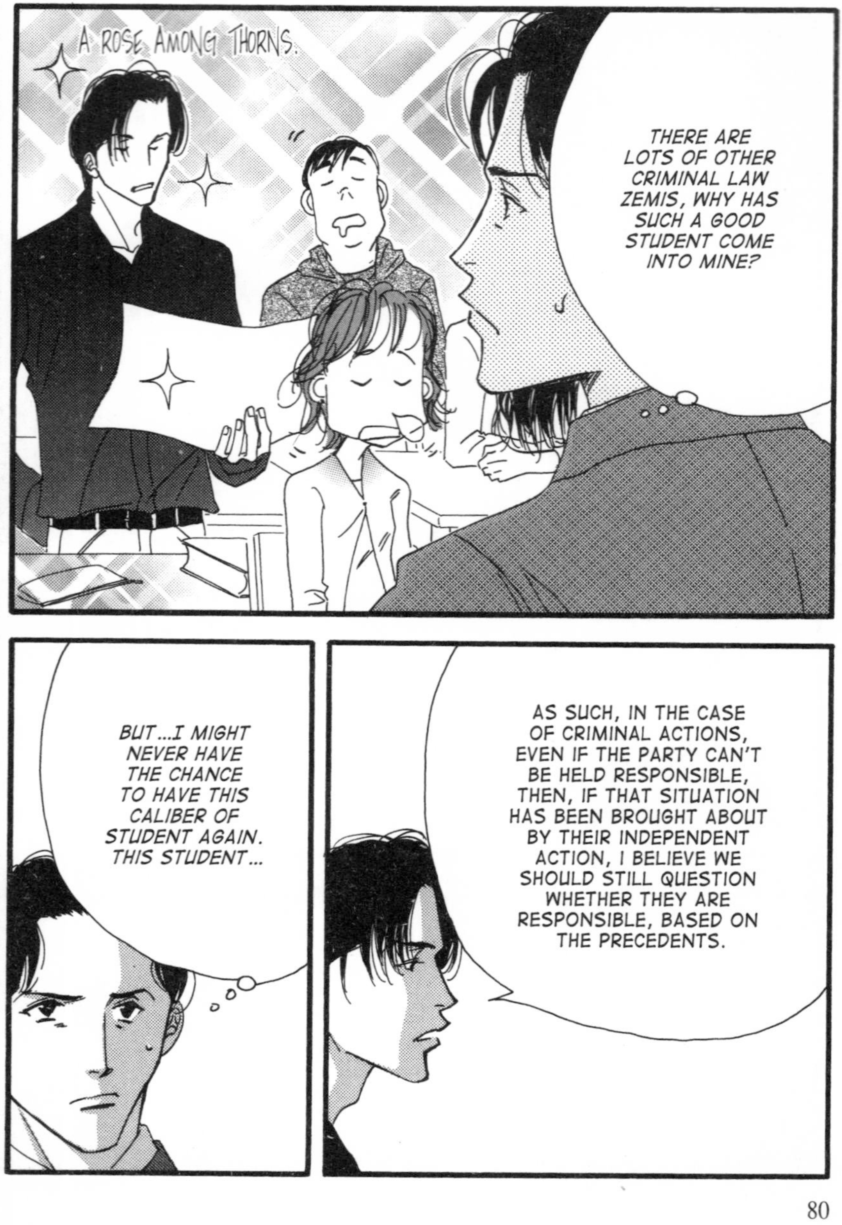
THERE ARE LOTS OF OTHER CRIMINAL LAW ZEMIS, WHY HAS SUCH A GOOD STUDENT COME INTO MINE?
A ROSE AMONG THORNS.
AS SUCH, IN THE CASE OF CRIMINAL ACTIONS, EVEN IF THE PARTY CAN'T BE HELD RESPONSIBLE, THEN, IF THAT SITUATION HAS BEEN BROUGHT ABOUT BY THEIR INDEPENDENT ACTION, I BELIEVE WE SHOULD STILL QUESTION WHETHER THEY ARE RESPONSIBLE, BASED ON THE PRECEDENTS.
BUT...I MIGHT NEVER HAVE THE CHANCE TO HAVE THIS CALIBER OF STUDENT AGAIN. THIS STUDENT...

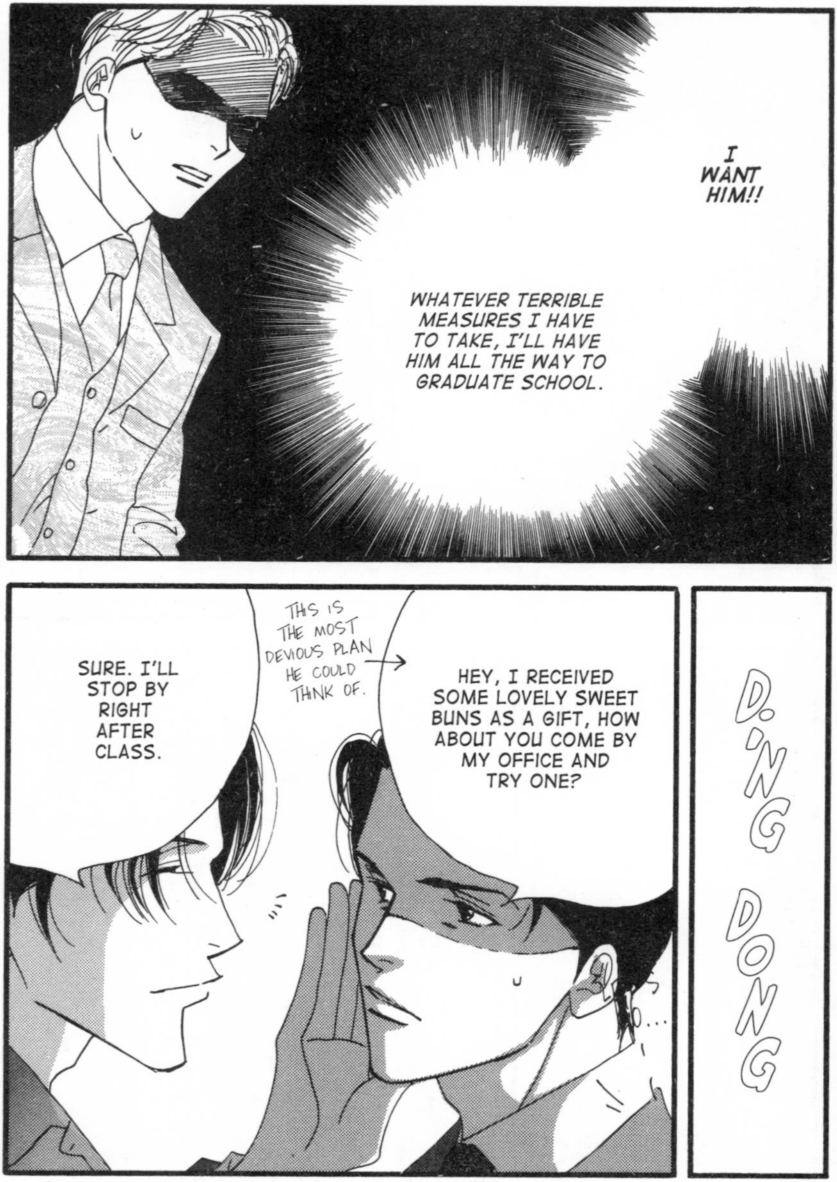
I WANT HIM!!
WHATEVER TERRIBLE MEASURES I HAVE TO TAKE, I'LL HAVE HIM ALL THE WAY TO GRADUATE SCHOOL.
DING DONG
HEY, I RECEIVED SOME LOVELY SWEET BUNS AS A GIFT, HOW ABOUT YOU COME BY MY OFFICE AND TRY ONE?
THIS IS THE MOST DEVIOUS PLAN HE COULD THINK OF.
SURE. I'LL STOP BY RIGHT AFTER CLASS.

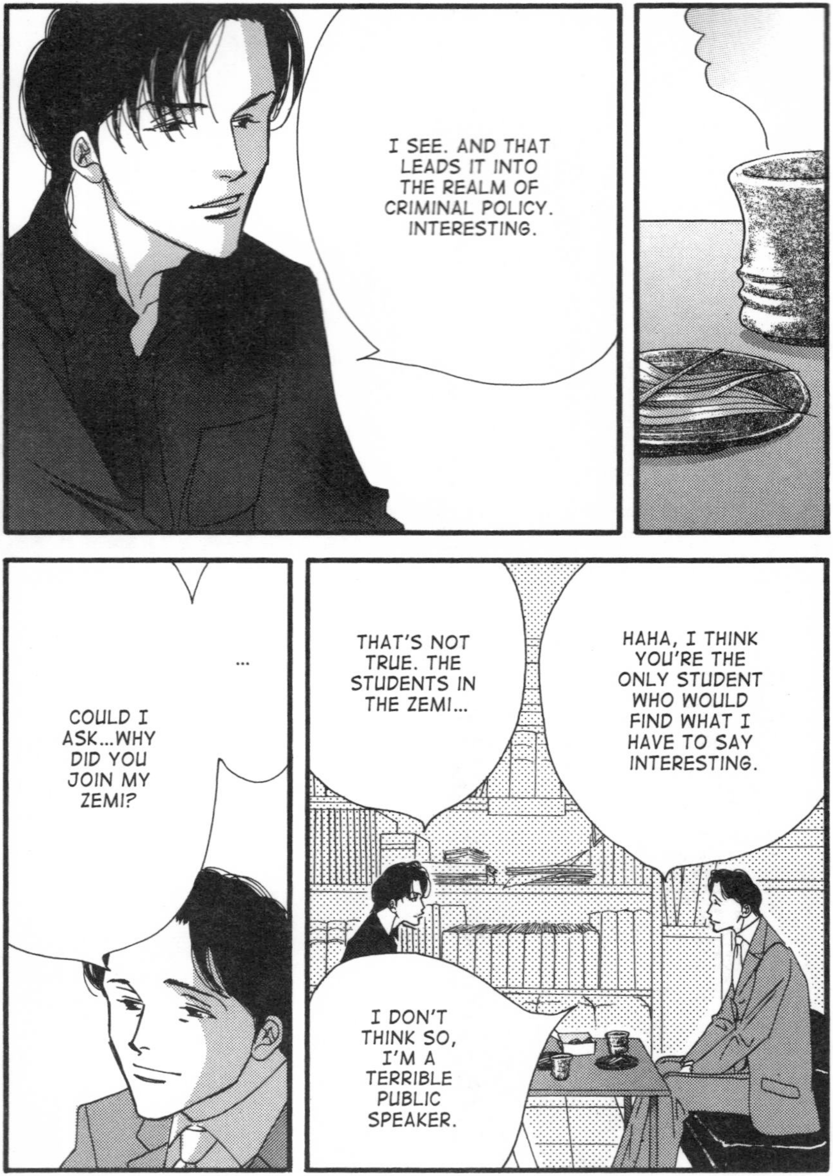
I SEE. AND THAT LEADS IT INTO THE REALM OF CRIMINAL POLICY. INTERESTING.
HAHA, I THINK YOU'RE THE ONLY STUDENT WHO WOULD FIND WHAT I HAVE TO SAY INTERESTING.
THAT'S NOT TRUE. THE STUDENTS IN THE ZEMI...
I DON'T THINK SO, I'M A TERRIBLE PUBLIC SPEAKER.
...
COULD I ASK...WHY DID YOU JOIN MY ZEMI?

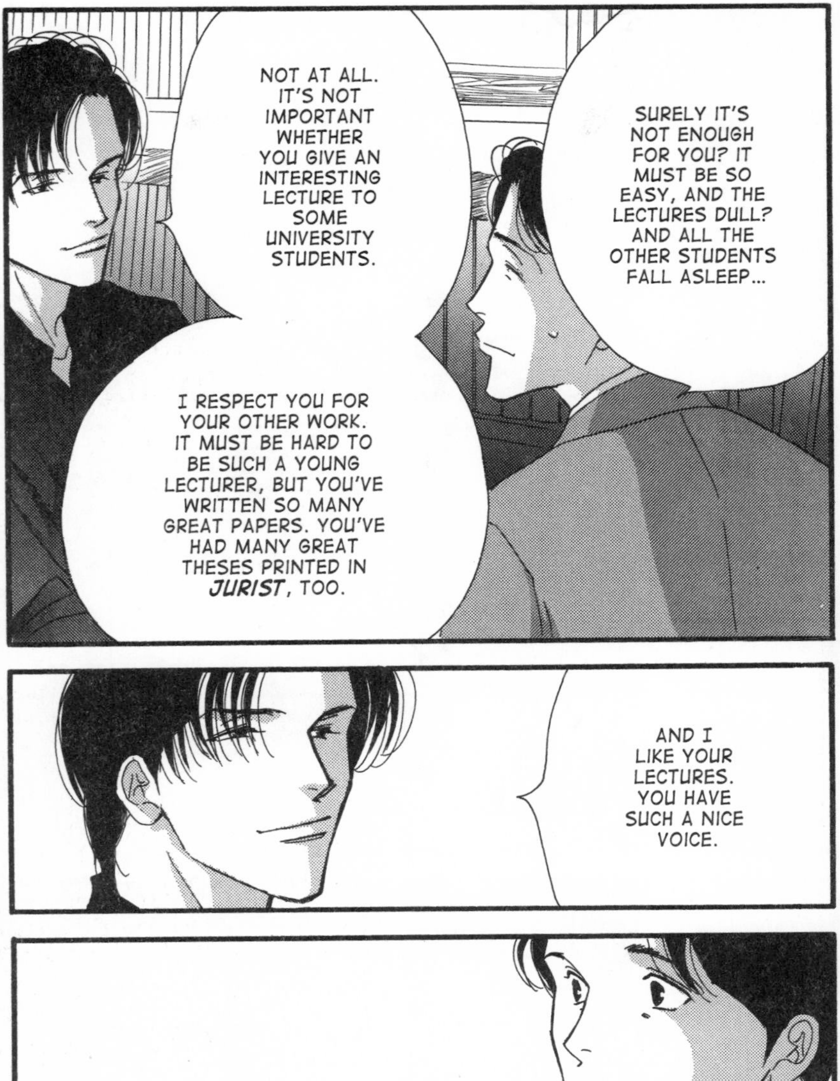
SURELY IT'S NOT ENOUGH FOR YOU? IT MUST BE SO EASY, AND THE LECTURES DULL? AND ALL THE OTHER STUDENTS FALL ASLEEP...
NOT AT ALL. IT'S NOT IMPORTANT WHETHER YOU GIVE AN INTERESTING LECTURE TO SOME UNIVERSITY STUDENTS.
I RESPECT YOU FOR YOUR OTHER WORK. IT MUST BE HARD TO BE SUCH A YOUNG LECTURER, BUT YOU'VE WRITTEN SO MANY GREAT PAPERS. YOU'VE HAD MANY GREAT THESES PRINTED IN *JURIST*, TOO.
AND I LIKE YOUR LECTURES. YOU HAVE SUCH A NICE VOICE.

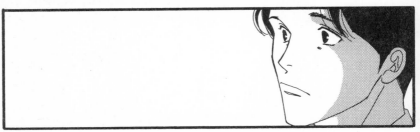

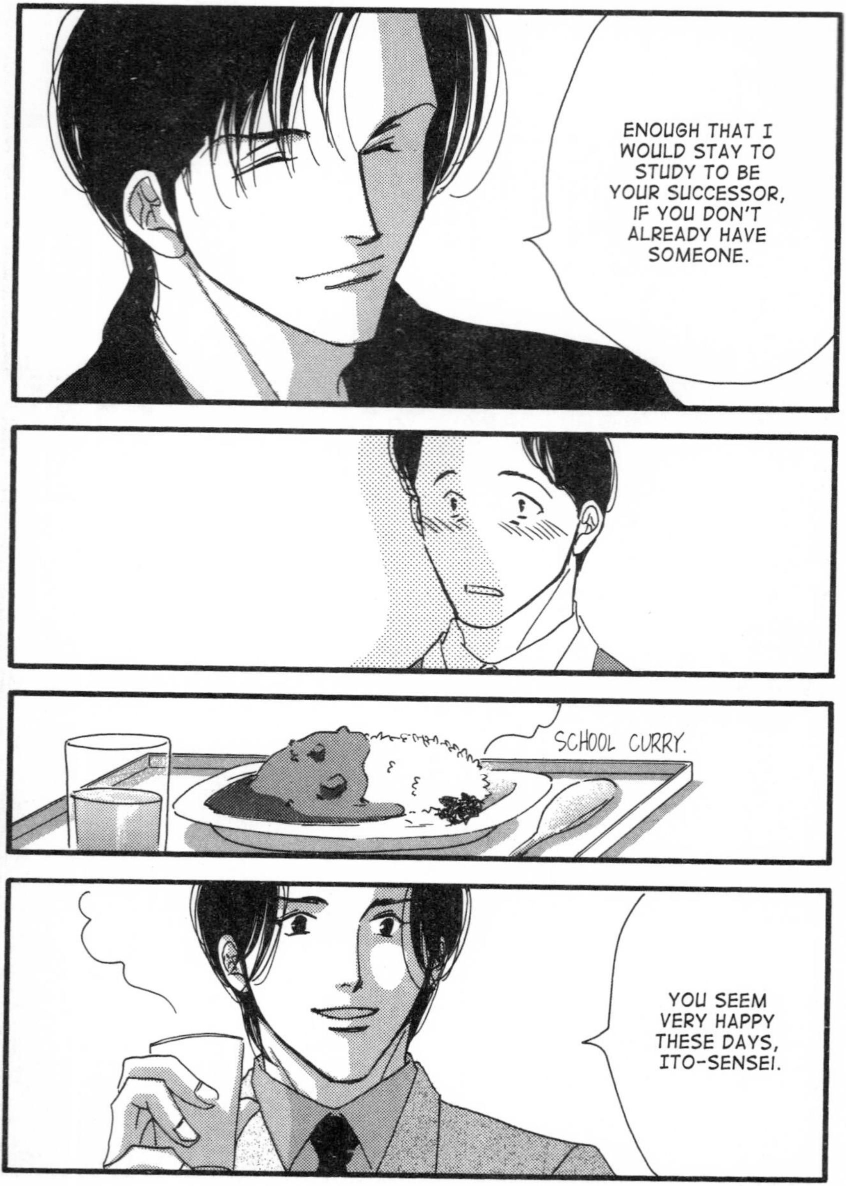
ENOUGH THAT I WOULD STAY TO STUDY TO BE YOUR SUCCESSOR, IF YOU DON'T ALREADY HAVE SOMEONE.
SCHOOL CURRY.
YOU SEEM VERY HAPPY THESE DAYS, ITO-SENSEI.

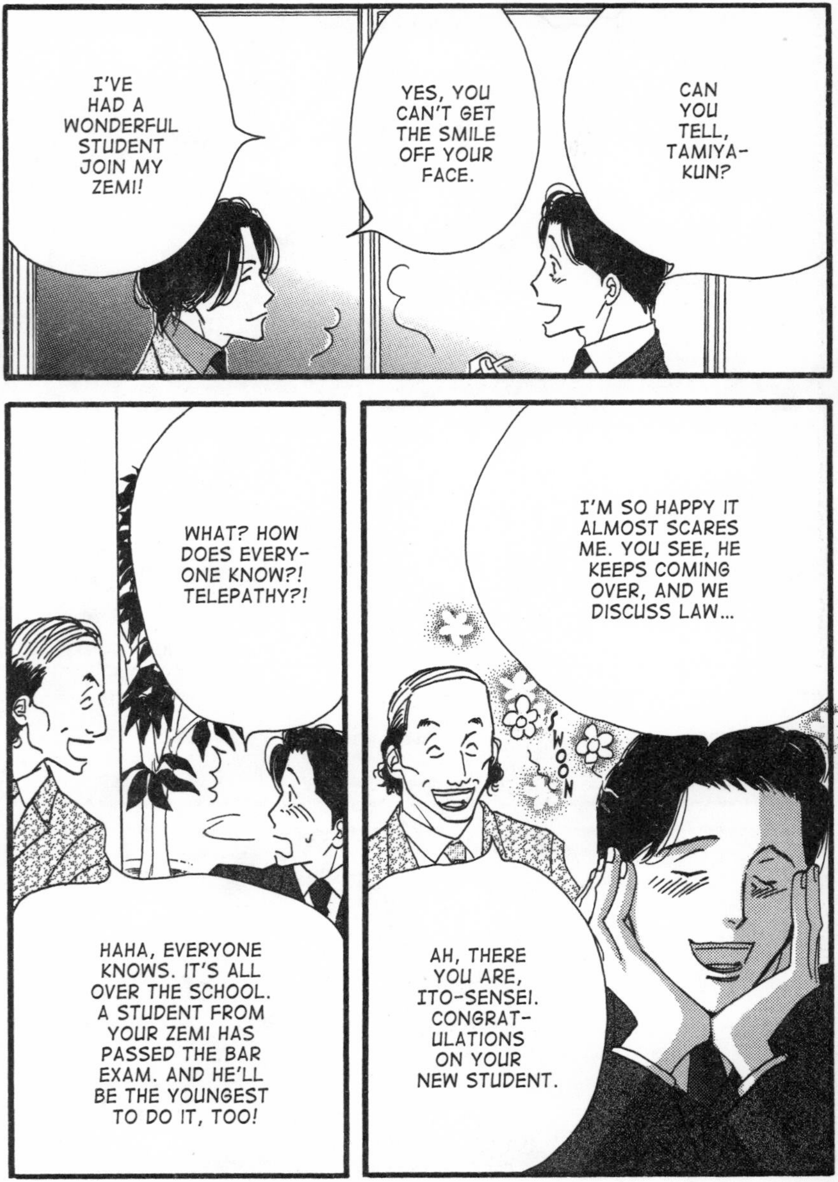
I'VE HAD A WONDERFUL STUDENT JOIN MY ZEMI!
YES, YOU CAN'T GET THE SMILE OFF YOUR FACE.
CAN YOU TELL, TAMIYA-KUN?
WHAT? HOW DOES EVERY-ONE KNOW?! TELEPATHY?!
HAHA, EVERYONE KNOWS. IT'S ALL OVER THE SCHOOL. A STUDENT FROM YOUR ZEMI HAS PASSED THE BAR EXAM. AND HE'LL BE THE YOUNGEST TO DO IT, TOO!
AH, THERE YOU ARE, ITO-SENSEI. CONGRAT-ULATIONS ON YOUR NEW STUDENT.
I'M SO HAPPY IT ALMOST SCARES ME. YOU SEE, HE KEEPS COMING OVER, AND WE DISCUSS LAW...
SWOON

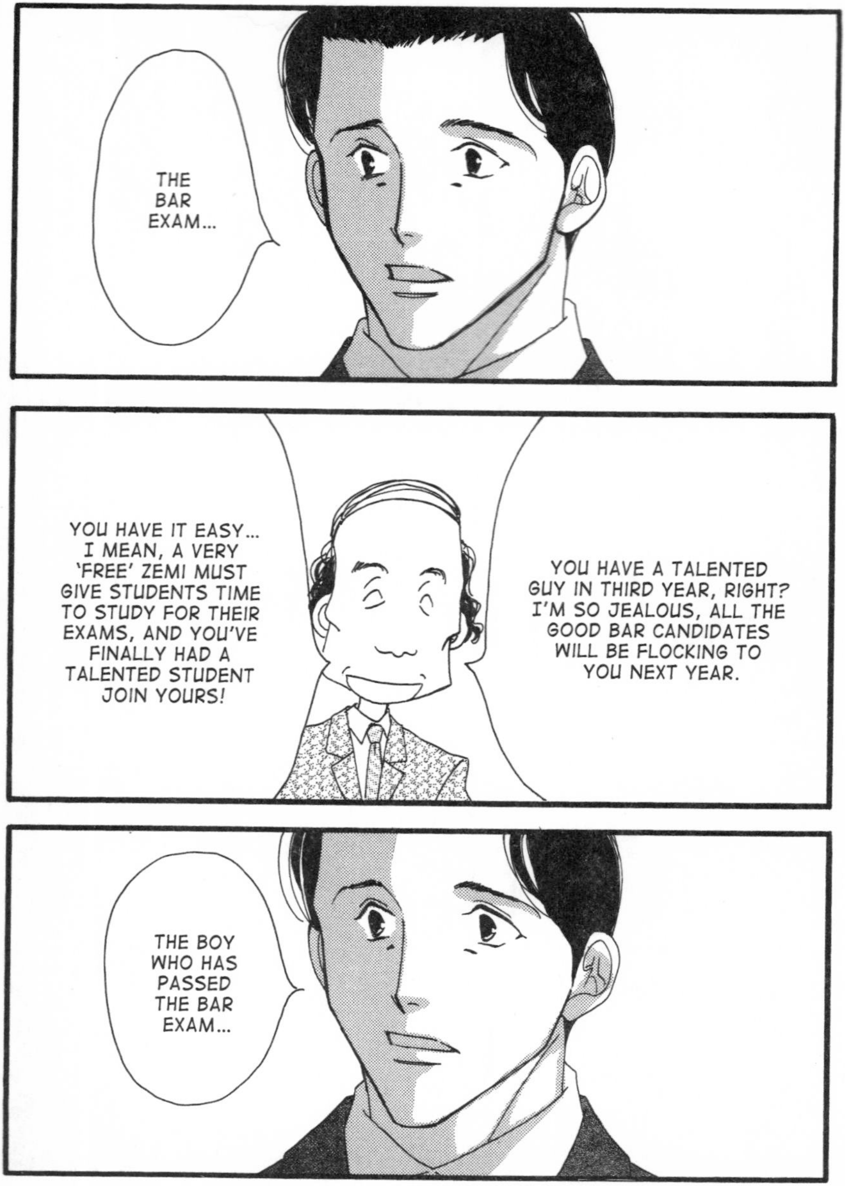
THE BAR EXAM...
YOU HAVE A TALENTED GUY IN THIRD YEAR, RIGHT? I'M SO JEALOUS, ALL THE GOOD BAR CANDIDATES WILL BE FLOCKING TO YOU NEXT YEAR.
YOU HAVE IT EASY... I MEAN, A VERY 'FREE' ZEMI MUST GIVE STUDENTS TIME TO STUDY FOR THEIR EXAMS, AND YOU'VE FINALLY HAD A TALENTED STUDENT JOIN YOURS!
THE BOY WHO HAS PASSED THE BAR EXAM...

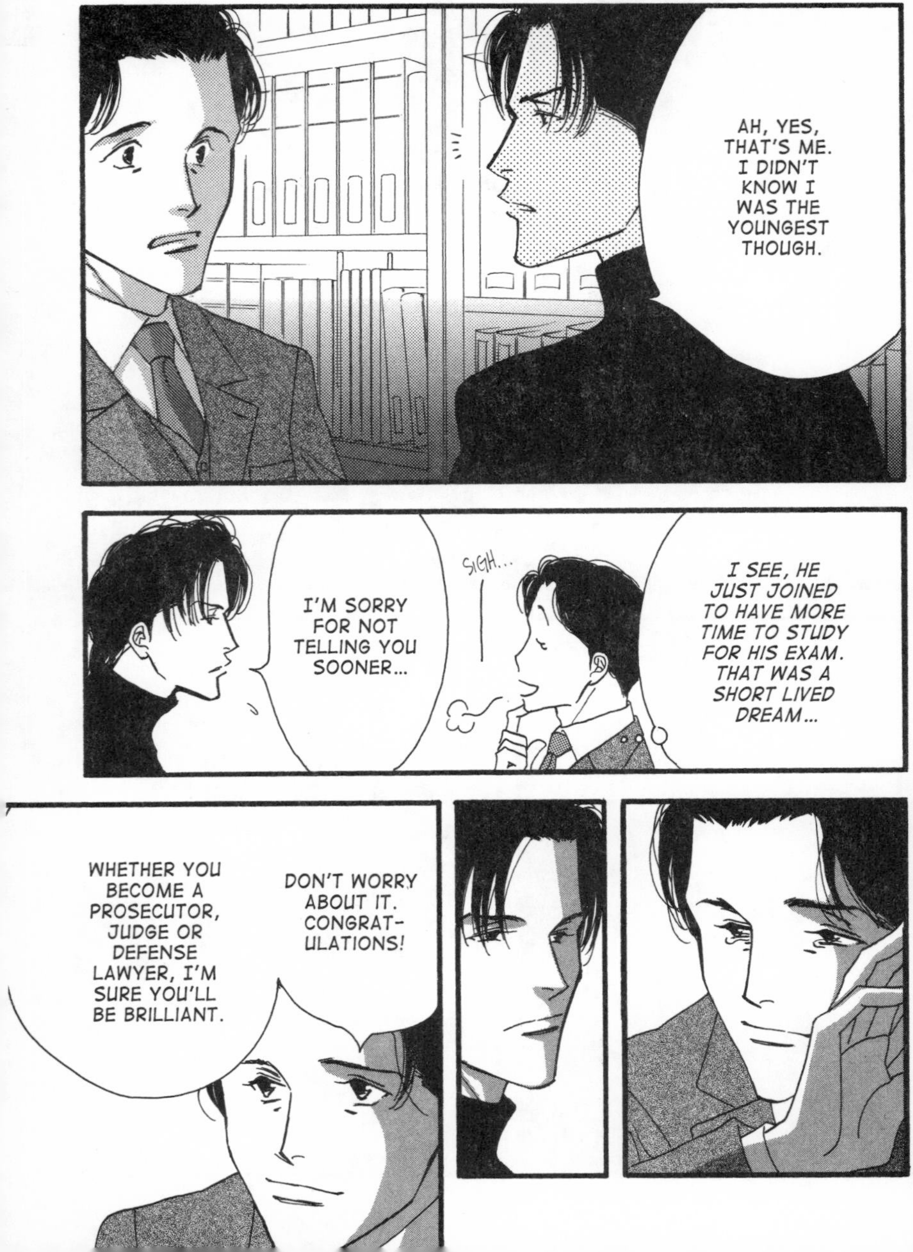
AH, YES, THAT'S ME. I DIDN'T KNOW I WAS THE YOUNGEST THOUGH.
I SEE, HE JUST JOINED TO HAVE MORE TIME TO STUDY FOR HIS EXAM. THAT WAS A SHORT LIVED DREAM...
SIGH...
I'M SORRY FOR NOT TELLING YOU SOONER...
DON'T WORRY ABOUT IT. CONGRAT-ULATIONS!
WHETHER YOU BECOME A PROSECUTOR, JUDGE OR DEFENSE LAWYER, I'M SURE YOU'LL BE BRILLIANT.

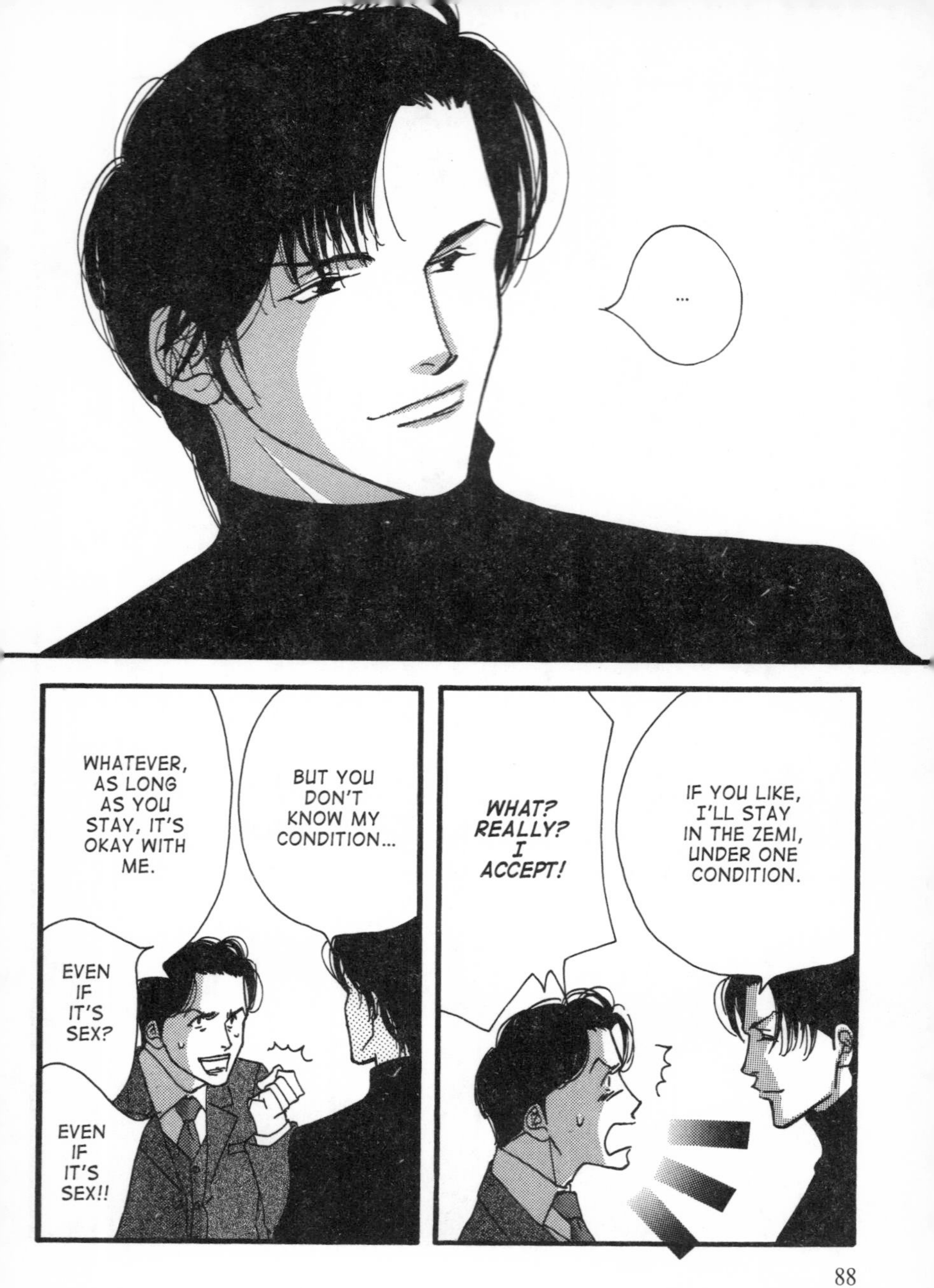
...
IF YOU LIKE, I'LL STAY IN THE ZEMI, UNDER ONE CONDITION.
WHAT? REALLY? I ACCEPT!
BUT YOU DON'T KNOW MY CONDITION...
WHATEVER, AS LONG AS YOU STAY, IT'S OKAY WITH ME.
EVEN IF IT'S SEX?
EVEN IF IT'S SEX!!

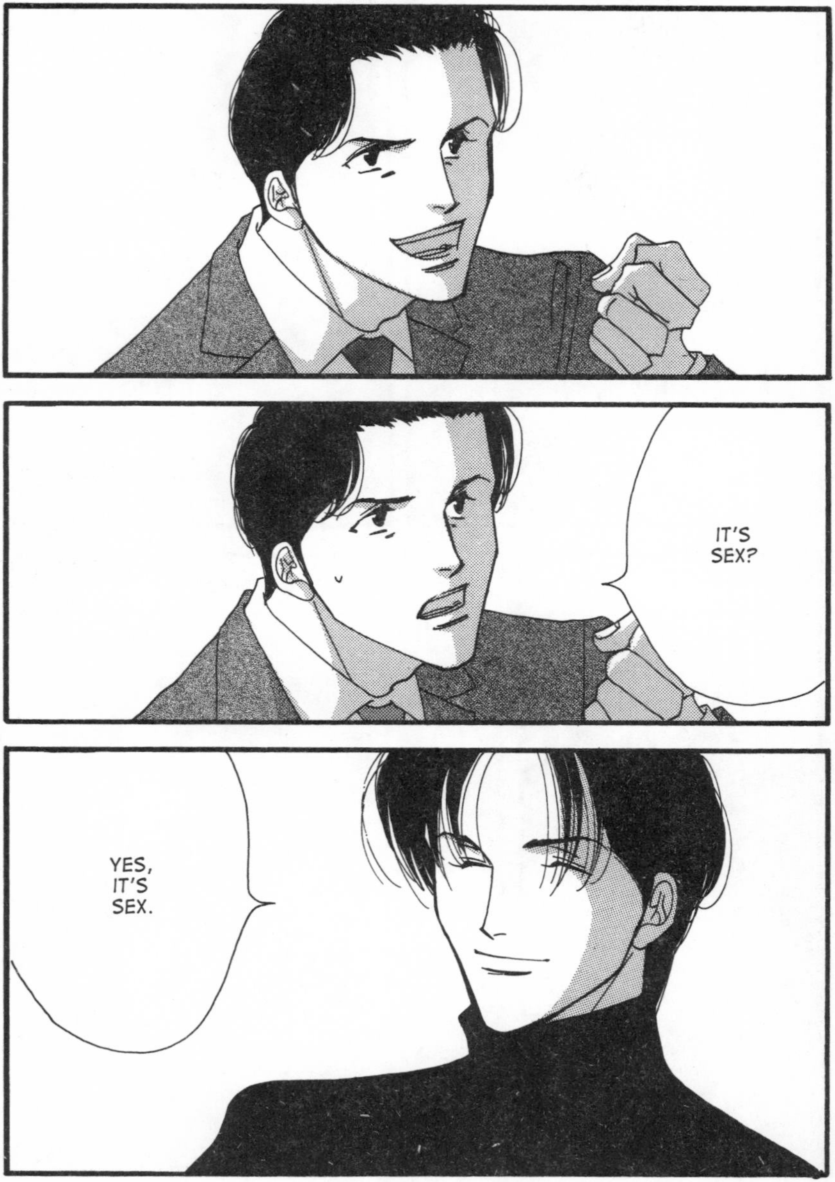
IT'S SEX?
YES, IT'S SEX.

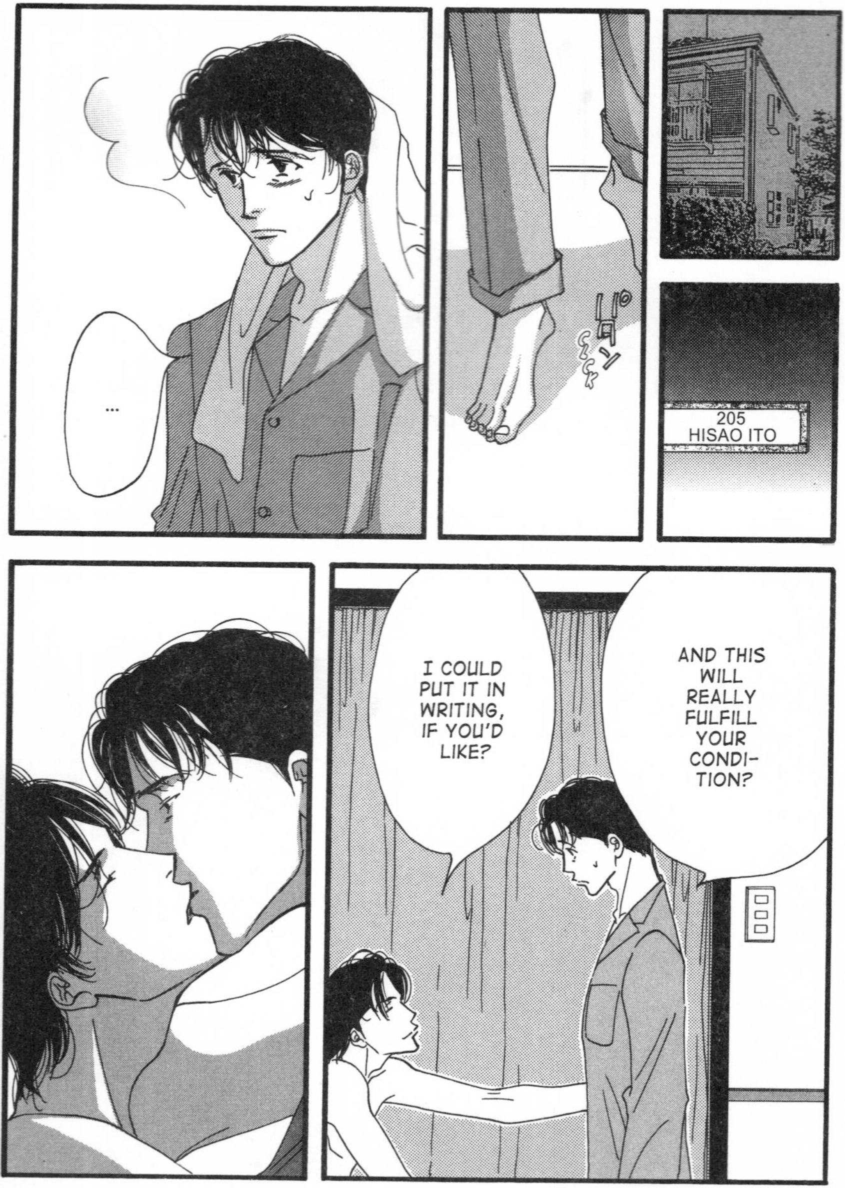
205
HISAO ITO
CLICK
...
AND THIS WILL REALLY FULFILL YOUR CONDITION?
I COULD PUT IT IN WRITING, IF YOU'D LIKE?

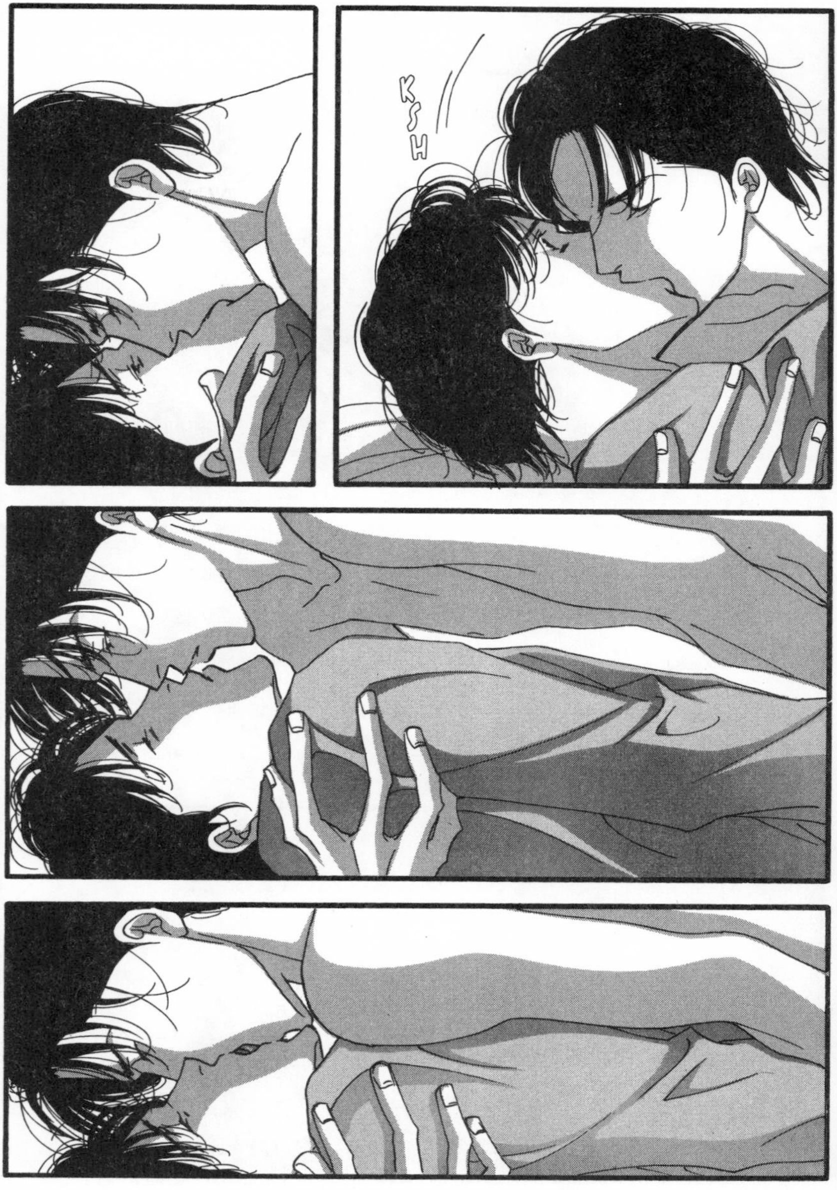
KSH

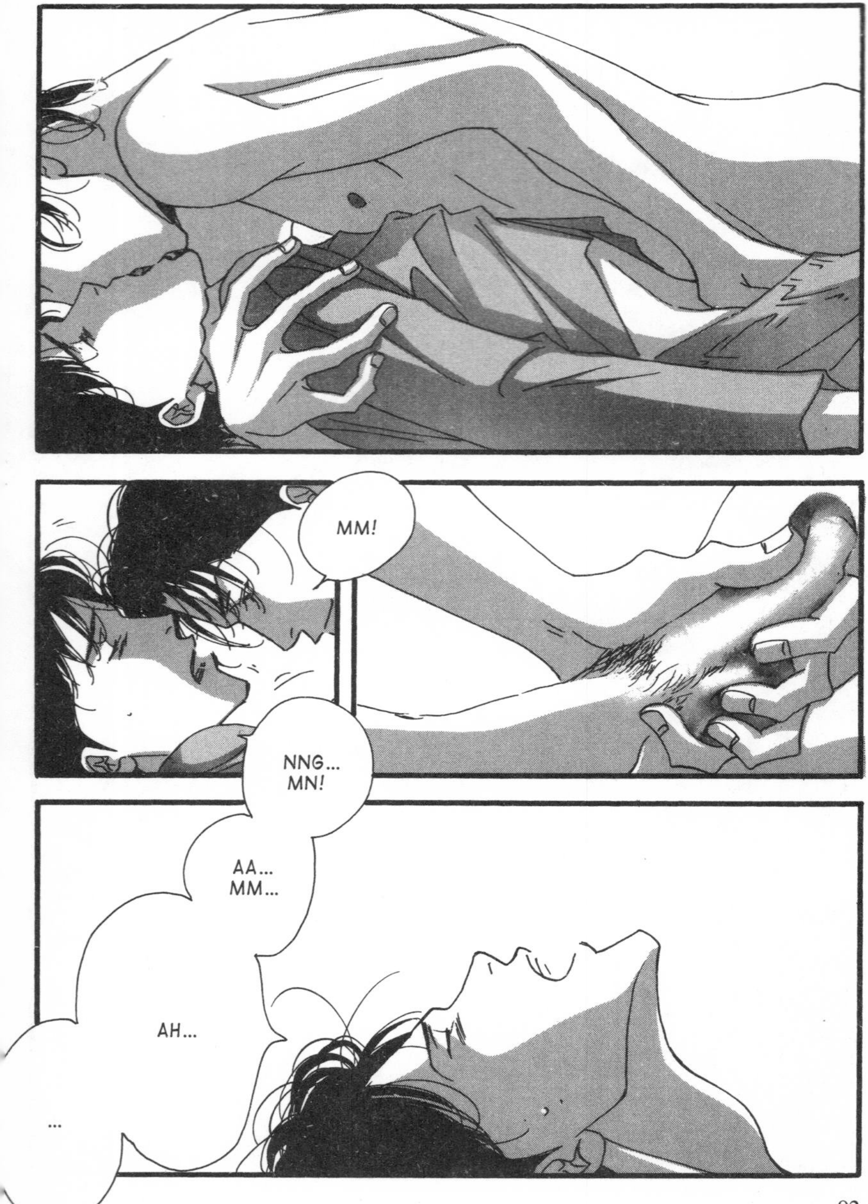
MM!
NNG... MN!
AA... MM...
AH...
...

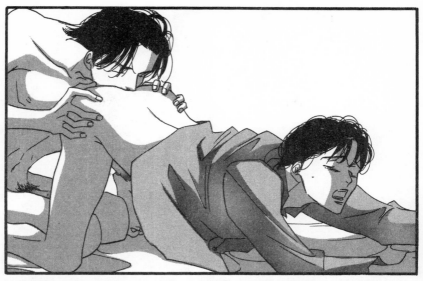

!

AH...
AH...

AH...!

THIS
IS...
SO...

I CAN'T
BELIEVE...
IT'S
GOING
IN...!

AH...
AAH...!

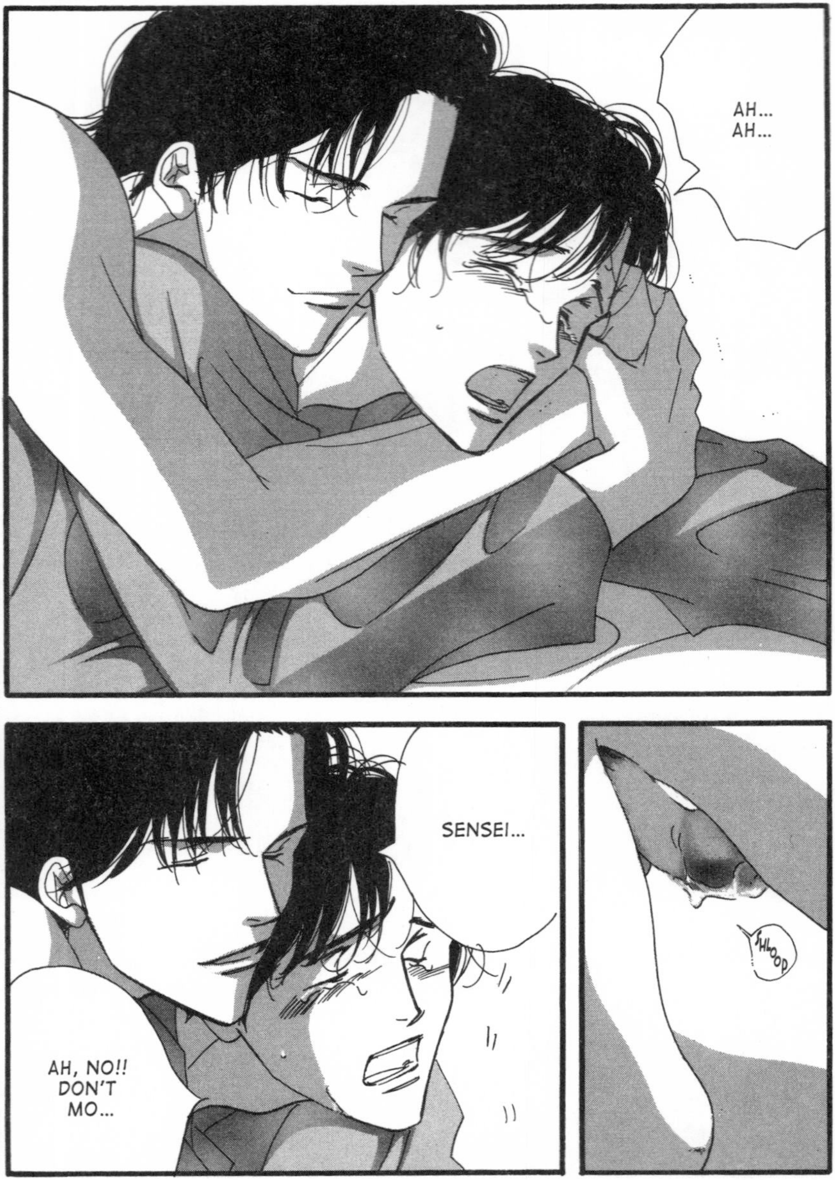
AH...
AH...
SHLOOP
SENSEI...
AH, NO!!
DON'T
MO...

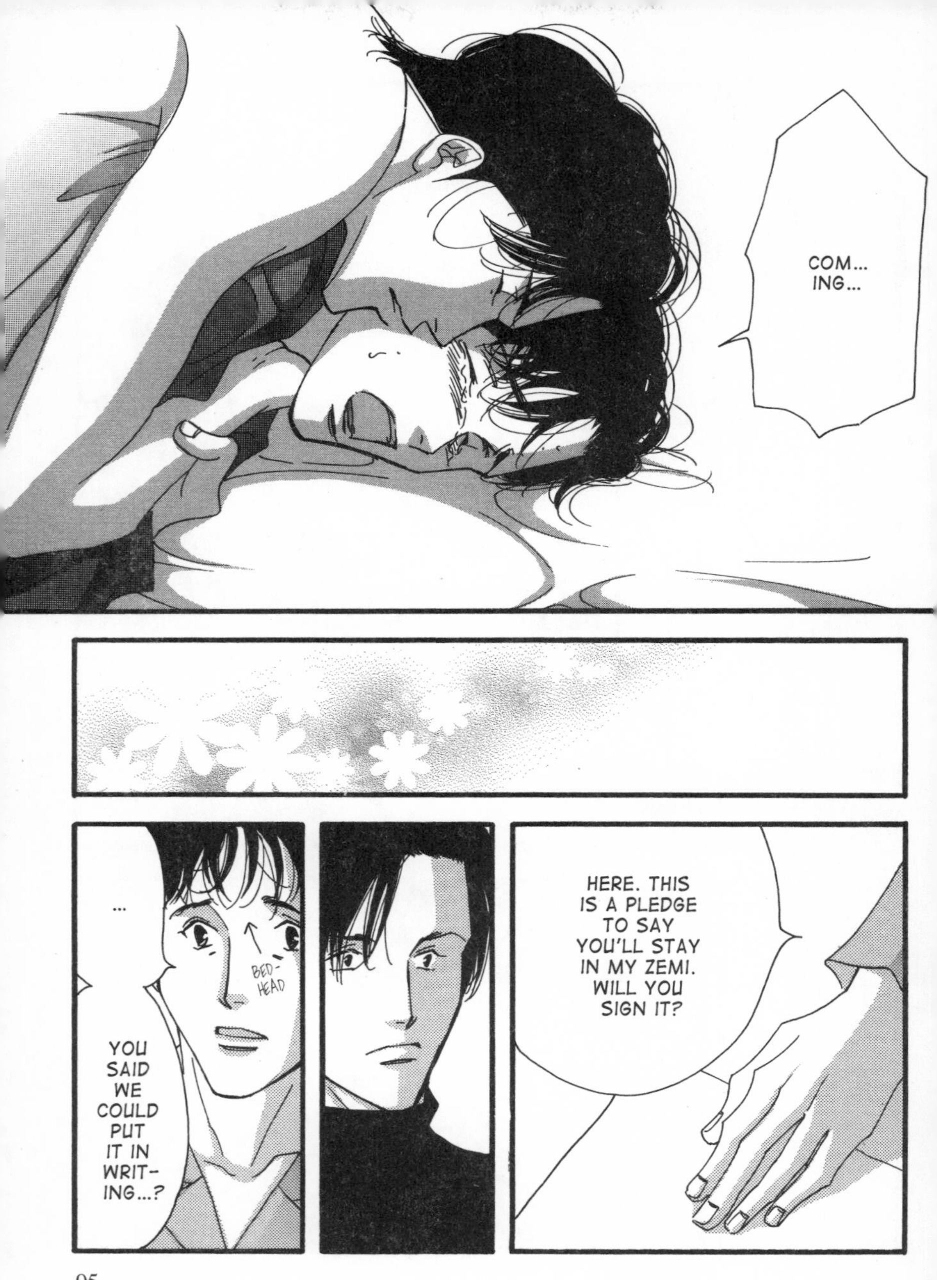
COM... ING...
HERE. THIS IS A PLEDGE TO SAY YOU'LL STAY IN MY ZEMI. WILL YOU SIGN IT?
...
BED-HEAD
YOU SAID WE COULD PUT IT IN WRITING...?

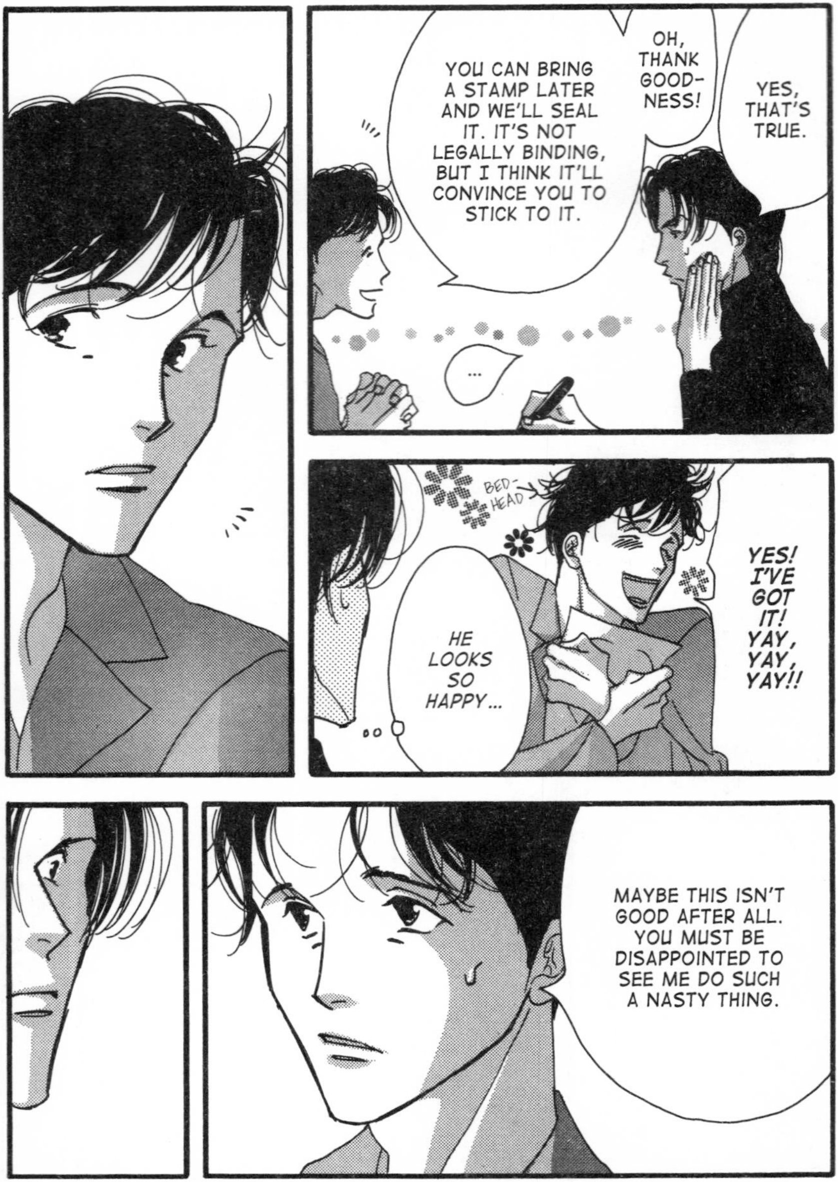
YES, THAT'S TRUE.
OH, THANK GOODNESS!
YOU CAN BRING A STAMP LATER AND WE'LL SEAL IT. IT'S NOT LEGALLY BINDING, BUT I THINK IT'LL CONVINCE YOU TO STICK TO IT.
...
YES! I'VE GOT IT! YAY, YAY, YAY!!
BED-HEAD
HE LOOKS SO HAPPY...
MAYBE THIS ISN'T GOOD AFTER ALL. YOU MUST BE DISAPPOINTED TO SEE ME DO SUCH A NASTY THING.

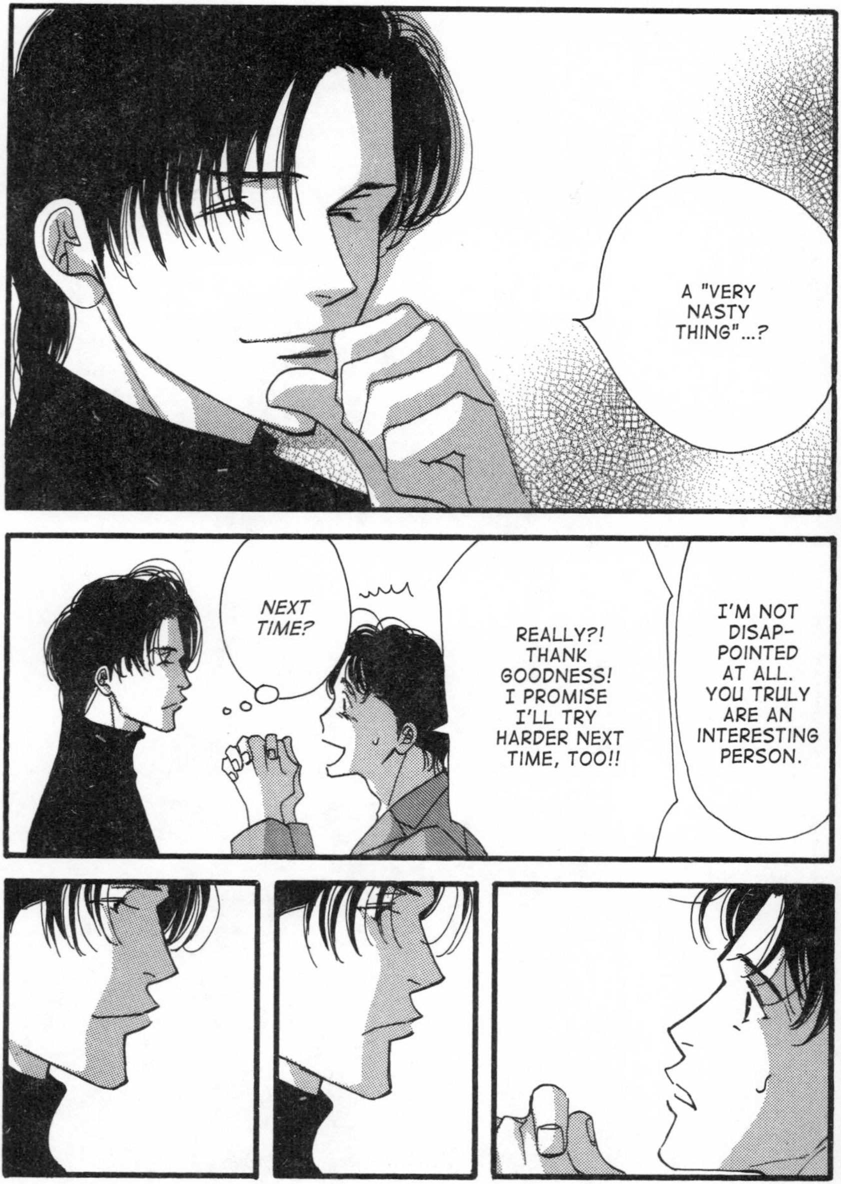
A "VERY NASTY THING"...?
I'M NOT DISAP-POINTED AT ALL. YOU TRULY ARE AN INTERESTING PERSON.
REALLY?! THANK GOODNESS! I PROMISE I'LL TRY HARDER NEXT TIME, TOO!!
NEXT TIME?

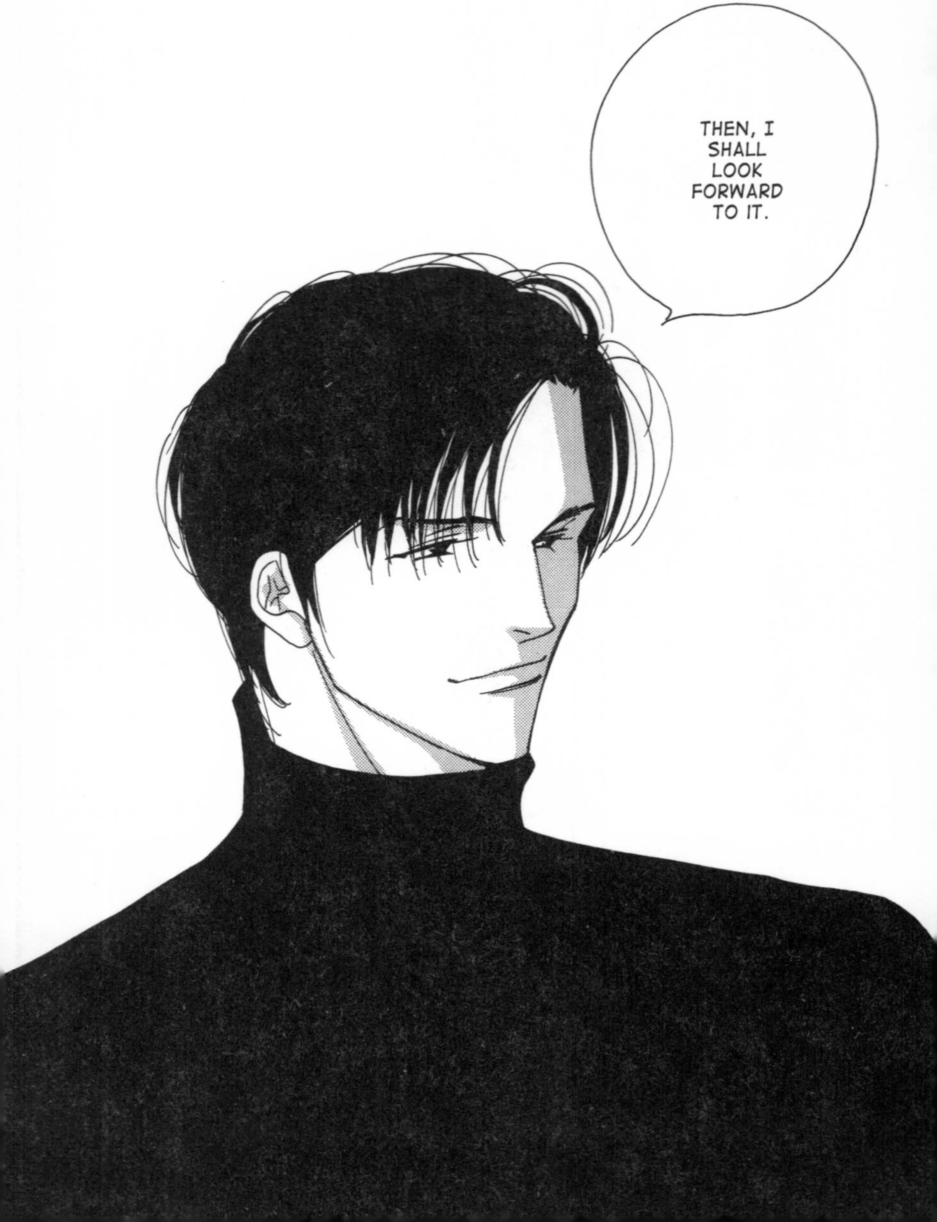
THEN, I SHALL LOOK FORWARD TO IT.

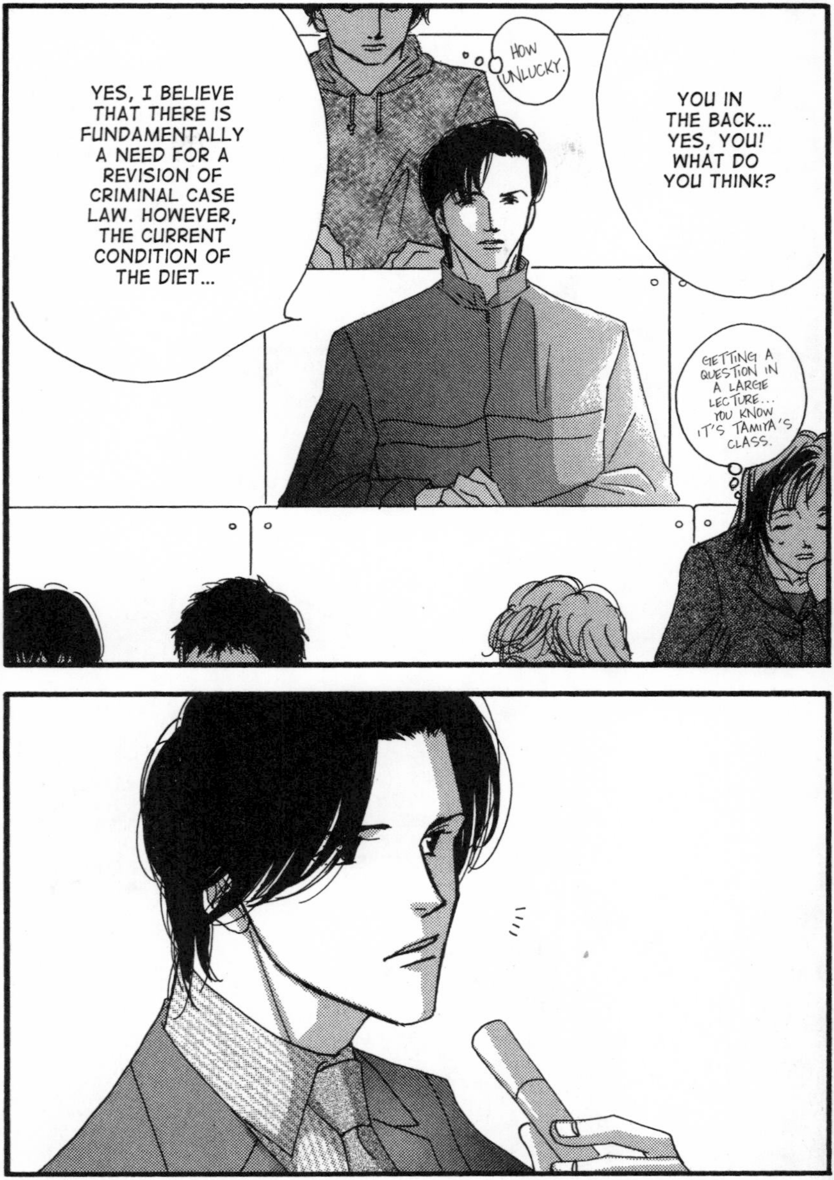
YOU IN THE BACK... YES, YOU! WHAT DO YOU THINK?
HOW UNLUCKY.
YES, I BELIEVE THAT THERE IS FUNDAMENTALLY A NEED FOR A REVISION OF CRIMINAL CASE LAW. HOWEVER, THE CURRENT CONDITION OF THE DIET...
GETTING A QUESTION IN A LARGE LECTURE... YOU KNOW IT'S TAMIYA'S CLASS.

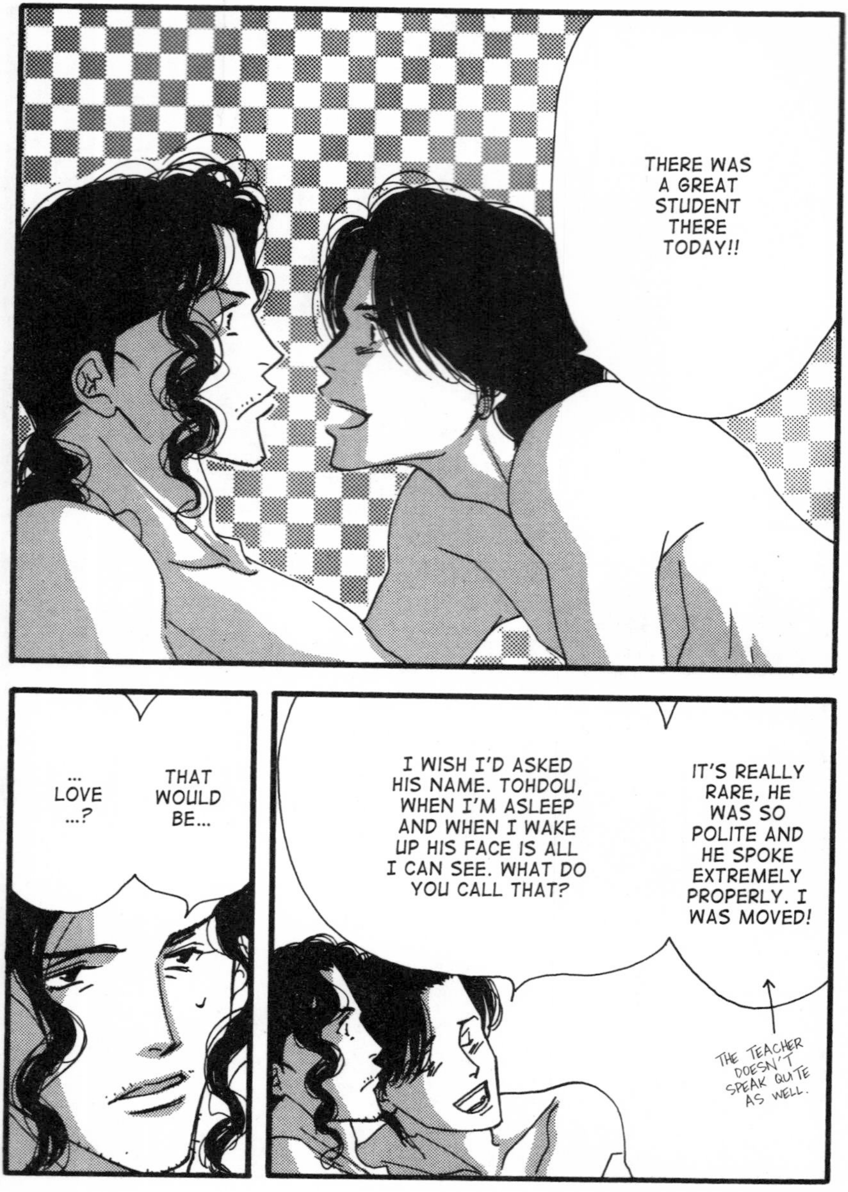
THERE WAS A GREAT STUDENT THERE TODAY!!
IT'S REALLY RARE, HE WAS SO POLITE AND HE SPOKE EXTREMELY PROPERLY. I WAS MOVED!
I WISH I'D ASKED HIS NAME. TOHDOU, WHEN I'M ASLEEP AND WHEN I WAKE UP HIS FACE IS ALL I CAN SEE. WHAT DO YOU CALL THAT?
THE TEACHER DOESN'T SPEAK QUITE AS WELL.
THAT WOULD BE...
... LOVE ...?

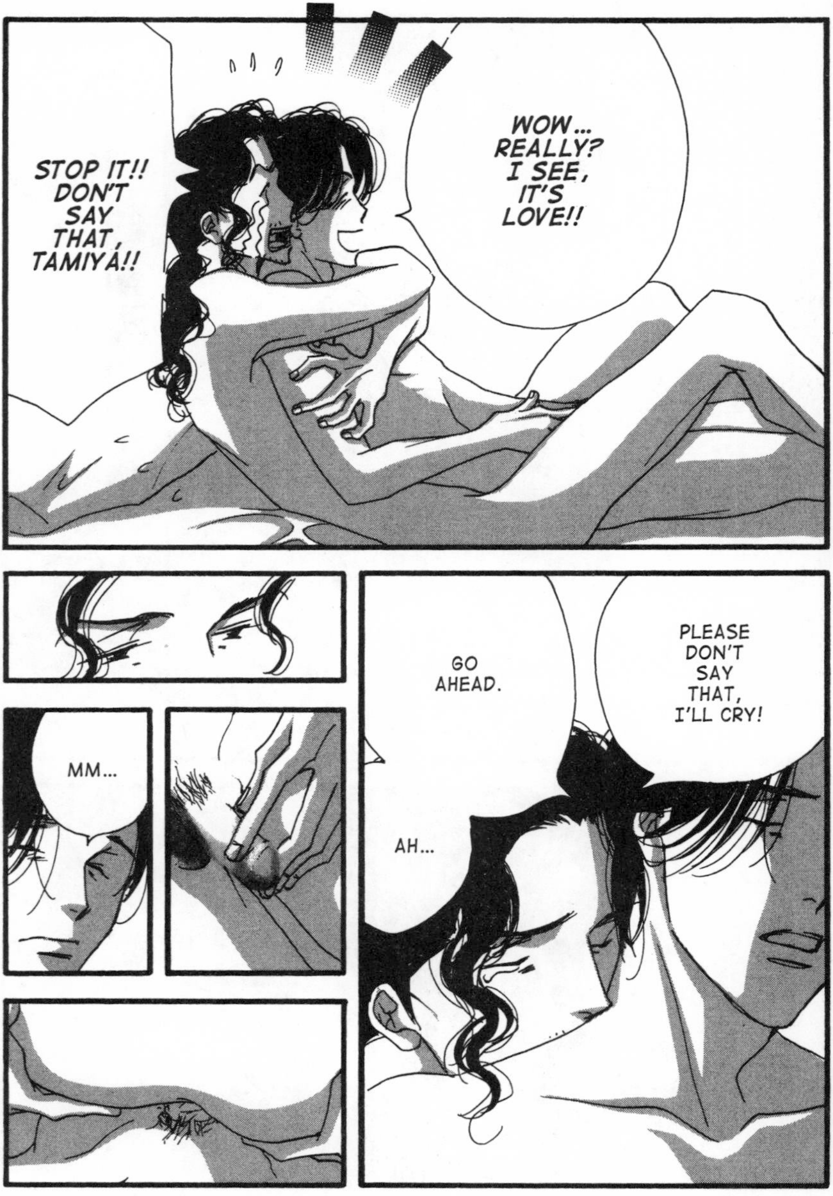
WOW... REALLY? I SEE, IT'S LOVE!!
STOP IT!! DON'T SAY THAT, TAMIYA!!
PLEASE DON'T SAY THAT, I'LL CRY!
GO AHEAD.
AH...
MM...

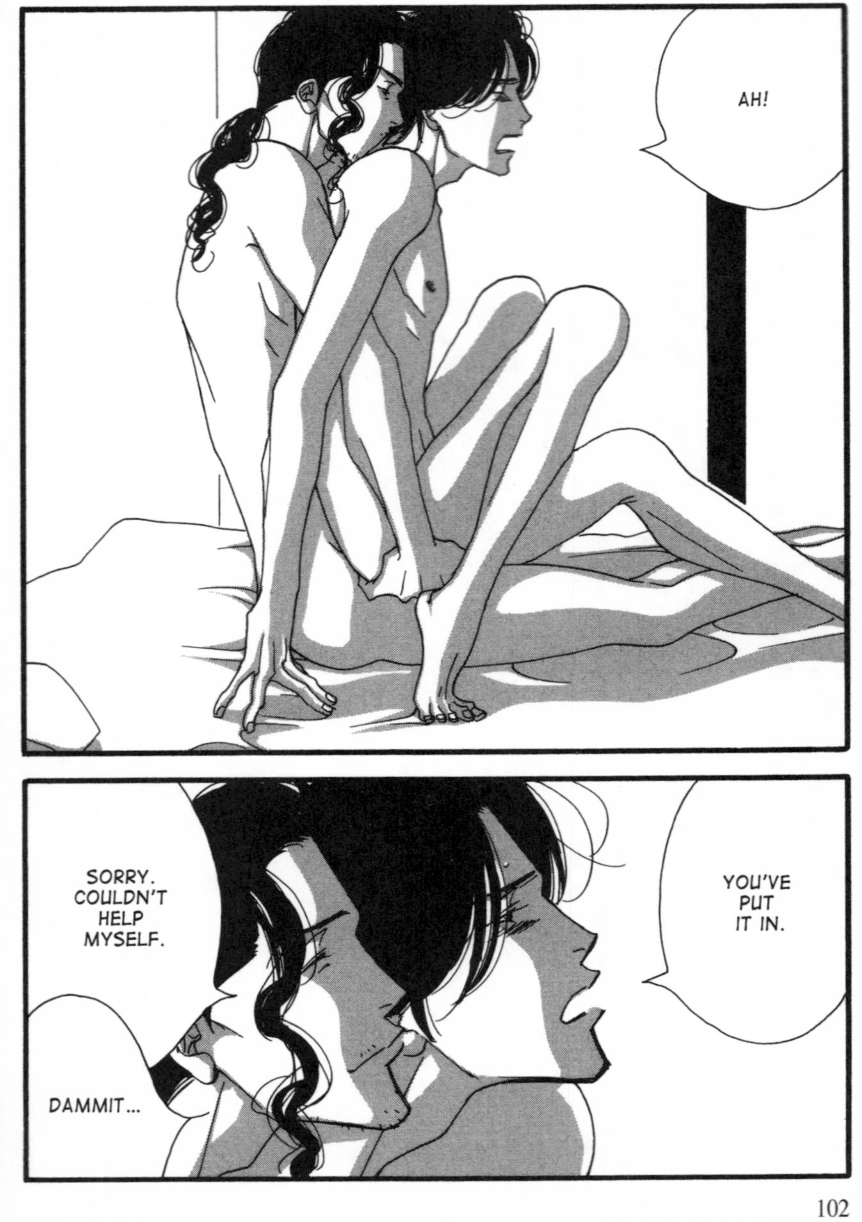
AH!
YOU'VE PUT IT IN.
SORRY. COULDN'T HELP MYSELF.
DAMMIT...

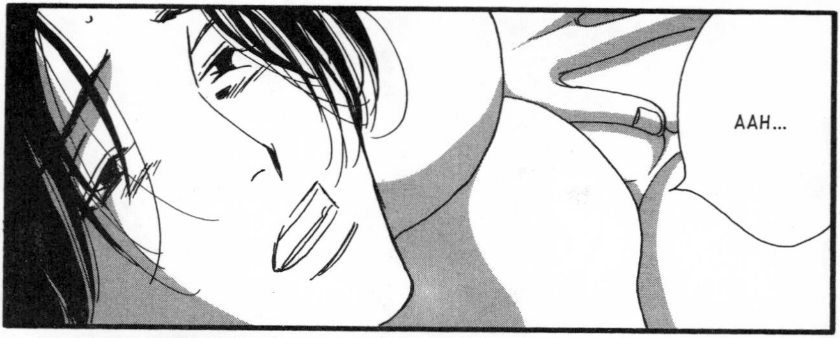
AAH...
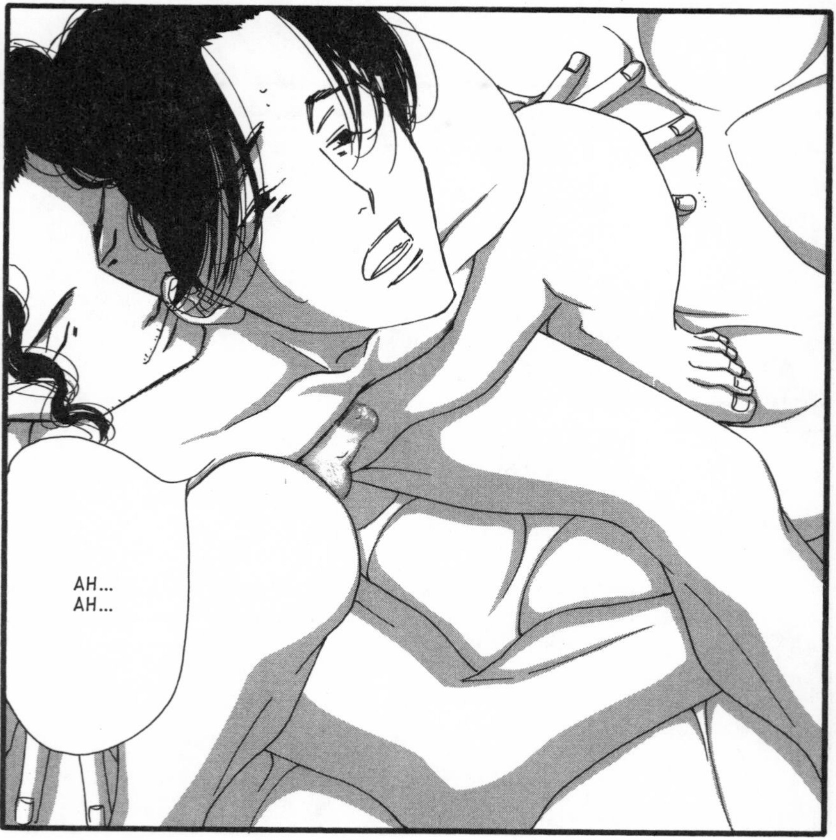
AH...
AH...

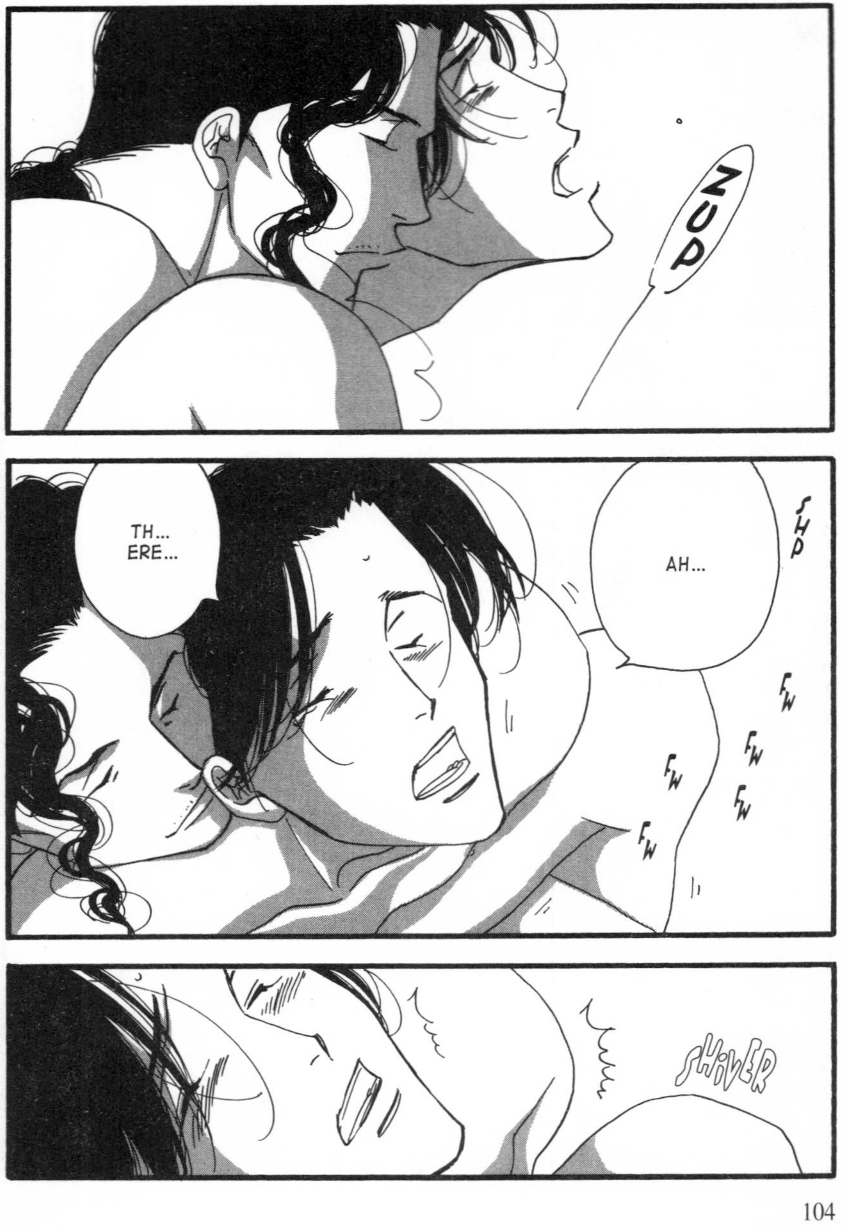
ZUP
SHP
AH...
TH... ERE...
FW
FW
FW
FW
FW
SHIVER

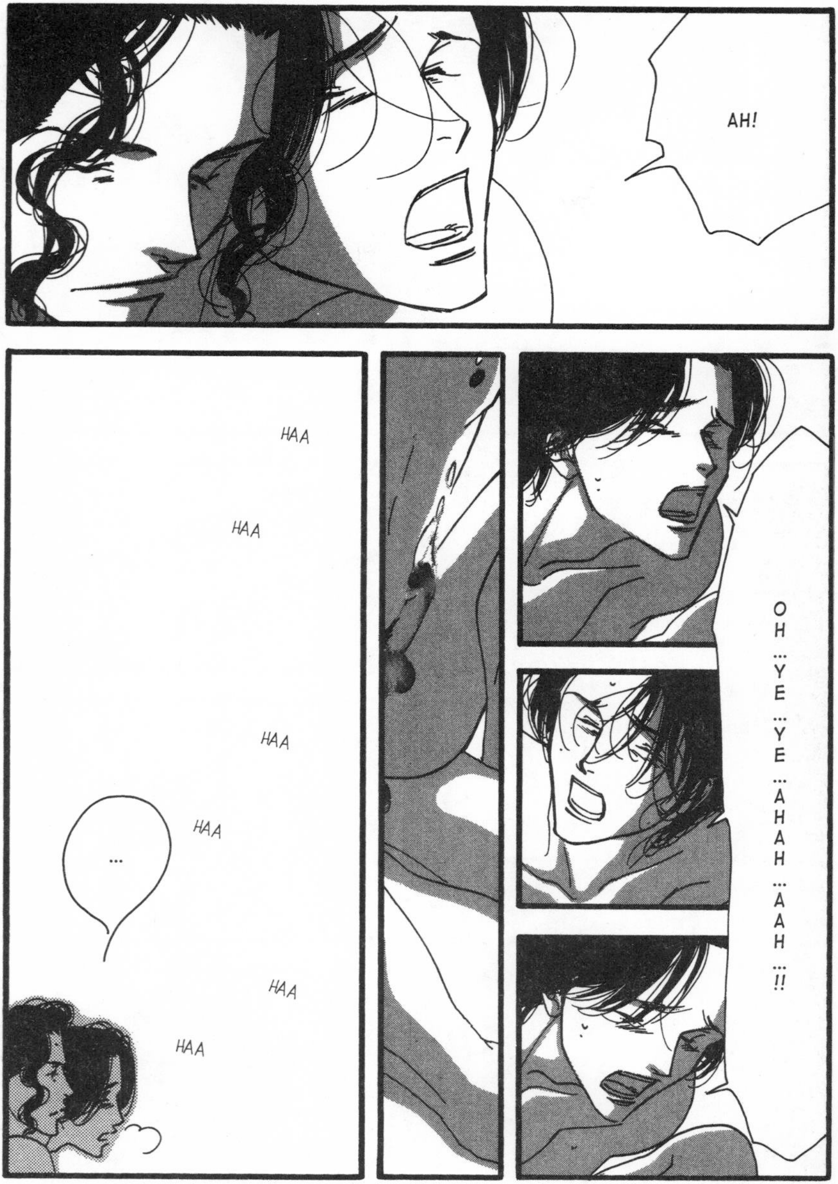
AH!
OH...YE...YE...AHAH...AAH...!!
HAA
HAA
HAA
HAA
...
HAA
HAA

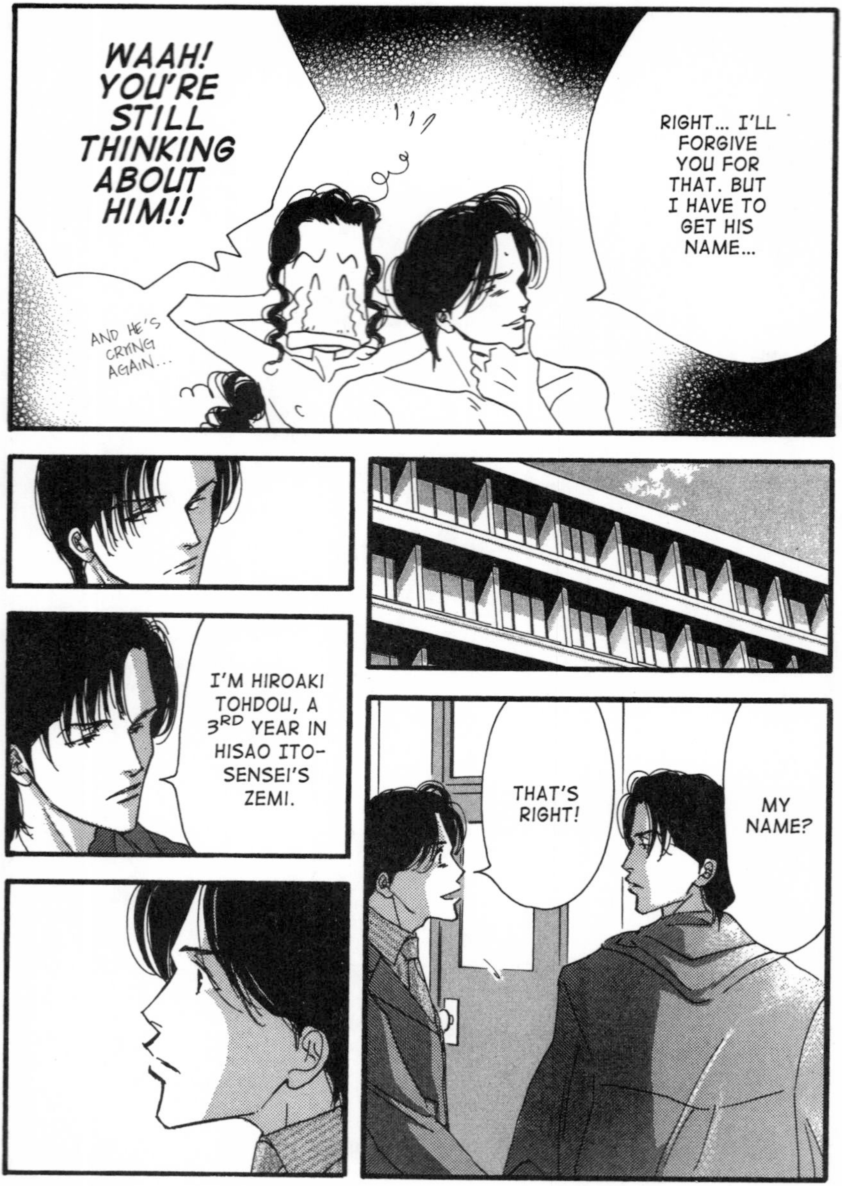
RIGHT... I'LL FORGIVE YOU FOR THAT. BUT I HAVE TO GET HIS NAME...
WAAH! YOU'RE STILL THINKING ABOUT HIM!!
AND HE'S CRYING AGAIN...
MY NAME?
THAT'S RIGHT!
I'M HIROAKI TOHDOU, A 3RD YEAR IN HISAO ITO-SENSEI'S ZEMI.

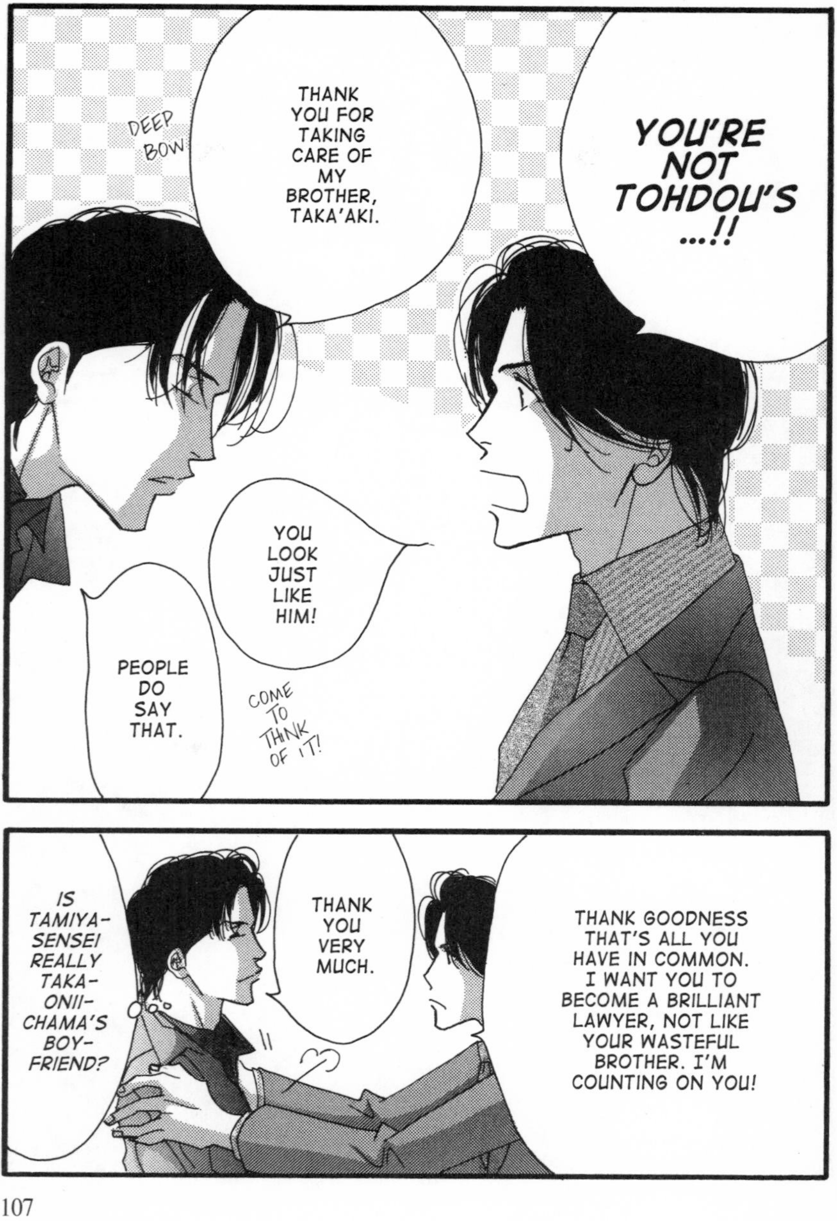
YOU'RE NOT TOHDOU'S ...!!
THANK YOU FOR TAKING CARE OF MY BROTHER, TAKA'AKI.
DEEP BOW
YOU LOOK JUST LIKE HIM!
COME TO THINK OF IT!
PEOPLE DO SAY THAT.
THANK GOODNESS THAT'S ALL YOU HAVE IN COMMON. I WANT YOU TO BECOME A BRILLIANT LAWYER, NOT LIKE YOUR WASTEFUL BROTHER. I'M COUNTING ON YOU!
THANK YOU VERY MUCH.
IS TAMIYA-SENSEI REALLY TAKA-ONII-CHAMA'S BOY-FRIEND?

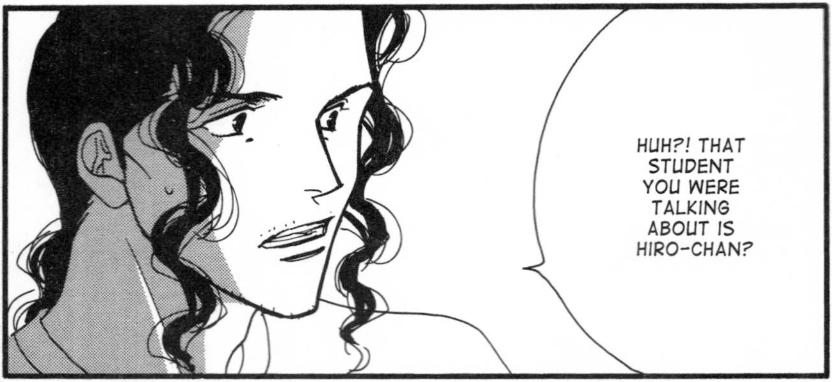
HUH?! THAT STUDENT YOU WERE TALKING ABOUT IS HIRO-CHAN?

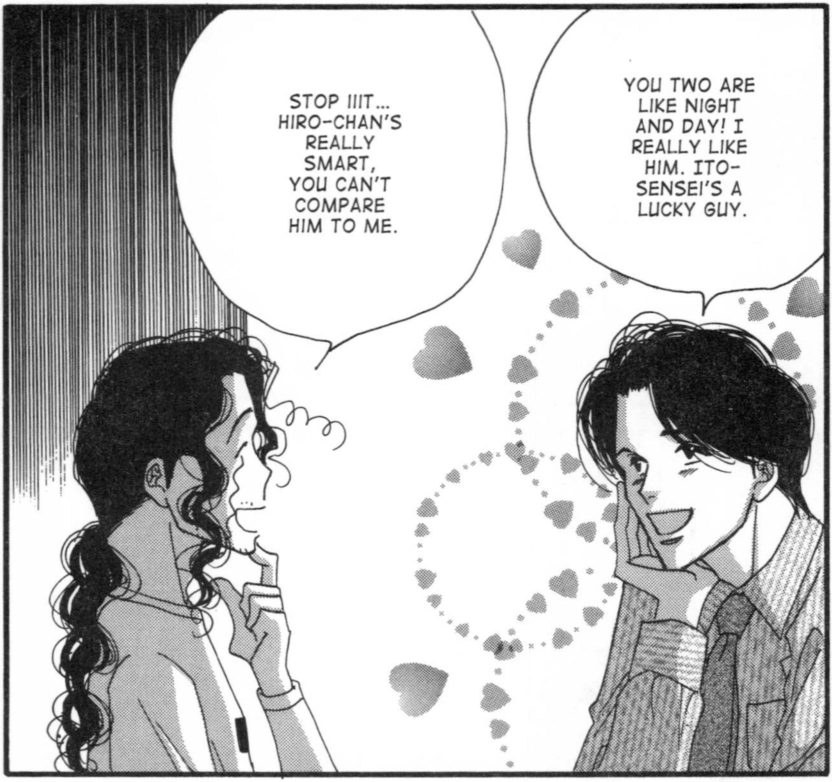
YOU TWO ARE LIKE NIGHT AND DAY! I REALLY LIKE HIM. ITO-SENSEI'S A LUCKY GUY.
STOP IIIT... HIRO-CHAN'S REALLY SMART, YOU CAN'T COMPARE HIM TO ME.

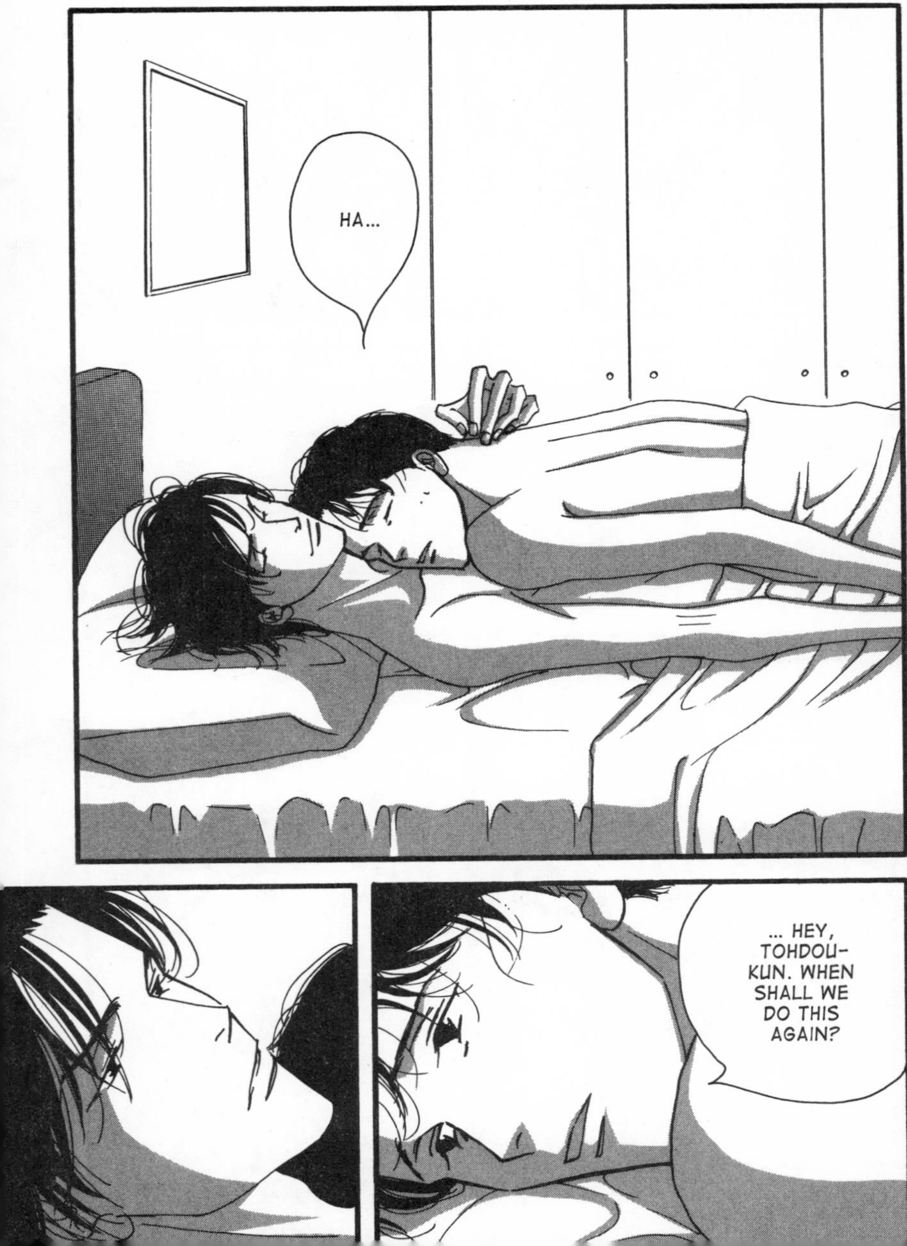
HA...
... HEY, TOHDOU-KUN. WHEN SHALL WE DO THIS AGAIN?

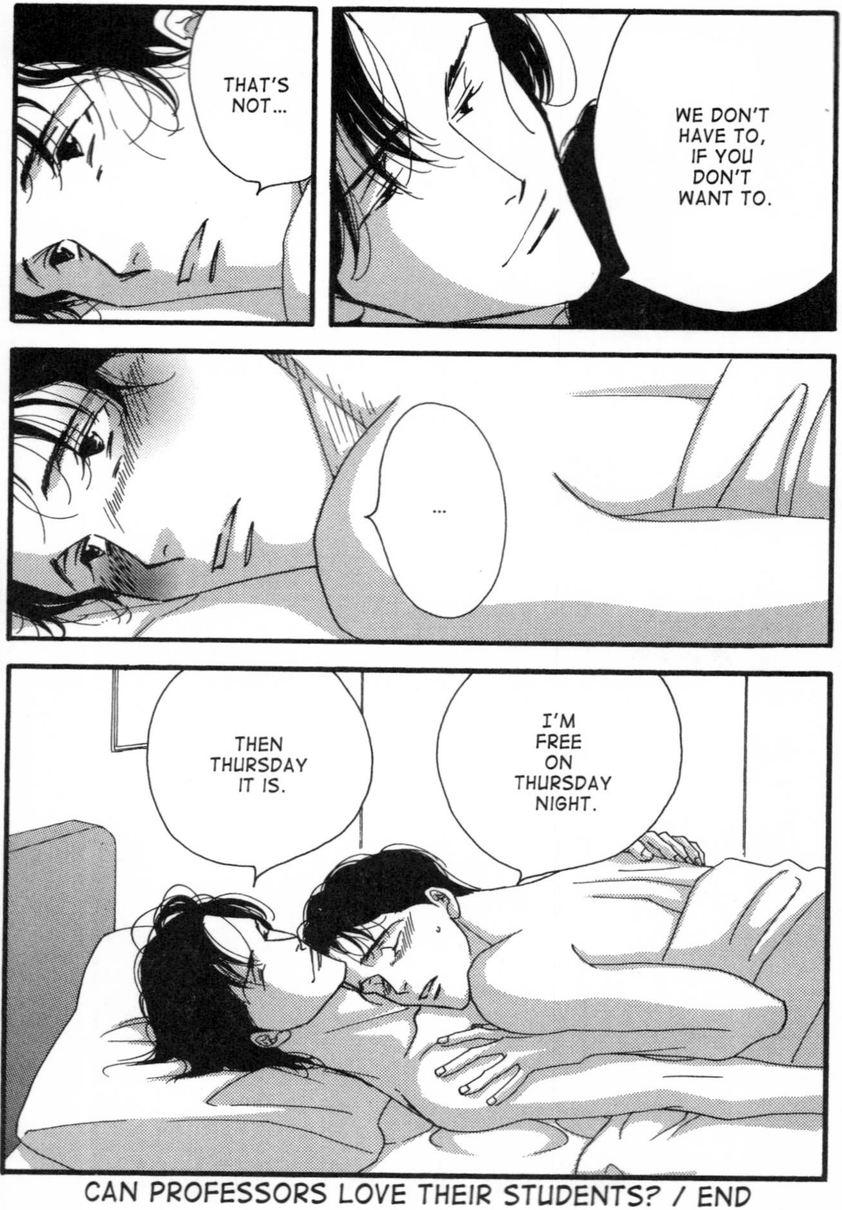
WE DON'T HAVE TO, IF YOU DON'T WANT TO.
THAT'S NOT...
...
I'M FREE ON THURSDAY NIGHT.
THEN THURSDAY IT IS.

CAN PROFESSORS LOVE THEIR STUDENTS? / END

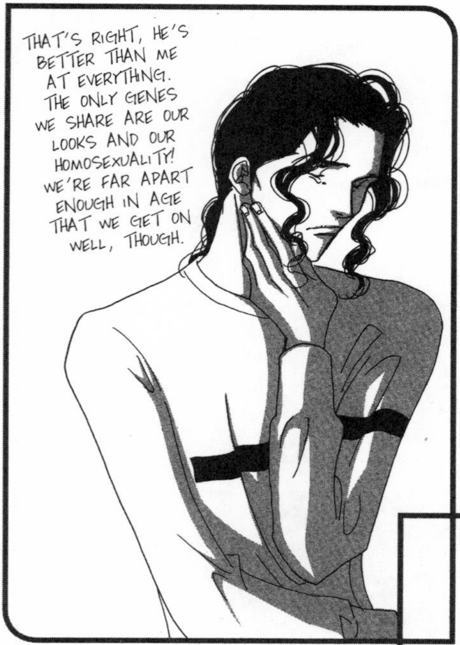
THAT'S RIGHT, HE'S BETTER THAN ME AT EVERYTHING. THE ONLY GENES WE SHARE ARE OUR LOOKS AND OUR HOMOSEXUALITY! WE'RE FAR APART ENOUGH IN AGE THAT WE GET ON WELL, THOUGH.

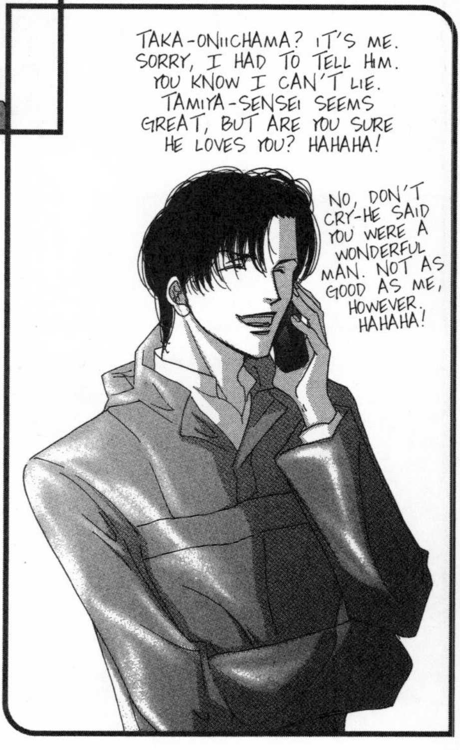
TAKA-ONIICHAMA? IT'S ME. SORRY, I HAD TO TELL HIM. YOU KNOW I CAN'T LIE. TAMIYA-SENSEI SEEMS GREAT, BUT ARE YOU SURE HE LOVES YOU? HAHAHA!
NO, DON'T CRY-HE SAID YOU WERE A WONDERFUL MAN. NOT AS GOOD AS ME, HOWEVER. HAHAHA!

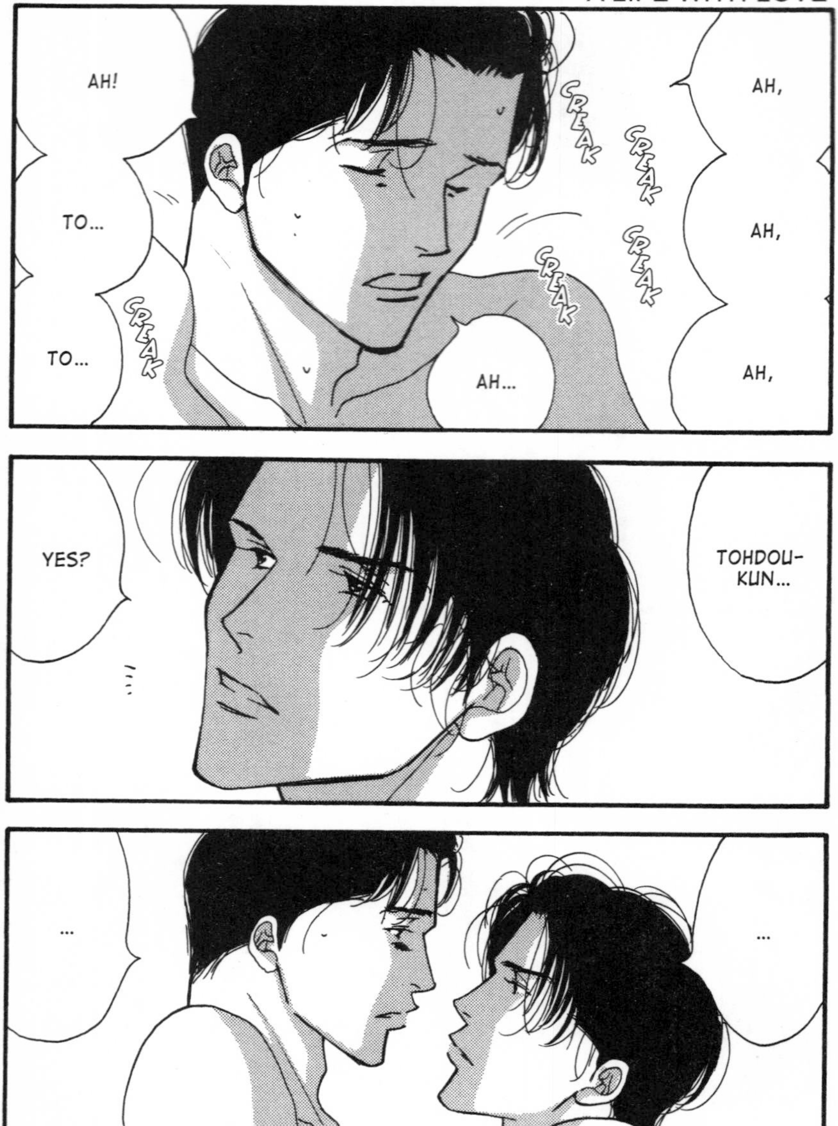
AH,
AH,
AH,
CREAK
CREAK
CREAK
CREAK
AH...
AH!
TO...
CREAK
TO...
TOHDOU-KUN...
YES?
...
...

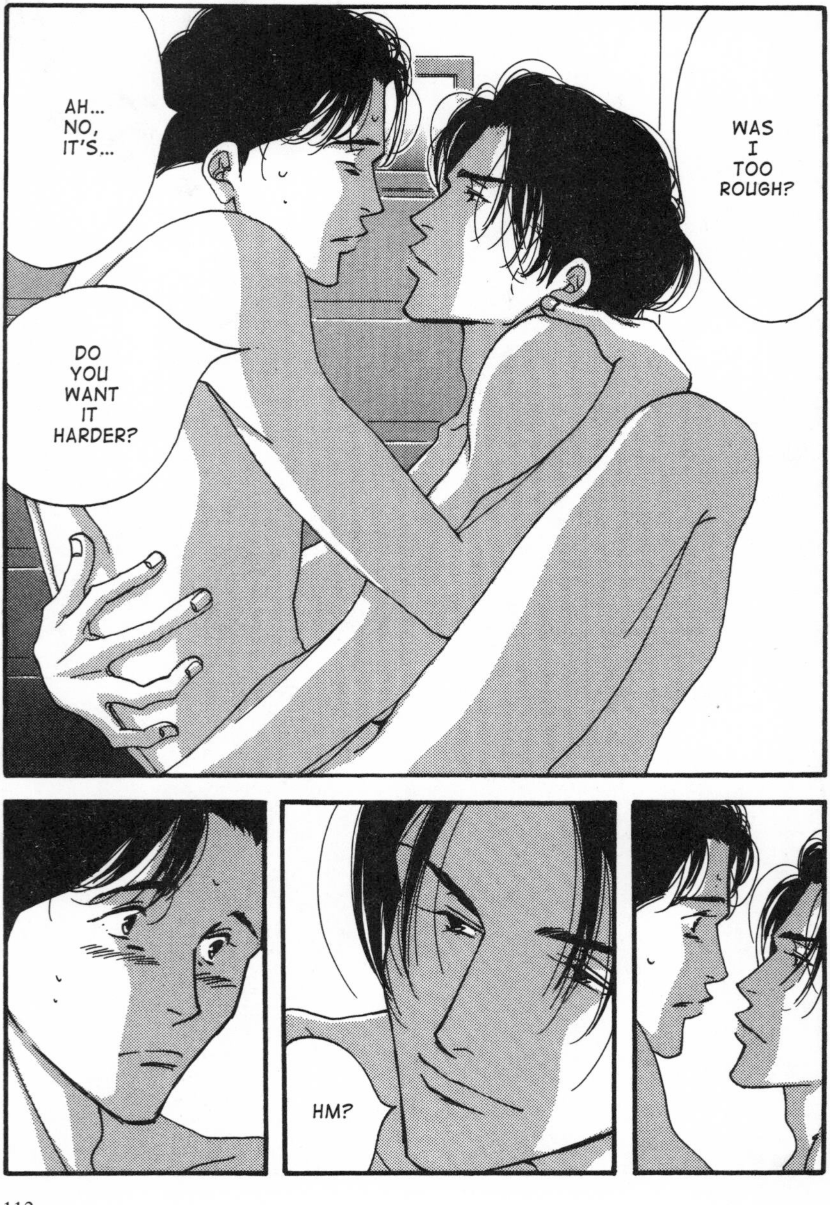
WAS I TOO ROUGH?
AH... NO, IT'S...
DO YOU WANT IT HARDER?
HM?

...HARDER!

A LIFE WITH LOVE

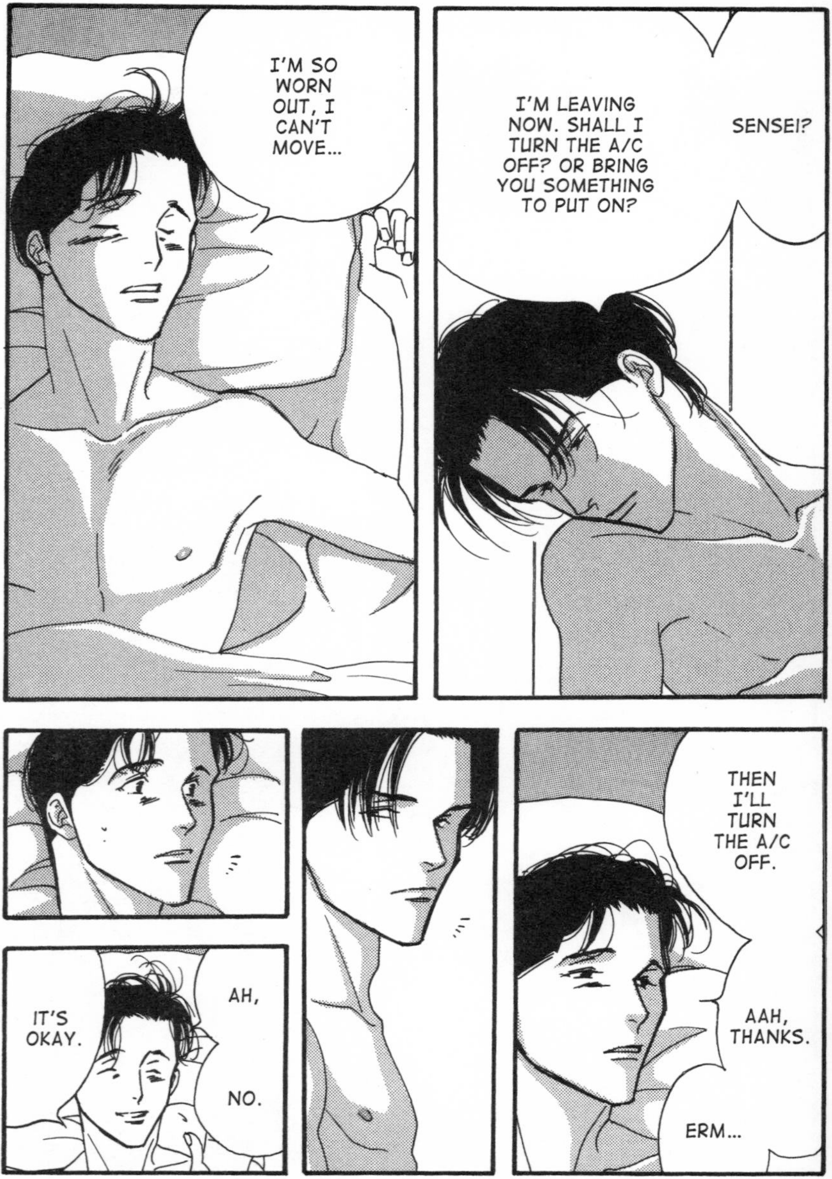
SENSEI?
I'M LEAVING NOW. SHALL I TURN THE A/C OFF? OR BRING YOU SOMETHING TO PUT ON?
I'M SO WORN OUT, I CAN'T MOVE...
THEN I'LL TURN THE A/C OFF.
AAH, THANKS.
ERM...
AH,
NO.
IT'S OKAY.

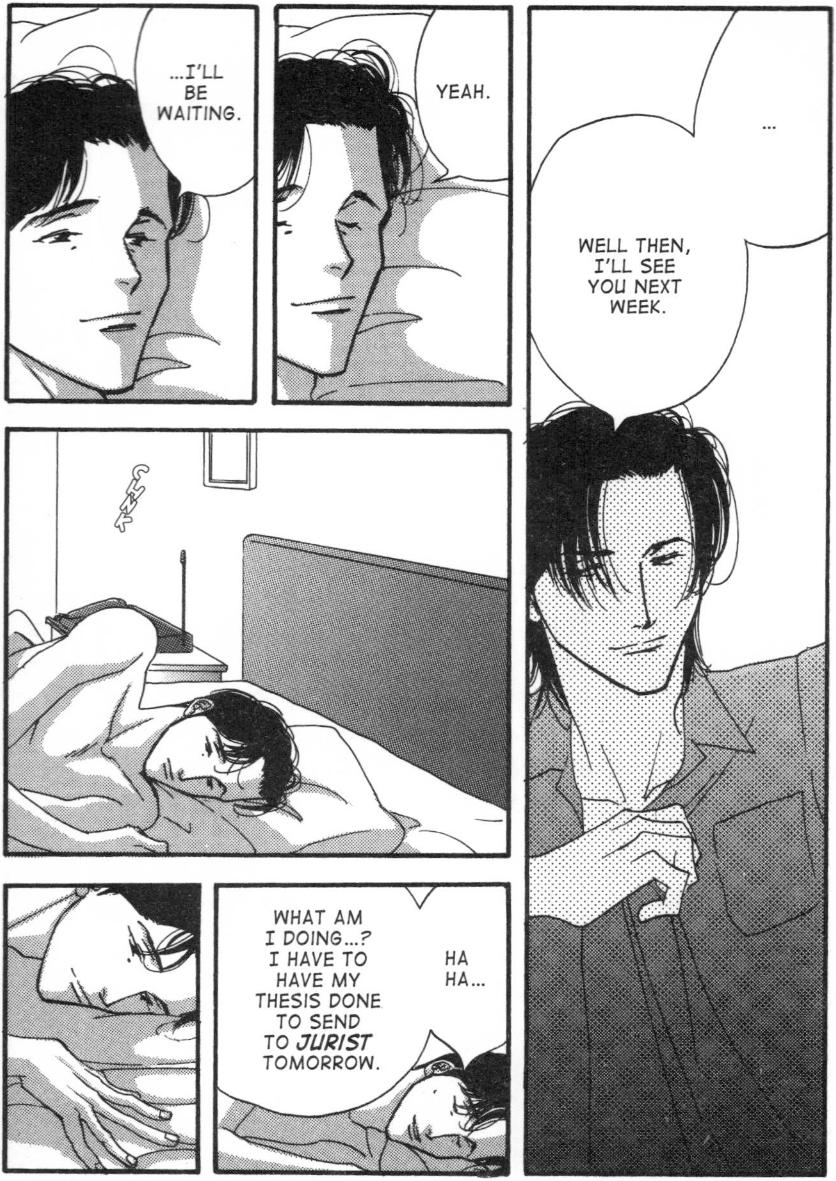
...
WELL THEN, I'LL SEE YOU NEXT WEEK.
YEAH.
...I'LL BE WAITING.
CLINK
WHAT AM I DOING...? I HAVE TO HAVE MY THESIS DONE TO SEND TO *JURIST* TOMORROW.
HA HA...

WHAT
AM I
DOING...

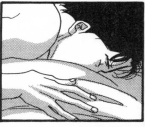

ジュリスト

JURIST

WHAT
THE HELL
WERE YOU
DOING?

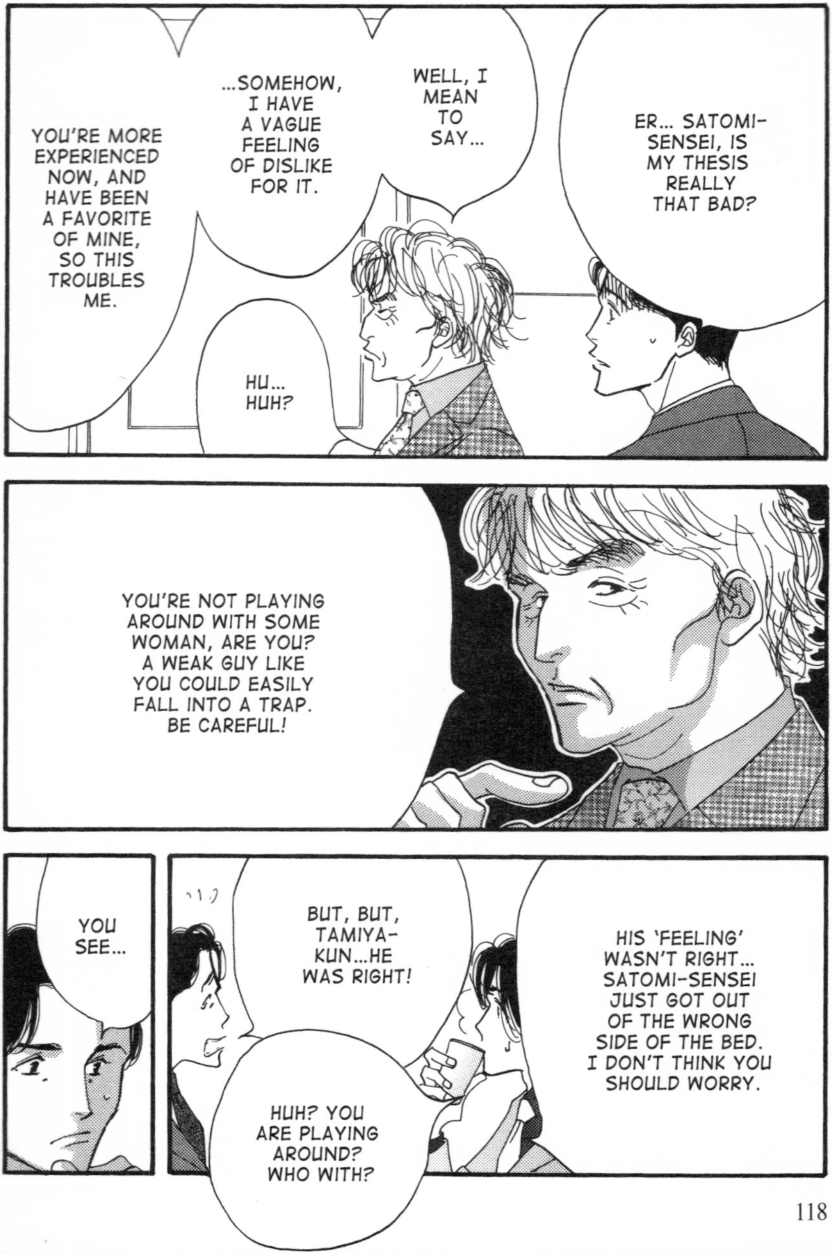
ER... SATOMI-SENSEI, IS MY THESIS REALLY THAT BAD?
WELL, I MEAN TO SAY...
...SOMEHOW, I HAVE A VAGUE FEELING OF DISLIKE FOR IT.
YOU'RE MORE EXPERIENCED NOW, AND HAVE BEEN A FAVORITE OF MINE, SO THIS TROUBLES ME.
HU... HUH?
YOU'RE NOT PLAYING AROUND WITH SOME WOMAN, ARE YOU? A WEAK GUY LIKE YOU COULD EASILY FALL INTO A TRAP. BE CAREFUL!
HIS 'FEELING' WASN'T RIGHT... SATOMI-SENSEI JUST GOT OUT OF THE WRONG SIDE OF THE BED. I DON'T THINK YOU SHOULD WORRY.
BUT, BUT, TAMIYA-KUN...HE WAS RIGHT!
HUH? YOU ARE PLAYING AROUND? WHO WITH?
YOU SEE...

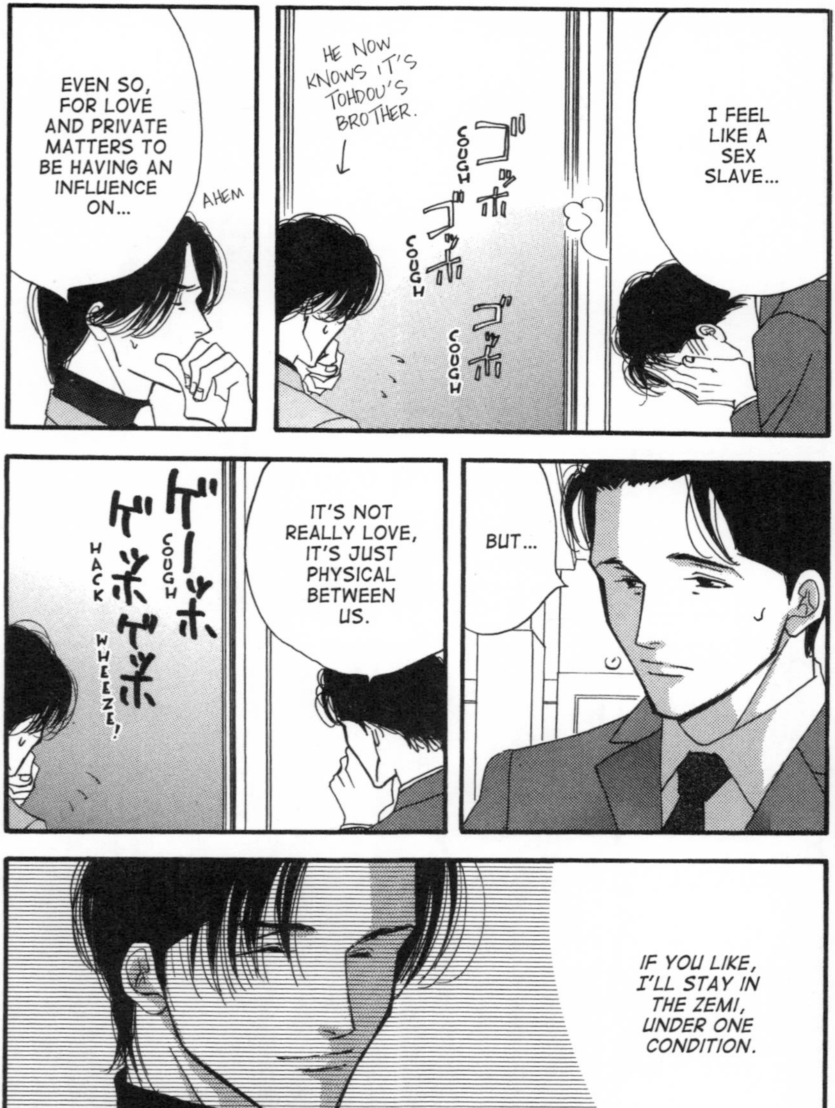
I FEEL LIKE A SEX SLAVE...
ゴッホ
COUGH
ゴッホ
COUGH
HE NOW KNOWS IT'S TOHDOU'S BROTHER.
ゴッホ
COUGH
EVEN SO, FOR LOVE AND PRIVATE MATTERS TO BE HAVING AN INFLUENCE ON...
AHEM
BUT...
IT'S NOT REALLY LOVE, IT'S JUST PHYSICAL BETWEEN US.
ゲーッホ
COUGH
ゲッホゲッホ
HACK
WHEEZE!
IF YOU LIKE, I'LL STAY IN THE ZEMI, UNDER ONE CONDITION.

YES, IT'S SEX.
YES,
THIS...
...ISN'T LOVE.
DING DONG
RIGHT, NEXT WEEK WE'LL START "WAIVING CHARGES WITH THE CONSENT OF THE VICTIM"
AH, FINISHED!
WANNA GET A DRINK?

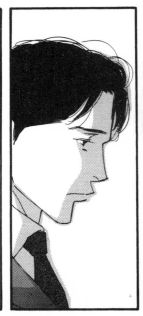

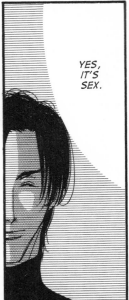

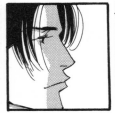

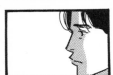

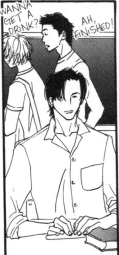

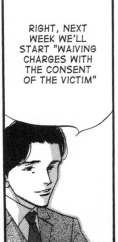

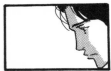

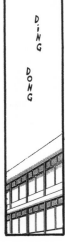

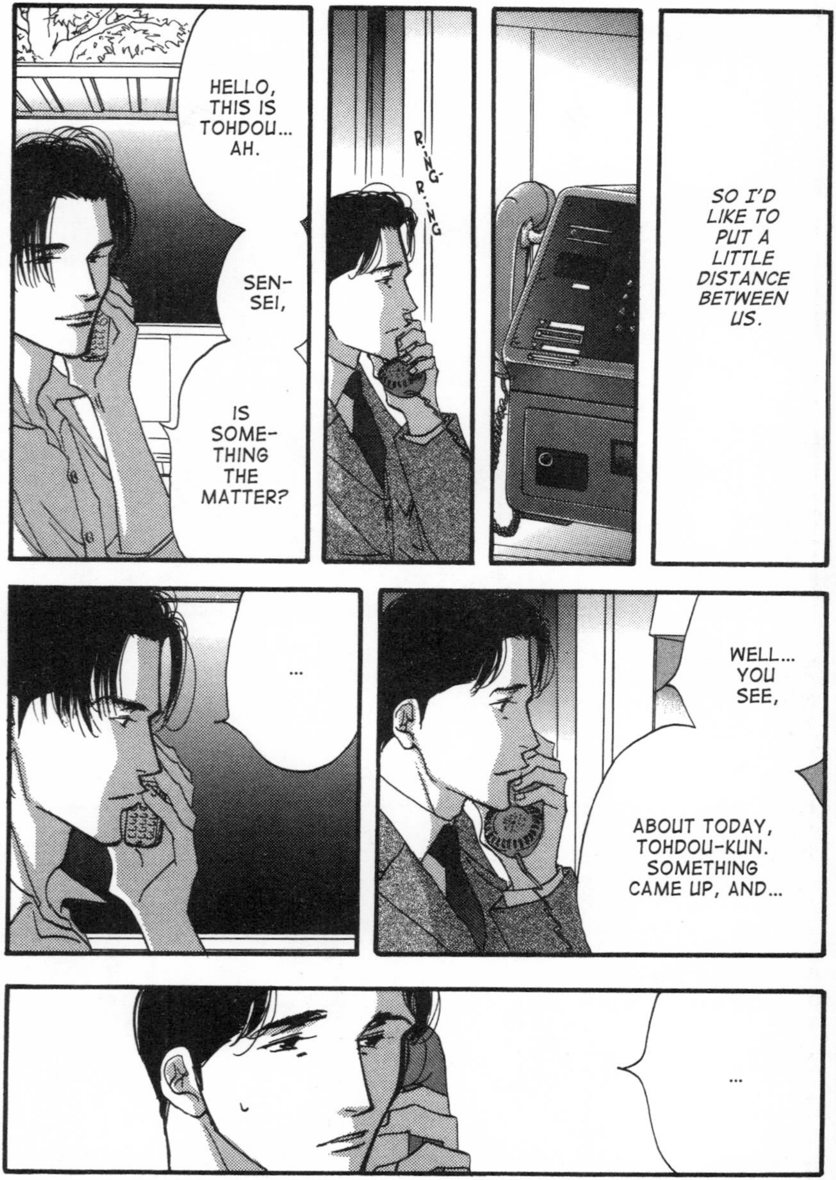

SO I'D LIKE TO PUT A LITTLE DISTANCE BETWEEN US.
R..NG R..NG
HELLO, THIS IS TOHDOU... AH.
SEN-SEI,
IS SOMETHING THE MATTER?
WELL... YOU SEE,
ABOUT TODAY, TOHDOU-KUN. SOMETHING CAME UP, AND...
...
...

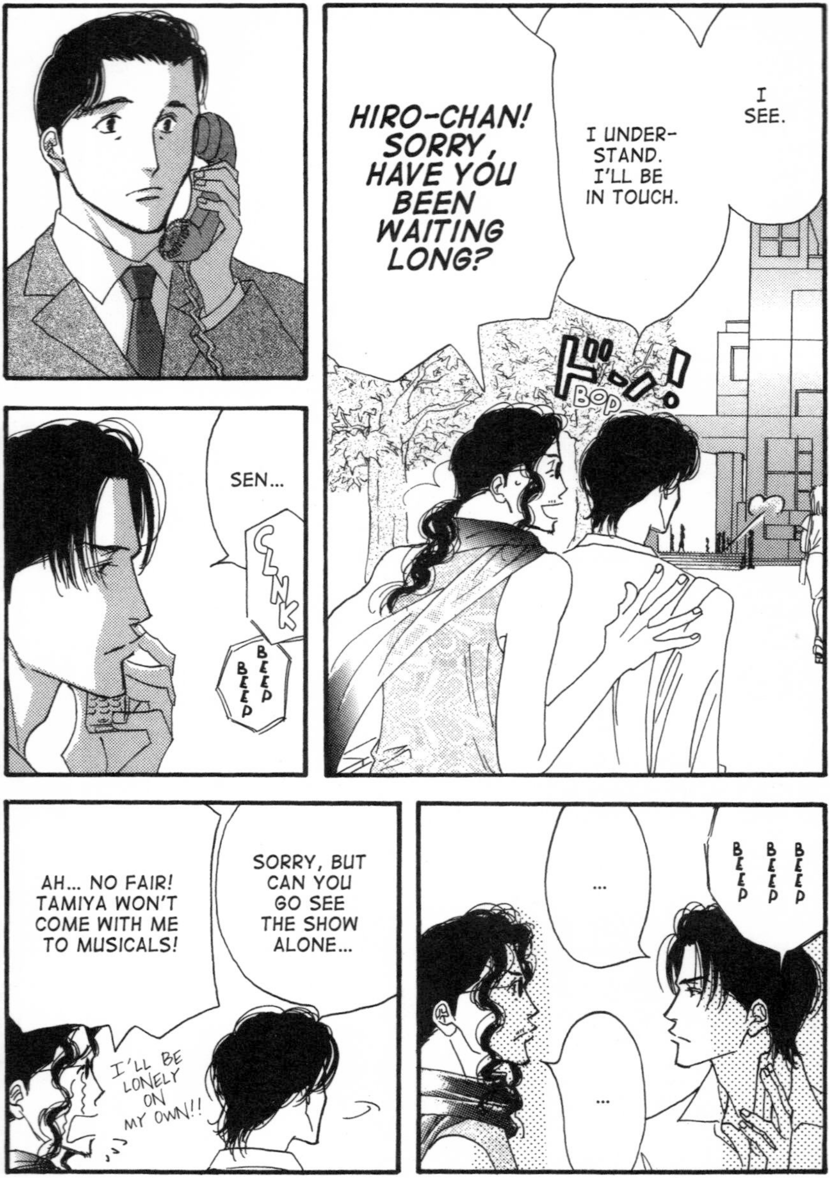
I SEE.
I UNDERSTAND. I'LL BE IN TOUCH.
HIRO-CHAN! SORRY, HAVE YOU BEEN WAITING LONG?
BOP
SEN...
CLNK
BEEP BEEP
BEEP BEEP BEEP
...
...
SORRY, BUT CAN YOU GO SEE THE SHOW ALONE...
AH... NO FAIR! TAMIYA WON'T COME WITH ME TO MUSICALS!
I'LL BE LONELY ON MY OWN!!

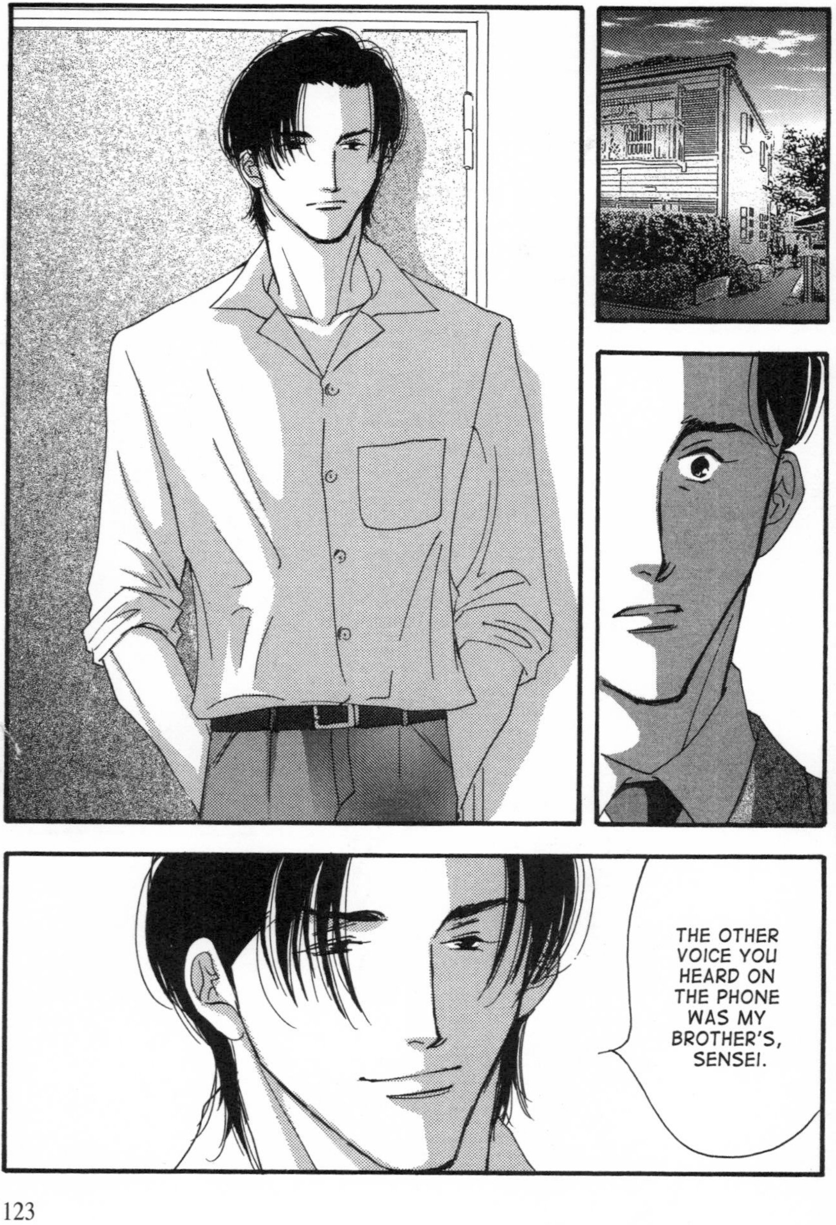
THE OTHER VOICE YOU HEARD ON THE PHONE WAS MY BROTHER'S, SENSEI.

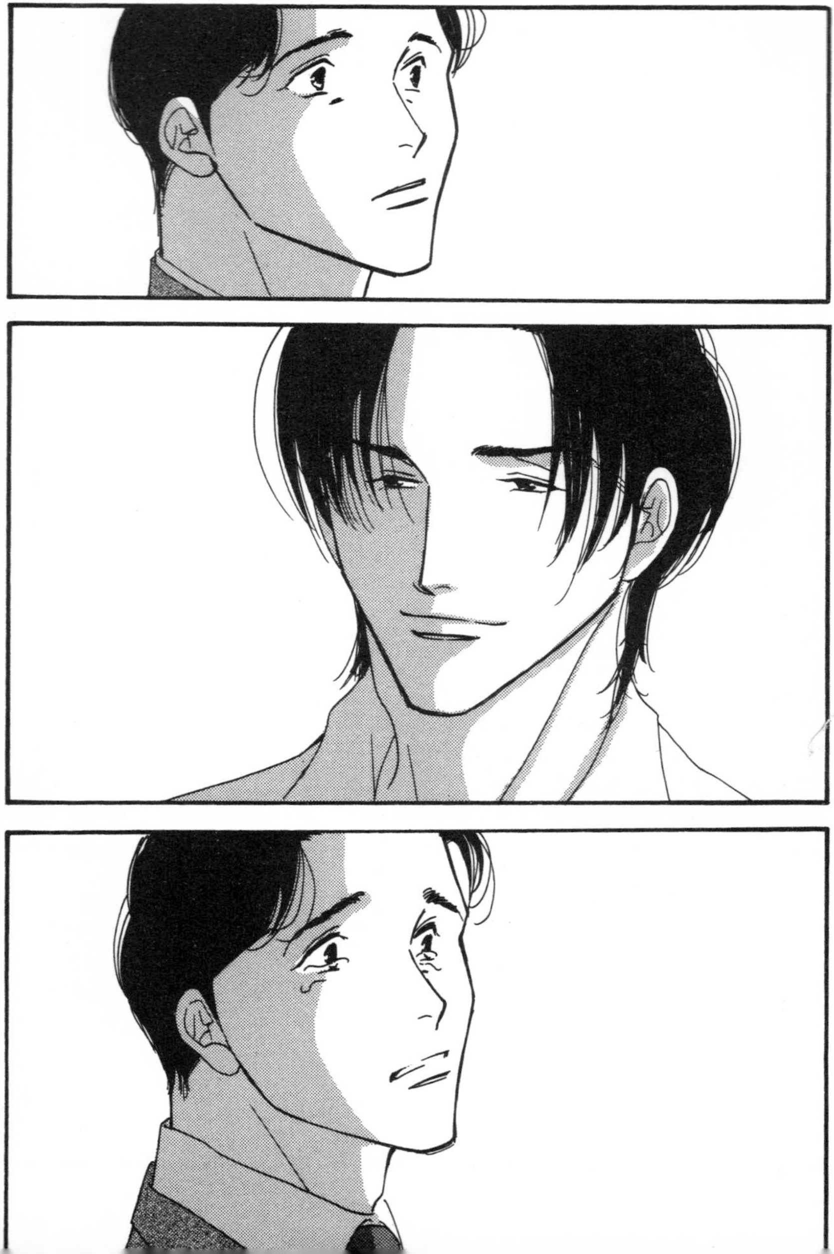

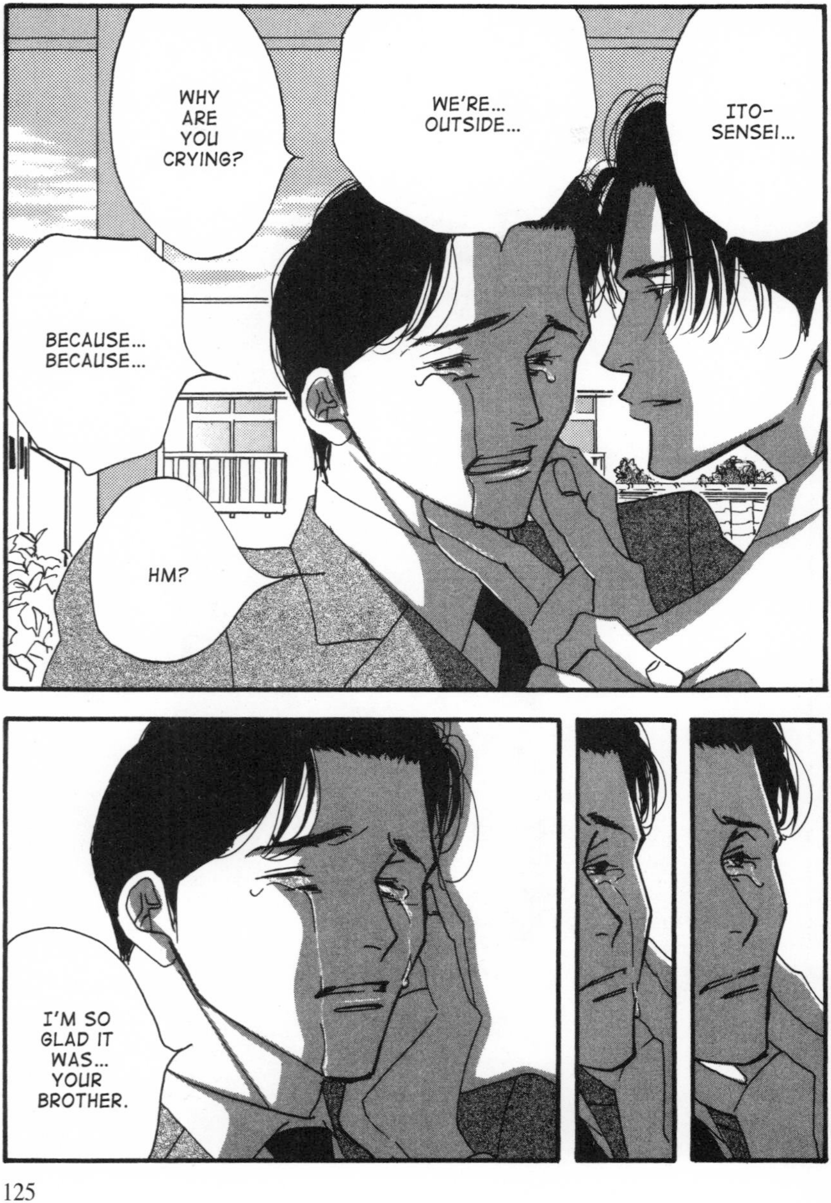
ITO-SENSEI...
WE'RE... OUTSIDE...
WHY ARE YOU CRYING?
BECAUSE... BECAUSE...
HM?
I'M SO GLAD IT WAS... YOUR BROTHER.

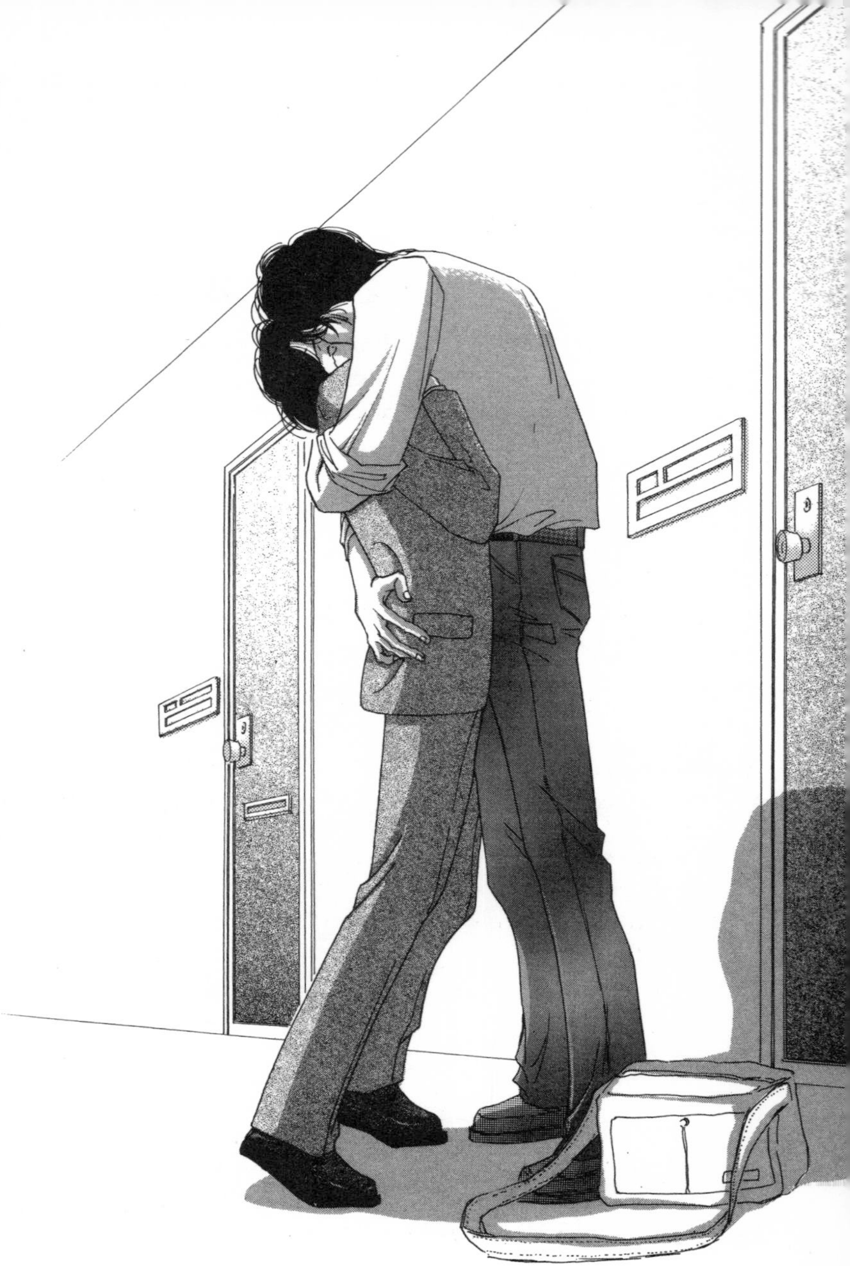

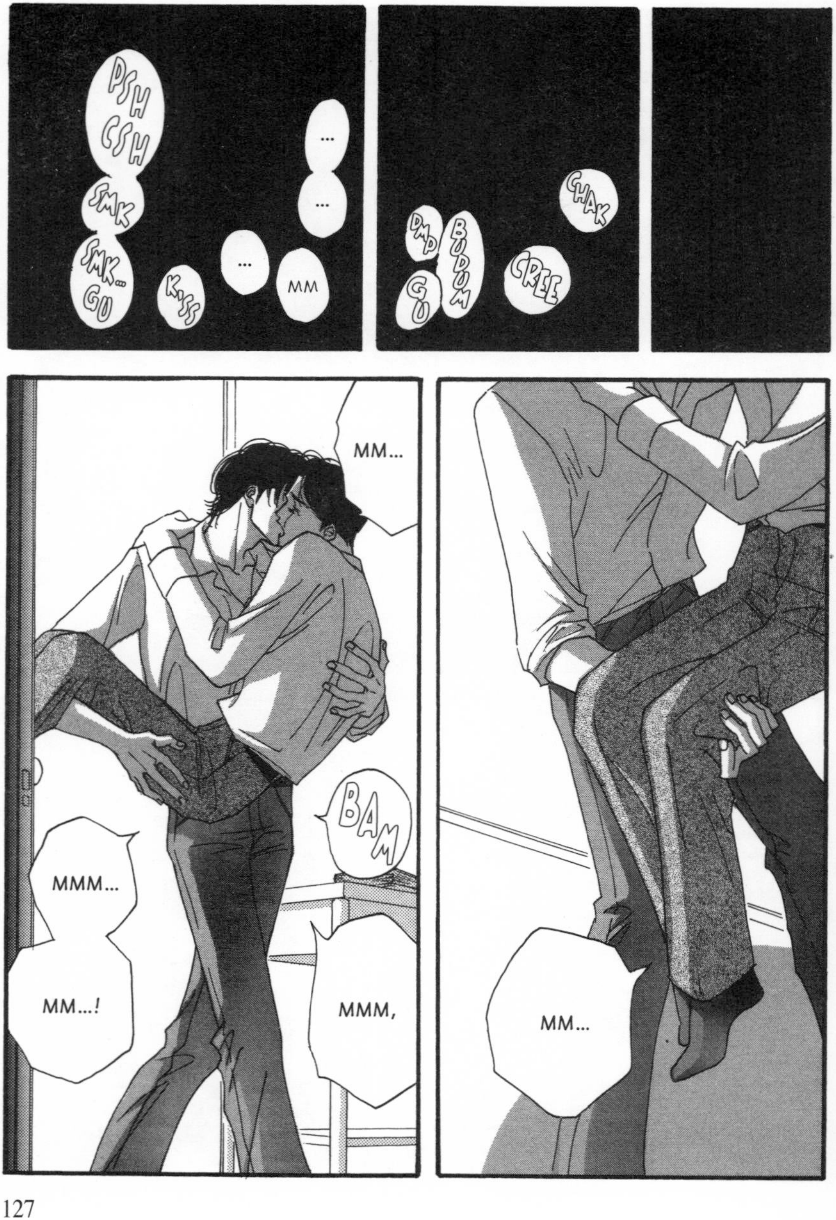
CHAK
CREE
BUDUM
DMP
GU
...
...
MM
...
KISS
PSH CSH
SMK
SMK... GU
MM...
MM...
BAM
MMM,
MMM...
MM...!

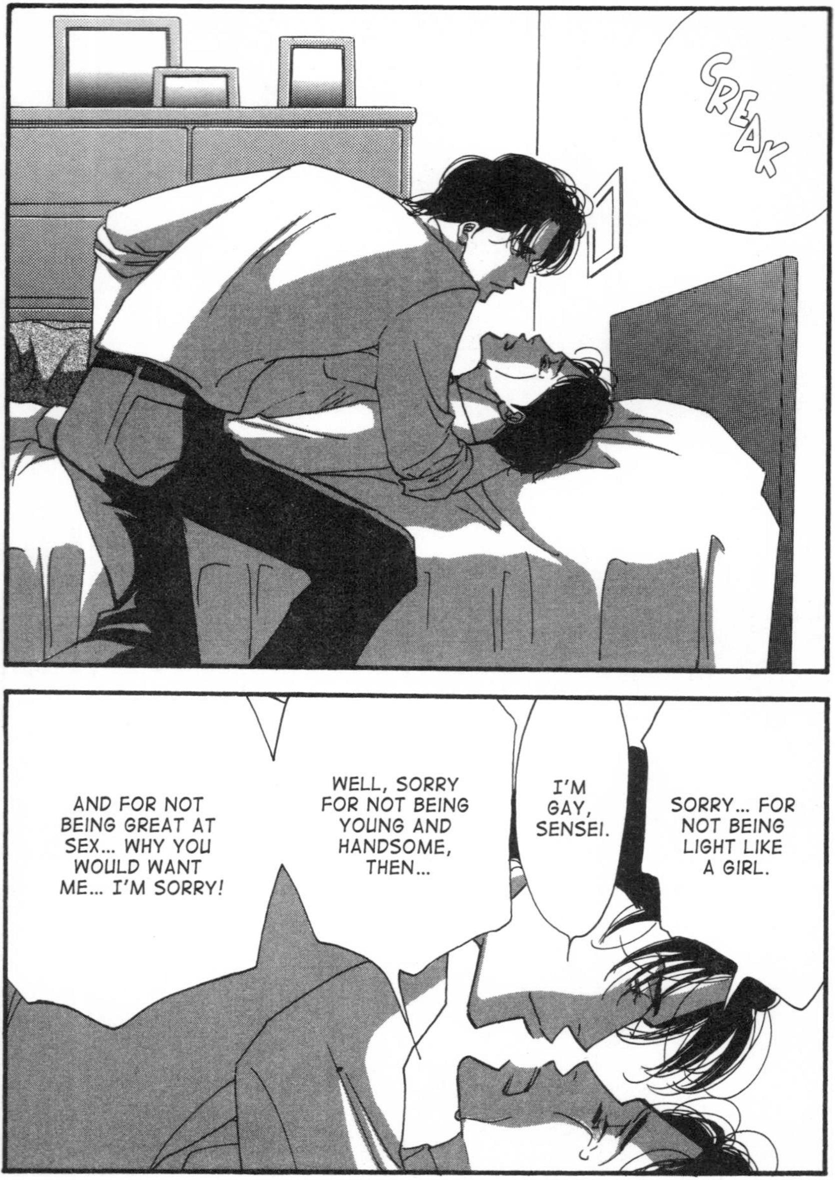
CREAK
SORRY... FOR NOT BEING LIGHT LIKE A GIRL.
I'M GAY, SENSEI.
WELL, SORRY FOR NOT BEING YOUNG AND HANDSOME, THEN...
AND FOR NOT BEING GREAT AT SEX... WHY YOU WOULD WANT ME... I'M SORRY!

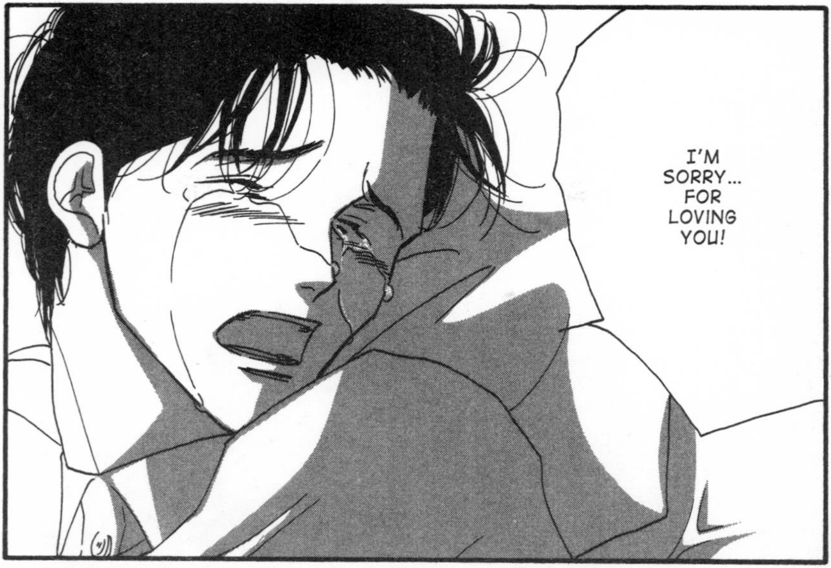
I'M SORRY... FOR LOVING YOU!

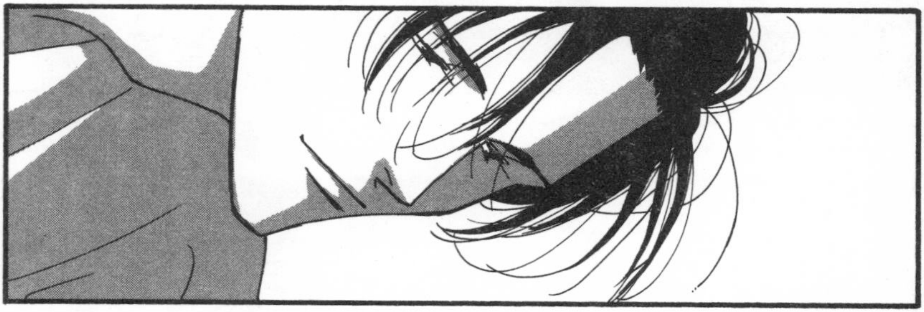

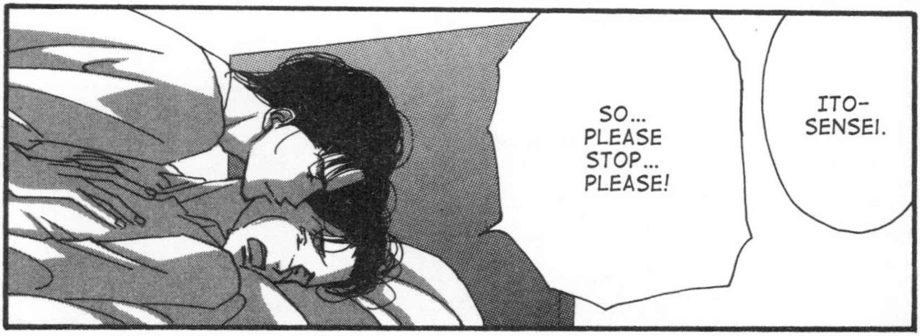
ITO-SENSEI.
SO... PLEASE STOP... PLEASE!

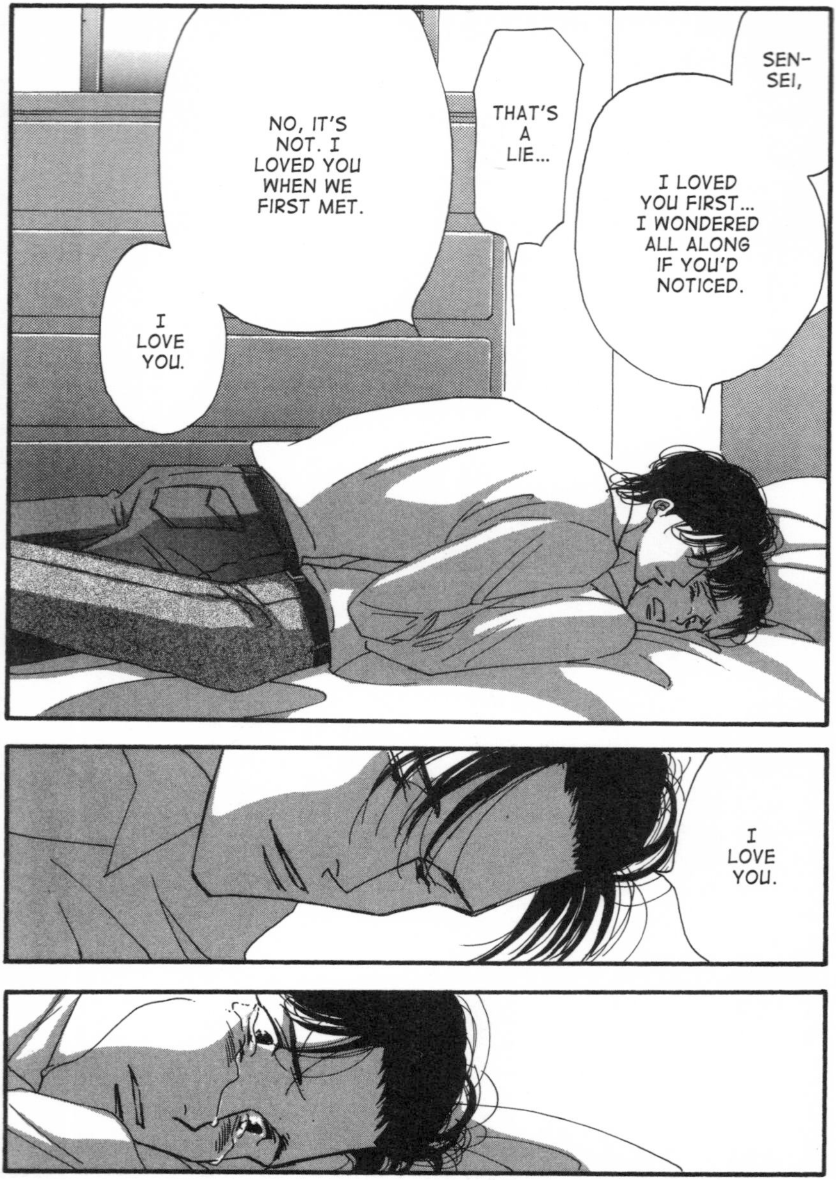
SEN-SEI,
I LOVED YOU FIRST... I WONDERED ALL ALONG IF YOU'D NOTICED.
THAT'S A LIE...
NO, IT'S NOT. I LOVED YOU WHEN WE FIRST MET.
I LOVE YOU.
I LOVE YOU.

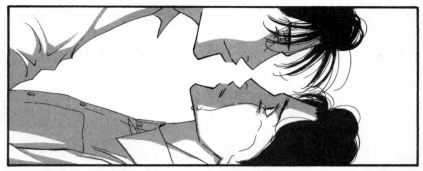

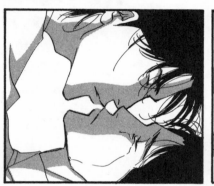

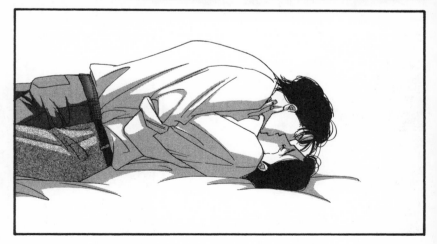

ONLY YOU...

I LOVE YOU, SENSEI.

NO...

I LOVE YOU.

AH... AH...

SHIVER

AH.

AAH!! DON'T TOUCH... NO...!!

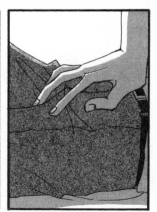

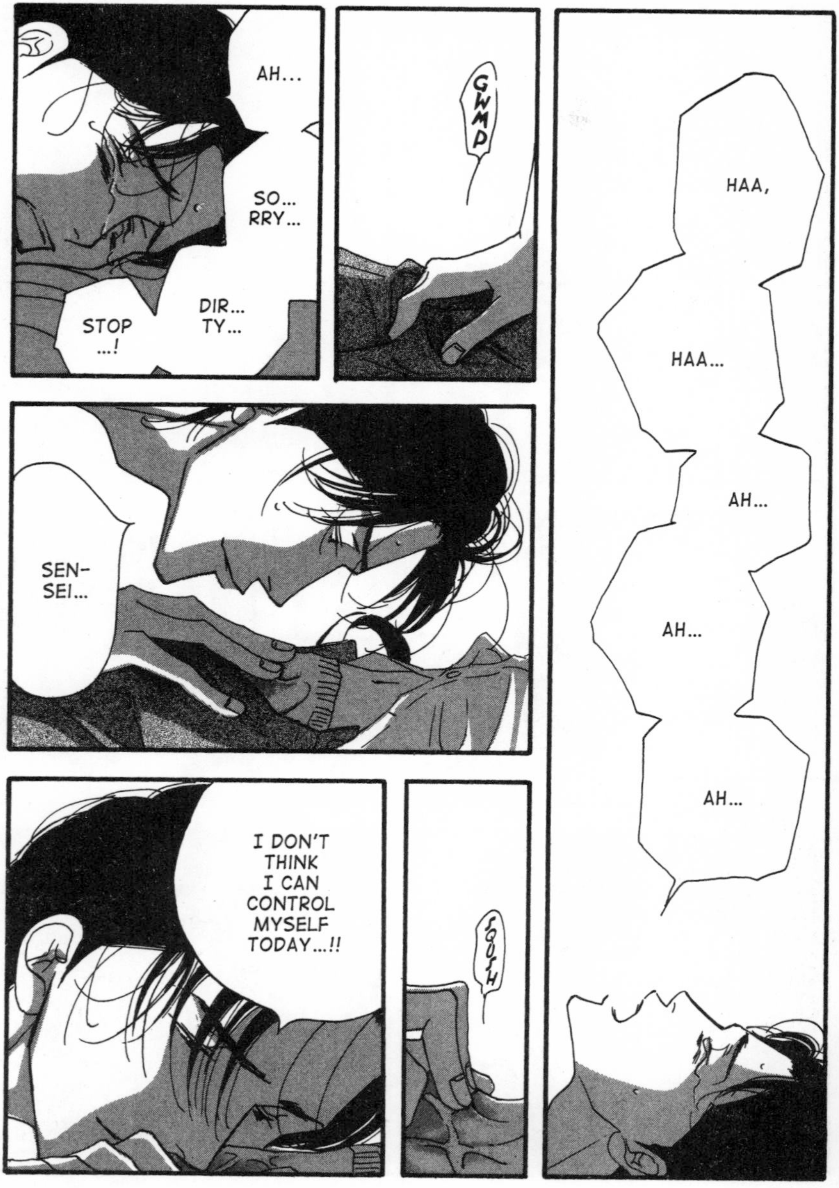
HAA, HAA... AH... AH... AH...
GWMP
AH...
SO... RRY...
DIR... TY...
STOP ...!
SEN-SEI...
SQUSH
I DON'T THINK I CAN CONTROL MYSELF TODAY...!!

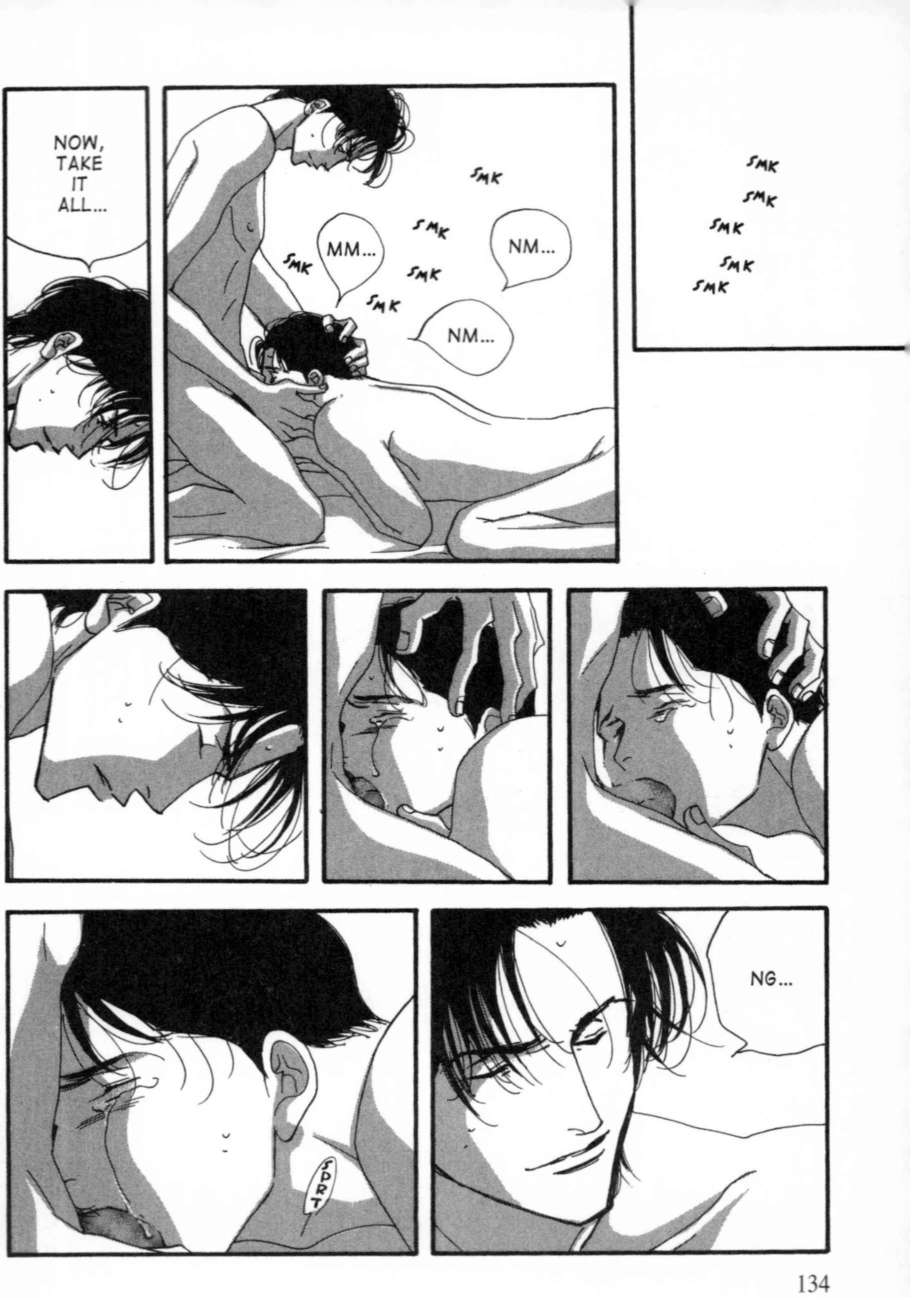
SMK
SMK
SMK
SMK
SMK
SMK
NM...
SMK
MM...
SMK
SMK
SMK
NM...
NOW, TAKE IT ALL...
NG...
SPRT

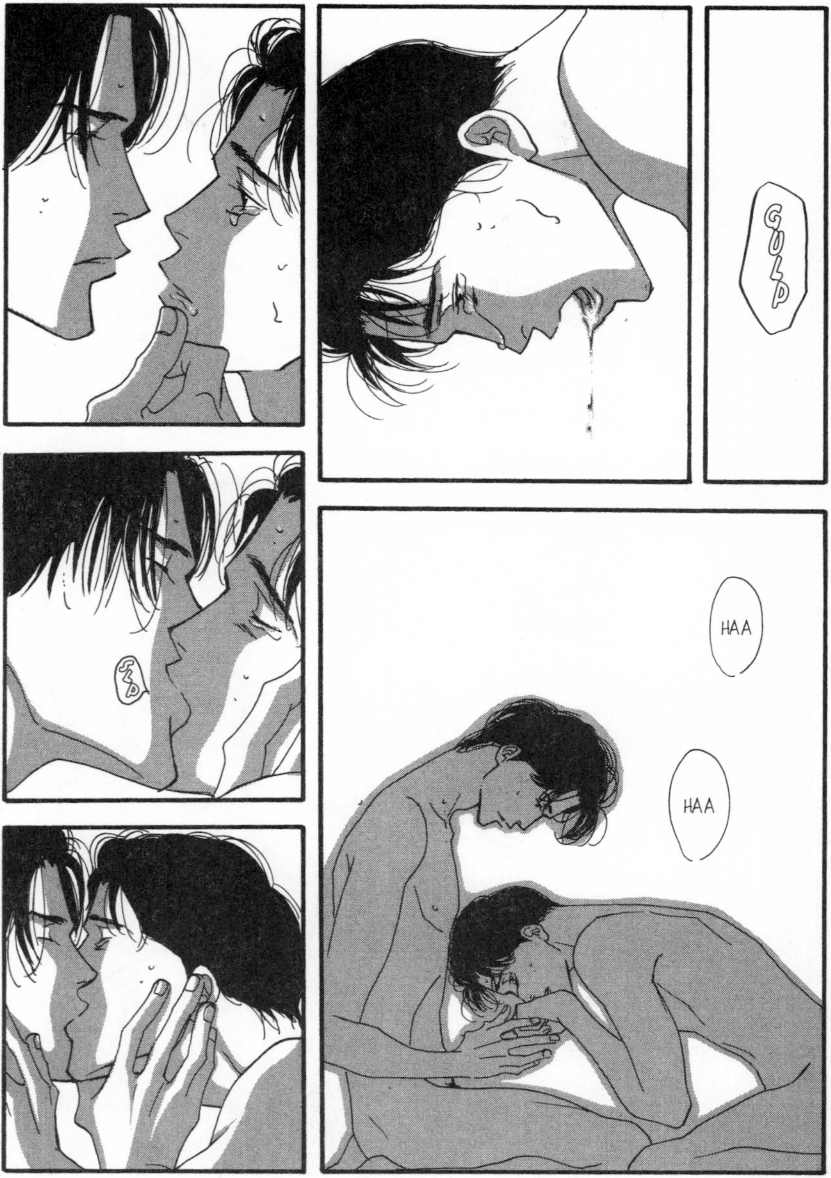
GULP
HAA
HAA
SLP

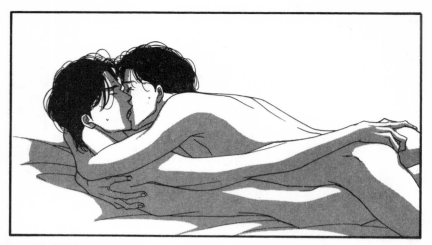

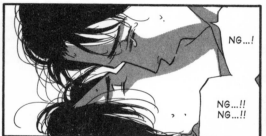

NG...!
NG...!! NG...!!
... NO WAY!
LIKE I SAID, I CAN'T CONTROL MYSELF.
THAT WAS FAST...! AH...!

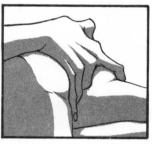

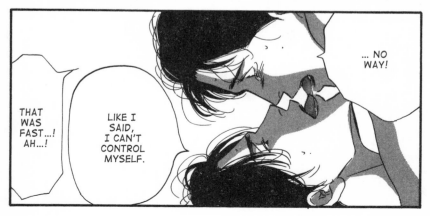

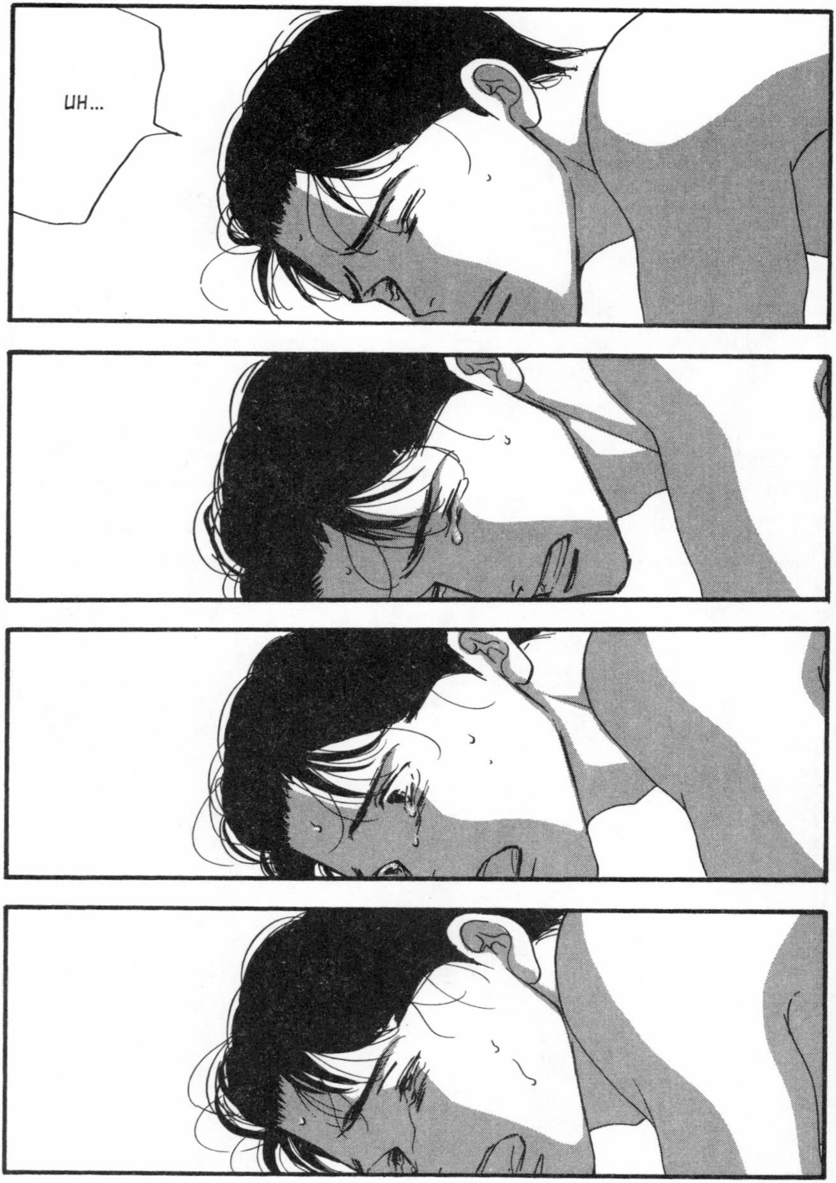
UH...

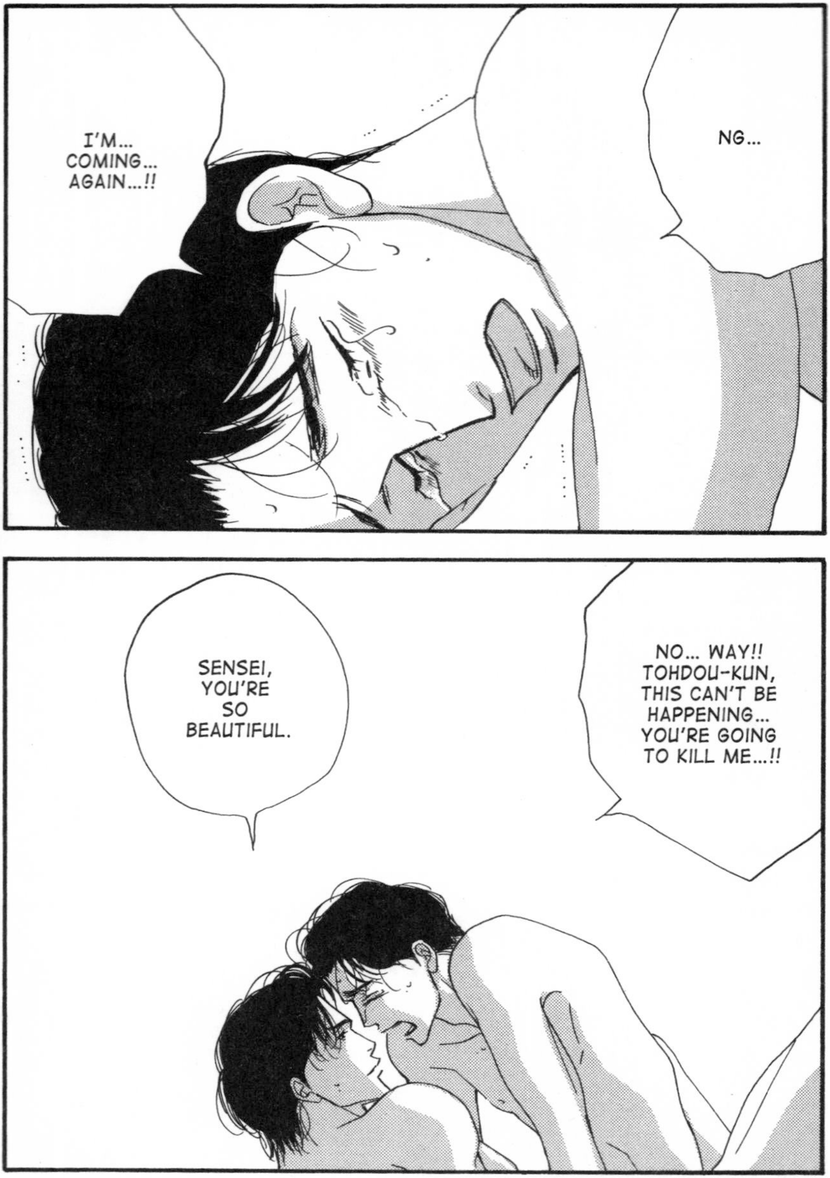
NG...
I'M... COMING... AGAIN...!!
NO... WAY!! TOHDOU-KUN, THIS CAN'T BE HAPPENING... YOU'RE GOING TO KILL ME...!!
SENSEI, YOU'RE SO BEAUTIFUL.

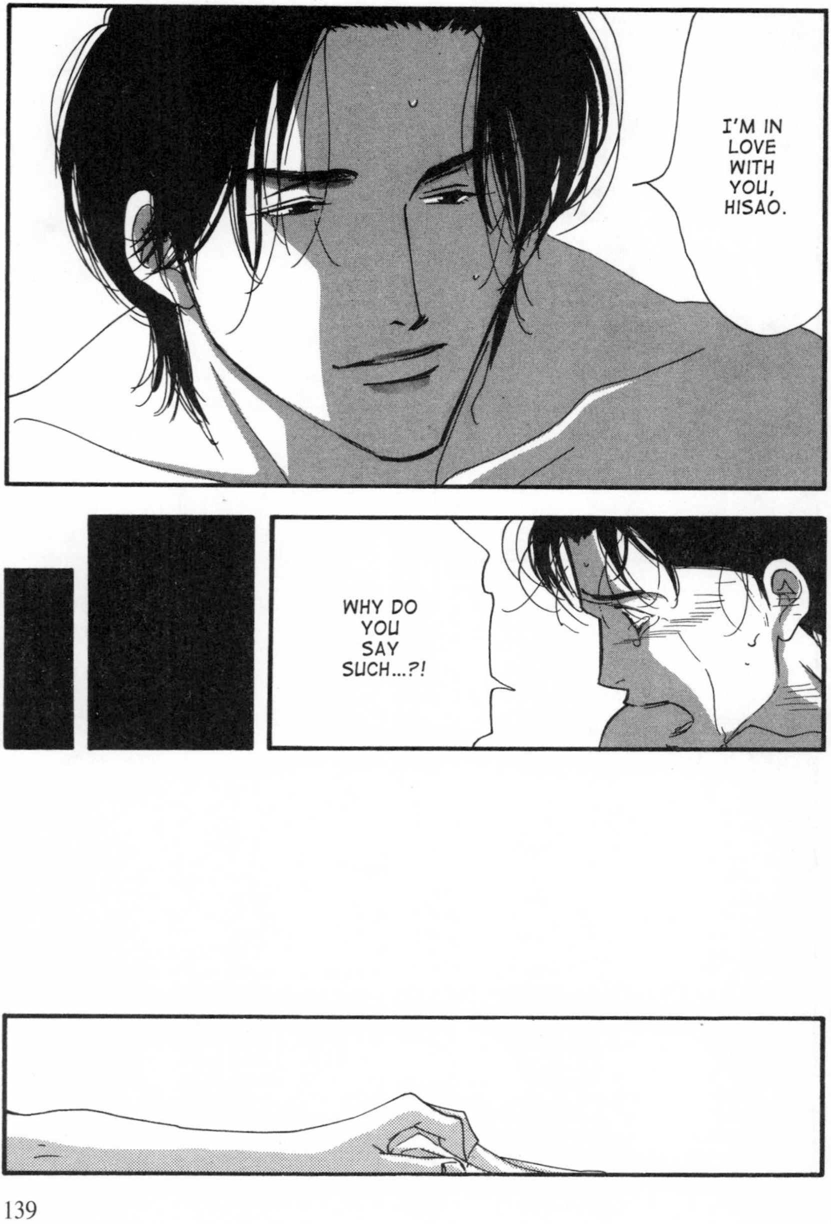
I'M IN LOVE WITH YOU, HISAO.
WHY DO YOU SAY SUCH...?!

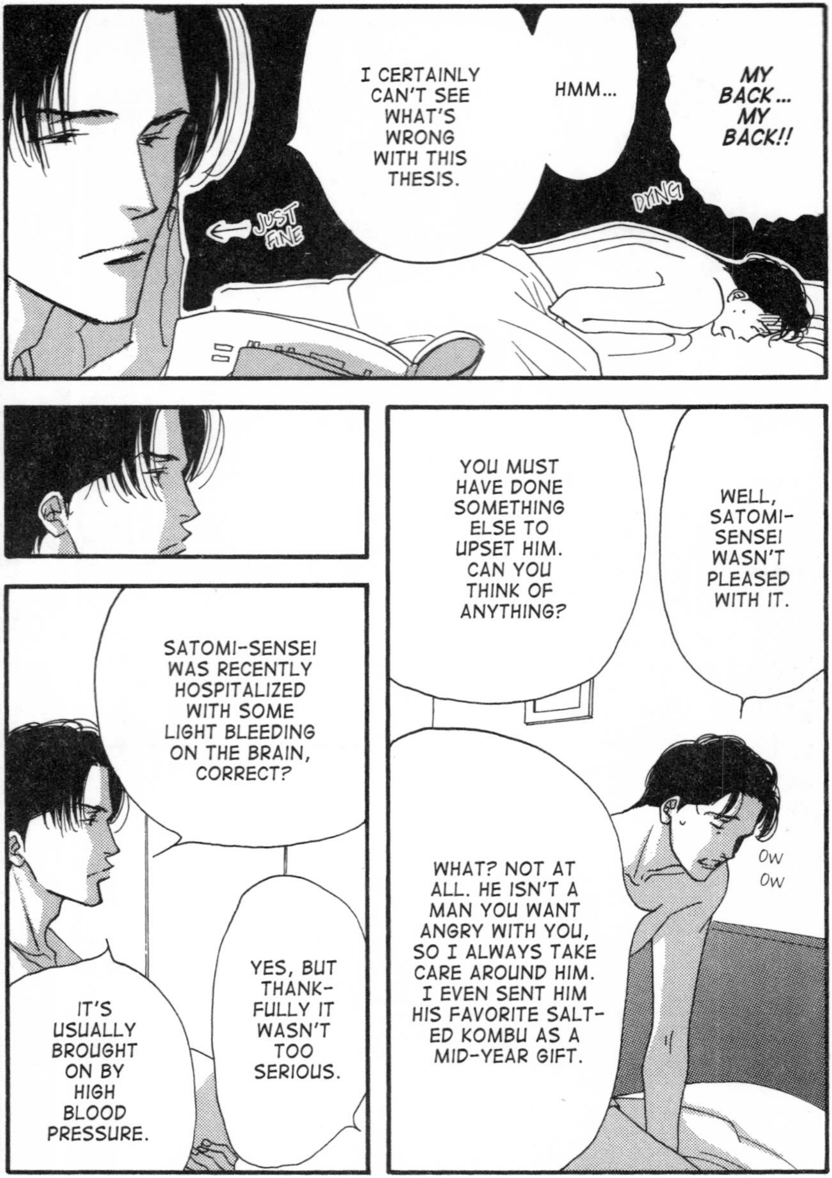
MY BACK... MY BACK!!
HMM...
I CERTAINLY CAN'T SEE WHAT'S WRONG WITH THIS THESIS.
DYING!
JUST FINE
WELL, SATOMI-SENSEI WASN'T PLEASED WITH IT.
YOU MUST HAVE DONE SOMETHING ELSE TO UPSET HIM. CAN YOU THINK OF ANYTHING?
OW OW
WHAT? NOT AT ALL. HE ISN'T A MAN YOU WANT ANGRY WITH YOU, SO I ALWAYS TAKE CARE AROUND HIM. I EVEN SENT HIM HIS FAVORITE SALT-ED KOMBU AS A MID-YEAR GIFT.
SATOMI-SENSEI WAS RECENTLY HOSPITALIZED WITH SOME LIGHT BLEEDING ON THE BRAIN, CORRECT?
YES, BUT THANK-FULLY IT WASN'T TOO SERIOUS.
IT'S USUALLY BROUGHT ON BY HIGH BLOOD PRESSURE.

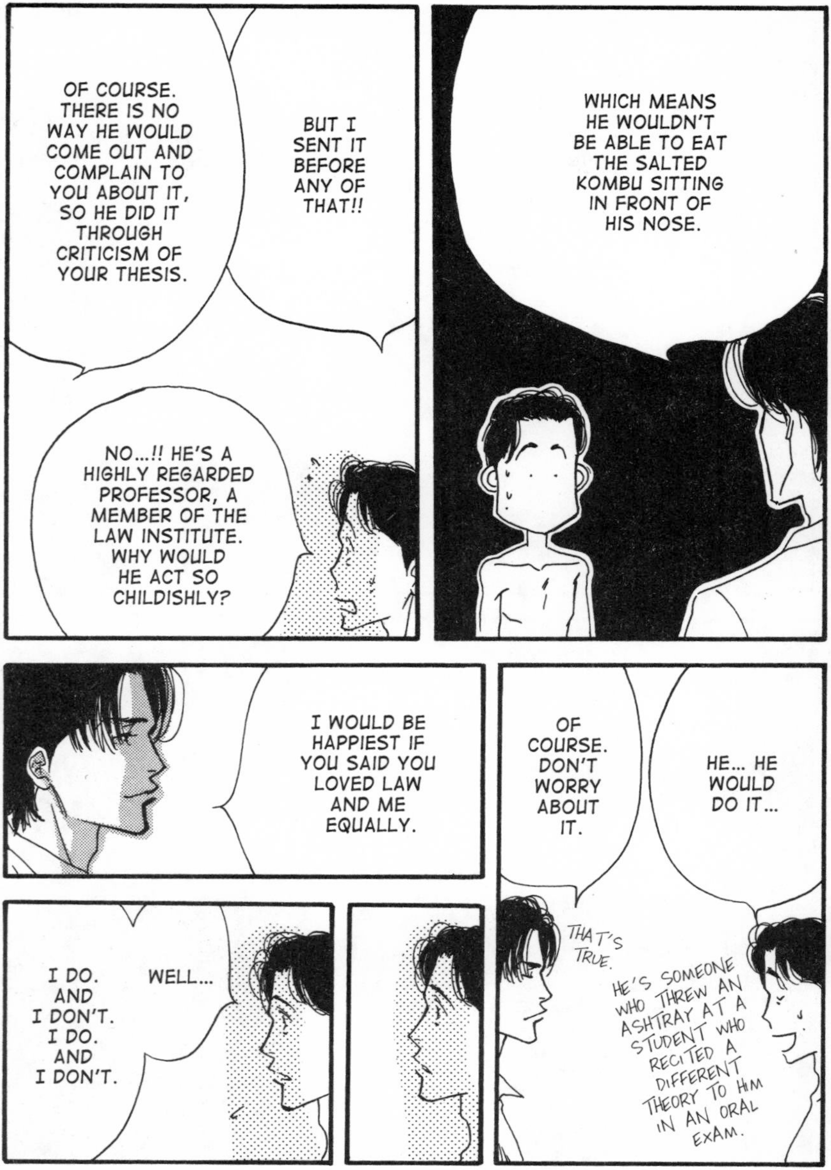
WHICH MEANS HE WOULDN'T BE ABLE TO EAT THE SALTED KOMBU SITTING IN FRONT OF HIS NOSE.
BUT I SENT IT BEFORE ANY OF THAT!!
OF COURSE. THERE IS NO WAY HE WOULD COME OUT AND COMPLAIN TO YOU ABOUT IT, SO HE DID IT THROUGH CRITICISM OF YOUR THESIS.
NO...!! HE'S A HIGHLY REGARDED PROFESSOR, A MEMBER OF THE LAW INSTITUTE. WHY WOULD HE ACT SO CHILDISHLY?
HE... HE WOULD DO IT...
OF COURSE. DON'T WORRY ABOUT IT.
HE'S SOMEONE WHO THREW AN ASHTRAY AT A STUDENT WHO RECITED A DIFFERENT THEORY TO HIM IN AN ORAL EXAM.
THAT'S TRUE.
I WOULD BE HAPPIEST IF YOU SAID YOU LOVED LAW AND ME EQUALLY.
WELL...
I DO. AND I DON'T. I DO. AND I DON'T.

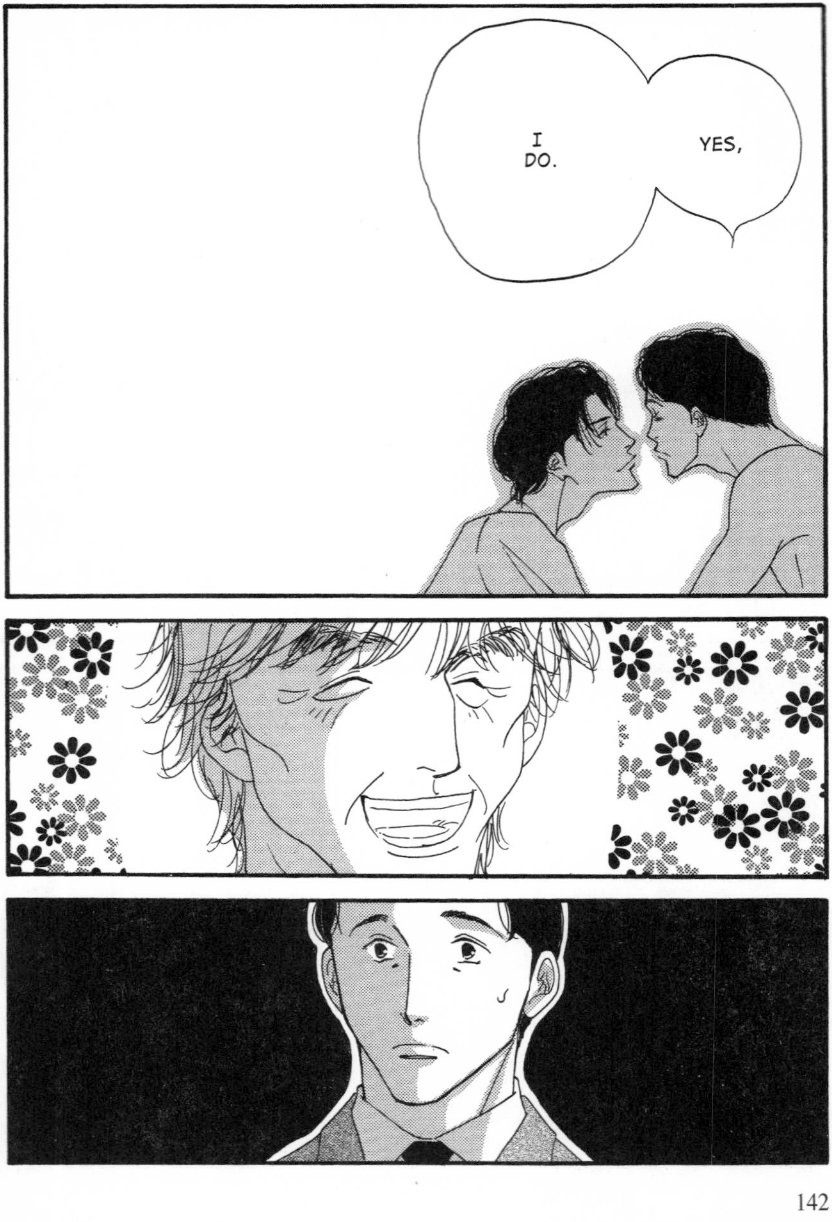
YES,
I DO.

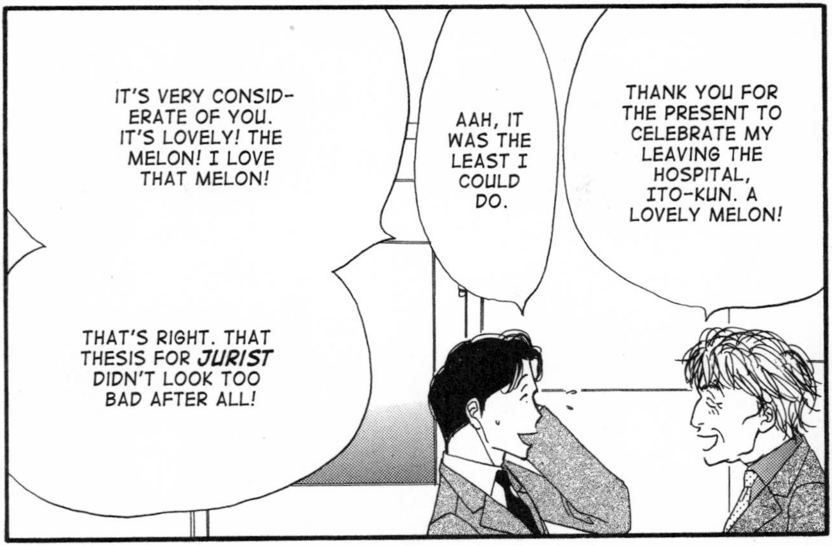
THANK YOU FOR THE PRESENT TO CELEBRATE MY LEAVING THE HOSPITAL, ITO-KUN. A LOVELY MELON!
AAH, IT WAS THE LEAST I COULD DO.
IT'S VERY CONSID-ERATE OF YOU. IT'S LOVELY! THE MELON! I LOVE THAT MELON!
THAT'S RIGHT. THAT THESIS FOR *JURIST* DIDN'T LOOK TOO BAD AFTER ALL!

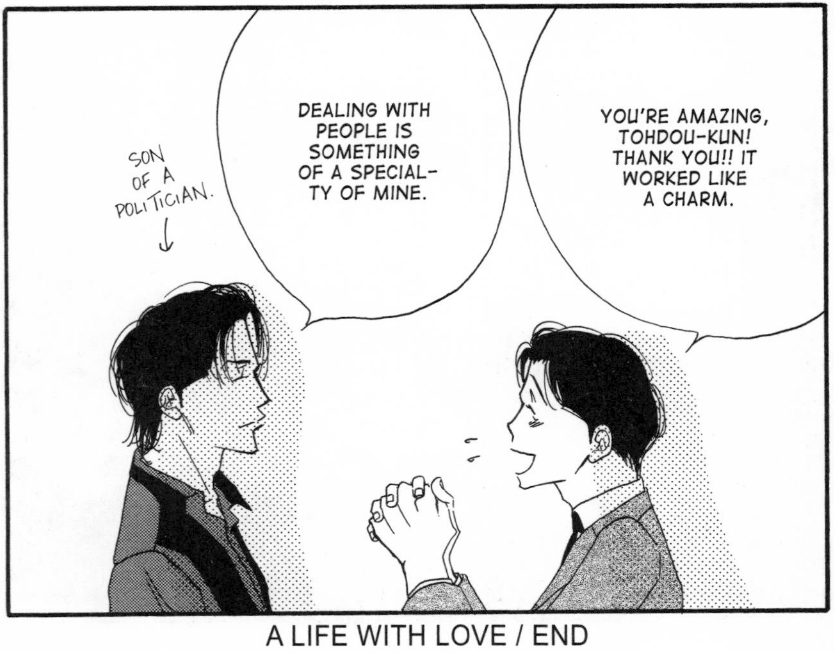
YOU'RE AMAZING, TOHDOU-KUN! THANK YOU!! IT WORKED LIKE A CHARM.
DEALING WITH PEOPLE IS SOMETHING OF A SPECIAL-TY OF MINE.
SON OF A POLITICIAN.

A LIFE WITH LOVE / END

OUR LIFE

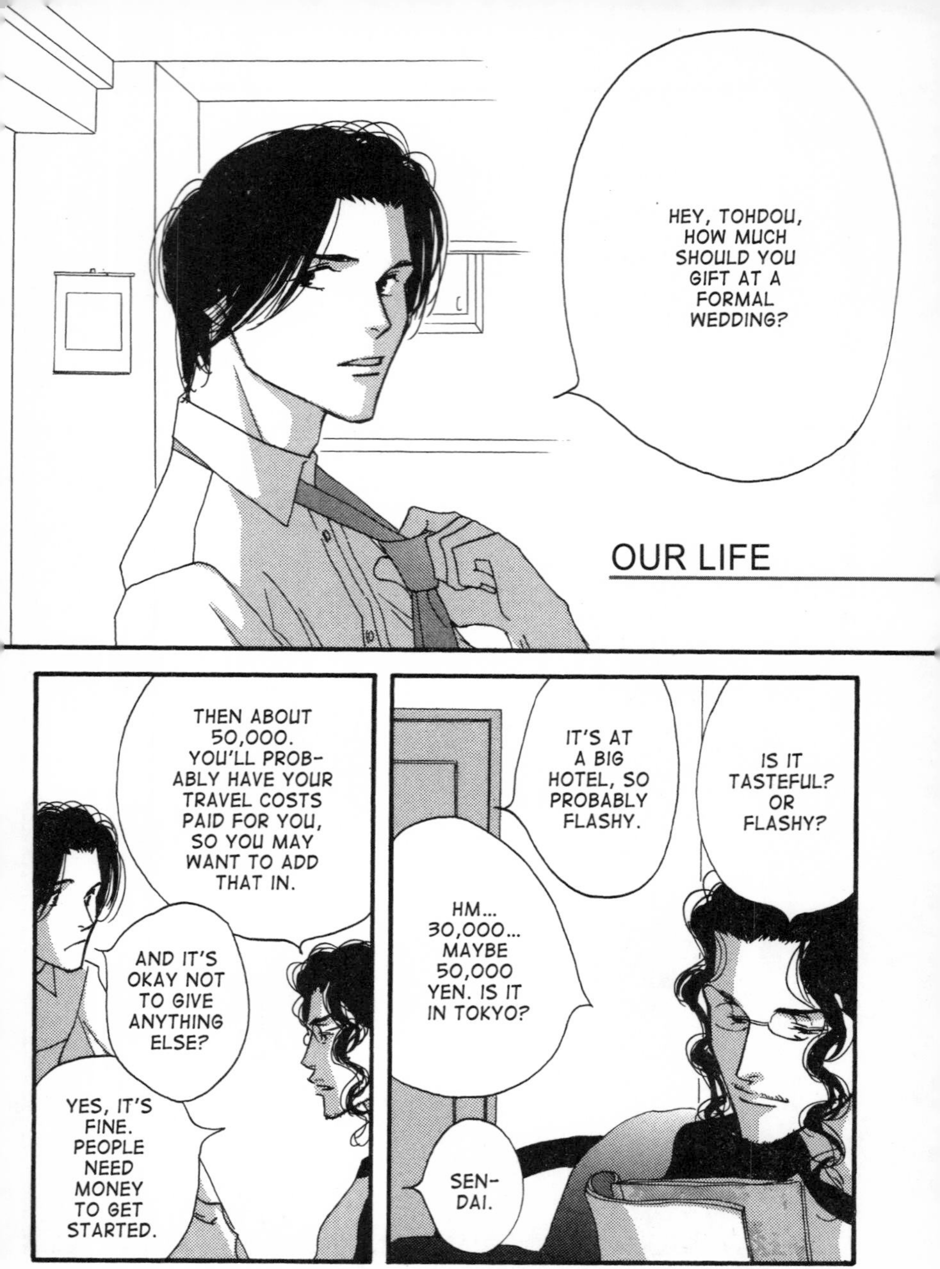
HEY, TOHDOU, HOW MUCH SHOULD YOU GIFT AT A FORMAL WEDDING?
IS IT TASTEFUL? OR FLASHY?
IT'S AT A BIG HOTEL, SO PROBABLY FLASHY.
HM... 30,000... MAYBE 50,000 YEN. IS IT IN TOKYO?
SEN-DAI.
THEN ABOUT 50,000. YOU'LL PROB-ABLY HAVE YOUR TRAVEL COSTS PAID FOR YOU, SO YOU MAY WANT TO ADD THAT IN.
AND IT'S OKAY NOT TO GIVE ANYTHING ELSE?
YES, IT'S FINE. PEOPLE NEED MONEY TO GET STARTED.

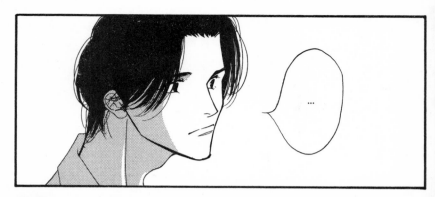

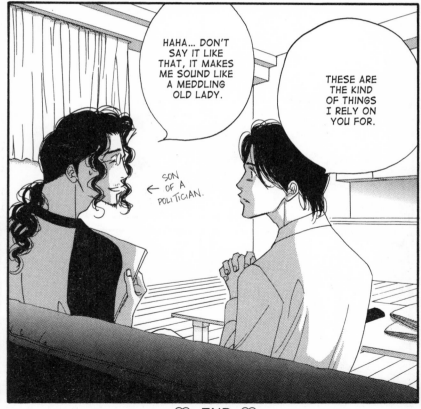

...
THESE ARE THE KIND OF THINGS I RELY ON YOU FOR.
HAHA... DON'T SAY IT LIKE THAT, IT MAKES ME SOUND LIKE A MEDDLING OLD LADY.
← SON OF A POLITICIAN.

♡ END ♡

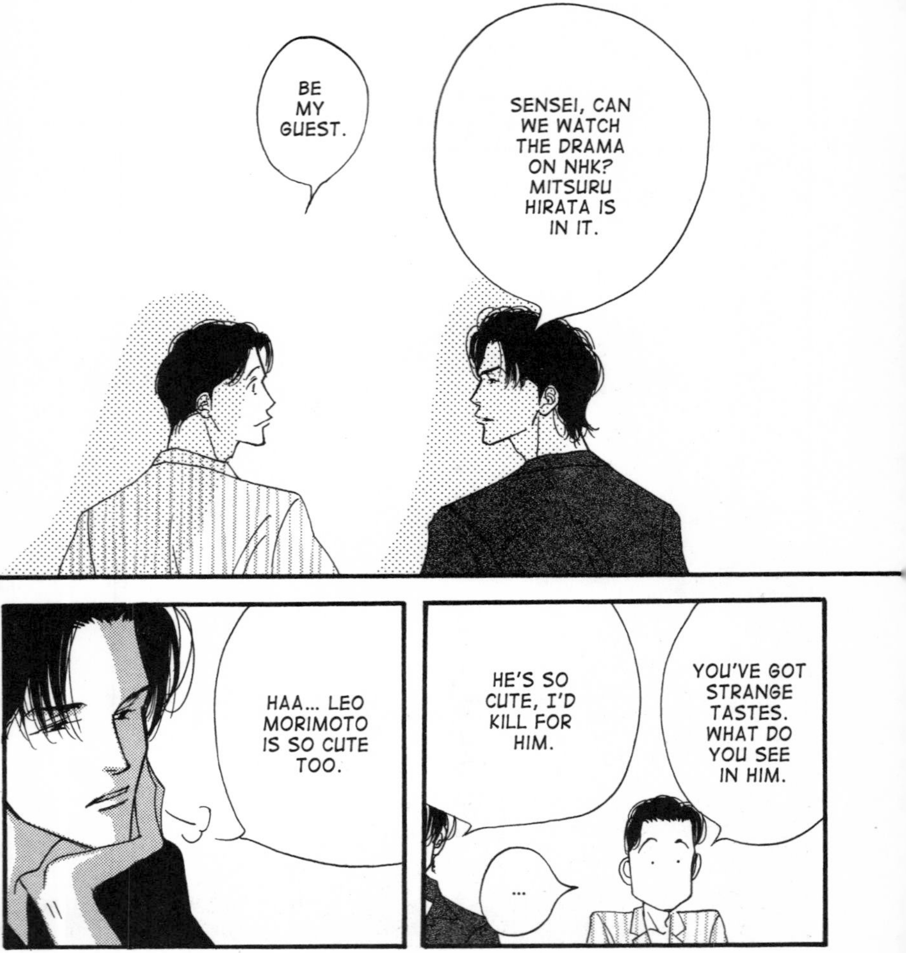
SENSEI, CAN WE WATCH THE DRAMA ON NHK? MITSURU HIRATA IS IN IT.
BE MY GUEST.
YOU'VE GOT STRANGE TASTES. WHAT DO YOU SEE IN HIM.
HE'S SO CUTE, I'D KILL FOR HIM.
...
HAA... LEO MORIMOTO IS SO CUTE TOO.

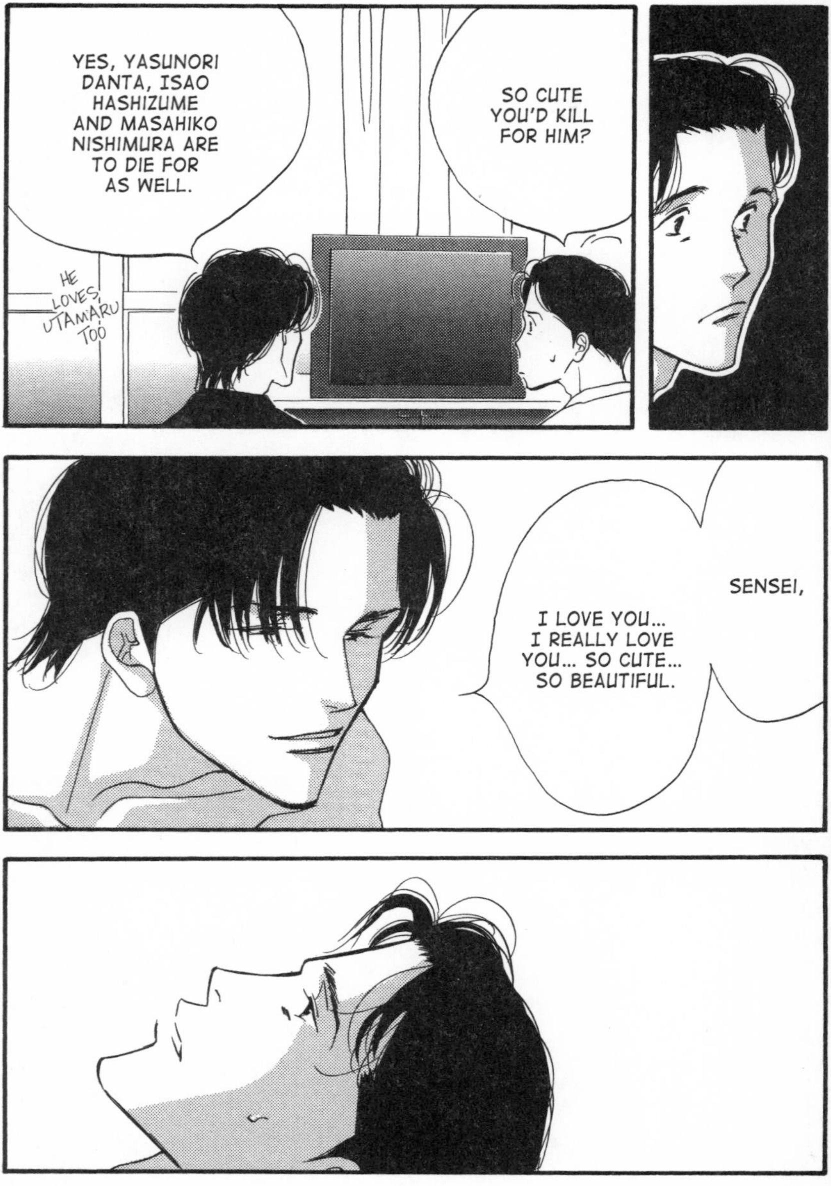
SO CUTE YOU'D KILL FOR HIM?
YES, YASUNORI DANTA, ISAO HASHIZUME AND MASAHIKO NISHIMURA ARE TO DIE FOR AS WELL.
HE LOVES UTAMARU TOO
SENSEI,
I LOVE YOU... I REALLY LOVE YOU... SO CUTE... SO BEAUTIFUL.

I GET IT NOW...
LIKES THEM MIDDLE-AGED.

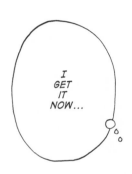

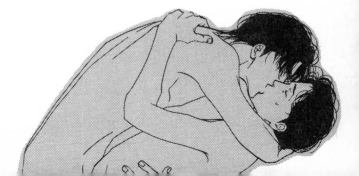

♡ END ♡

I CAN'T SAY IT, BUT I LOVE YOU

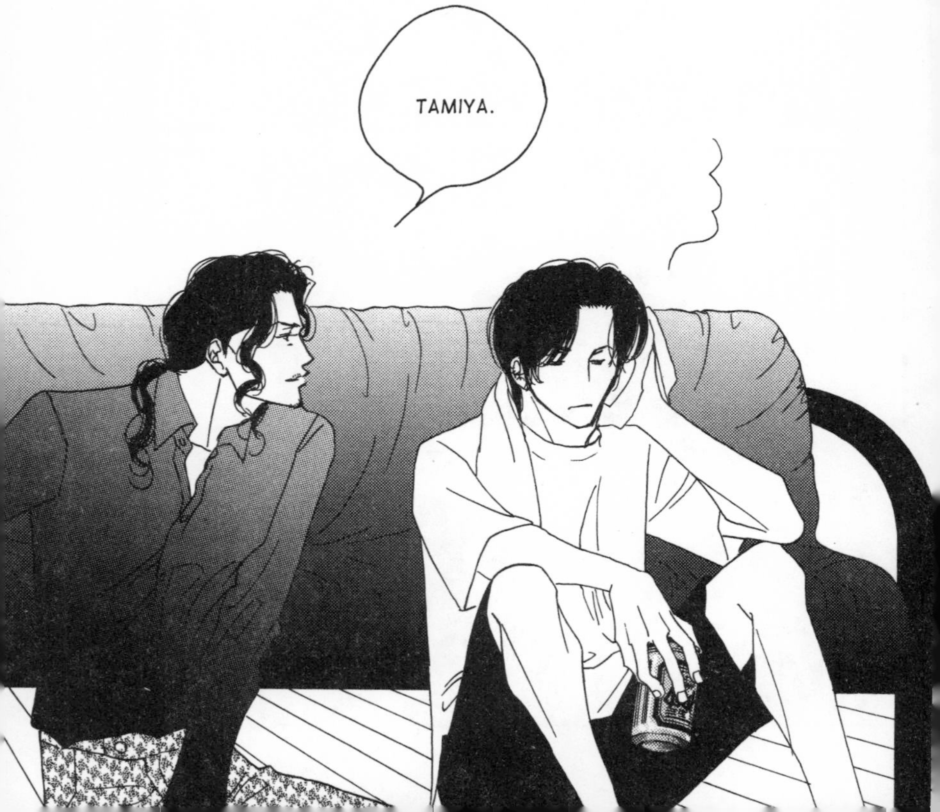
TAMIYA.

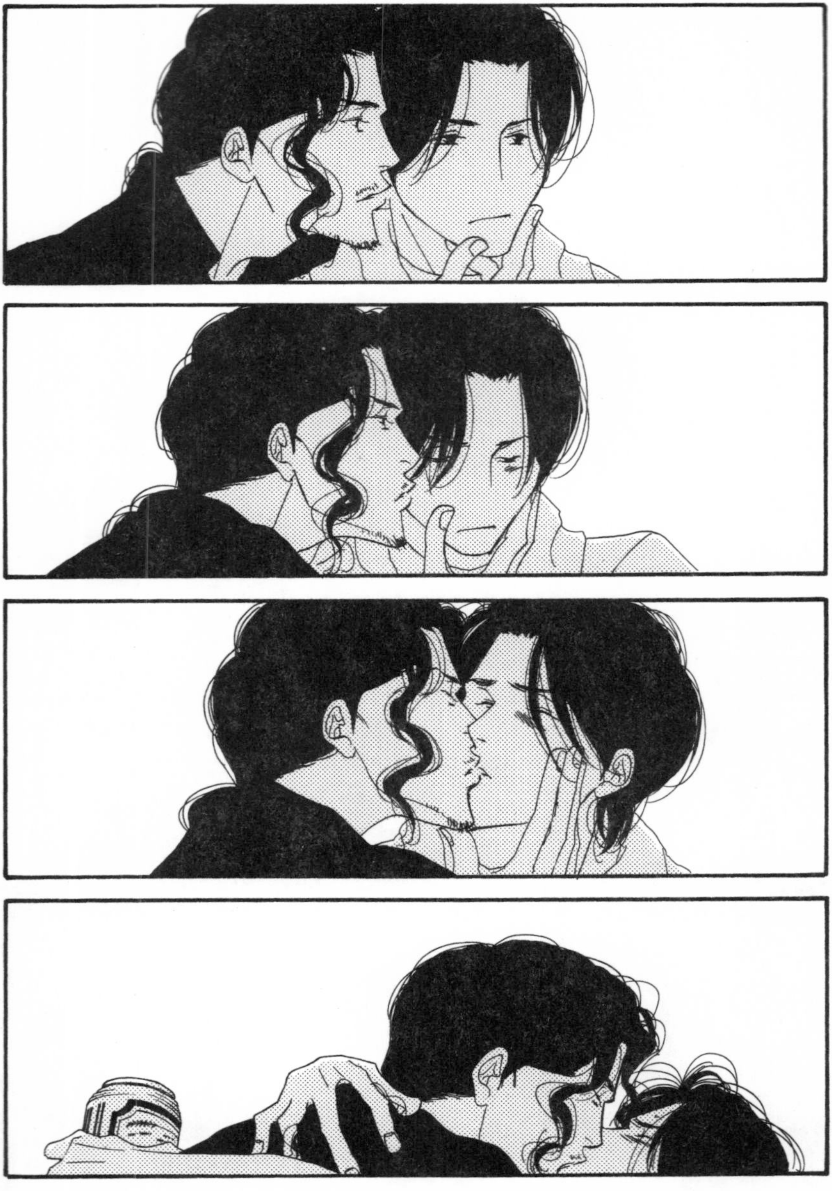

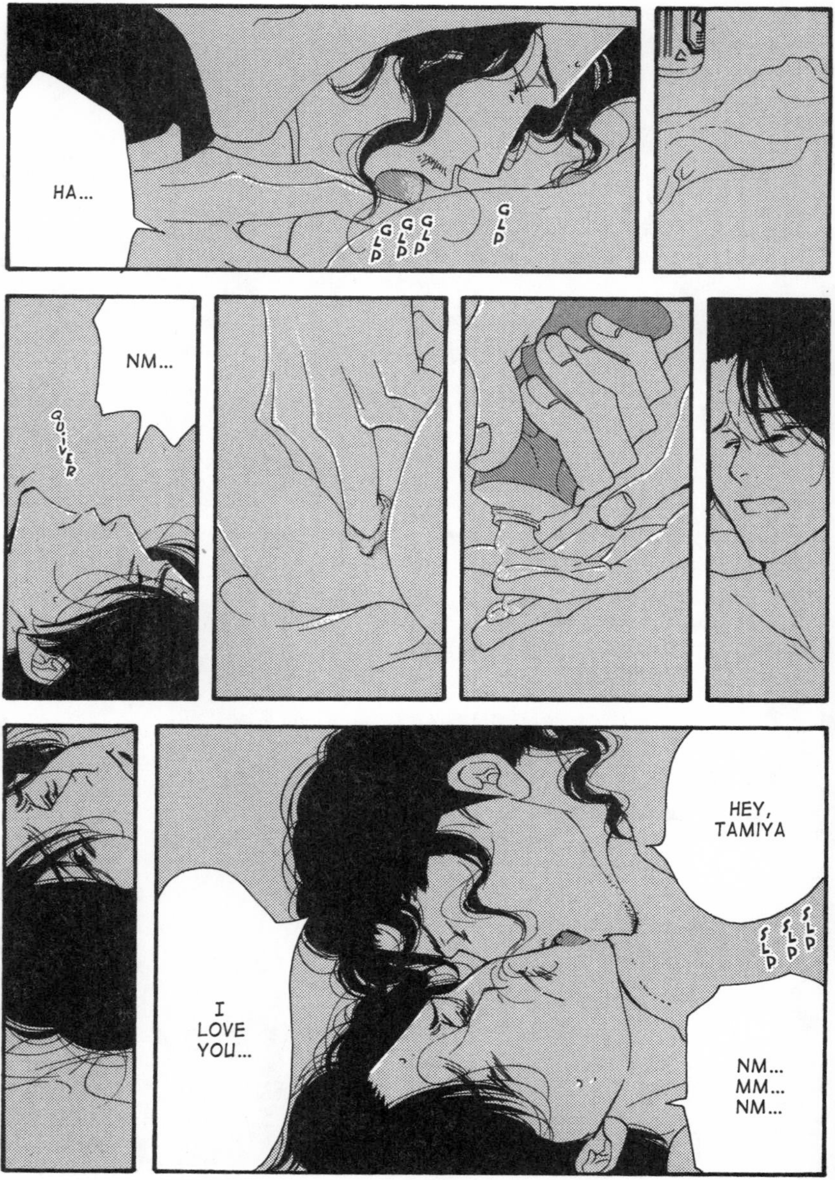
GLP
GLP
GLP
GLP
HA...
NM...
QUIVER
HEY, TAMIYA
SLP
SLP
SLP
NM... MM... NM...
I LOVE YOU...

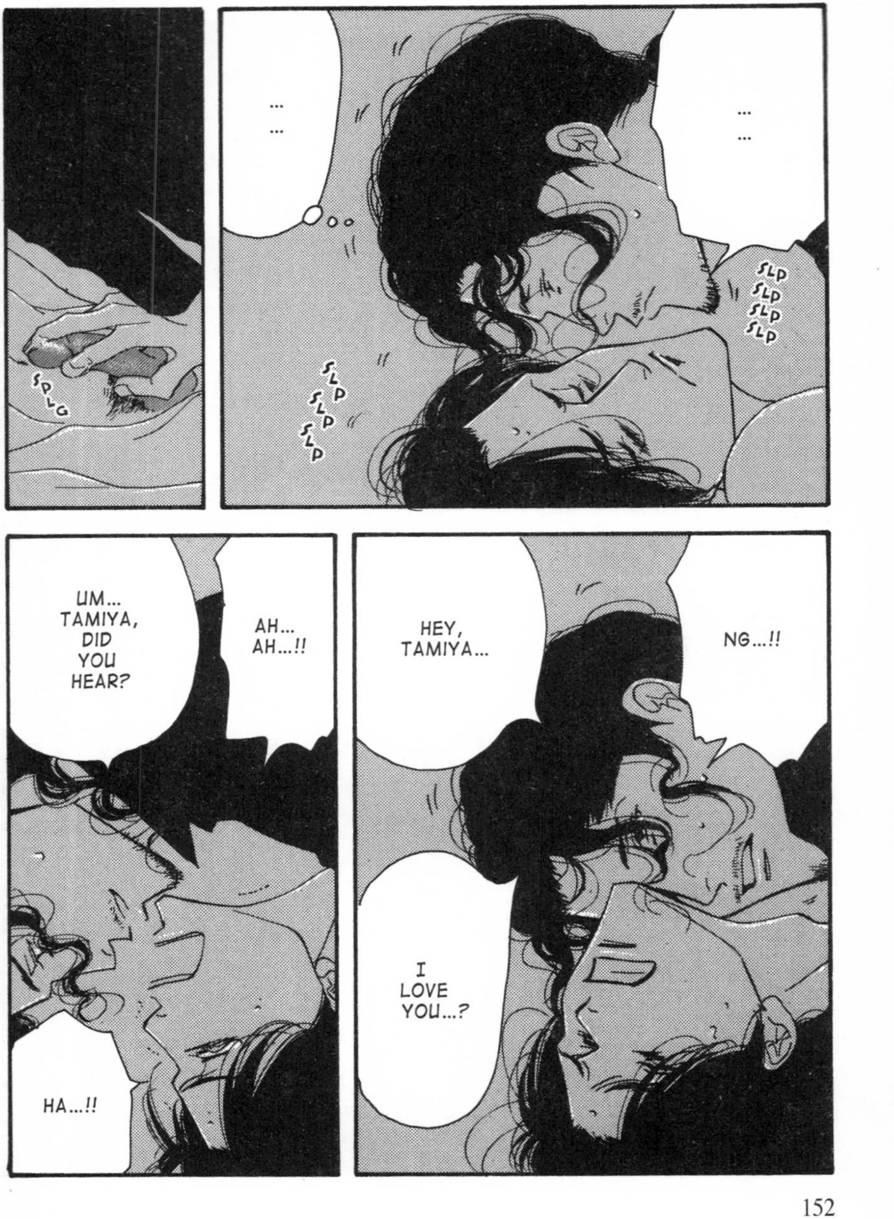

... ...
... ...
SLP SLP SLP SLP
SLP SLP SLP
SPLG
NG...!!
HEY, TAMIYA...
I LOVE YOU...?
AH... AH...!!
UM... TAMIYA, DID YOU HEAR?
HA...!!

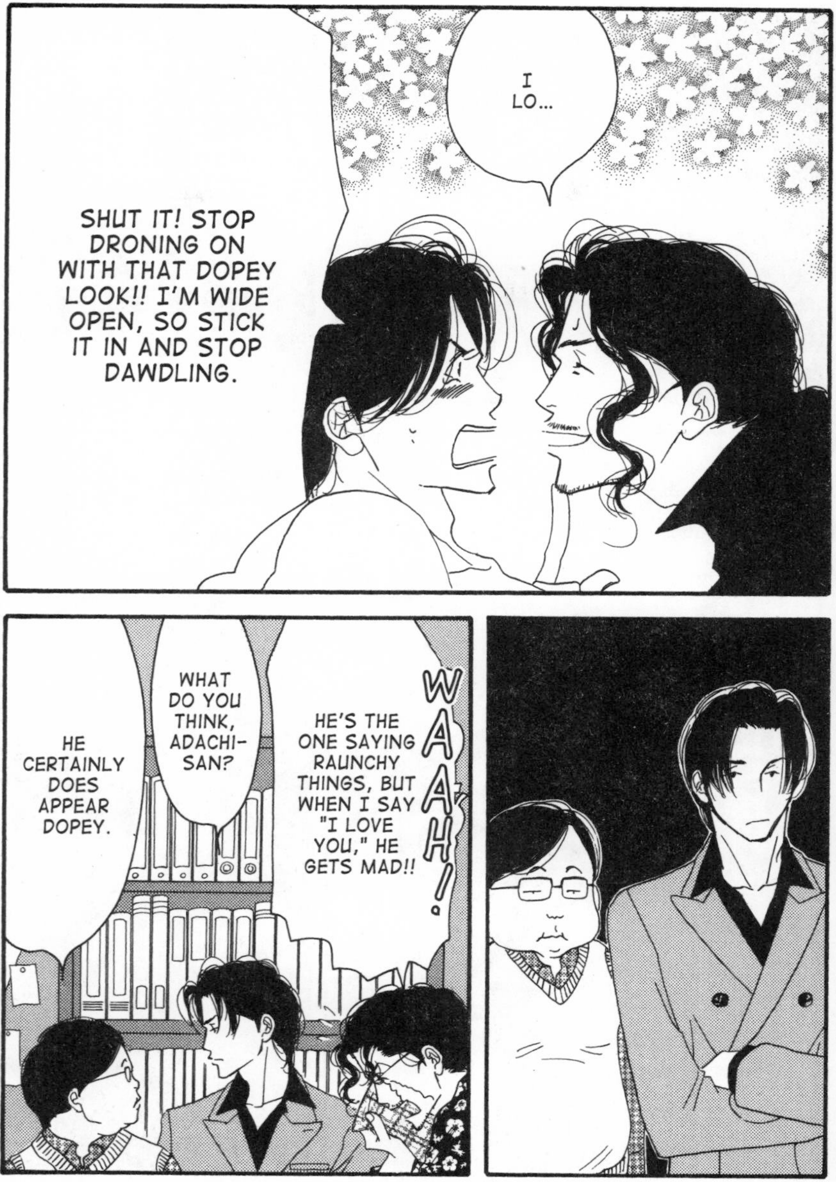
I LO...
SHUT IT! STOP DRONING ON WITH THAT DOPEY LOOK!! I'M WIDE OPEN, SO STICK IT IN AND STOP DAWDLING.
WAAAH!
HE'S THE ONE SAYING RAUNCHY THINGS, BUT WHEN I SAY "I LOVE YOU," HE GETS MAD!!
WHAT DO YOU THINK, ADACHI-SAN?
HE CERTAINLY DOES APPEAR DOPEY.

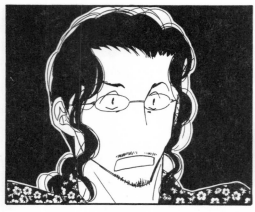

BOSS,
BROTHER,
IF YOU KEPT ON SAYING 'I LOVE YOU' AS A WAY OF ASKING 'HEY, DO YOU LOVE ME?' THEN THAT WOULD BE ANNOYING, BORING AND A LITTLE TOO MUCH, I THINK.
SOB SOB SOB
IT APPEARS THAT'S WHAT HAPPENED.
MY BROTHER DOES DO GIRLY THINGS LIKE GIVING HAND-KNIT BIRTHDAY PRESENTS, AFTER ALL.
HE'S A FEMALE INSIDE.
IF WE LEAVE HIM HE'LL GET EVEN WORSE. WE SHOULD THINK OF A PLAN.

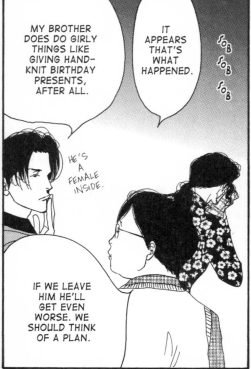

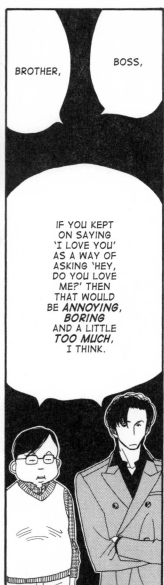

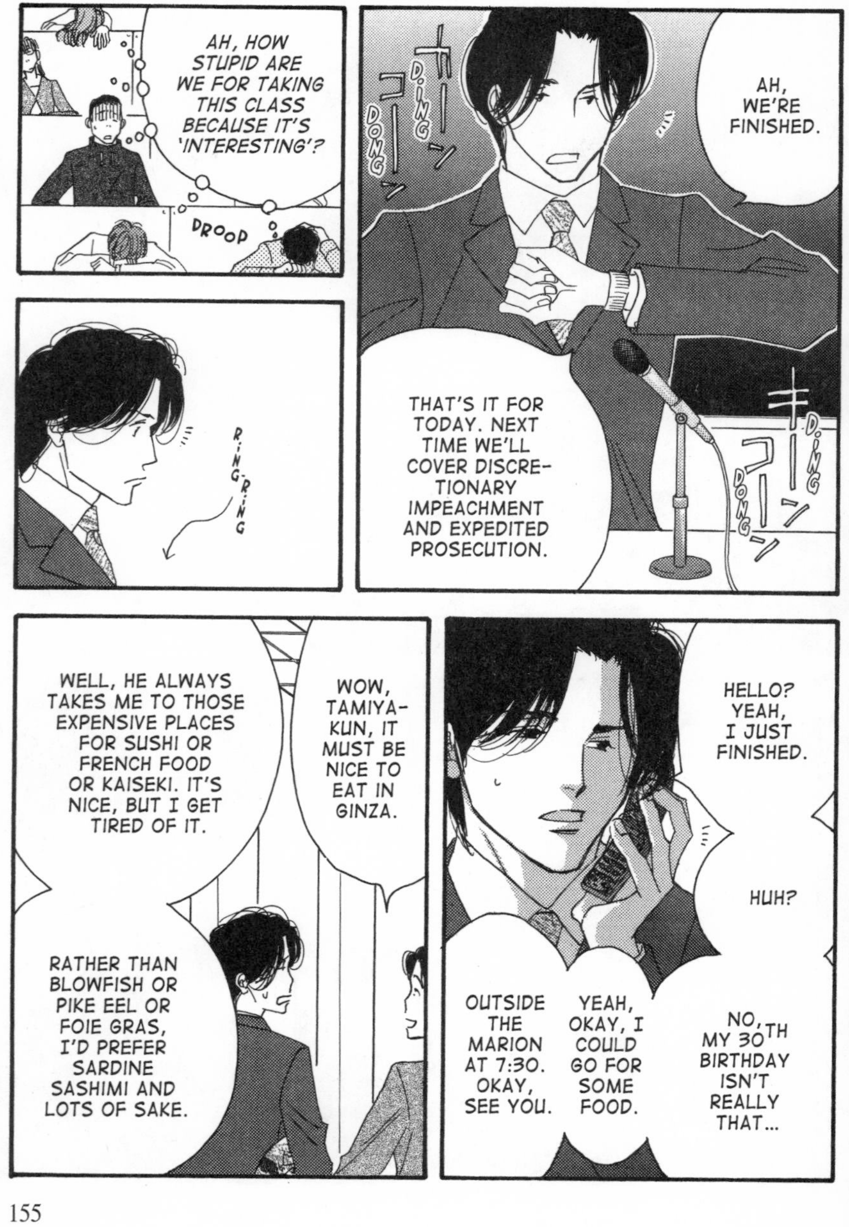
AH, WE'RE FINISHED.
DING DONG
DING DONG
THAT'S IT FOR TODAY. NEXT TIME WE'LL COVER DISCRETIONARY IMPEACHMENT AND EXPEDITED PROSECUTION.
AH, HOW STUPID ARE WE FOR TAKING THIS CLASS BECAUSE IT'S 'INTERESTING'?
DROOP
RING RING
HELLO? YEAH, I JUST FINISHED.
HUH?
NO, MY 30TH BIRTHDAY ISN'T REALLY THAT...
YEAH, OKAY, I COULD GO FOR SOME FOOD.
OUTSIDE THE MARION AT 7:30. OKAY, SEE YOU.
WOW, TAMIYA-KUN, IT MUST BE NICE TO EAT IN GINZA.
WELL, HE ALWAYS TAKES ME TO THOSE EXPENSIVE PLACES FOR SUSHI OR FRENCH FOOD OR KAISEKI. IT'S NICE, BUT I GET TIRED OF IT.
RATHER THAN BLOWFISH OR PIKE EEL OR FOIE GRAS, I'D PREFER SARDINE SASHIMI AND LOTS OF SAKE.

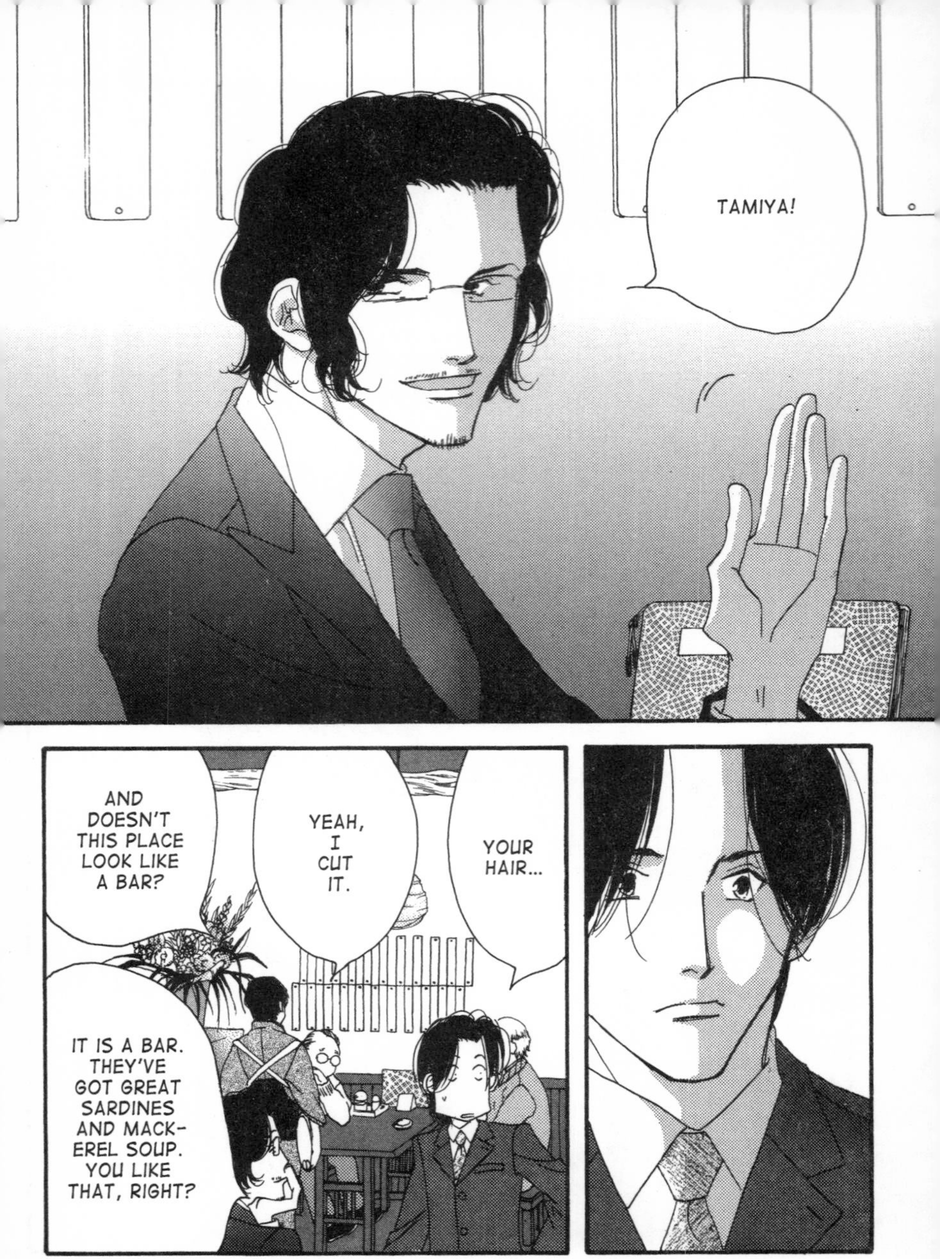
TAMIYA!
YOUR HAIR...
YEAH, I CUT IT.
AND DOESN'T THIS PLACE LOOK LIKE A BAR?
IT IS A BAR. THEY'VE GOT GREAT SARDINES AND MACK-EREL SOUP. YOU LIKE THAT, RIGHT?

HAPPY BIRTHDAY, TAMIYA.

CHOMP

SORRY TO KEEP YOU WAITING, HERE'S YOUR SARDINE SASHIMI.

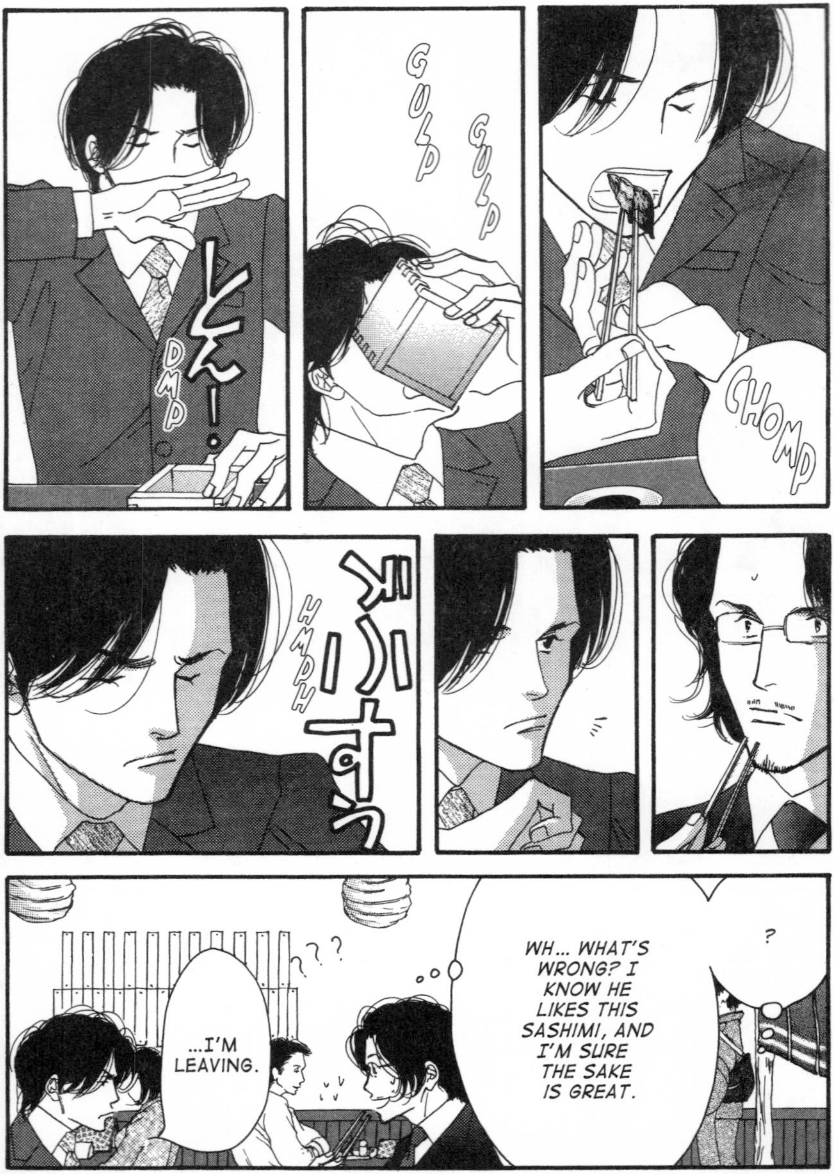
CHOMP
GULP
GULP
とん！
DMP
ふーすう
HMPH
?
WH... WHAT'S WRONG? I KNOW HE LIKES THIS SASHIMI, AND I'M SURE THE SAKE IS GREAT.
...I'M LEAVING.
???

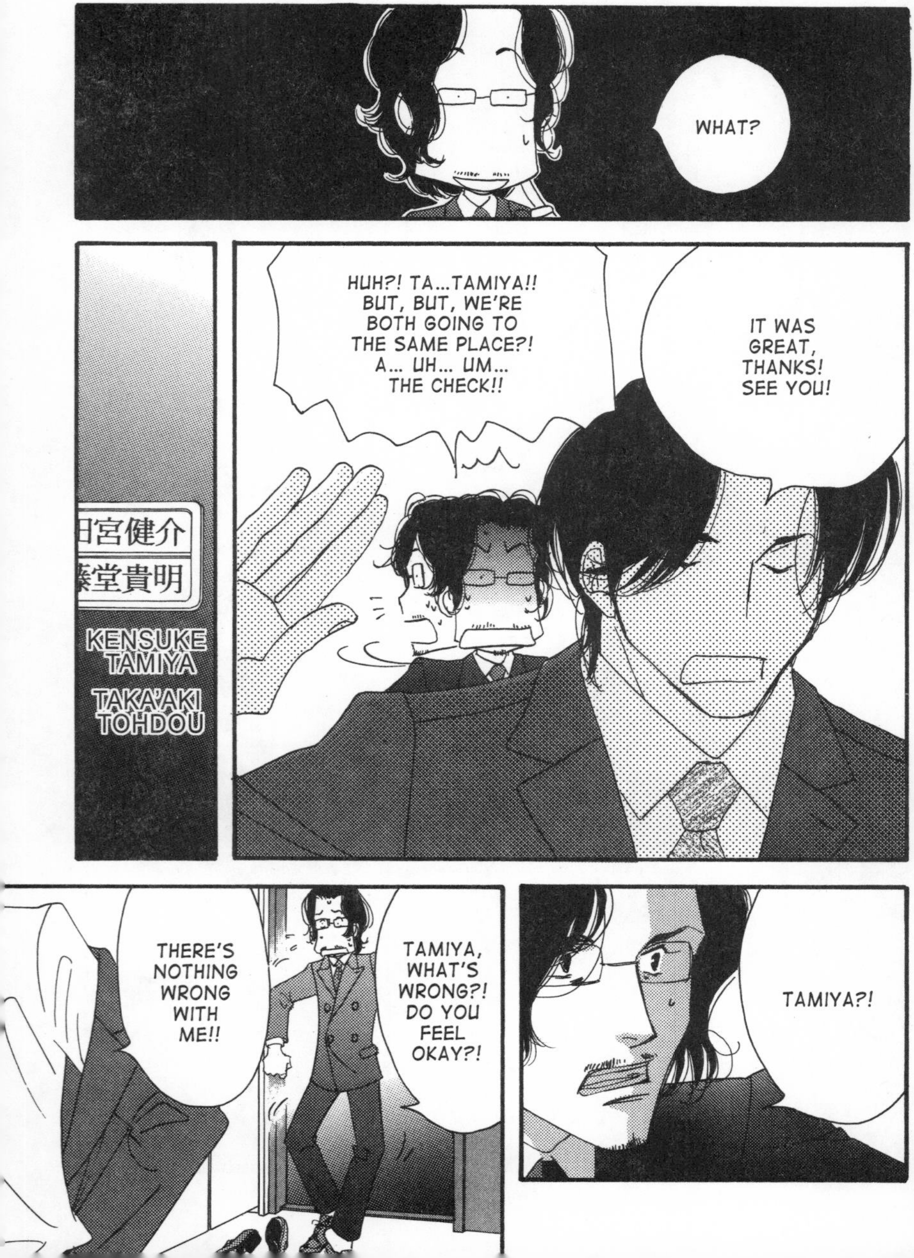
WHAT?
IT WAS GREAT, THANKS! SEE YOU!
HUH?! TA...TAMIYA!! BUT, BUT, WE'RE BOTH GOING TO THE SAME PLACE?! A... UH... UM... THE CHECK!!
KENSUKE TAMIYA
TAKA'AKI TOHDOU
TAMIYA?!
TAMIYA, WHAT'S WRONG?! DO YOU FEEL OKAY?!
THERE'S NOTHING WRONG WITH ME!!

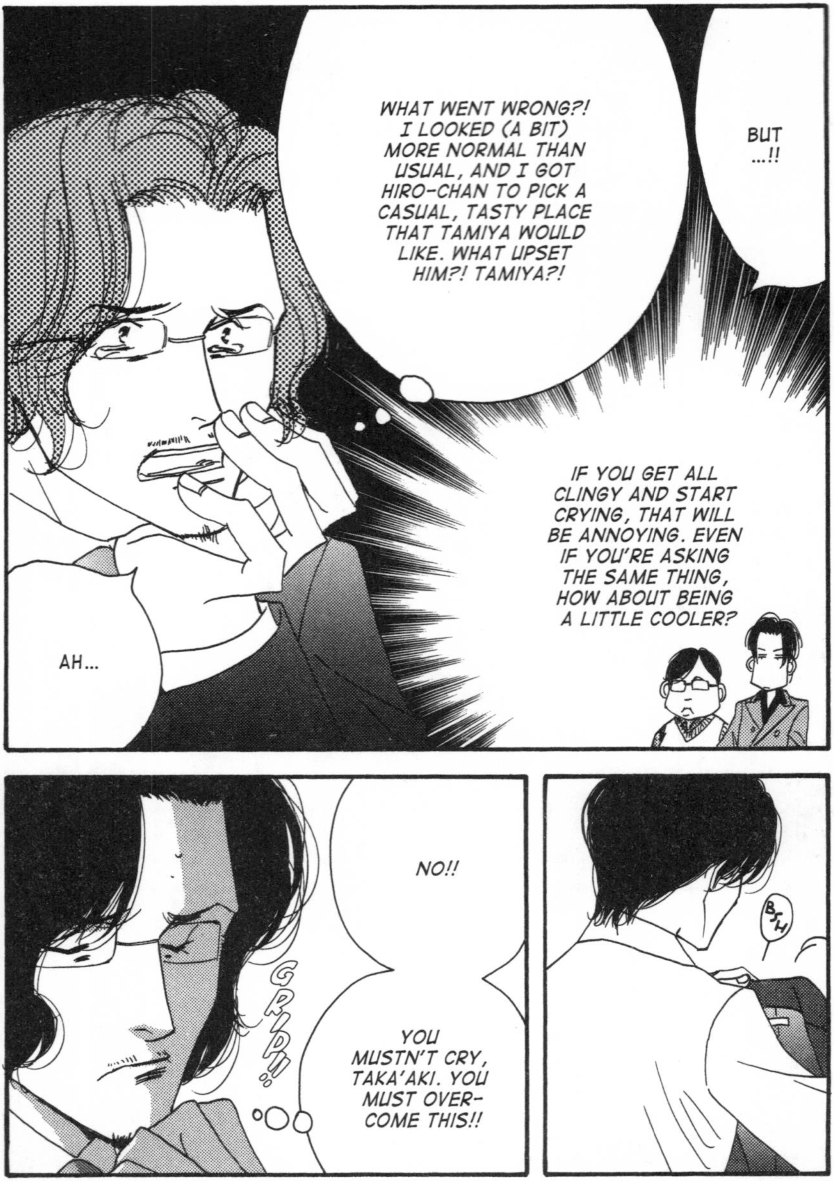

BUT ...!!
WHAT WENT WRONG?! I LOOKED (A BIT) MORE NORMAL THAN USUAL, AND I GOT HIRO-CHAN TO PICK A CASUAL, TASTY PLACE THAT TAMIYA WOULD LIKE. WHAT UPSET HIM?! TAMIYA?!
IF YOU GET ALL CLINGY AND START CRYING, THAT WILL BE ANNOYING. EVEN IF YOU'RE ASKING THE SAME THING, HOW ABOUT BEING A LITTLE COOLER?
AH...
BSH
NO!!
GRIP!!
YOU MUSTN'T CRY, TAKA'AKI. YOU MUST OVER-COME THIS!!

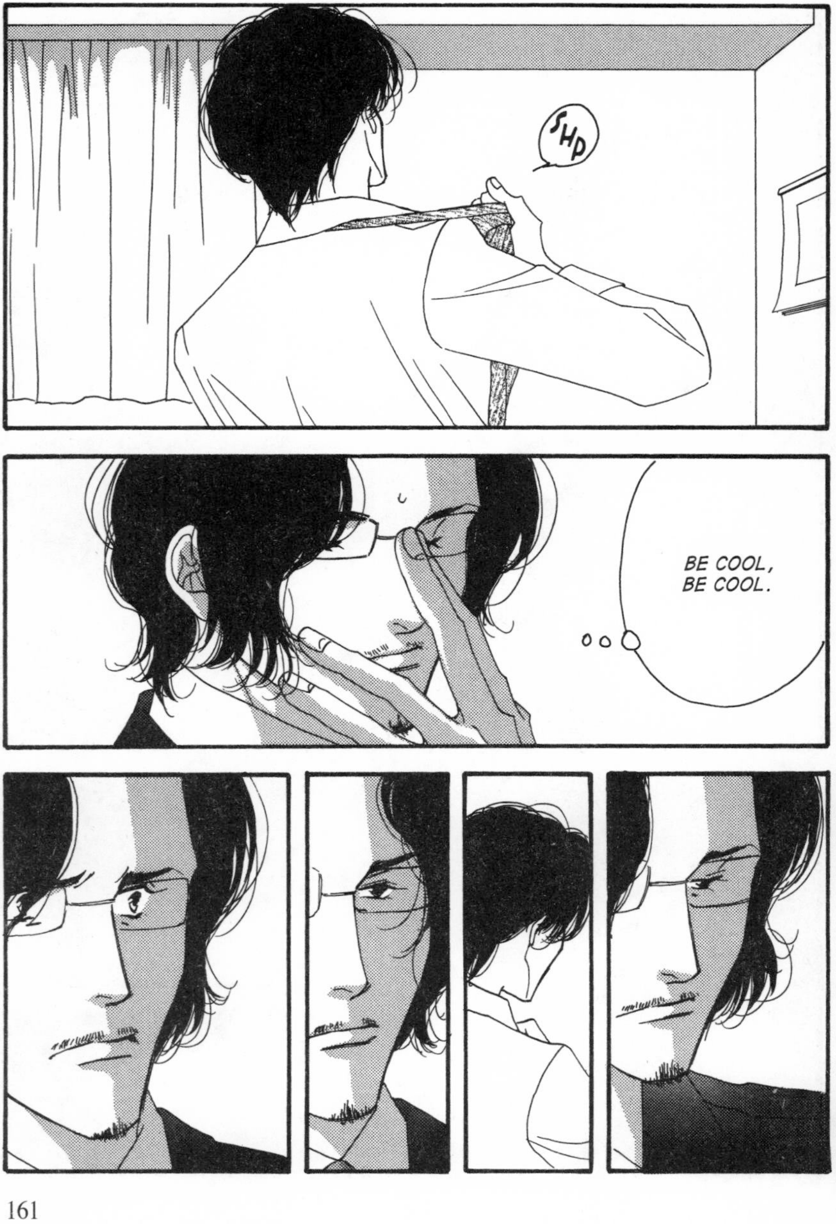
SHP
BE COOL,
BE COOL.

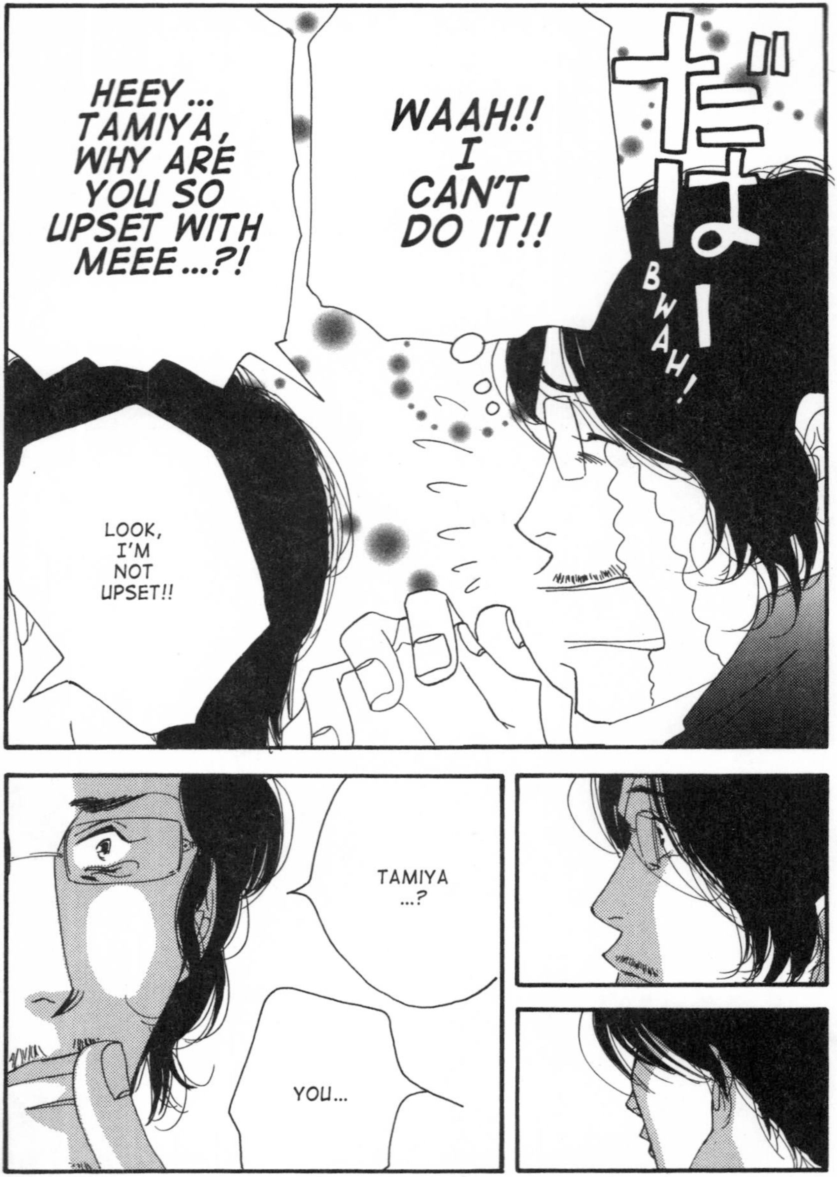
だばー
BWAAH!
WAAH!! I CAN'T DO IT!!
HEEY... TAMIYA, WHY ARE YOU SO UPSET WITH MEEE...?!
LOOK, I'M NOT UPSET!!
TAMIYA ...?
YOU...

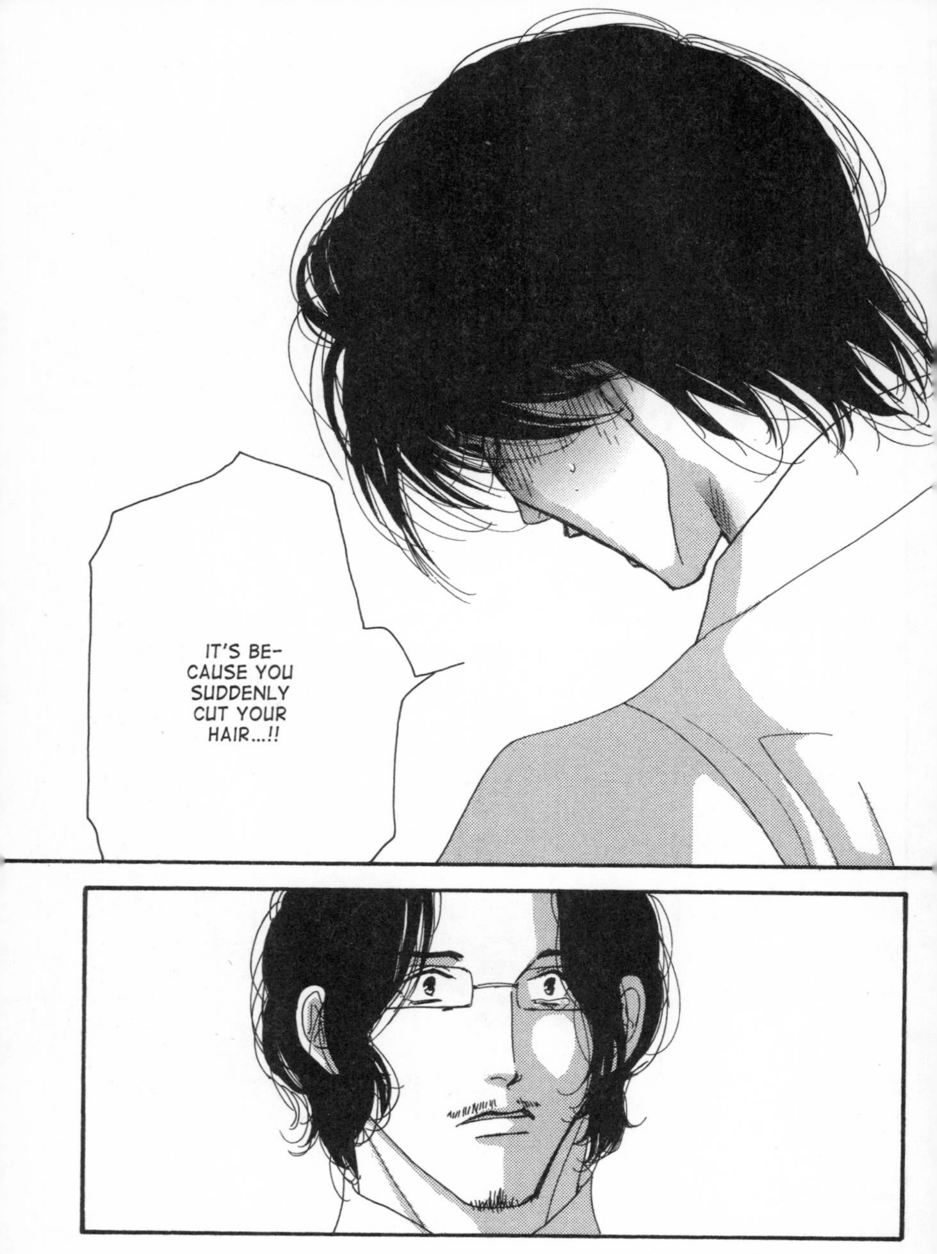
IT'S BE-CAUSE YOU SUDDENLY CUT YOUR HAIR...!!

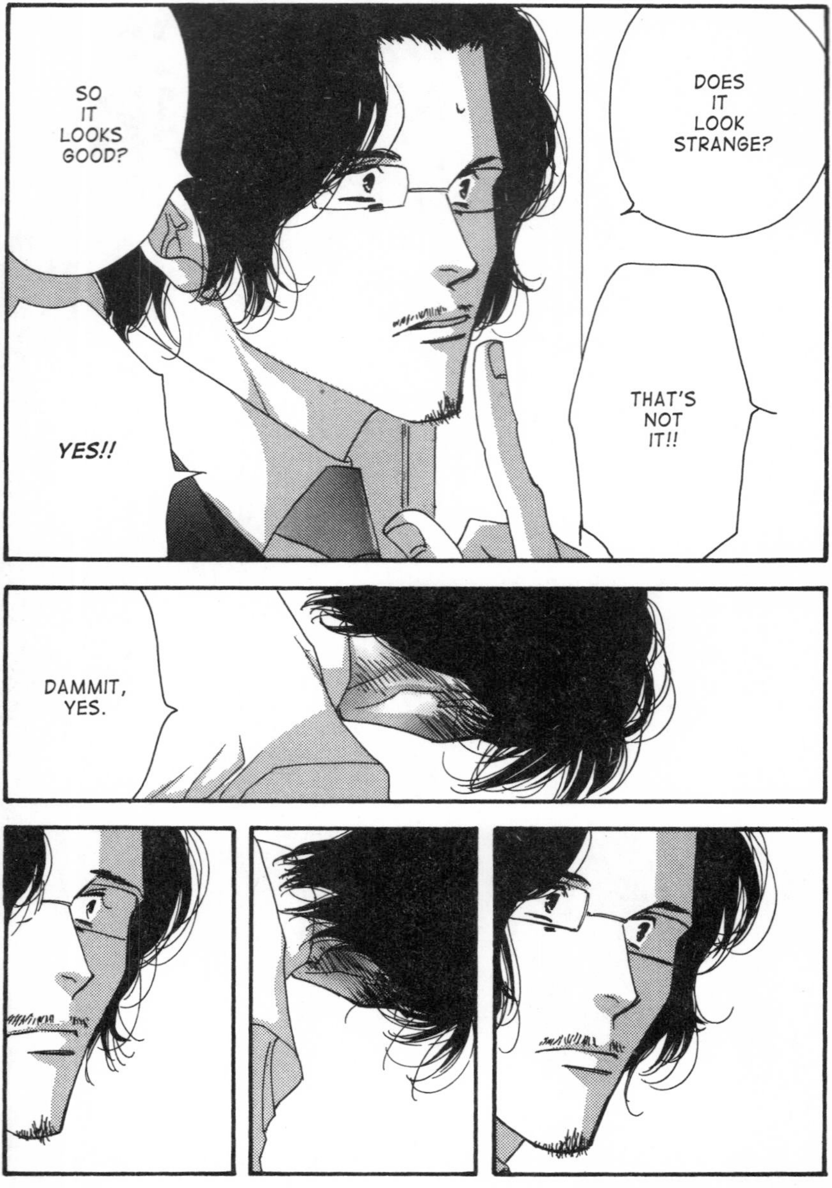
DOES IT LOOK STRANGE?
THAT'S NOT IT!!
SO IT LOOKS GOOD?
YES!!
DAMMIT, YES.

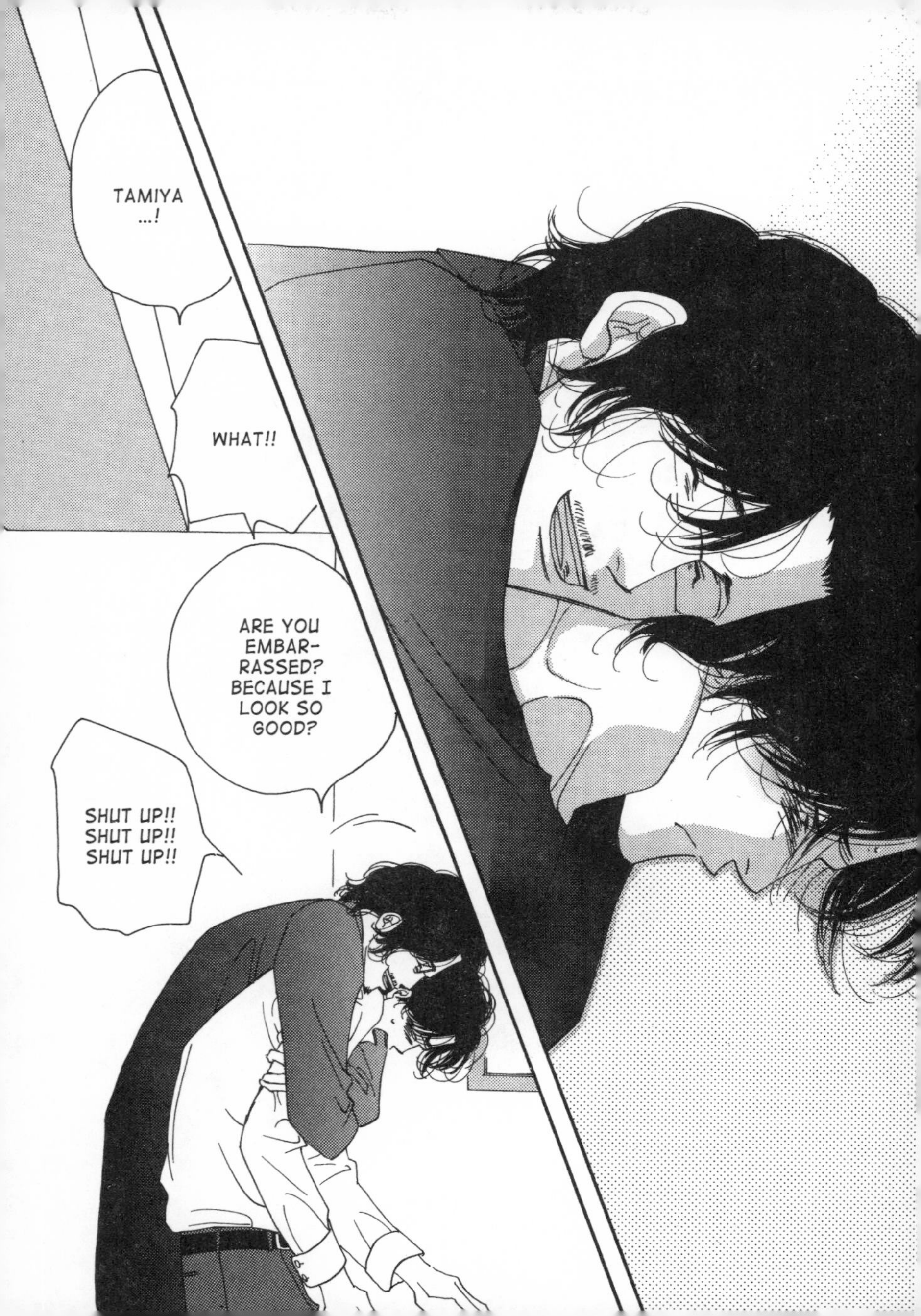
TAMIYA ...!
WHAT!!
ARE YOU EMBAR-RASSED? BECAUSE I LOOK SO GOOD?
SHUT UP!! SHUT UP!! SHUT UP!!

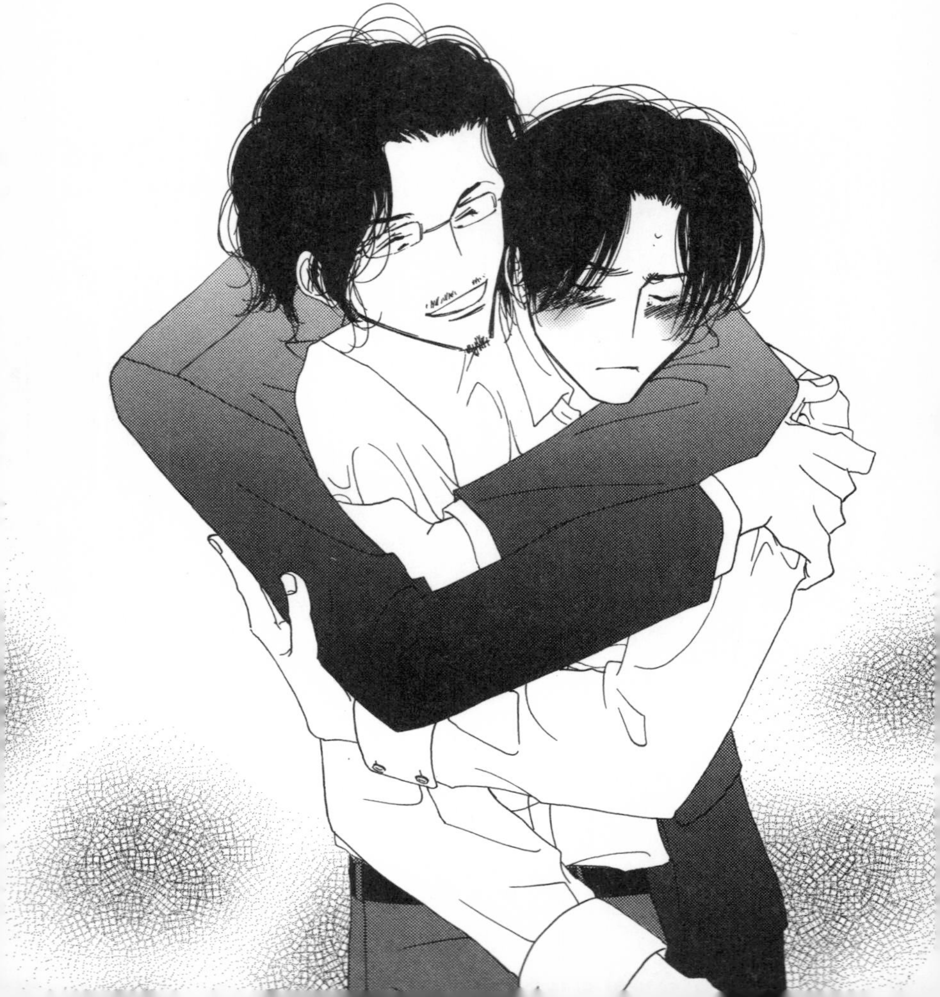

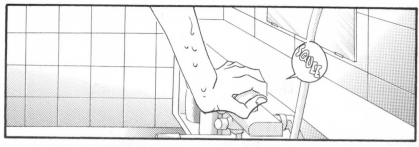

YOU'RE NOT ASLEEP, ARE YOU? WOULD YOU LET ME...?

TAMIYA?

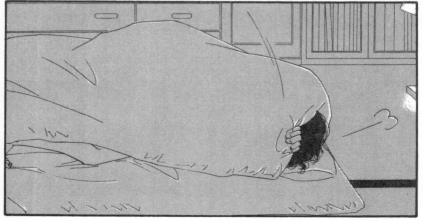

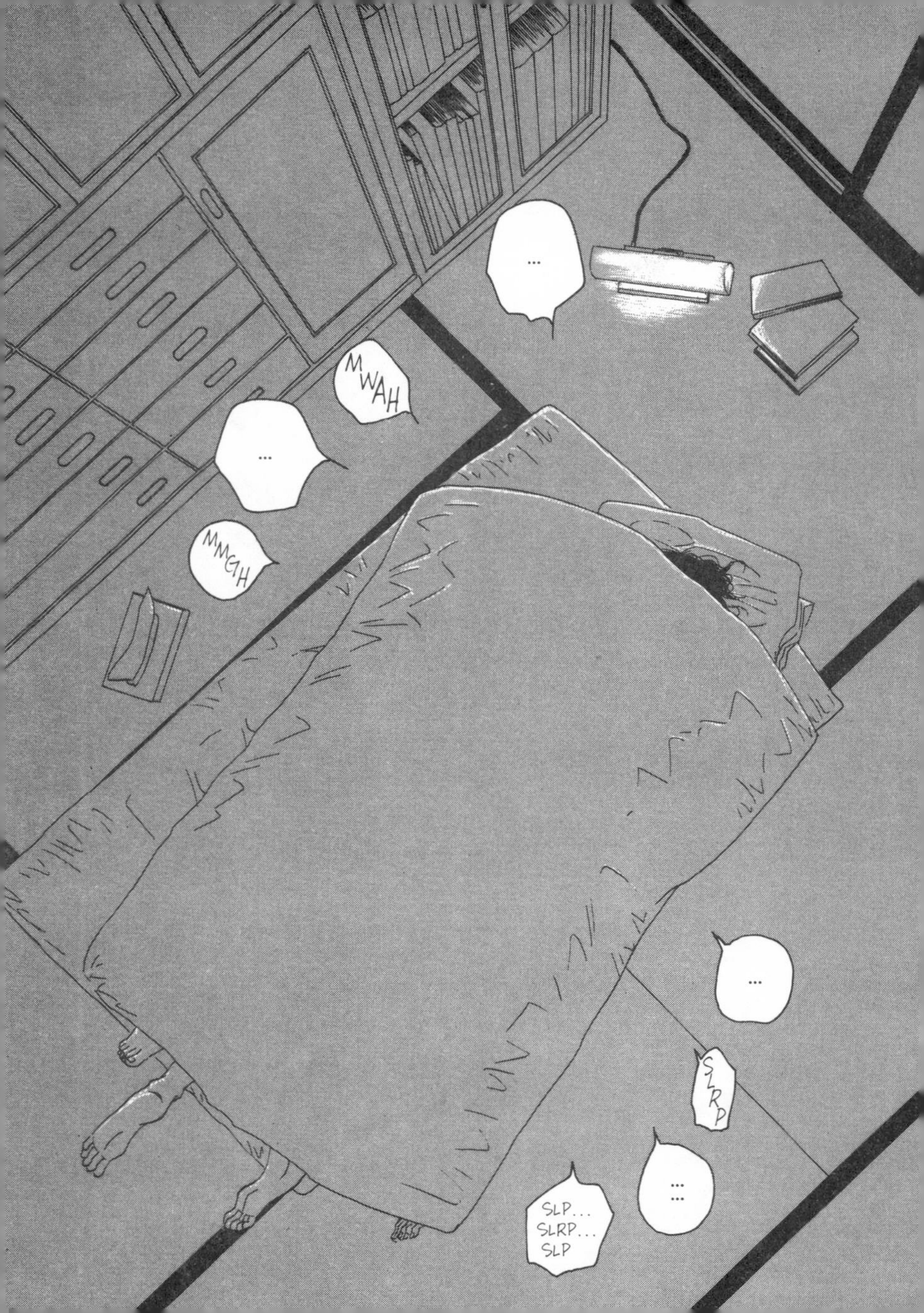
...
MWAH
...
MMGH
...
SLRP
... ...
SLP... SLRP... SLP

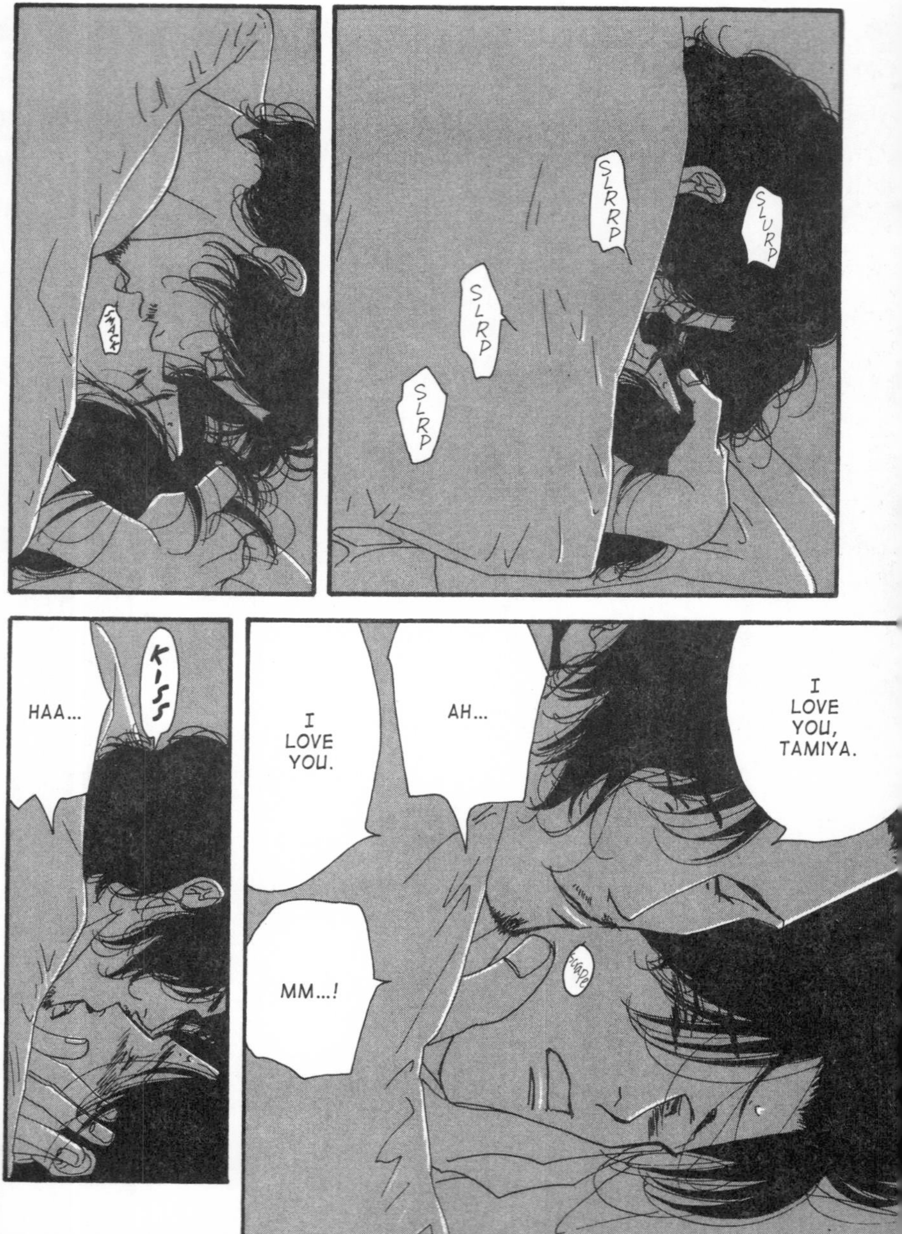
SLURP
SLRRP
SLRP
SLRP
SMACK
I LOVE YOU, TAMIYA.
AH...
I LOVE YOU.
scrape
MM...!
KISS
HAA...

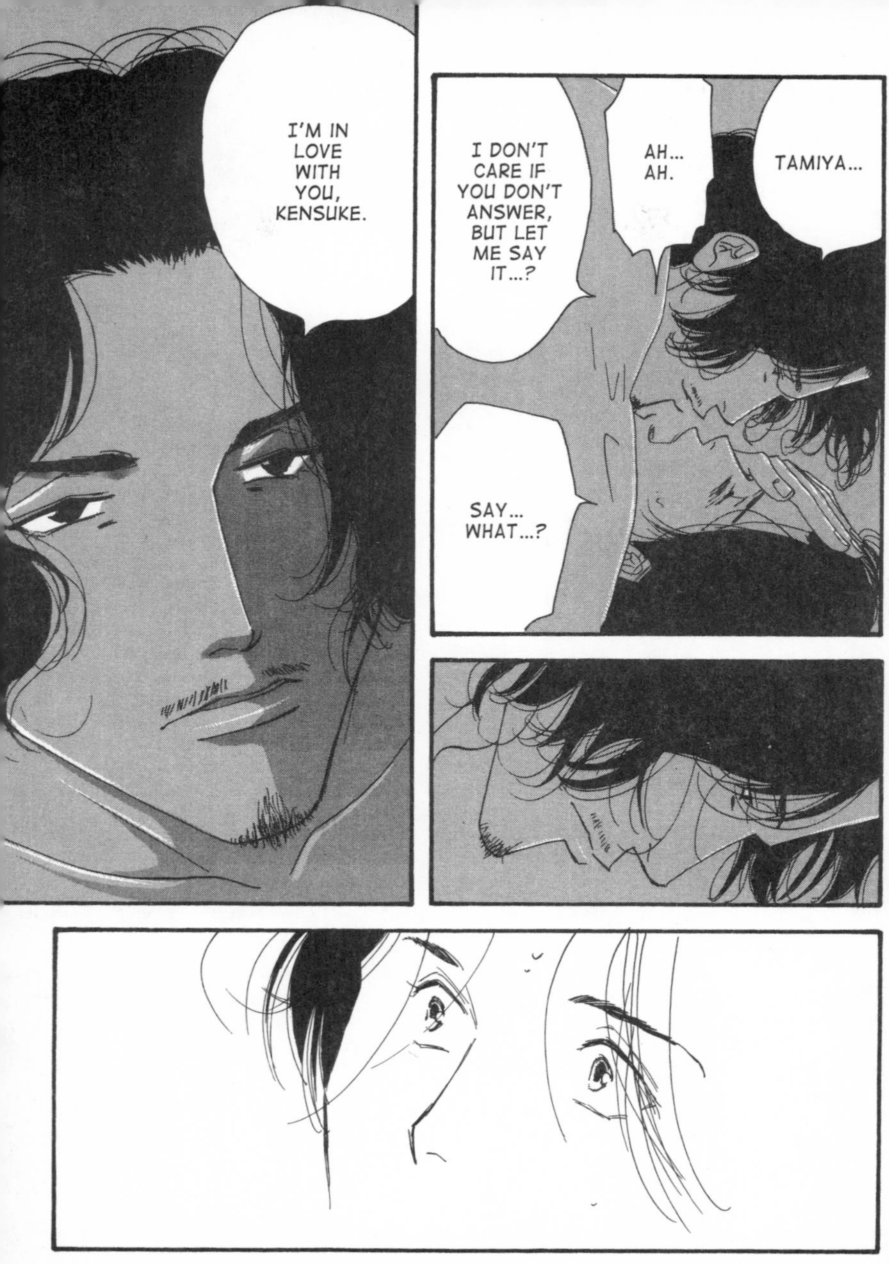
TAMIYA...
AH... AH.
I DON'T CARE IF YOU DON'T ANSWER, BUT LET ME SAY IT...?
SAY... WHAT...?
I'M IN LOVE WITH YOU, KENSUKE.

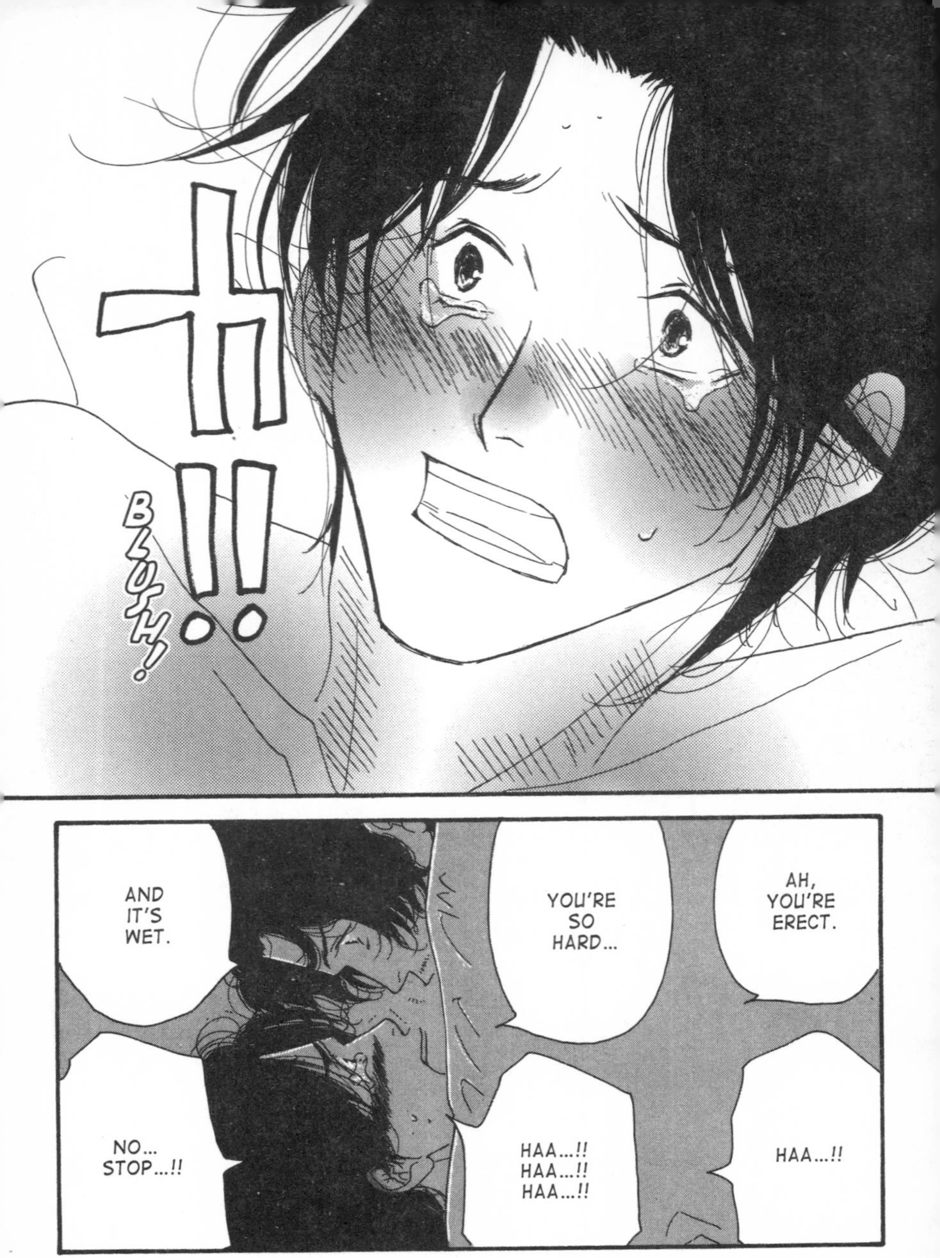
カ!!
BLUSH!
AH, YOU'RE ERECT.
YOU'RE SO HARD...
AND IT'S WET.
HAA...!!
HAA...!! HAA...!! HAA...!!
NO... STOP...!!

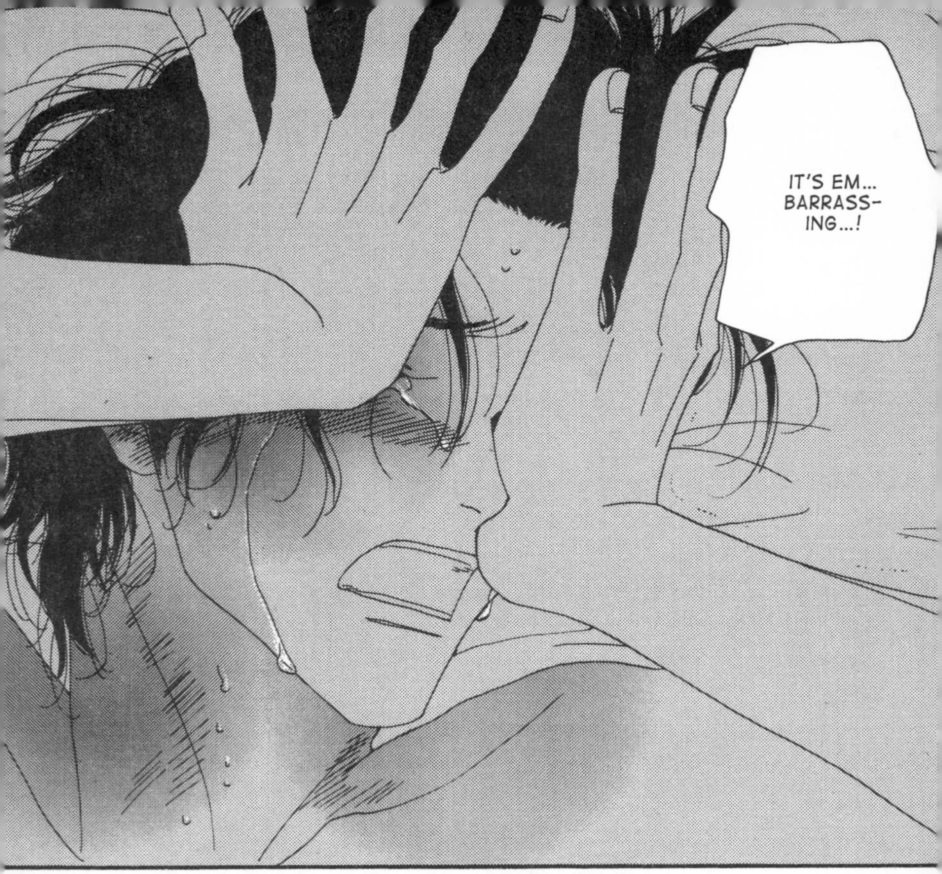
IT'S EM... BARRASS- ING...!

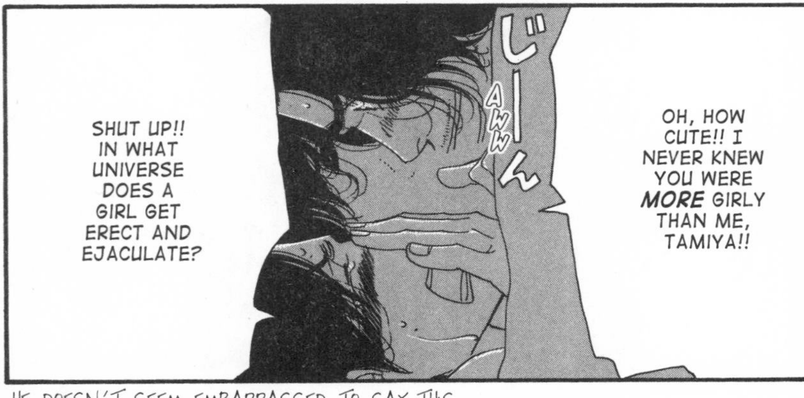
OH, HOW CUTE!! I NEVER KNEW YOU WERE **MORE** GIRLY THAN ME, TAMIYA!!
じーん
AWW
SHUT UP!! IN WHAT UNIVERSE DOES A GIRL GET ERECT AND EJACULATE?

HE DOESN'T SEEM EMBARRASSED TO SAY THIS.

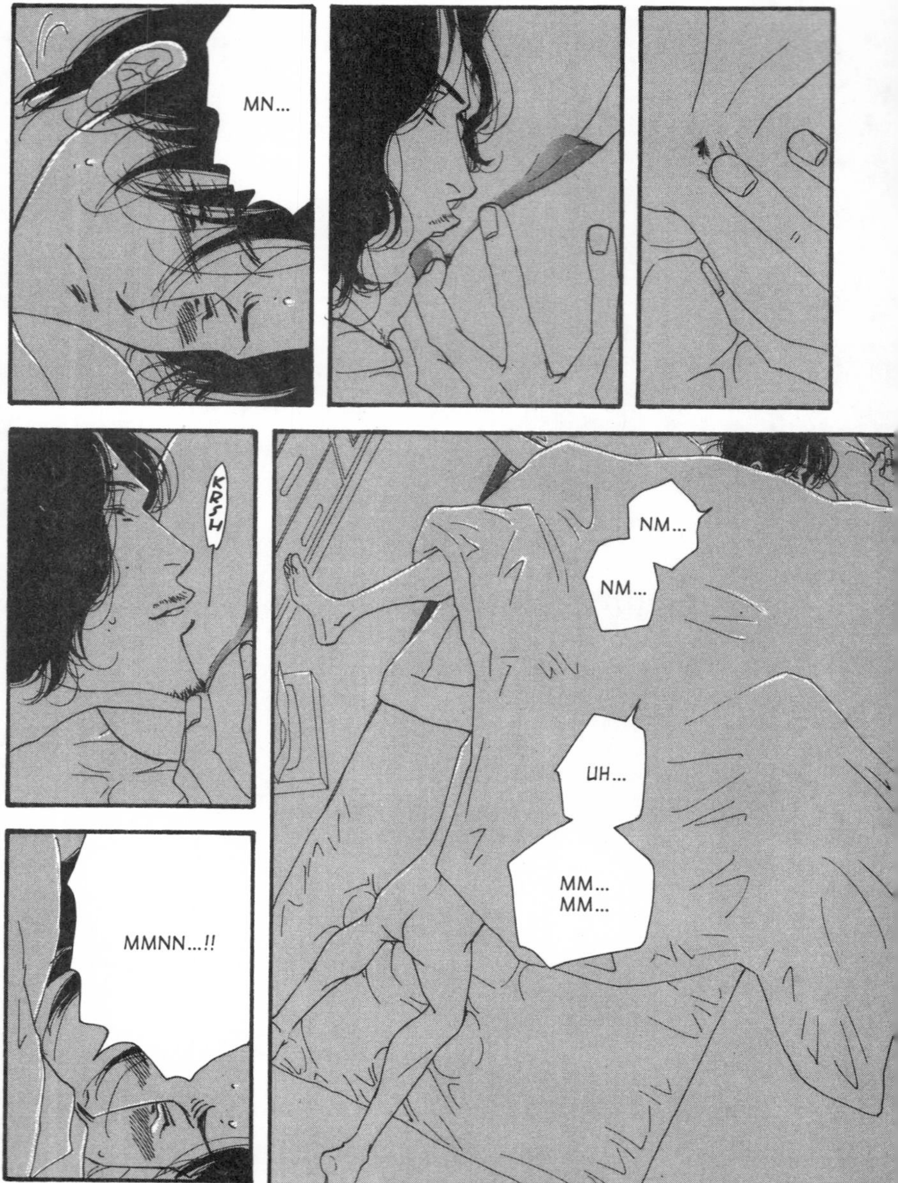
MN...
NM...
NM...
UH...
MM...
MM...
KRSH
MMNN...!!

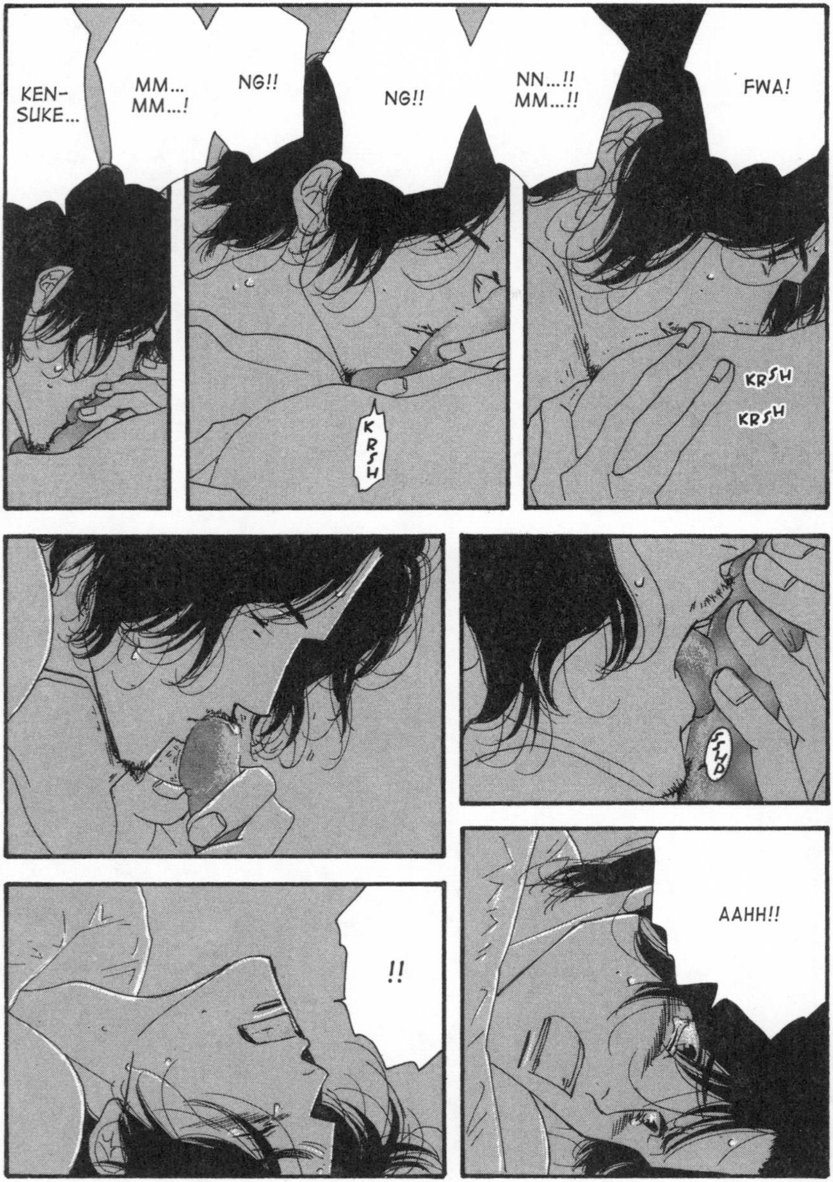
FWA!
KRSH
KRSH
NN...!! MM...!!
NG!!
KRSH
NG!!
MM... MM...!
KEN-SUKE...
AAHH!!
!!

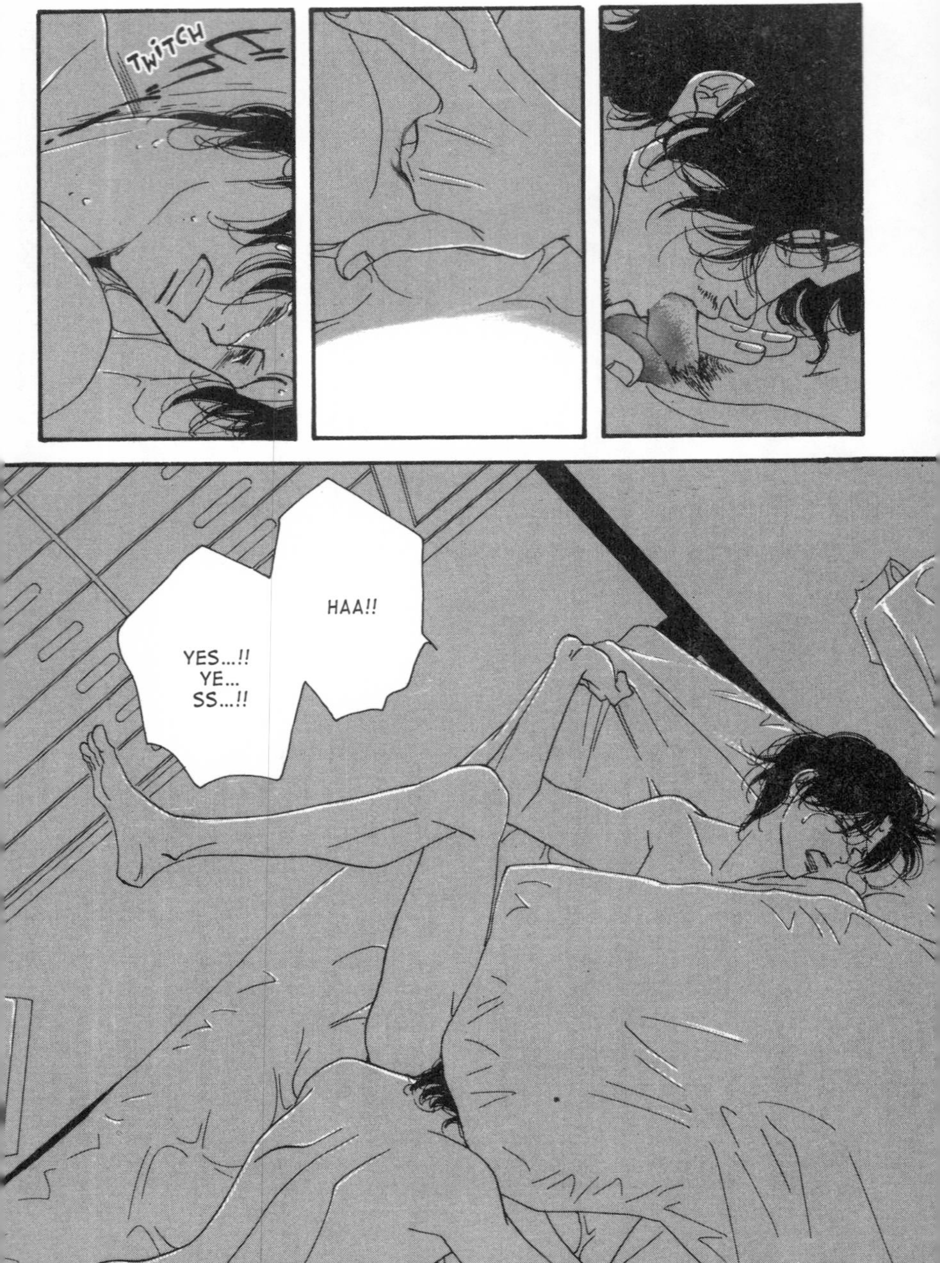
TWITCH
HAA!!
YES...!! YE... SS...!!

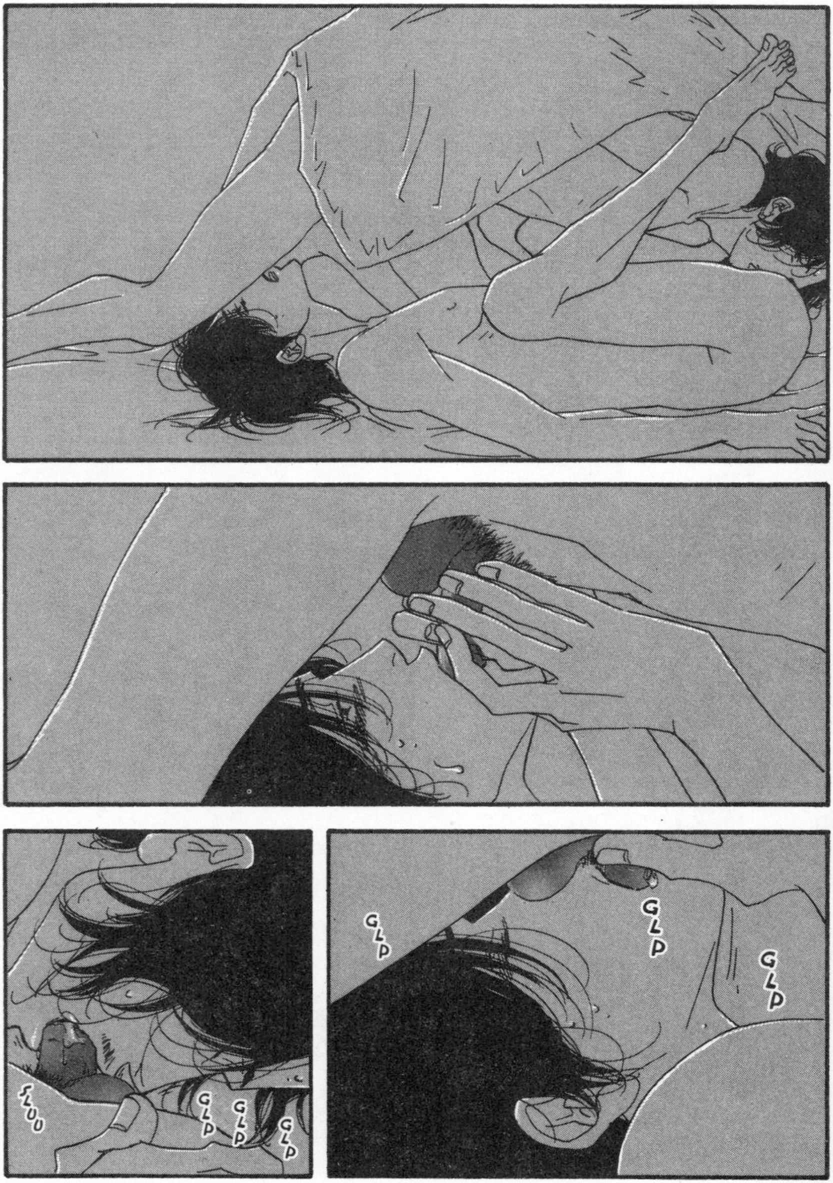
GLP
GLP
GLP
GLP
GLP
GLP
SLUU

SLP
SLP
SLRP
UH!
QUIVER
GNN
NNGH-GH...!!
GAH GUH
GAH
GAH
GAH

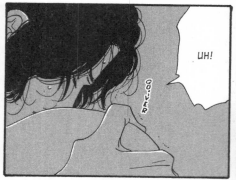

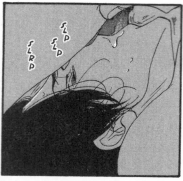

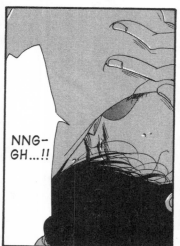

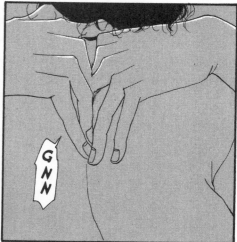

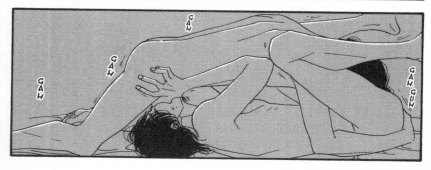

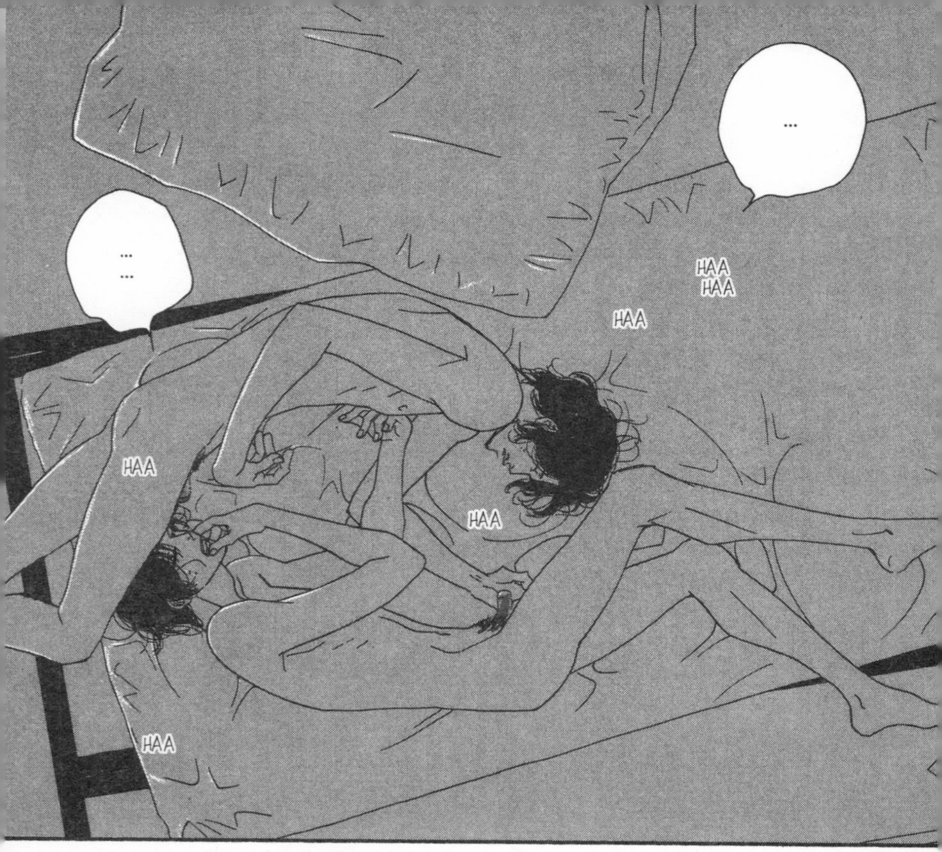
...
HAA HAA
HAA
...
...
HAA
HAA
HAA
HAA

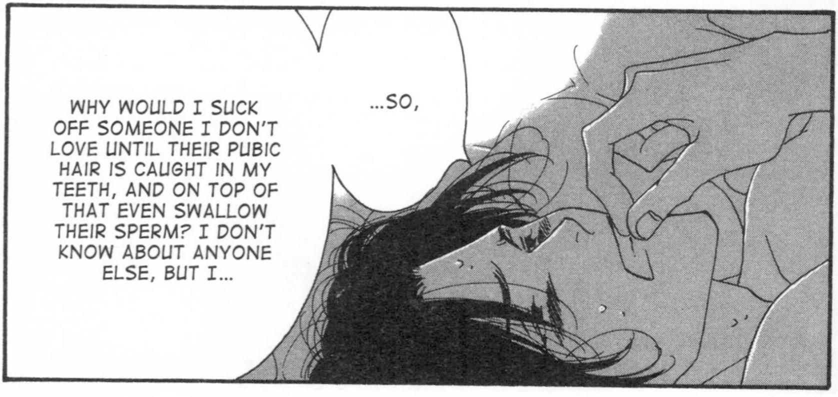
...SO,
WHY WOULD I SUCK OFF SOMEONE I DON'T LOVE UNTIL THEIR PUBIC HAIR IS CAUGHT IN MY TEETH, AND ON TOP OF THAT EVEN SWALLOW THEIR SPERM? I DON'T KNOW ABOUT ANYONE ELSE, BUT I...

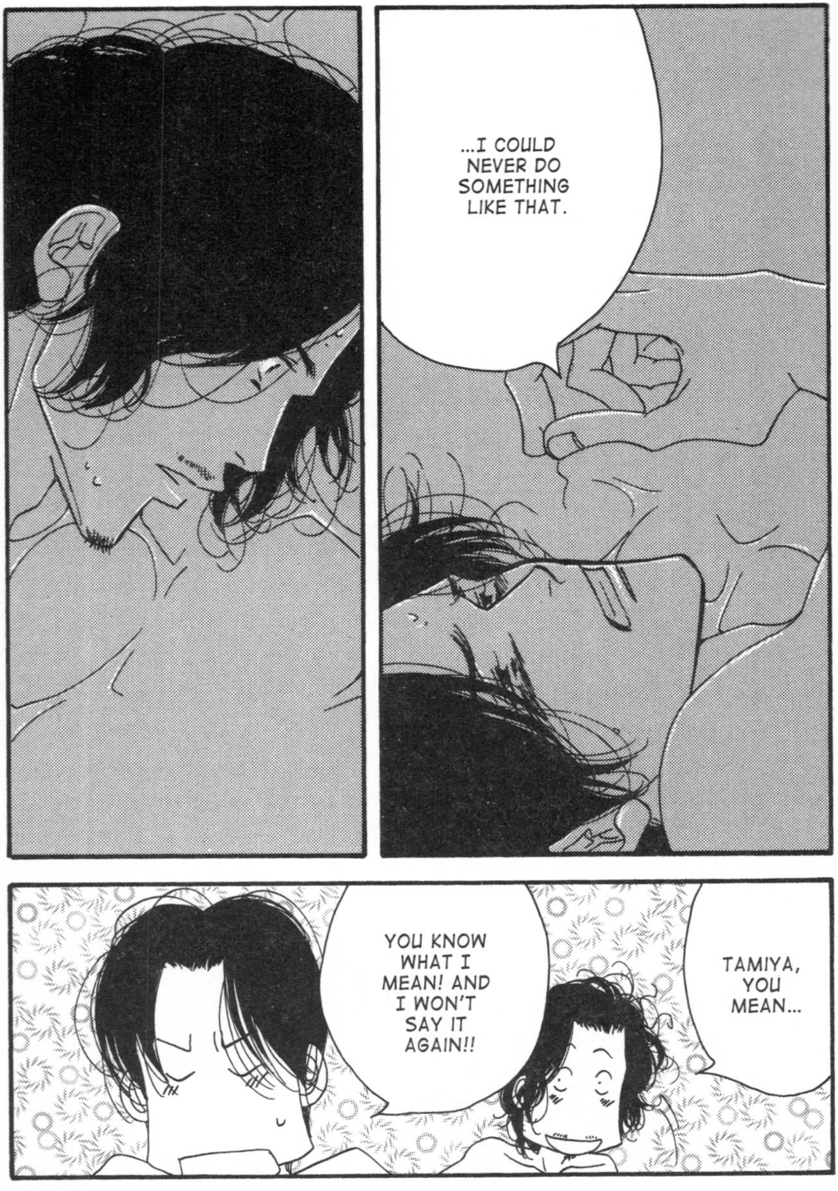
...I COULD NEVER DO SOMETHING LIKE THAT.
TAMIYA, YOU MEAN...
YOU KNOW WHAT I MEAN! AND I WON'T SAY IT AGAIN!!

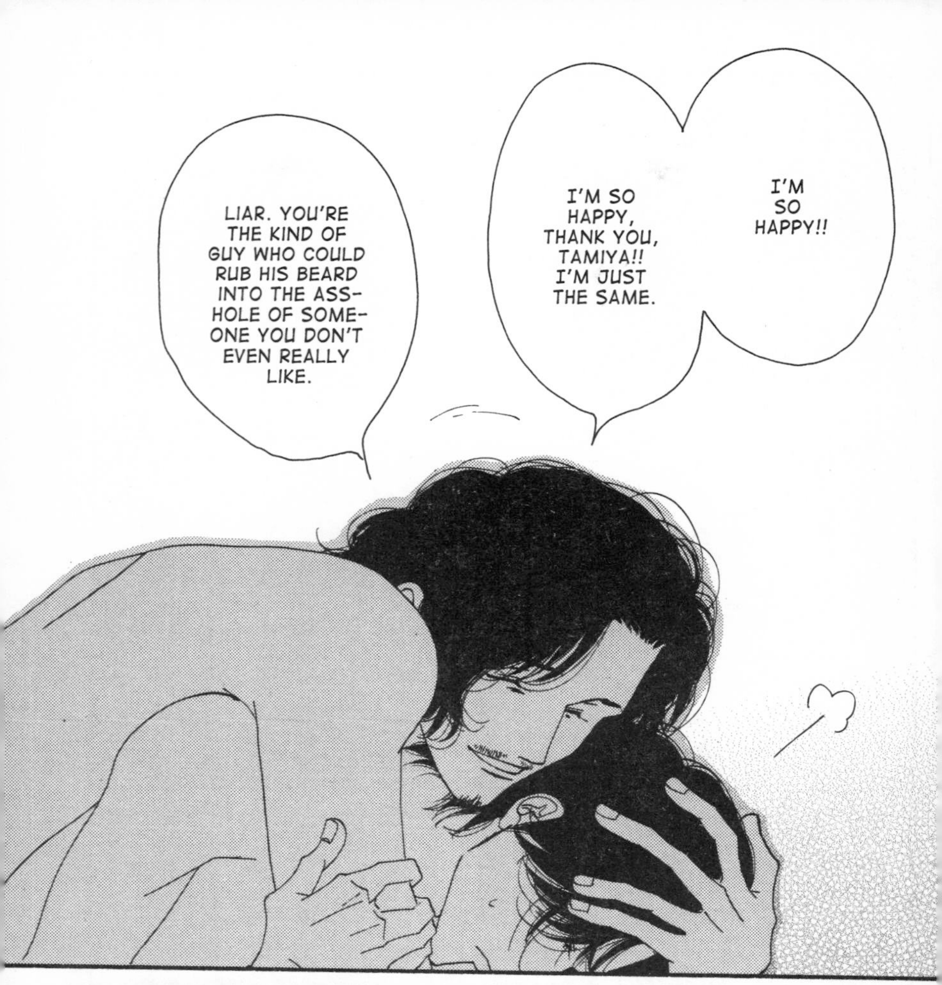
I'M SO HAPPY!!
I'M SO HAPPY, THANK YOU, TAMIYA!! I'M JUST THE SAME.
LIAR. YOU'RE THE KIND OF GUY WHO COULD RUB HIS BEARD INTO THE ASS-HOLE OF SOME-ONE YOU DON'T EVEN REALLY LIKE.

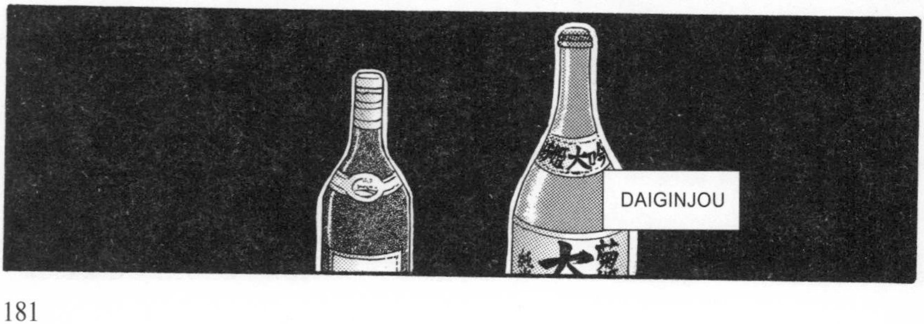
DAIGINJOU

YEP!! THE HAIRCUT WORKED!! THANKS, BOTH OF YOU!!

WHICH MEANS...

AND A GOOD VINTAGE CHILEAN WINE, TOO,

AH, DAIGINJOU.

MAY 2001 PLANNER

1	TUE	HOLIDAY	16	FRI
2	WED	WEEK!	17	SAT
			18	SUN
			19	MON
			20	TUE

HEY, HEY, HIRO-CHAN!!

DOESN'T THAT ANNOY YOU A LITTLE?

SO, IT WAS LOVE ALL ALONG AND THE BOSS JUST NEVER NOTICED?

NOT AT ALL!! BUT, ALL'S WELL THAT ENDS WELL!! BASICALLY, IT TURNS OUT THAT TAMIYA'S JUST REALLY SHY!

I'M GLAD. SO, DID YOU DO EVERY-THING ELSE LIKE WE TOLD YOU?

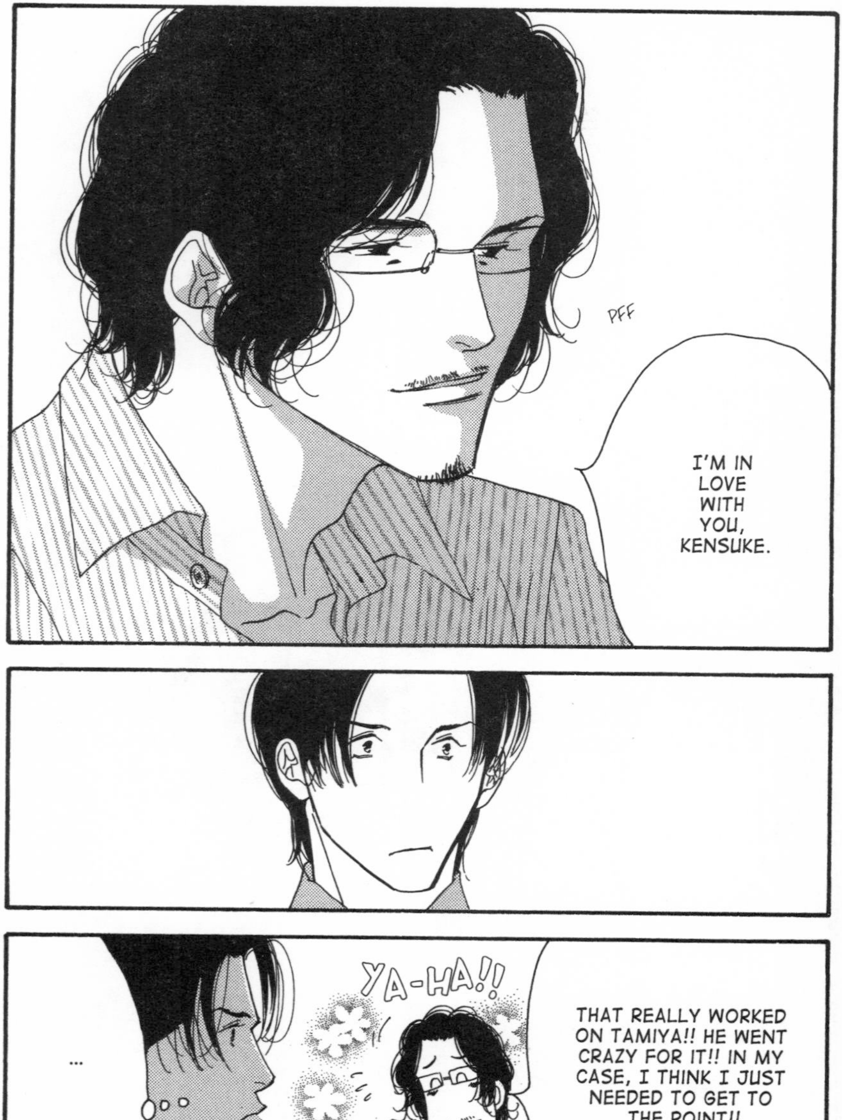
PFF
I'M IN LOVE WITH YOU, KENSUKE.
THAT REALLY WORKED ON TAMIYA!! HE WENT CRAZY FOR IT!! IN MY CASE, I THINK I JUST NEEDED TO GET TO THE POINT!!
YA-HA!!
...

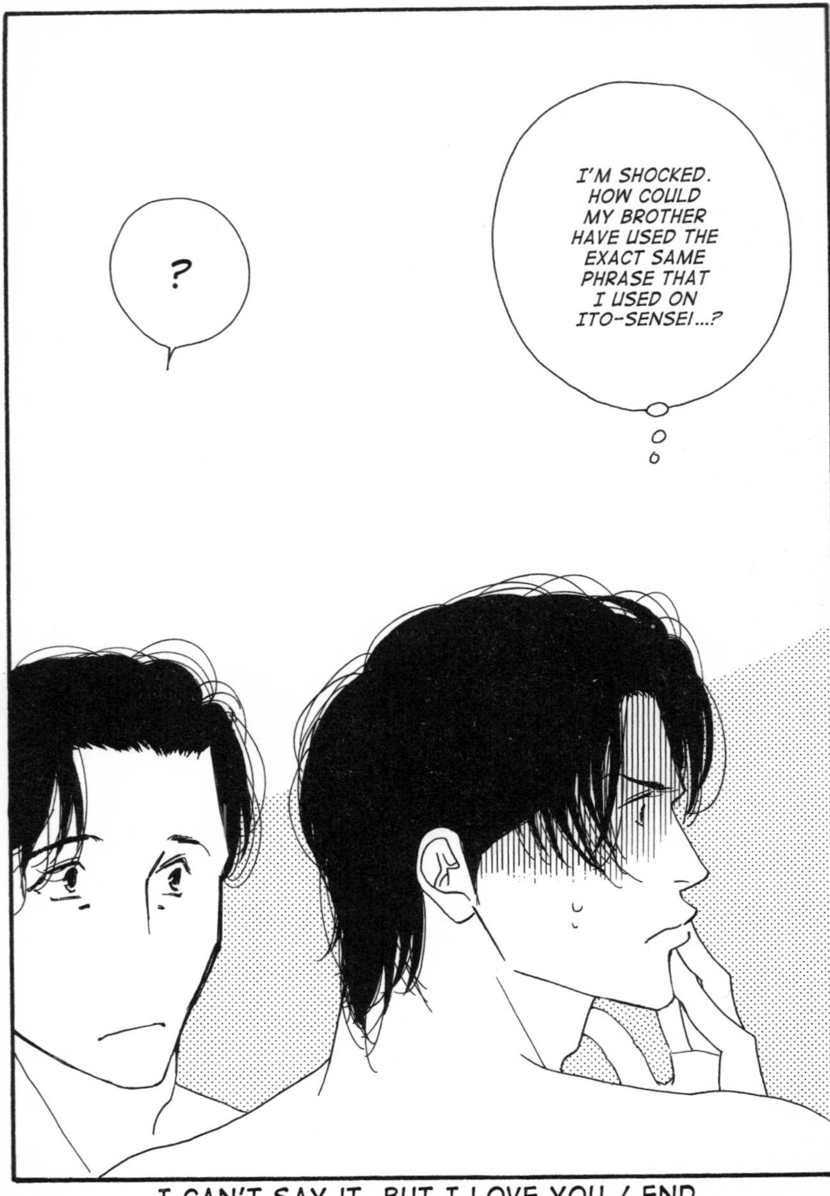
I'M SHOCKED. HOW COULD MY BROTHER HAVE USED THE EXACT SAME PHRASE THAT I USED ON ITO-SENSEI...?
?

I CAN'T SAY IT, BUT I LOVE YOU / END

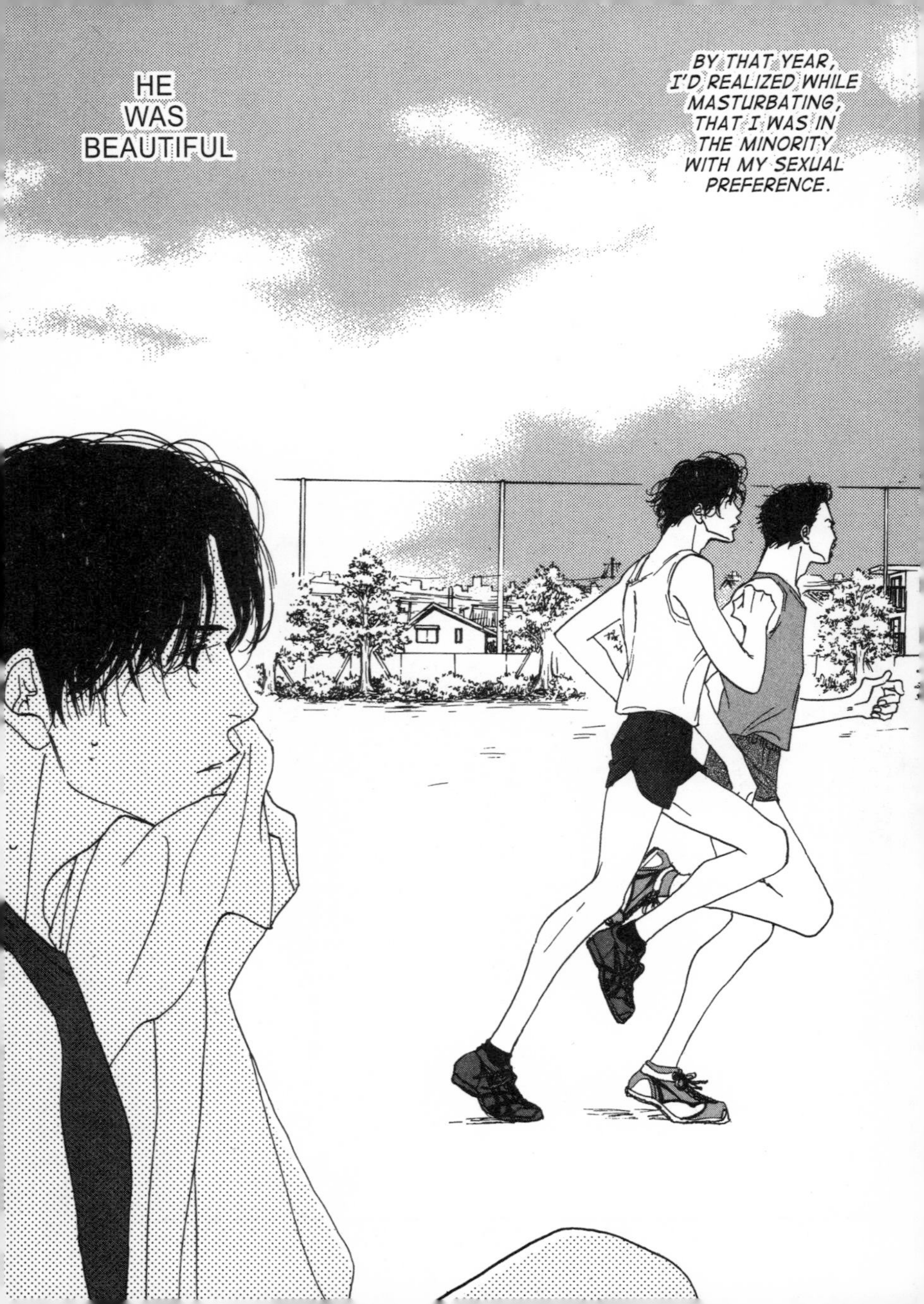
BY THAT YEAR, I'D REALIZED WHILE MASTURBATING, THAT I WAS IN THE MINORITY WITH MY SEXUAL PREFERENCE.
HE WAS BEAUTIFUL

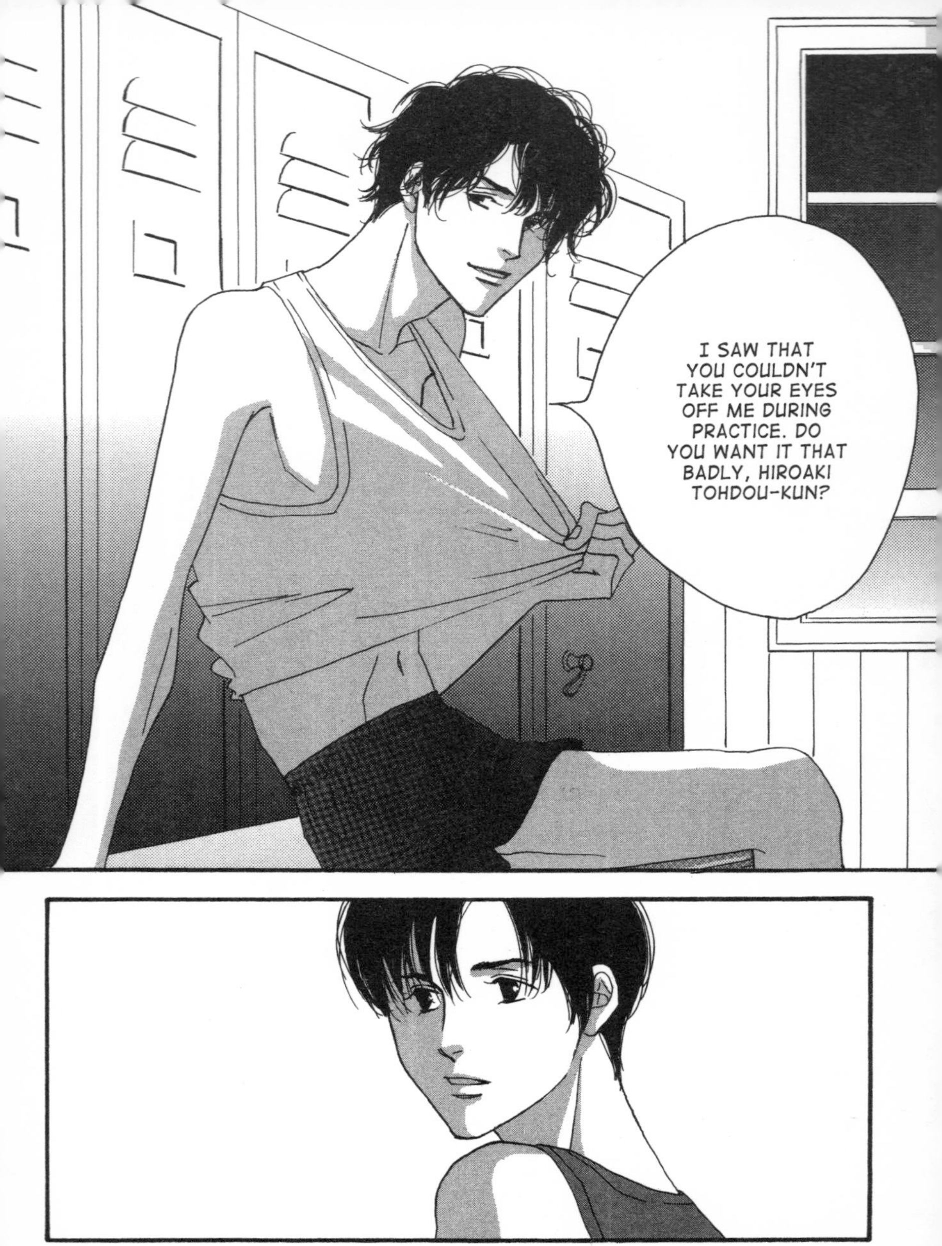
I SAW THAT YOU COULDN'T TAKE YOUR EYES OFF ME DURING PRACTICE. DO YOU WANT IT THAT BADLY, HIROAKI TOHDOU-KUN?

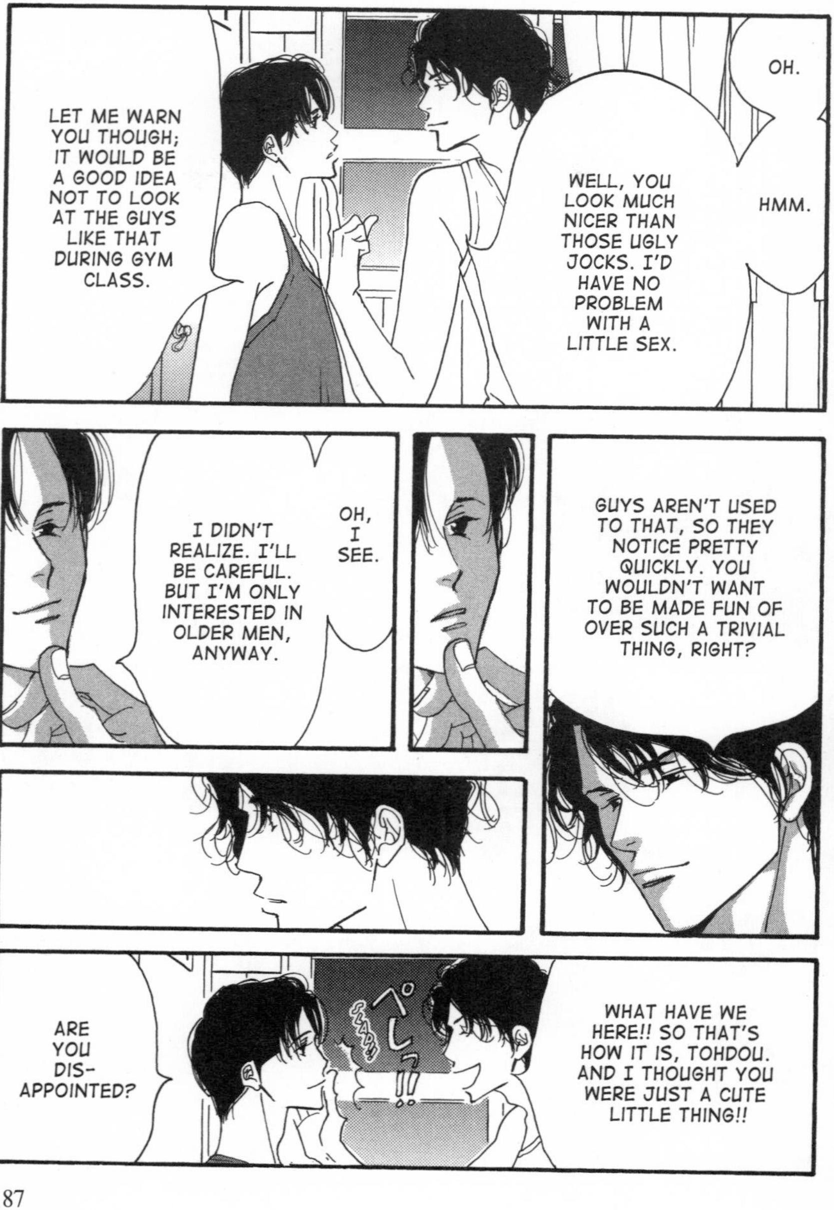
OH.
HMM.
WELL, YOU LOOK MUCH NICER THAN THOSE UGLY JOCKS. I'D HAVE NO PROBLEM WITH A LITTLE SEX.
LET ME WARN YOU THOUGH; IT WOULD BE A GOOD IDEA NOT TO LOOK AT THE GUYS LIKE THAT DURING GYM CLASS.
GUYS AREN'T USED TO THAT, SO THEY NOTICE PRETTY QUICKLY. YOU WOULDN'T WANT TO BE MADE FUN OF OVER SUCH A TRIVIAL THING, RIGHT?
OH, I SEE.
I DIDN'T REALIZE. I'LL BE CAREFUL. BUT I'M ONLY INTERESTED IN OLDER MEN, ANYWAY.
WHAT HAVE WE HERE!! SO THAT'S HOW IT IS, TOHDOU. AND I THOUGHT YOU WERE JUST A CUTE LITTLE THING!!
ぺしっ!!
SLAP!!
ARE YOU DIS-APPOINTED?

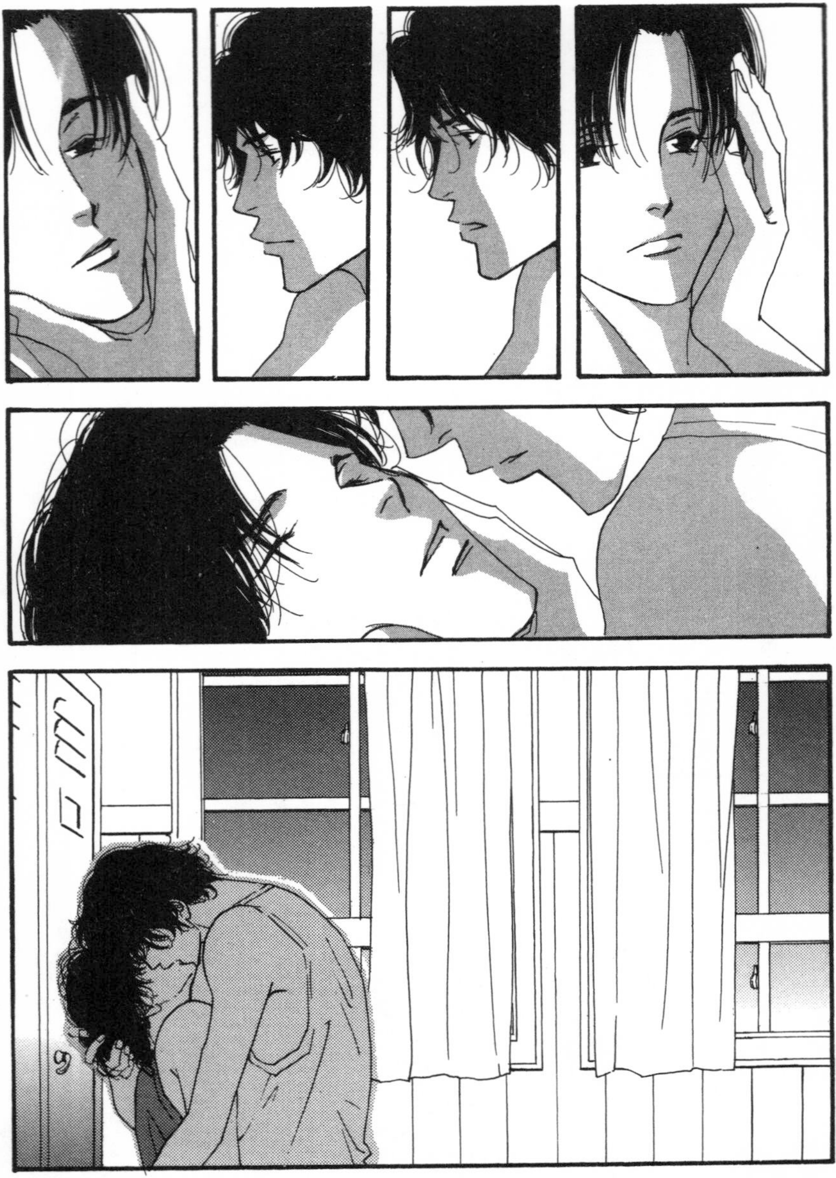

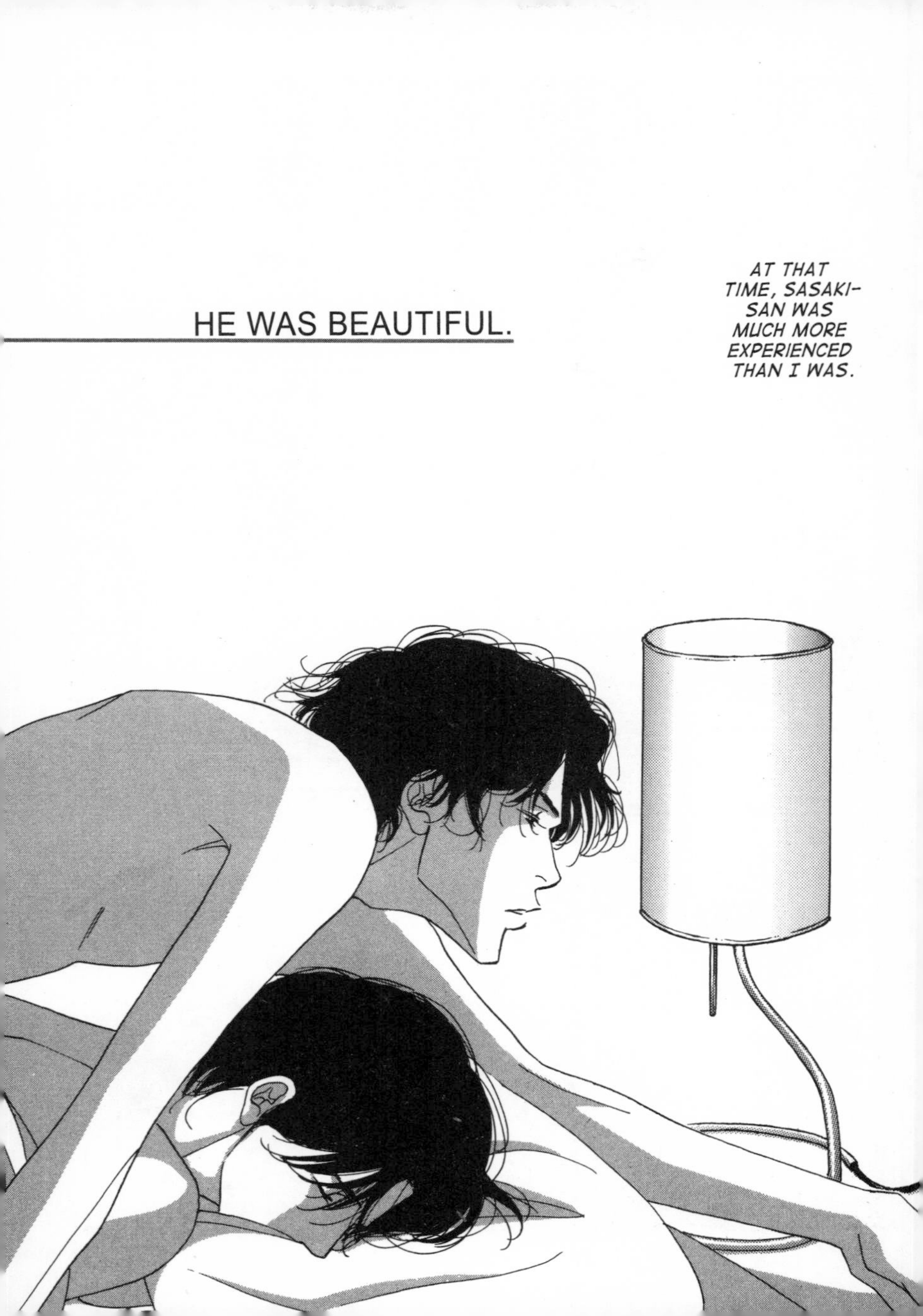
AT THAT TIME, SASAKI-SAN WAS MUCH MORE EXPERIENCED THAN I WAS.
HE WAS BEAUTIFUL.

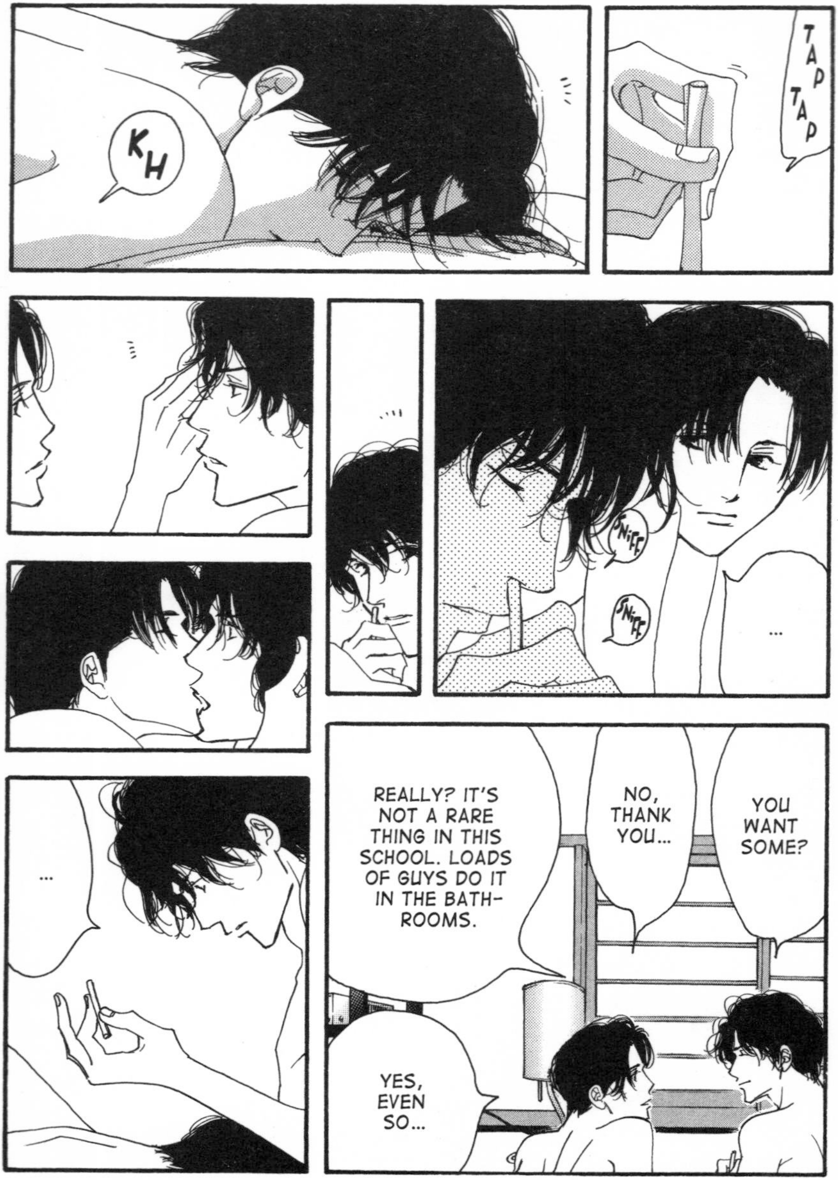
TAP TAP TAP
KH
SNIFF
SNIFF
...
YOU WANT SOME?
NO, THANK YOU...
REALLY? IT'S NOT A RARE THING IN THIS SCHOOL. LOADS OF GUYS DO IT IN THE BATH-ROOMS.
YES, EVEN SO...
...

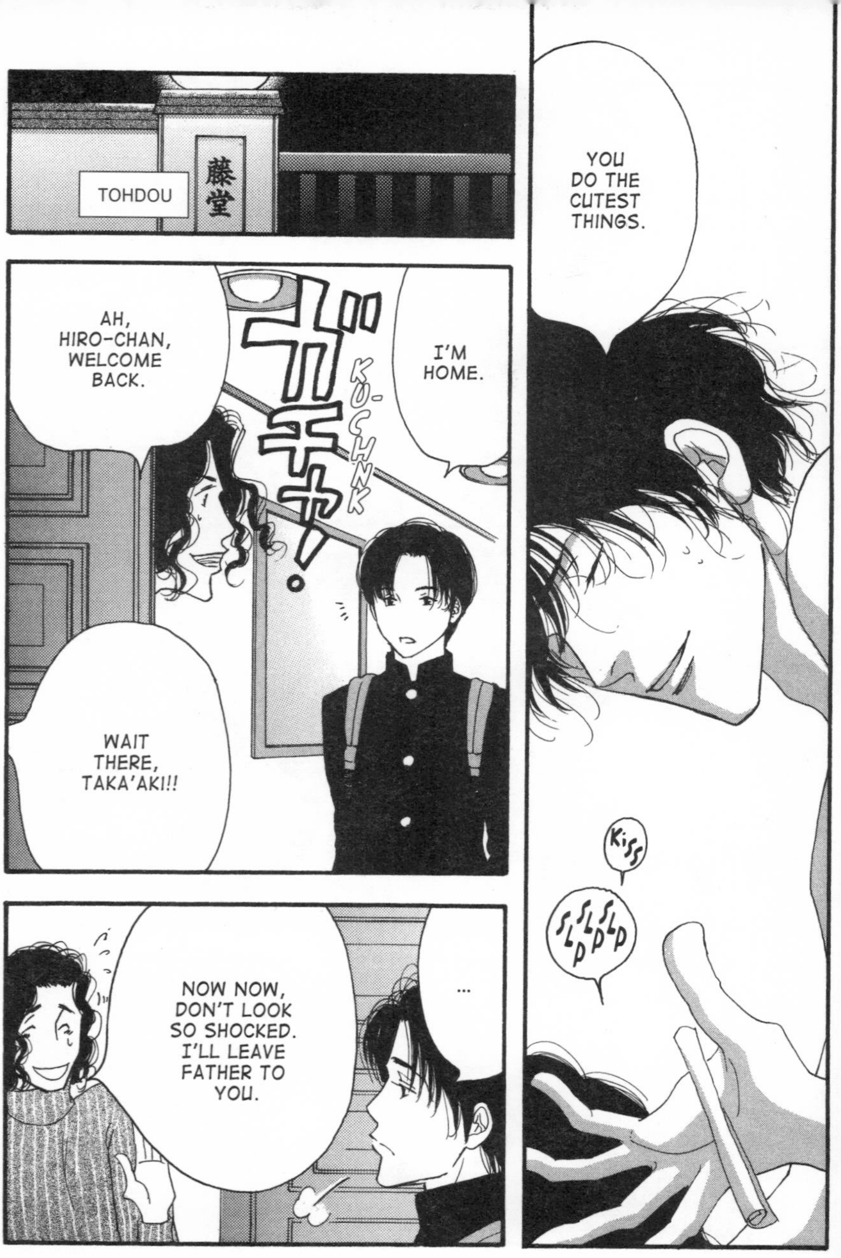
YOU DO THE CUTEST THINGS.
Kiss
SLP SLP SLP
藤堂
TOHDOU
I'M HOME.
ガチャ!
KU-CHNK
AH, HIRO-CHAN, WELCOME BACK.
WAIT THERE, TAKA'AKI!!
...
NOW NOW, DON'T LOOK SO SHOCKED. I'LL LEAVE FATHER TO YOU.

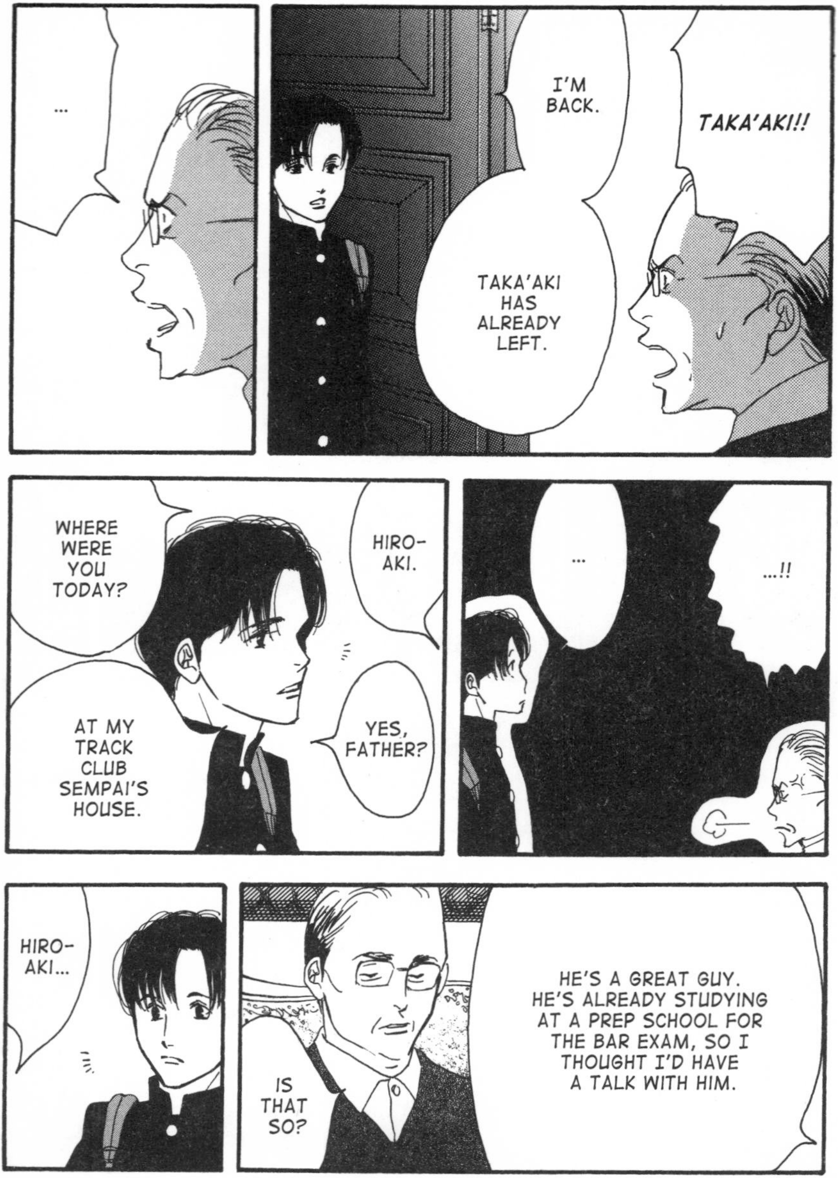
TAKA'AKI!!
I'M BACK.
TAKA'AKI HAS ALREADY LEFT.
...
...!!
...
HIRO-AKI.
WHERE WERE YOU TODAY?
YES, FATHER?
AT MY TRACK CLUB SEMPAI'S HOUSE.
HE'S A GREAT GUY. HE'S ALREADY STUDYING AT A PREP SCHOOL FOR THE BAR EXAM, SO I THOUGHT I'D HAVE A TALK WITH HIM.
IS THAT SO?
HIRO-AKI...

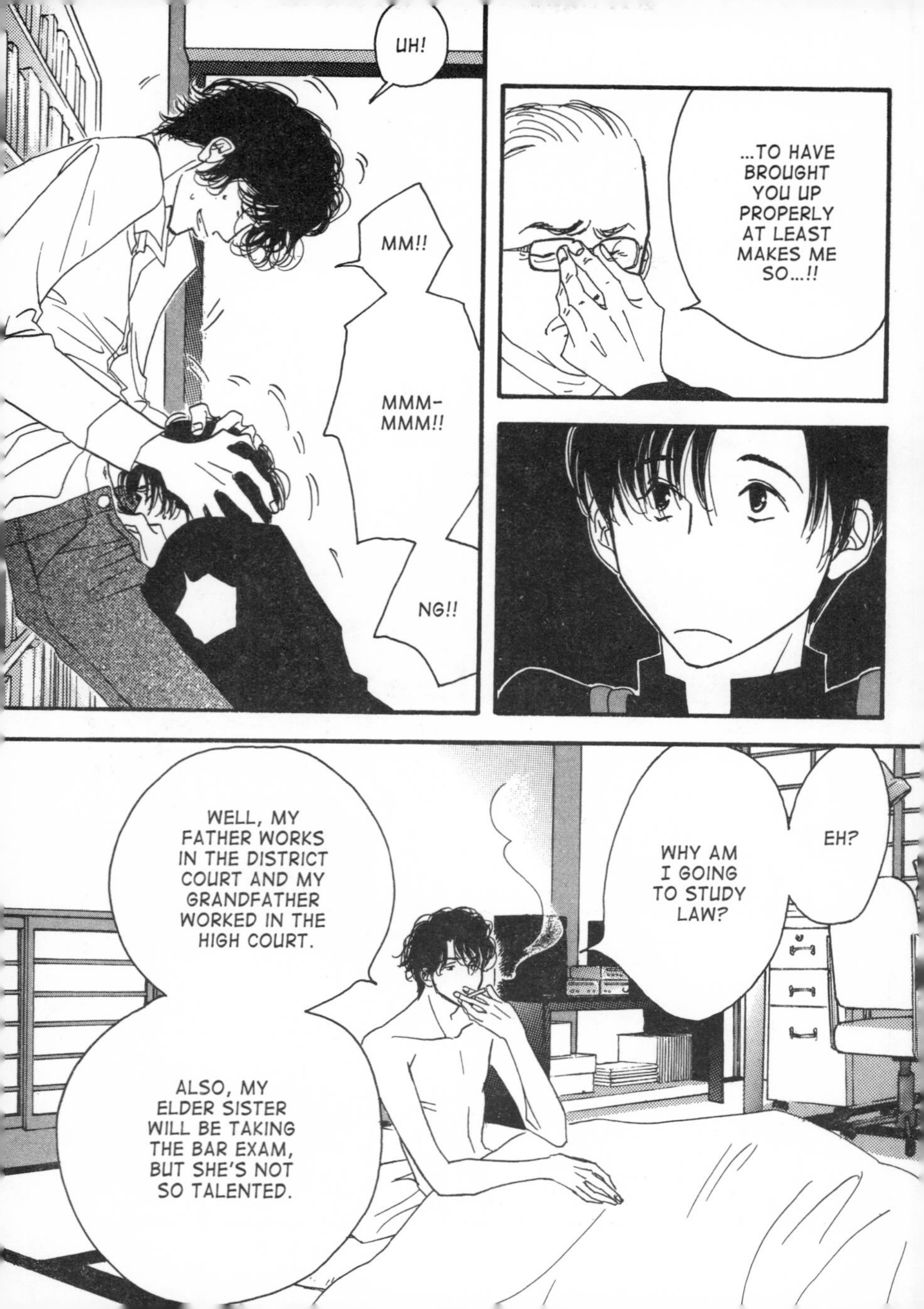
...TO HAVE BROUGHT YOU UP PROPERLY AT LEAST MAKES ME SO...!!
UH!
MM!!
MMM-MMM!!
NG!!
EH?
WHY AM I GOING TO STUDY LAW?
WELL, MY FATHER WORKS IN THE DISTRICT COURT AND MY GRANDFATHER WORKED IN THE HIGH COURT.
ALSO, MY ELDER SISTER WILL BE TAKING THE BAR EXAM, BUT SHE'S NOT SO TALENTED.

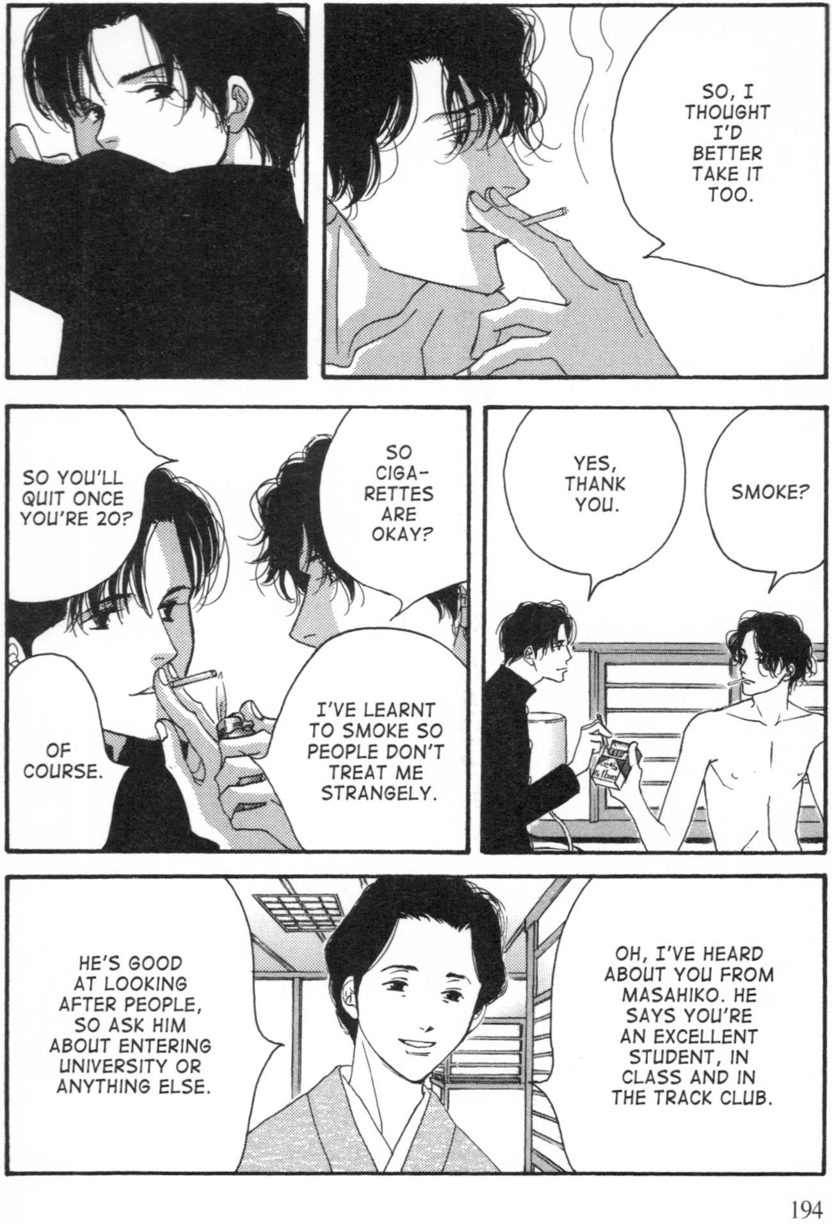
SO, I THOUGHT I'D BETTER TAKE IT TOO.
SMOKE?
YES, THANK YOU.
SO CIGA-RETTES ARE OKAY?
I'VE LEARNT TO SMOKE SO PEOPLE DON'T TREAT ME STRANGELY.
SO YOU'LL QUIT ONCE YOU'RE 20?
OF COURSE.
OH, I'VE HEARD ABOUT YOU FROM MASAHIKO. HE SAYS YOU'RE AN EXCELLENT STUDENT, IN CLASS AND IN THE TRACK CLUB.
HE'S GOOD AT LOOKING AFTER PEOPLE, SO ASK HIM ABOUT ENTERING UNIVERSITY OR ANYTHING ELSE.

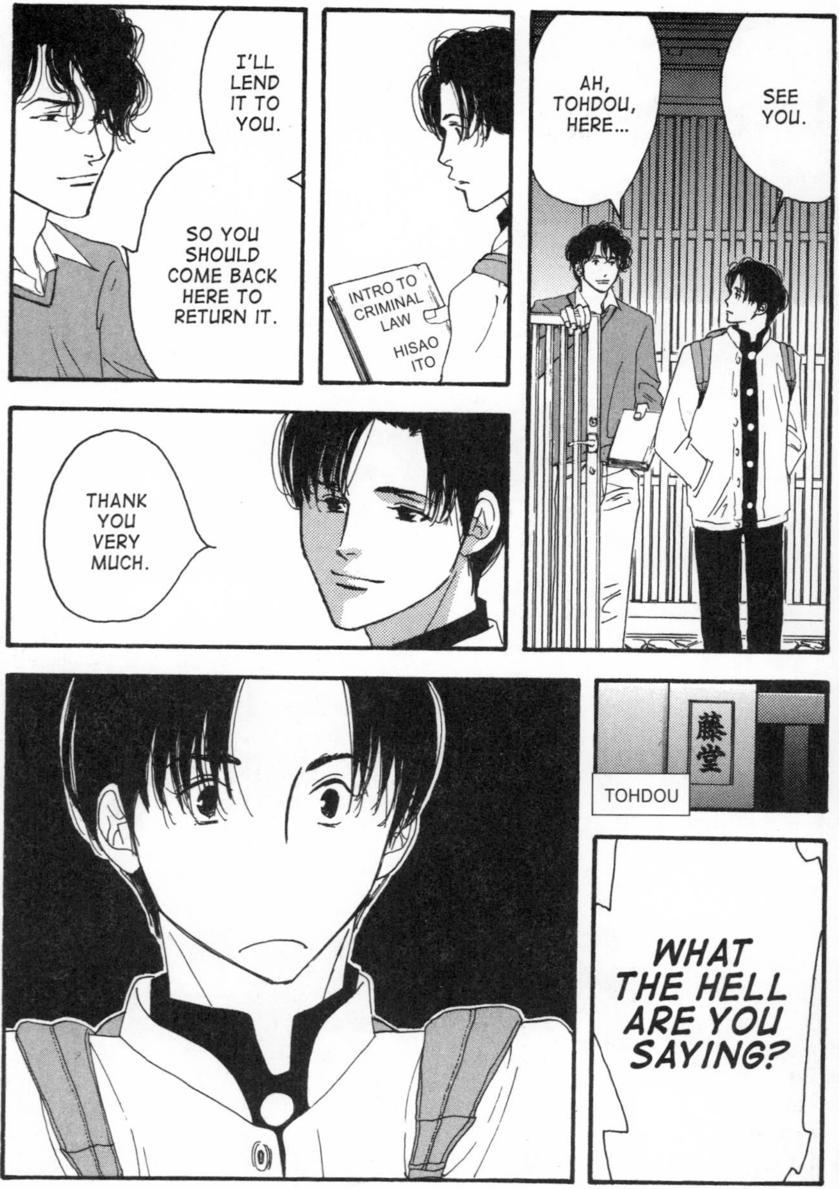
SEE YOU.
AH, TOHDOU, HERE...
INTRO TO CRIMINAL LAW
HISAO ITO
I'LL LEND IT TO YOU.
SO YOU SHOULD COME BACK HERE TO RETURN IT.
THANK YOU VERY MUCH.
藤堂
TOHDOU
WHAT THE HELL ARE YOU SAYING?

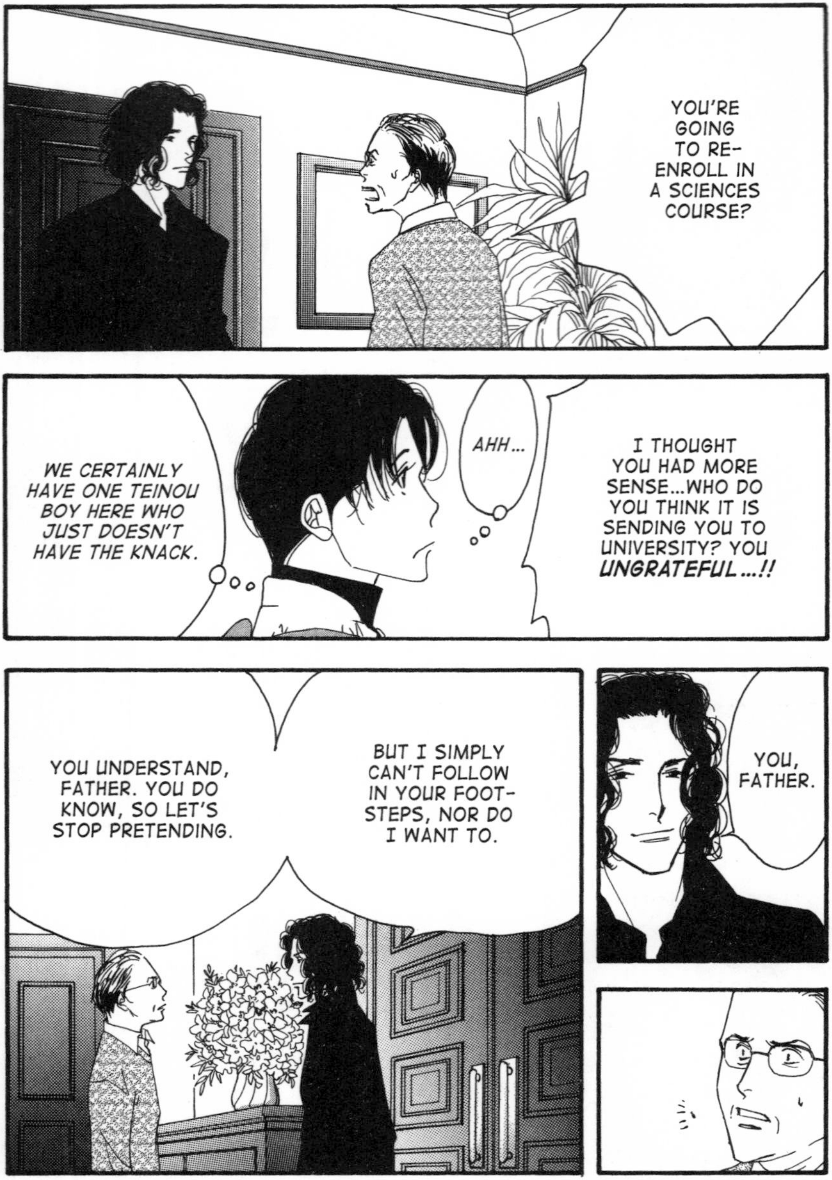
YOU'RE GOING TO RE-ENROLL IN A SCIENCES COURSE?
I THOUGHT YOU HAD MORE SENSE...WHO DO YOU THINK IT IS SENDING YOU TO UNIVERSITY? YOU UNGRATEFUL...!!
AHH...
WE CERTAINLY HAVE ONE TEINOU BOY HERE WHO JUST DOESN'T HAVE THE KNACK.
YOU, FATHER.
BUT I SIMPLY CAN'T FOLLOW IN YOUR FOOT-STEPS, NOR DO I WANT TO.
YOU UNDERSTAND, FATHER. YOU DO KNOW, SO LET'S STOP PRETENDING.

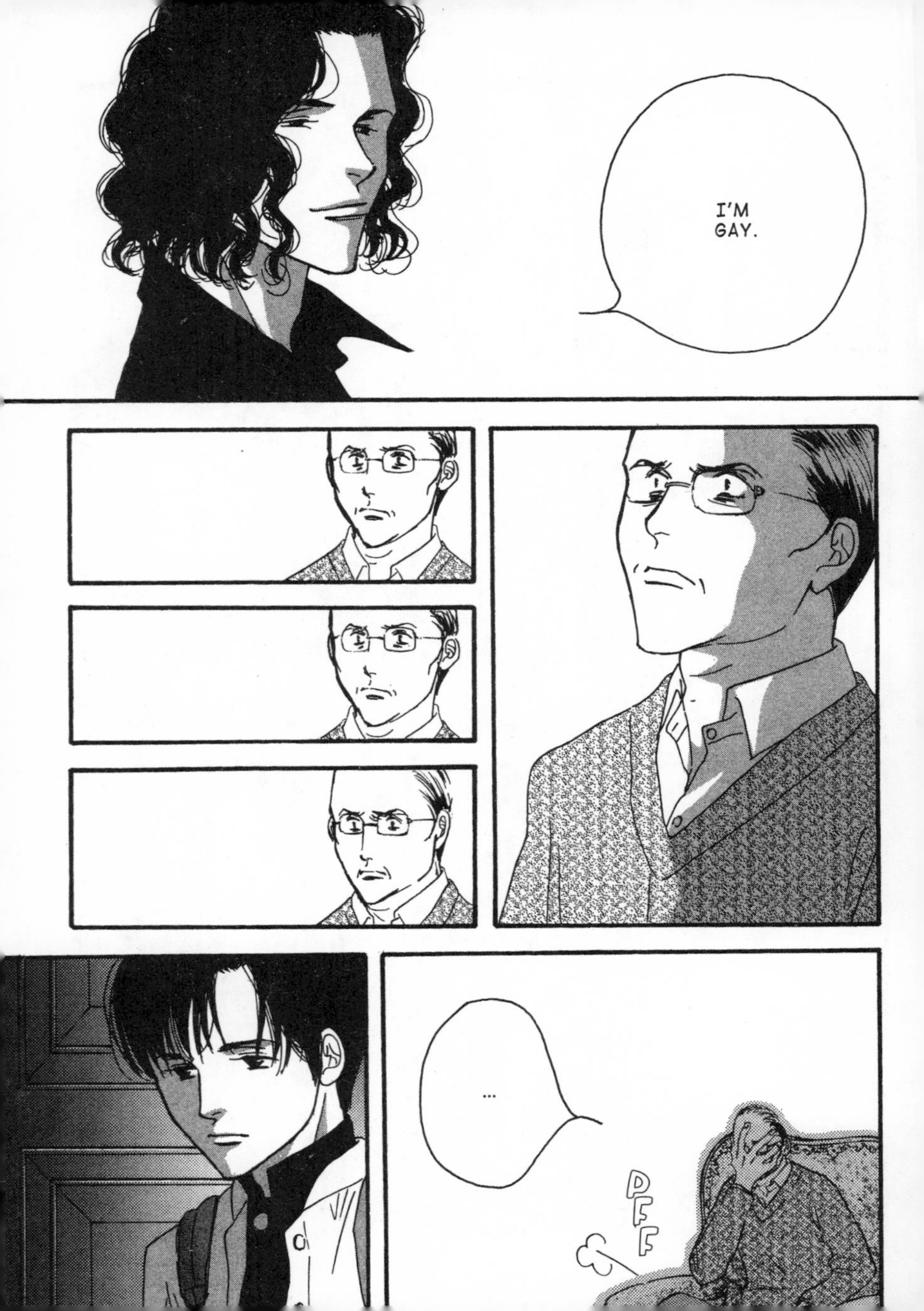
I'M GAY.
...
PFF

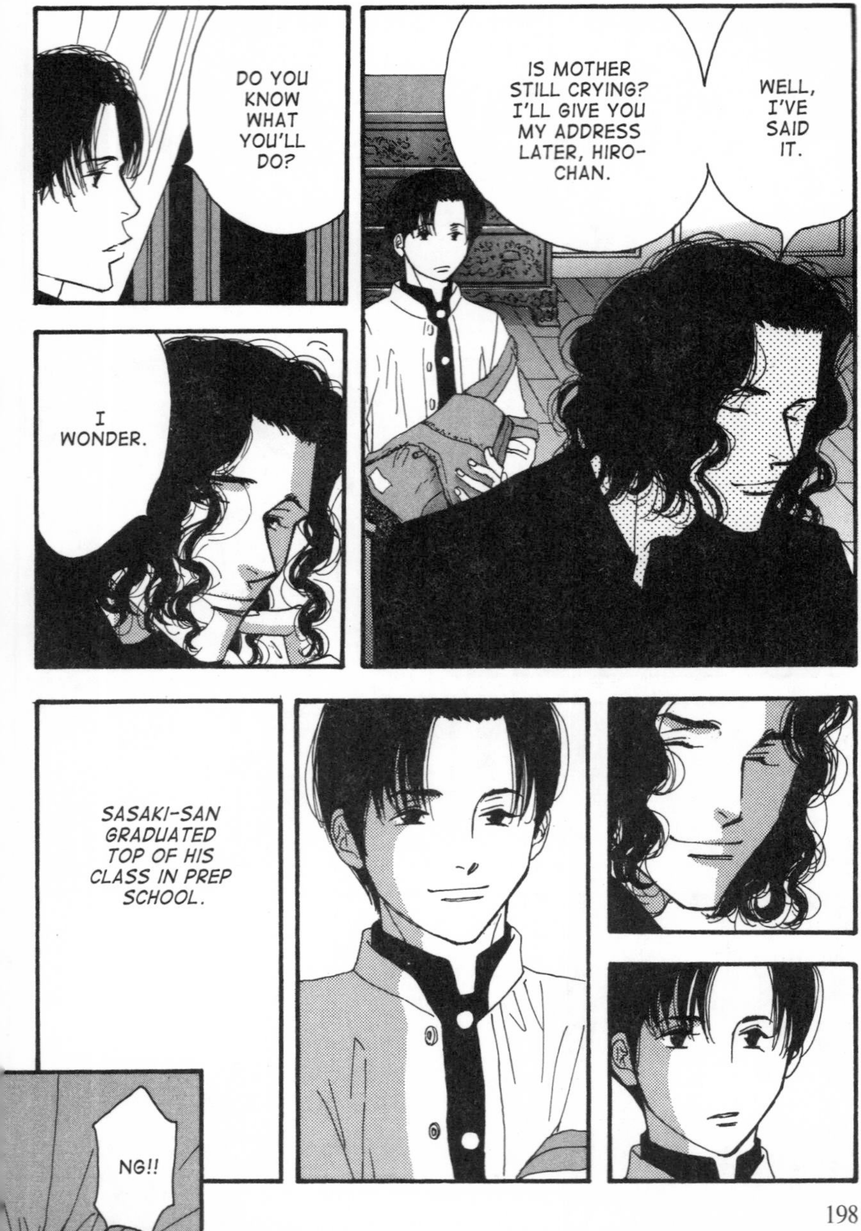
WELL, I'VE SAID IT.
IS MOTHER STILL CRYING? I'LL GIVE YOU MY ADDRESS LATER, HIRO-CHAN.
DO YOU KNOW WHAT YOU'LL DO?
I WONDER.
SASAKI-SAN GRADUATED TOP OF HIS CLASS IN PREP SCHOOL.
NG!!

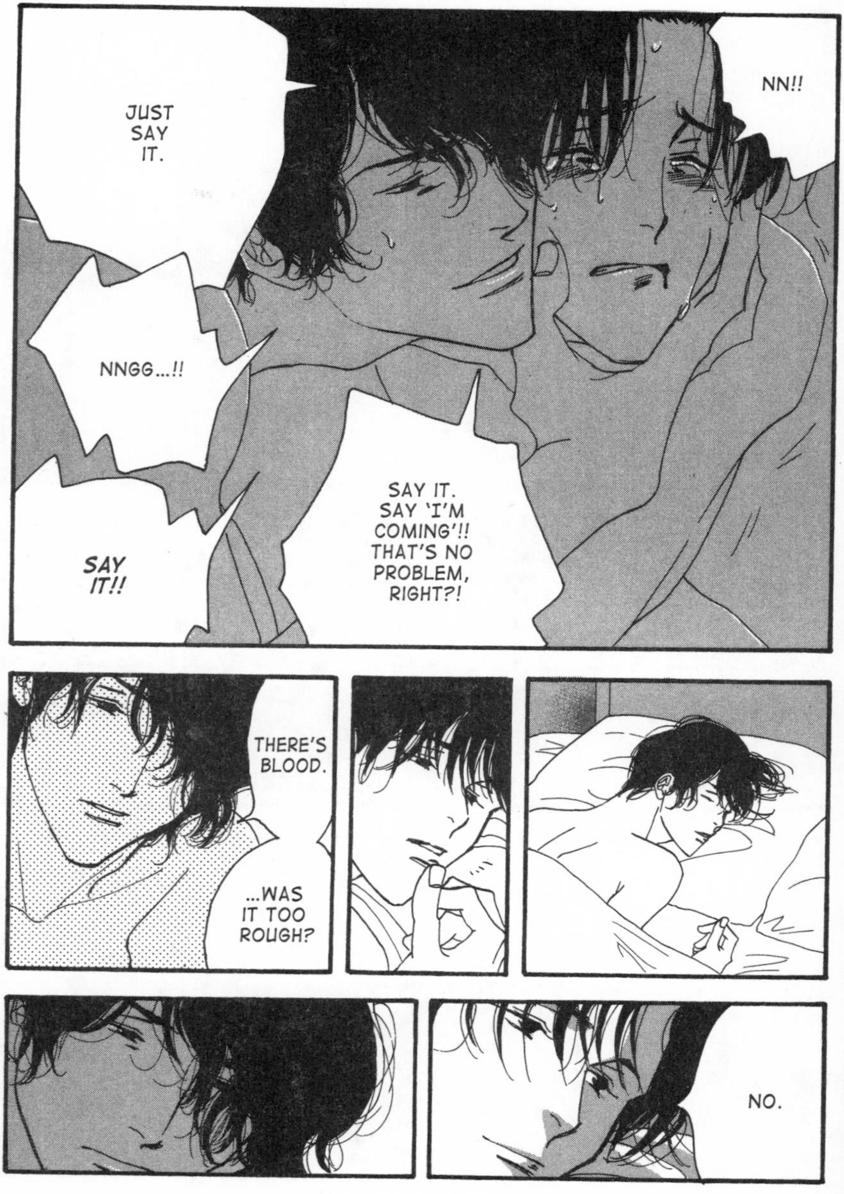
NN!!
JUST SAY IT.
NNGG...!!
SAY IT. SAY 'I'M COMING'!! THAT'S NO PROBLEM, RIGHT?!
SAY IT!!
THERE'S BLOOD.
...WAS IT TOO ROUGH?
NO.

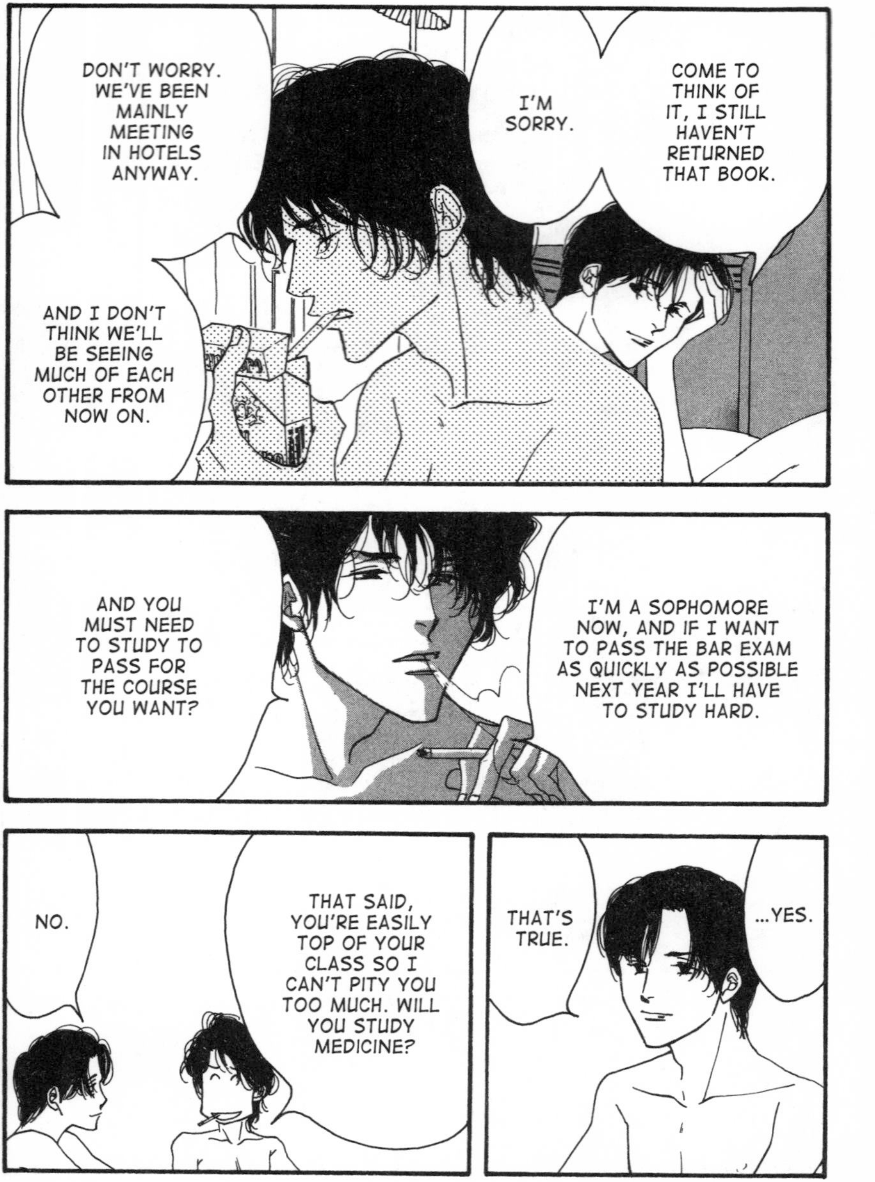
COME TO THINK OF IT, I STILL HAVEN'T RETURNED THAT BOOK.
I'M SORRY.
DON'T WORRY. WE'VE BEEN MAINLY MEETING IN HOTELS ANYWAY.
AND I DON'T THINK WE'LL BE SEEING MUCH OF EACH OTHER FROM NOW ON.
I'M A SOPHOMORE NOW, AND IF I WANT TO PASS THE BAR EXAM AS QUICKLY AS POSSIBLE NEXT YEAR I'LL HAVE TO STUDY HARD.
AND YOU MUST NEED TO STUDY TO PASS FOR THE COURSE YOU WANT?
...YES.
THAT'S TRUE.
THAT SAID, YOU'RE EASILY TOP OF YOUR CLASS SO I CAN'T PITY YOU TOO MUCH. WILL YOU STUDY MEDICINE?
NO.

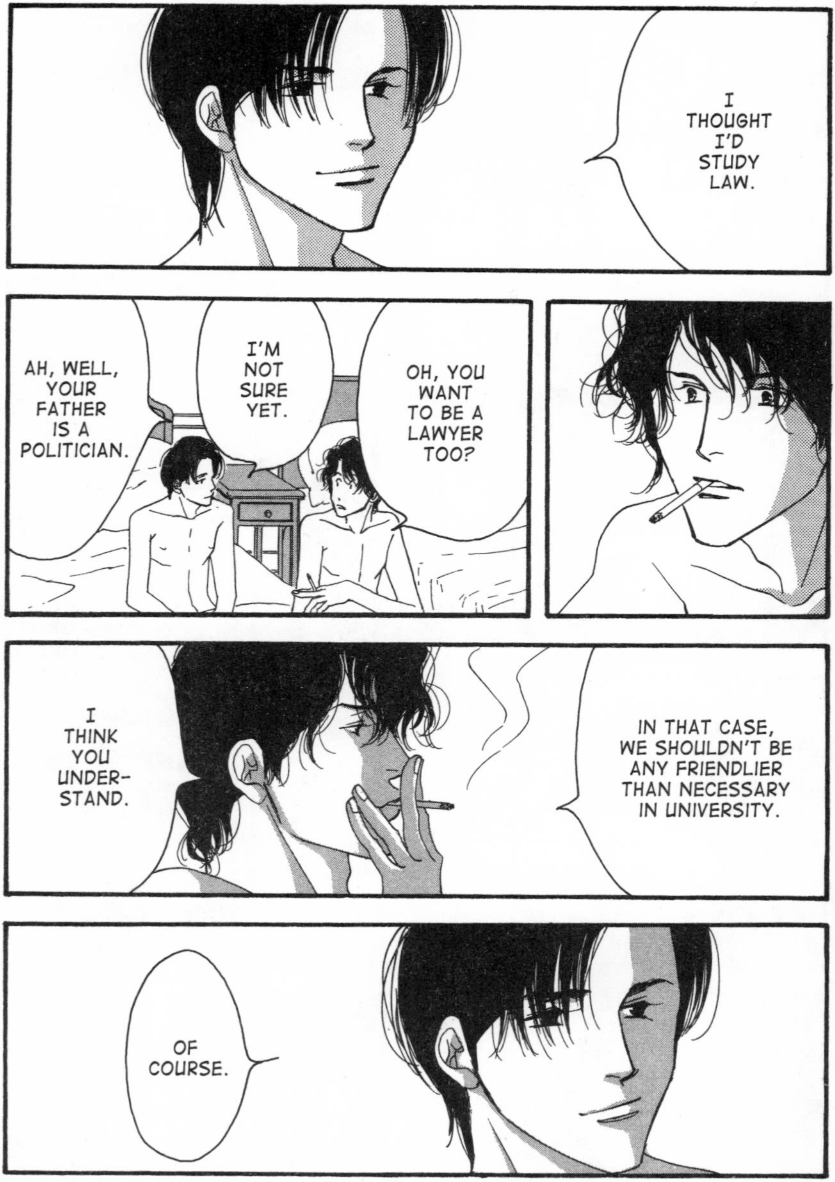
I THOUGHT I'D STUDY LAW.
OH, YOU WANT TO BE A LAWYER TOO?
I'M NOT SURE YET.
AH, WELL, YOUR FATHER IS A POLITICIAN.
IN THAT CASE, WE SHOULDN'T BE ANY FRIENDLIER THAN NECESSARY IN UNIVERSITY.
I THINK YOU UNDERSTAND.
OF COURSE.

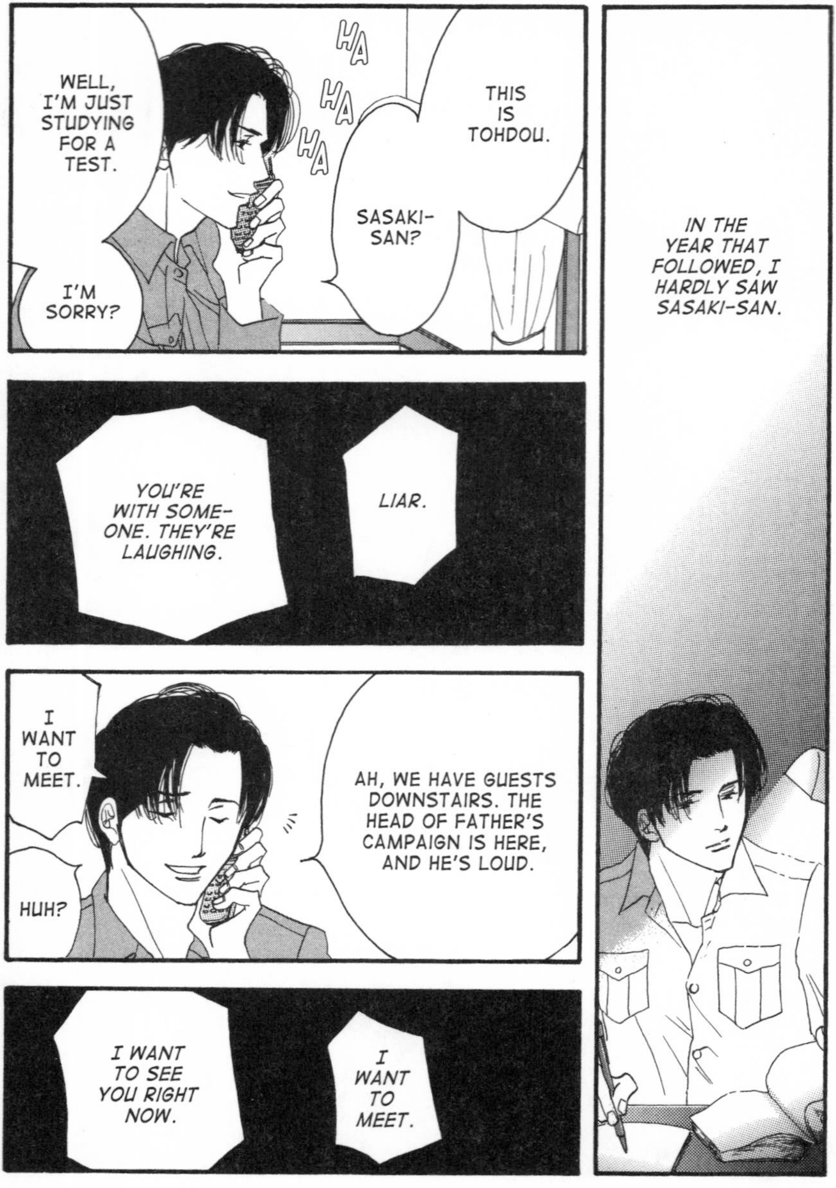
IN THE YEAR THAT FOLLOWED, I HARDLY SAW SASAKI-SAN.
HA HA HA
THIS IS TOHDOU.
SASAKI-SAN?
WELL, I'M JUST STUDYING FOR A TEST.
I'M SORRY?
LIAR.
YOU'RE WITH SOME-ONE. THEY'RE LAUGHING.
AH, WE HAVE GUESTS DOWNSTAIRS. THE HEAD OF FATHER'S CAMPAIGN IS HERE, AND HE'S LOUD.
I WANT TO MEET.
HUH?
I WANT TO MEET.
I WANT TO SEE YOU RIGHT NOW.

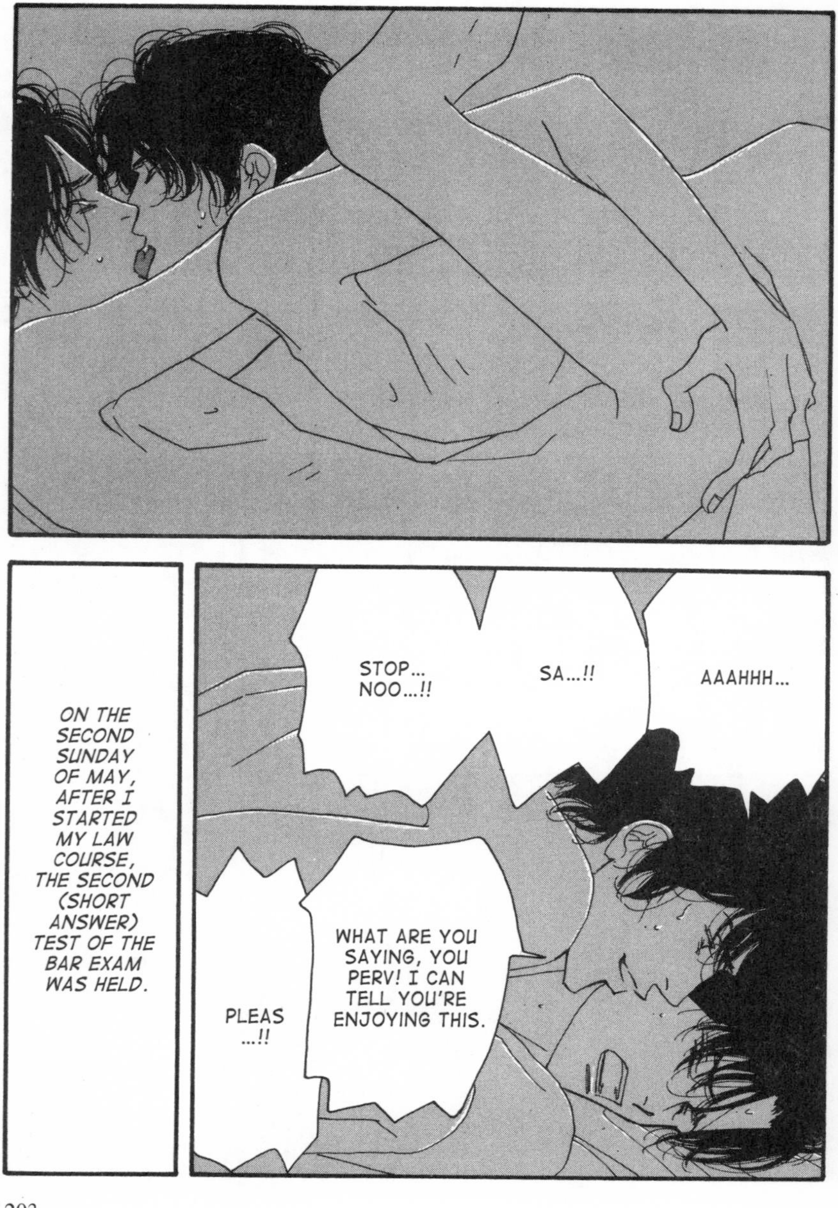
AAAHHH...
SA...!!
STOP... NOO...!!
WHAT ARE YOU SAYING, YOU PERV! I CAN TELL YOU'RE ENJOYING THIS.
PLEAS ...!!
ON THE SECOND SUNDAY OF MAY, AFTER I STARTED MY LAW COURSE, THE SECOND (SHORT ANSWER) TEST OF THE BAR EXAM WAS HELD.

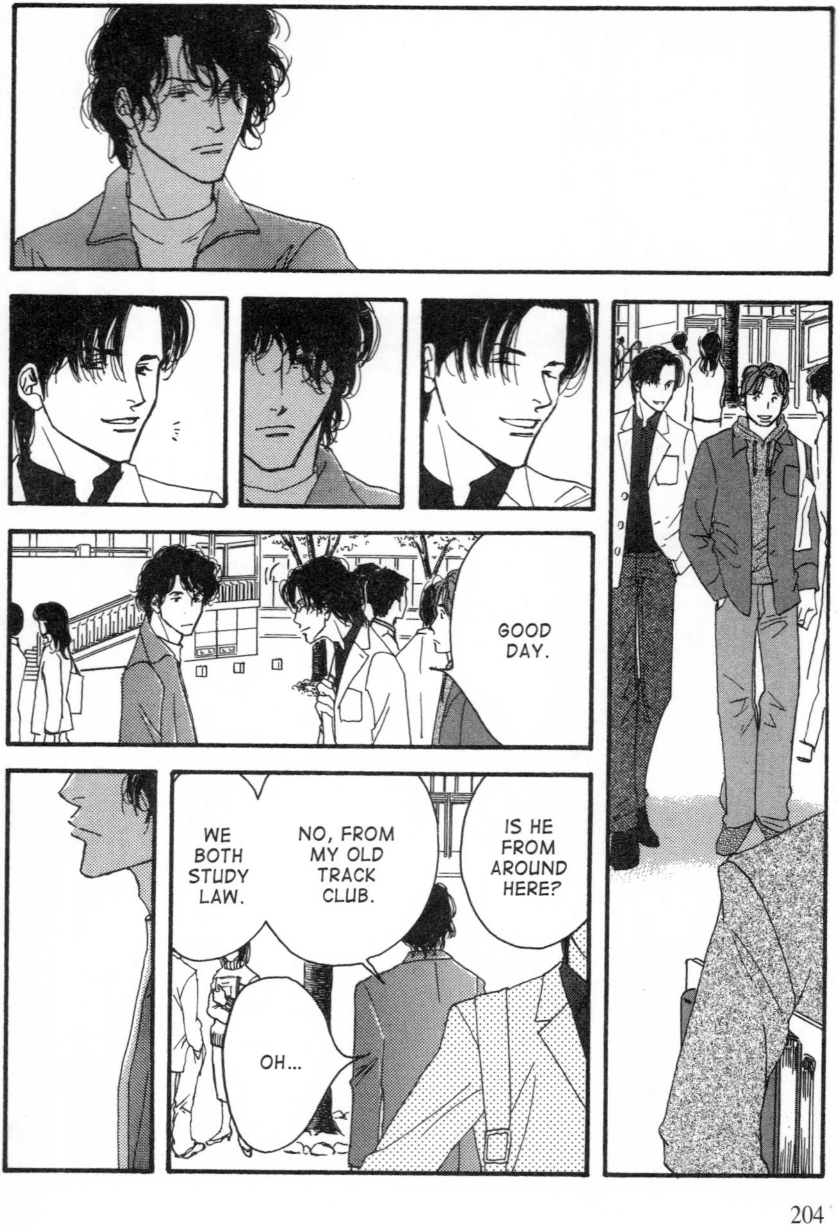
GOOD DAY.
IS HE FROM AROUND HERE?
NO, FROM MY OLD TRACK CLUB.
WE BOTH STUDY LAW.
OH...

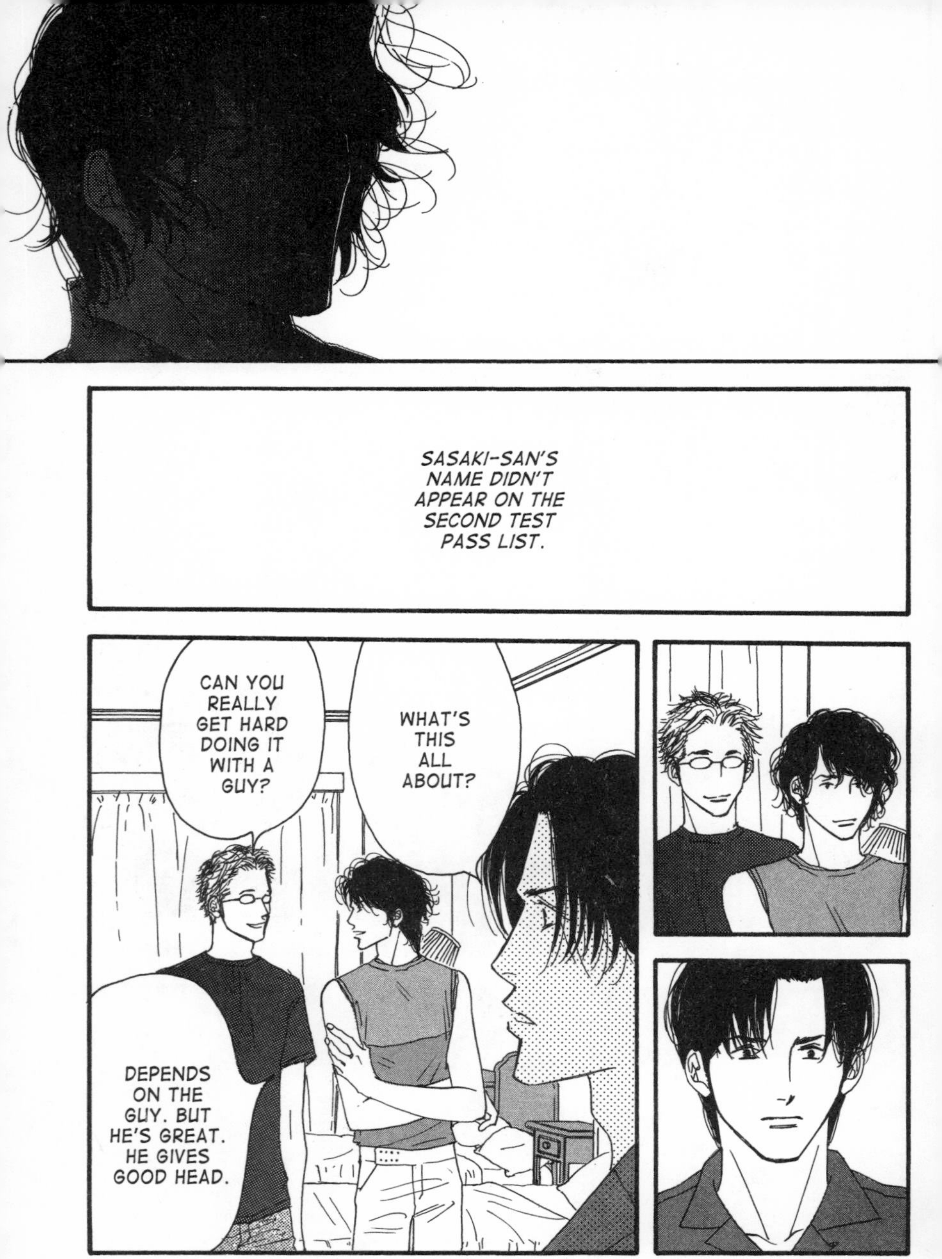
SASAKI-SAN'S NAME DIDN'T APPEAR ON THE SECOND TEST PASS LIST.
WHAT'S THIS ALL ABOUT?
CAN YOU REALLY GET HARD DOING IT WITH A GUY?
DEPENDS ON THE GUY. BUT HE'S GREAT. HE GIVES GOOD HEAD.

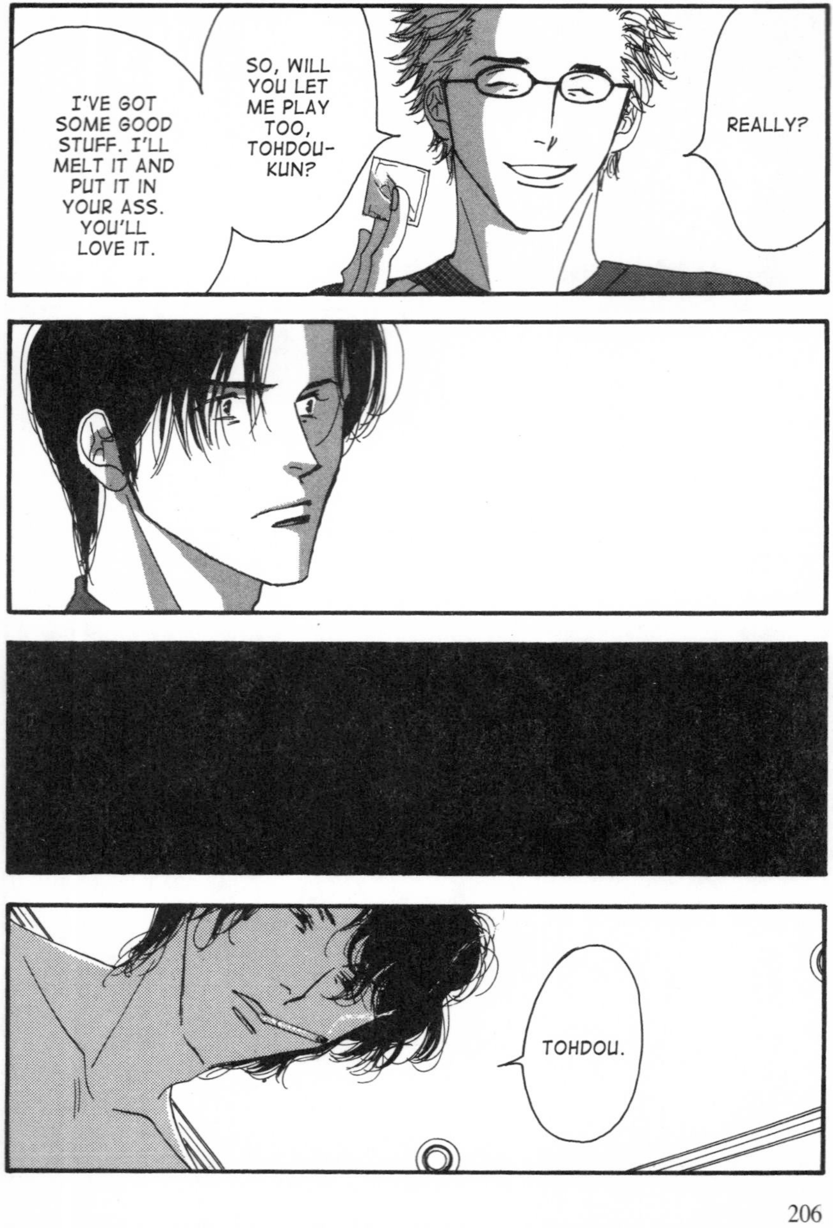
REALLY?
SO, WILL YOU LET ME PLAY TOO, TOHDOU-KUN?
I'VE GOT SOME GOOD STUFF. I'LL MELT IT AND PUT IT IN YOUR ASS. YOU'LL LOVE IT.
TOHDOU.

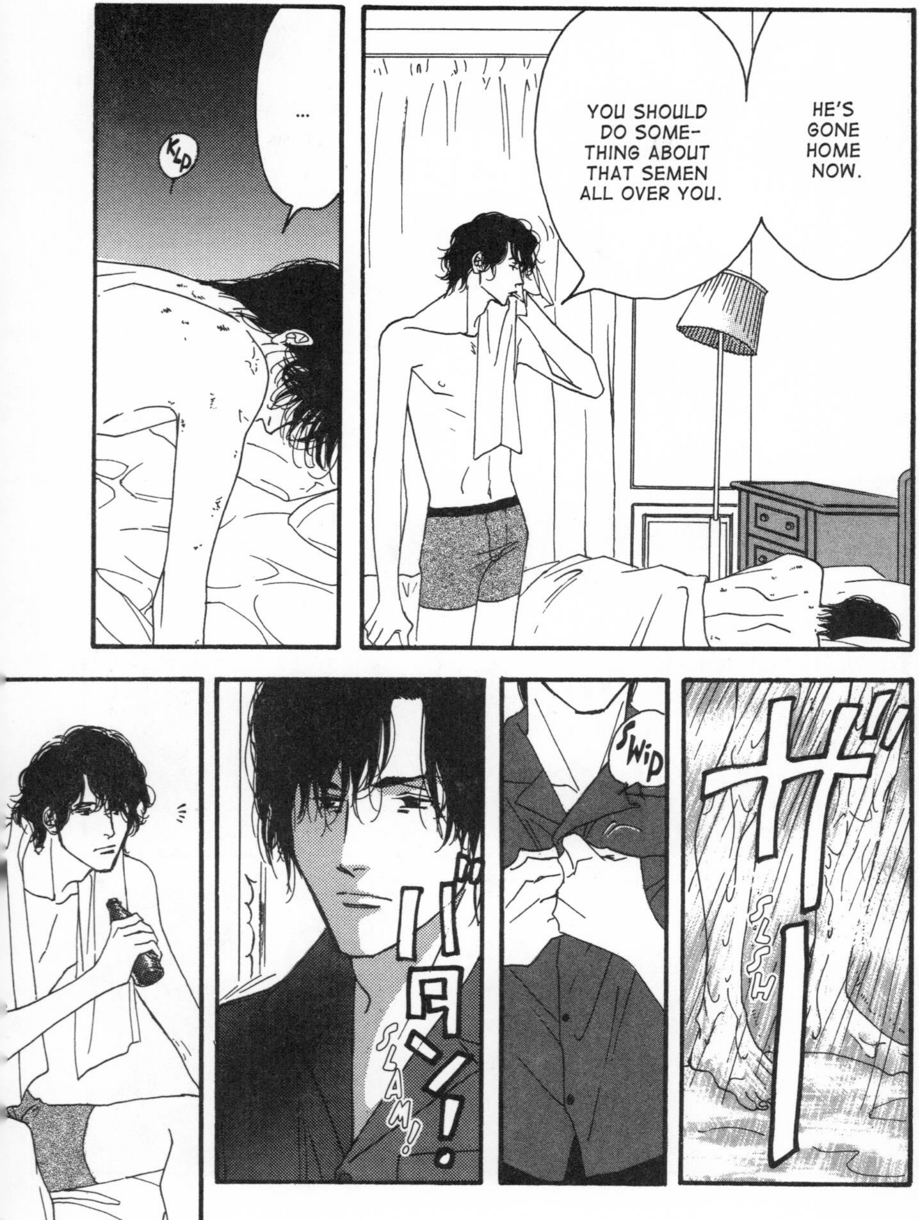
HE'S GONE HOME NOW.
YOU SHOULD DO SOME-THING ABOUT THAT SEMEN ALL OVER YOU.
...
KLP
SLSH
SWIP
SLAM!

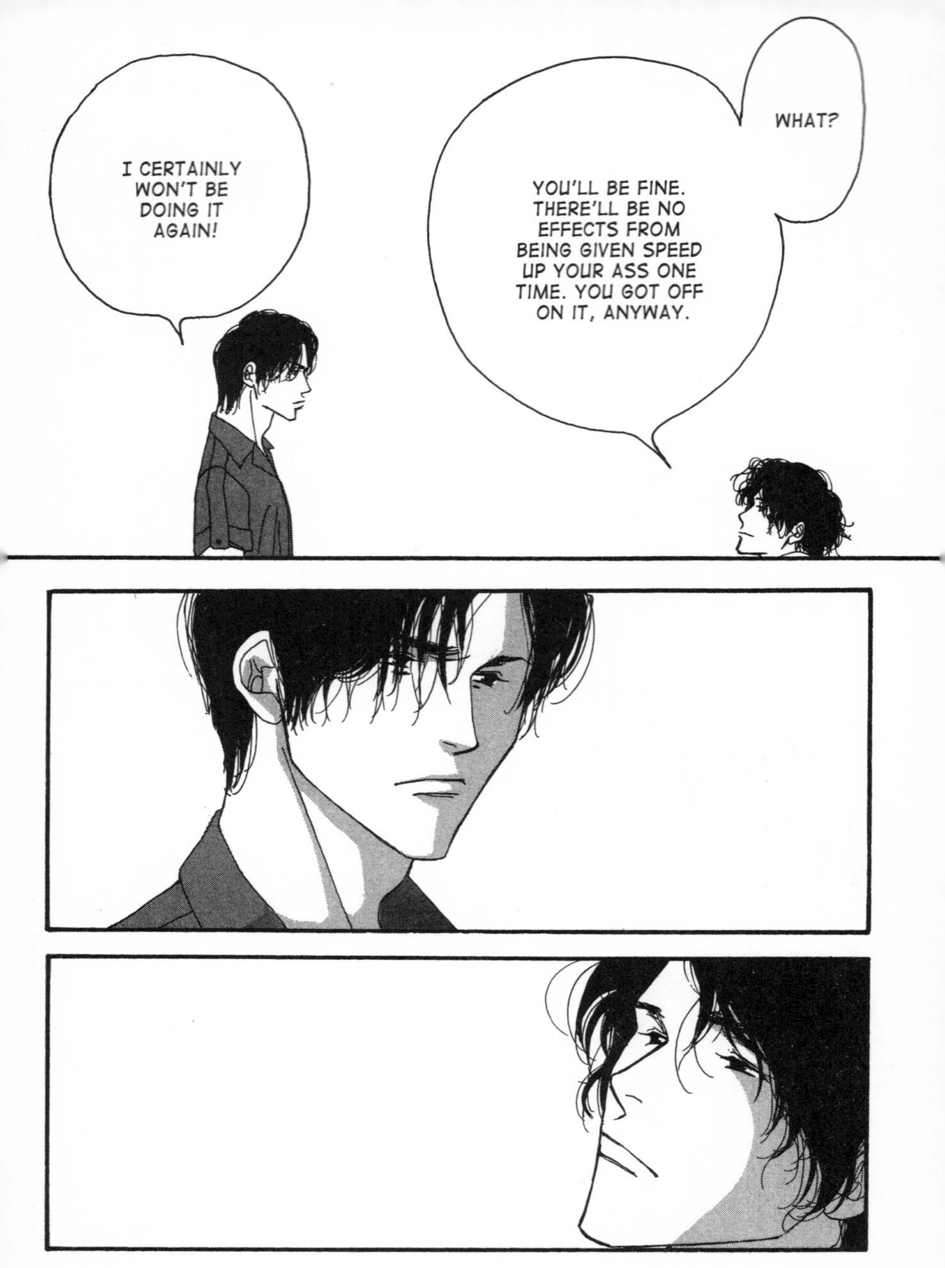
WHAT?
YOU'LL BE FINE. THERE'LL BE NO EFFECTS FROM BEING GIVEN SPEED UP YOUR ASS ONE TIME. YOU GOT OFF ON IT, ANYWAY.
I CERTAINLY WON'T BE DOING IT AGAIN!

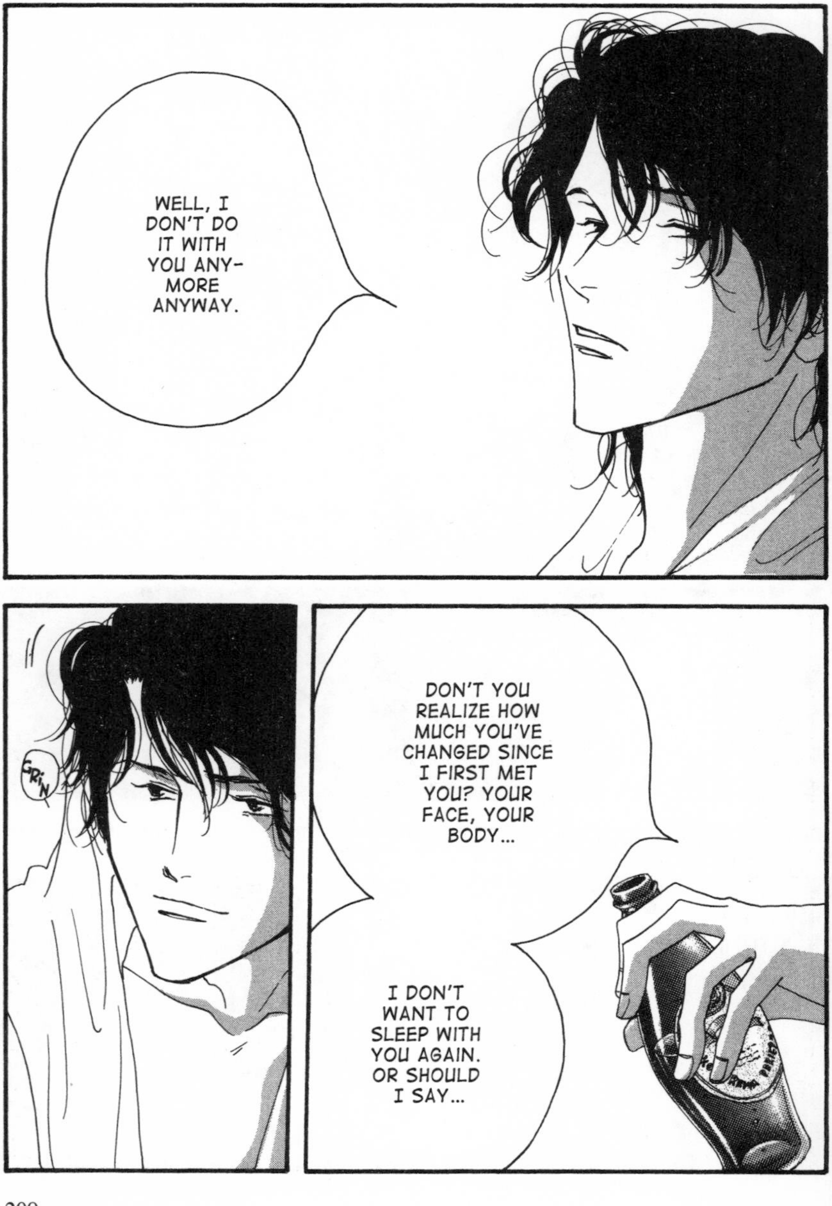
WELL, I DON'T DO IT WITH YOU ANY-MORE ANYWAY.
DON'T YOU REALIZE HOW MUCH YOU'VE CHANGED SINCE I FIRST MET YOU? YOUR FACE, YOUR BODY...
I DON'T WANT TO SLEEP WITH YOU AGAIN. OR SHOULD I SAY...
GRIN

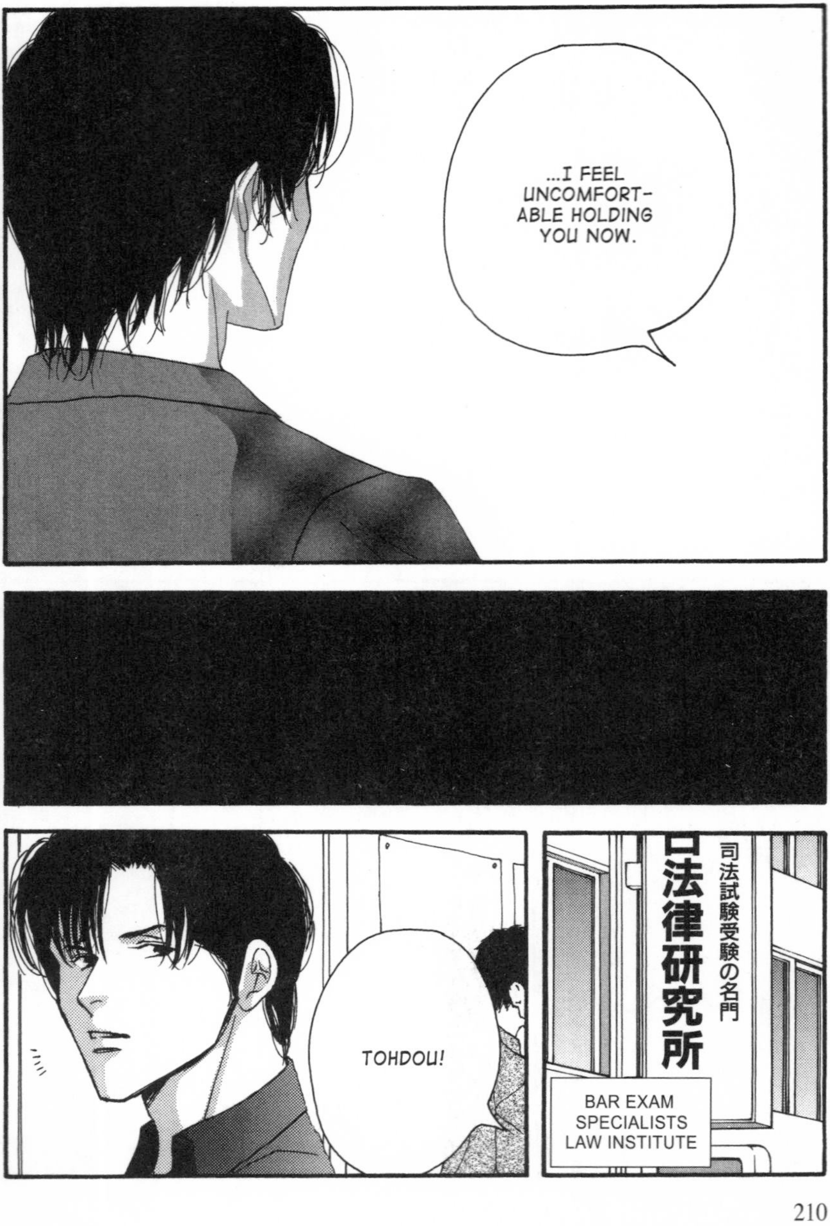
...I FEEL UNCOMFORT-ABLE HOLDING YOU NOW.
司法試験受験の名門
法律研究所
BAR EXAM SPECIALISTS LAW INSTITUTE
TOHDOU!

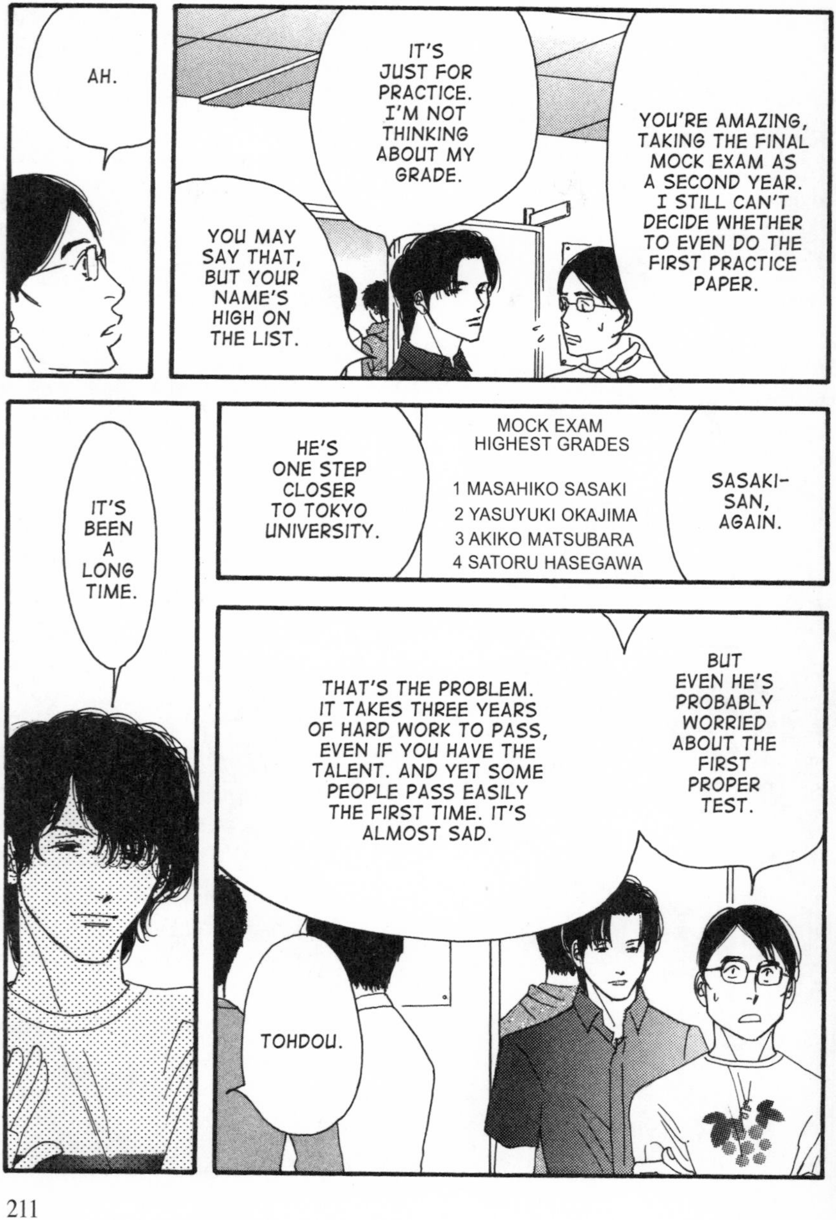
YOU'RE AMAZING, TAKING THE FINAL MOCK EXAM AS A SECOND YEAR. I STILL CAN'T DECIDE WHETHER TO EVEN DO THE FIRST PRACTICE PAPER.
IT'S JUST FOR PRACTICE. I'M NOT THINKING ABOUT MY GRADE.
YOU MAY SAY THAT, BUT YOUR NAME'S HIGH ON THE LIST.
AH.
SASAKI-SAN, AGAIN.
MOCK EXAM HIGHEST GRADES
1 MASAHIKO SASAKI
2 YASUYUKI OKAJIMA
3 AKIKO MATSUBARA
4 SATORU HASEGAWA
HE'S ONE STEP CLOSER TO TOKYO UNIVERSITY.
BUT EVEN HE'S PROBABLY WORRIED ABOUT THE FIRST PROPER TEST.
THAT'S THE PROBLEM. IT TAKES THREE YEARS OF HARD WORK TO PASS, EVEN IF YOU HAVE THE TALENT. AND YET SOME PEOPLE PASS EASILY THE FIRST TIME. IT'S ALMOST SAD.
TOHDOU.
IT'S BEEN A LONG TIME.

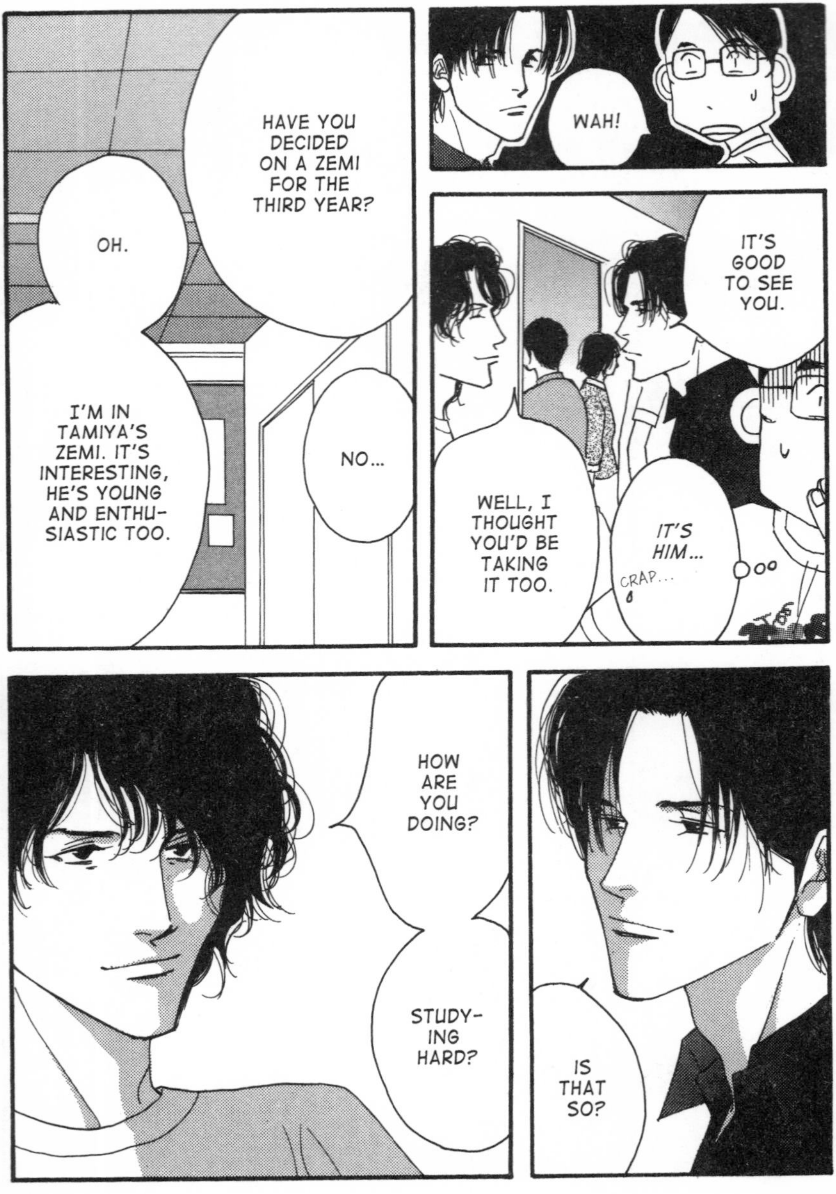
WAH!
IT'S GOOD TO SEE YOU.
IT'S HIM...
CRAP...
WELL, I THOUGHT YOU'D BE TAKING IT TOO.
HAVE YOU DECIDED ON A ZEMI FOR THE THIRD YEAR?
NO...
OH.
I'M IN TAMIYA'S ZEMI. IT'S INTERESTING, HE'S YOUNG AND ENTHU-SIASTIC TOO.
IS THAT SO?
HOW ARE YOU DOING?
STUDY-ING HARD?

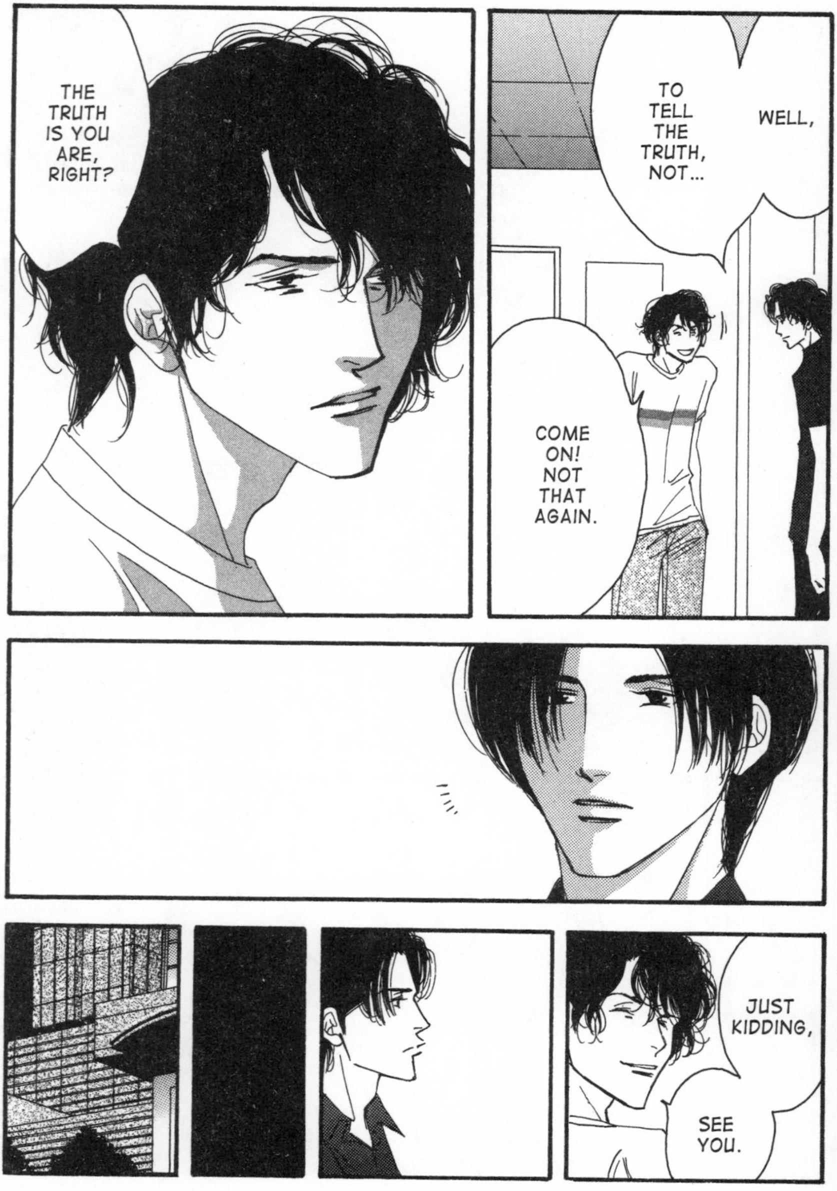
WELL,
TO TELL THE TRUTH, NOT...
COME ON! NOT THAT AGAIN.
THE TRUTH IS YOU ARE, RIGHT?
JUST KIDDING,
SEE YOU.

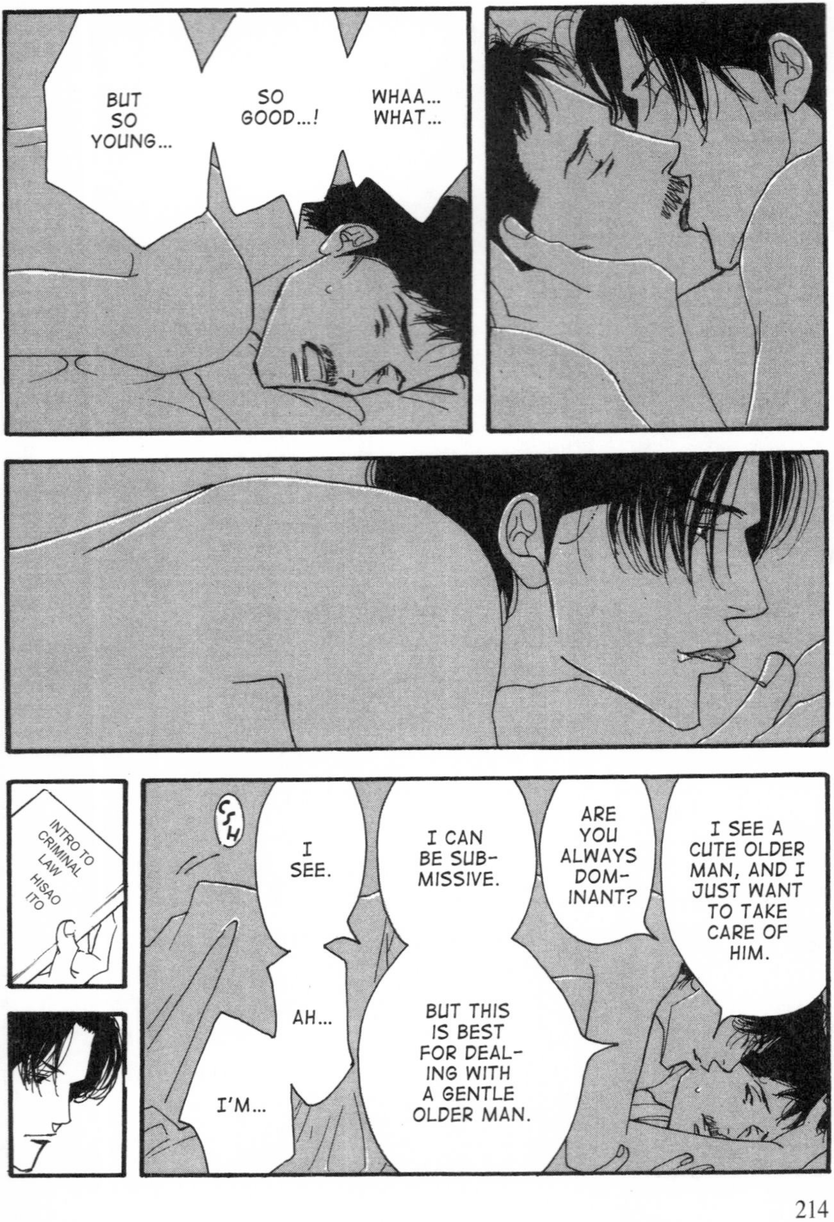
WHAA... WHAT...
SO GOOD...!
BUT SO YOUNG...
I SEE A CUTE OLDER MAN, AND I JUST WANT TO TAKE CARE OF HIM.
ARE YOU ALWAYS DOM-INANT?
I CAN BE SUB-MISSIVE.
I SEE.
CSH
BUT THIS IS BEST FOR DEAL-ING WITH A GENTLE OLDER MAN.
AH...
I'M...
INTRO TO CRIMINAL LAW
HISAO ITO

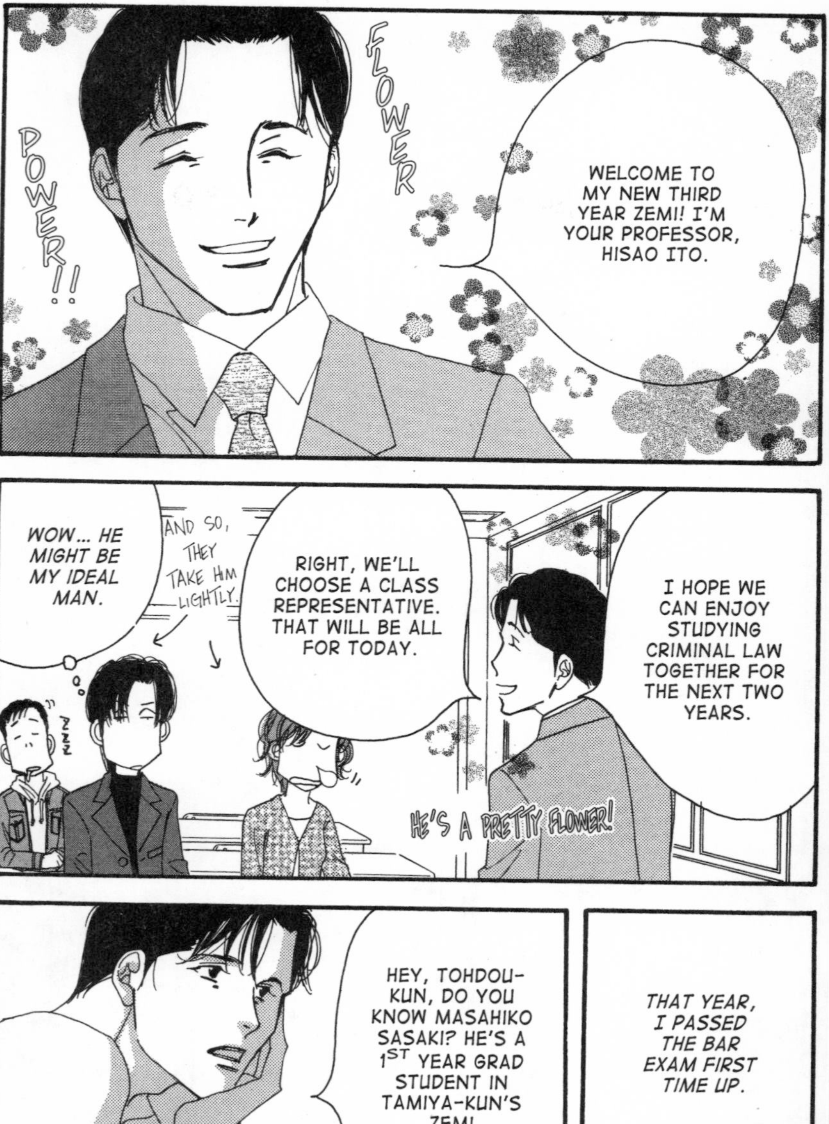
WELCOME TO MY NEW THIRD YEAR ZEMI! I'M YOUR PROFESSOR, HISAO ITO.
FLOWER
POWER!!
I HOPE WE CAN ENJOY STUDYING CRIMINAL LAW TOGETHER FOR THE NEXT TWO YEARS.
HE'S A PRETTY FLOWER!
RIGHT, WE'LL CHOOSE A CLASS REPRESENTATIVE. THAT WILL BE ALL FOR TODAY.
AND SO, THEY TAKE HIM LIGHTLY.
WOW... HE MIGHT BE MY IDEAL MAN.
ZZZ
THAT YEAR, I PASSED THE BAR EXAM FIRST TIME UP.
HEY, TOHDOU-KUN, DO YOU KNOW MASAHIKO SASAKI? HE'S A 1ST YEAR GRAD STUDENT IN TAMIYA-KUN'S ZEMI.

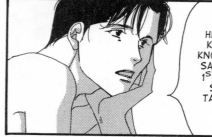

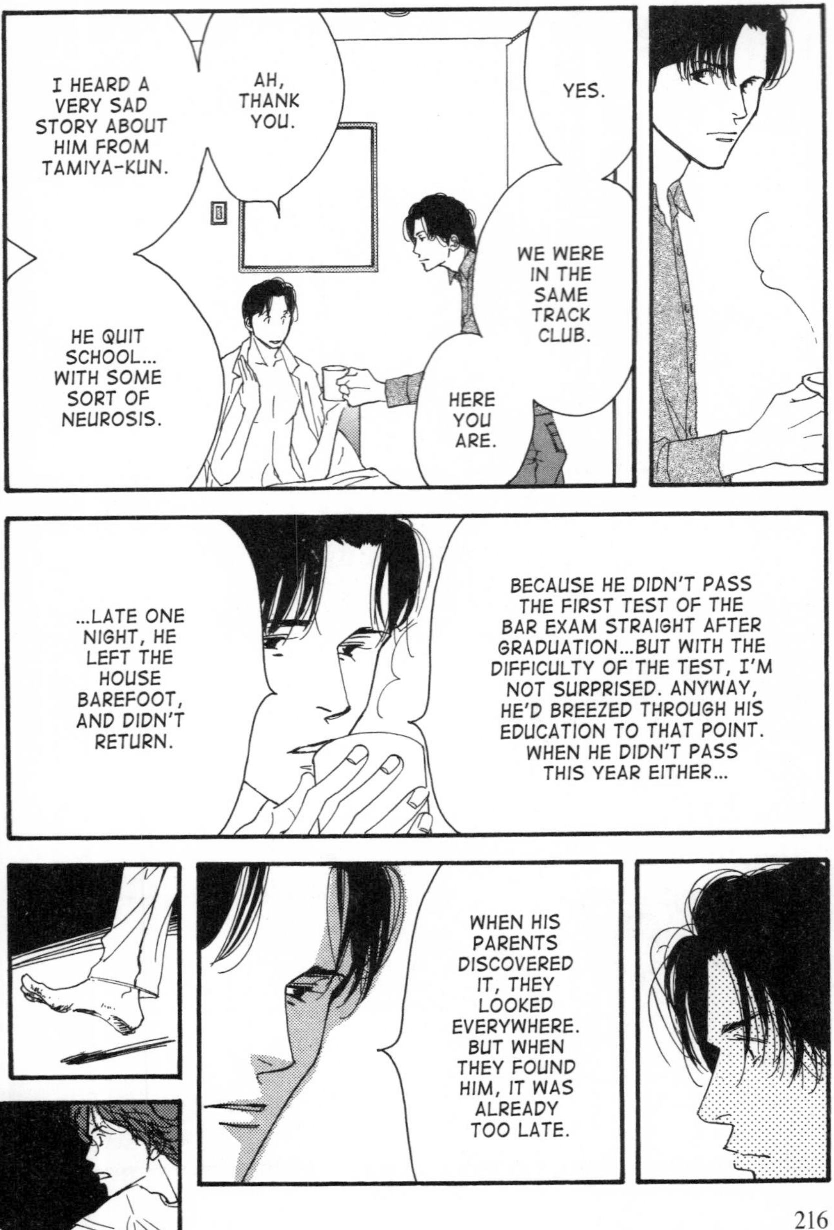
YES.
AH, THANK YOU.
I HEARD A VERY SAD STORY ABOUT HIM FROM TAMIYA-KUN.
WE WERE IN THE SAME TRACK CLUB.
HERE YOU ARE.
HE QUIT SCHOOL... WITH SOME SORT OF NEUROSIS.
BECAUSE HE DIDN'T PASS THE FIRST TEST OF THE BAR EXAM STRAIGHT AFTER GRADUATION...BUT WITH THE DIFFICULTY OF THE TEST, I'M NOT SURPRISED. ANYWAY, HE'D BREEZED THROUGH HIS EDUCATION TO THAT POINT. WHEN HE DIDN'T PASS THIS YEAR EITHER...
...LATE ONE NIGHT, HE LEFT THE HOUSE BAREFOOT, AND DIDN'T RETURN.
WHEN HIS PARENTS DISCOVERED IT, THEY LOOKED EVERYWHERE. BUT WHEN THEY FOUND HIM, IT WAS ALREADY TOO LATE.

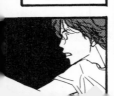

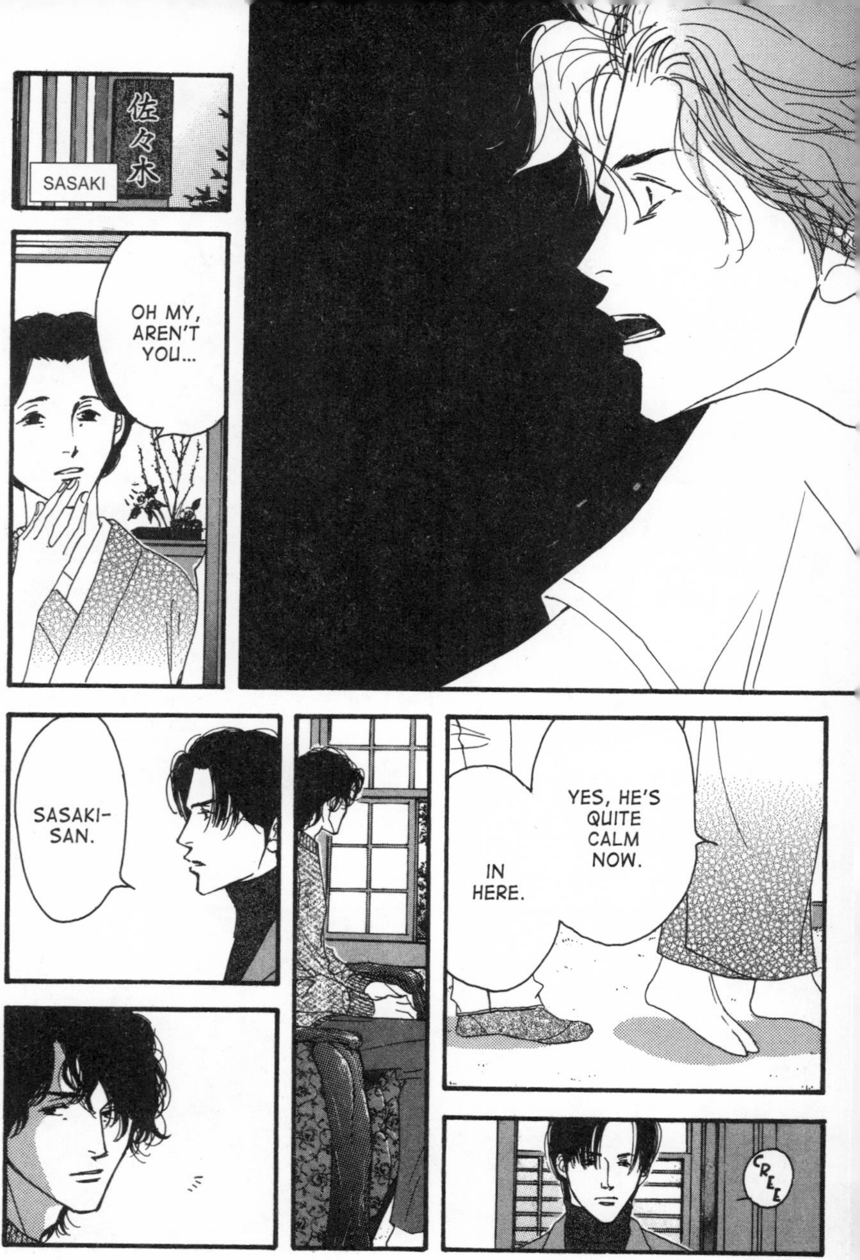
佐々木
SASAKI
OH MY, AREN'T YOU...
YES, HE'S QUITE CALM NOW.
IN HERE.
CREE
SASAKI-SAN.

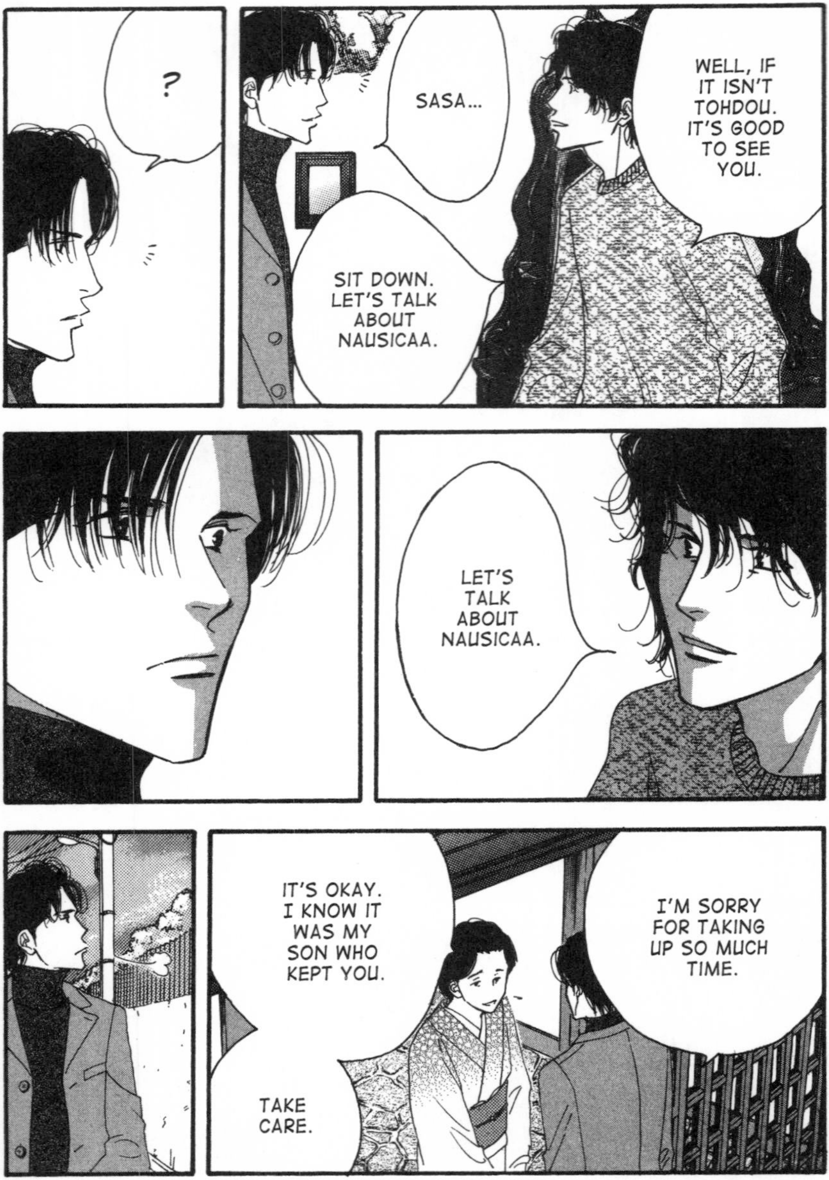
WELL, IF IT ISN'T TOHDOU. IT'S GOOD TO SEE YOU.
SASA...
SIT DOWN. LET'S TALK ABOUT NAUSICAA.
?
LET'S TALK ABOUT NAUSICAA.
I'M SORRY FOR TAKING UP SO MUCH TIME.
IT'S OKAY. I KNOW IT WAS MY SON WHO KEPT YOU.
TAKE CARE.

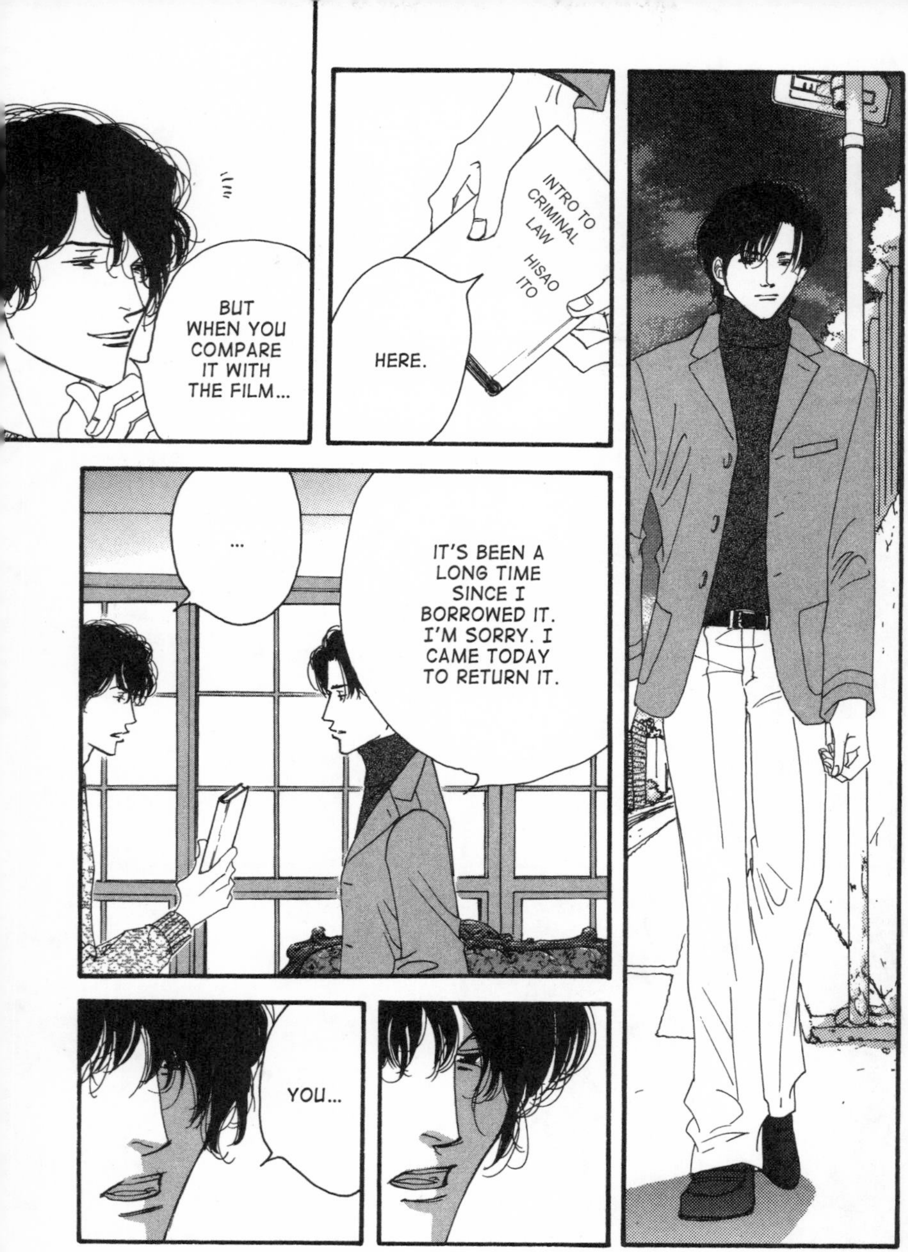
INTRO TO CRIMINAL LAW HISAO ITO
HERE.
BUT WHEN YOU COMPARE IT WITH THE FILM...
IT'S BEEN A LONG TIME SINCE I BORROWED IT. I'M SORRY. I CAME TODAY TO RETURN IT.
...
YOU...

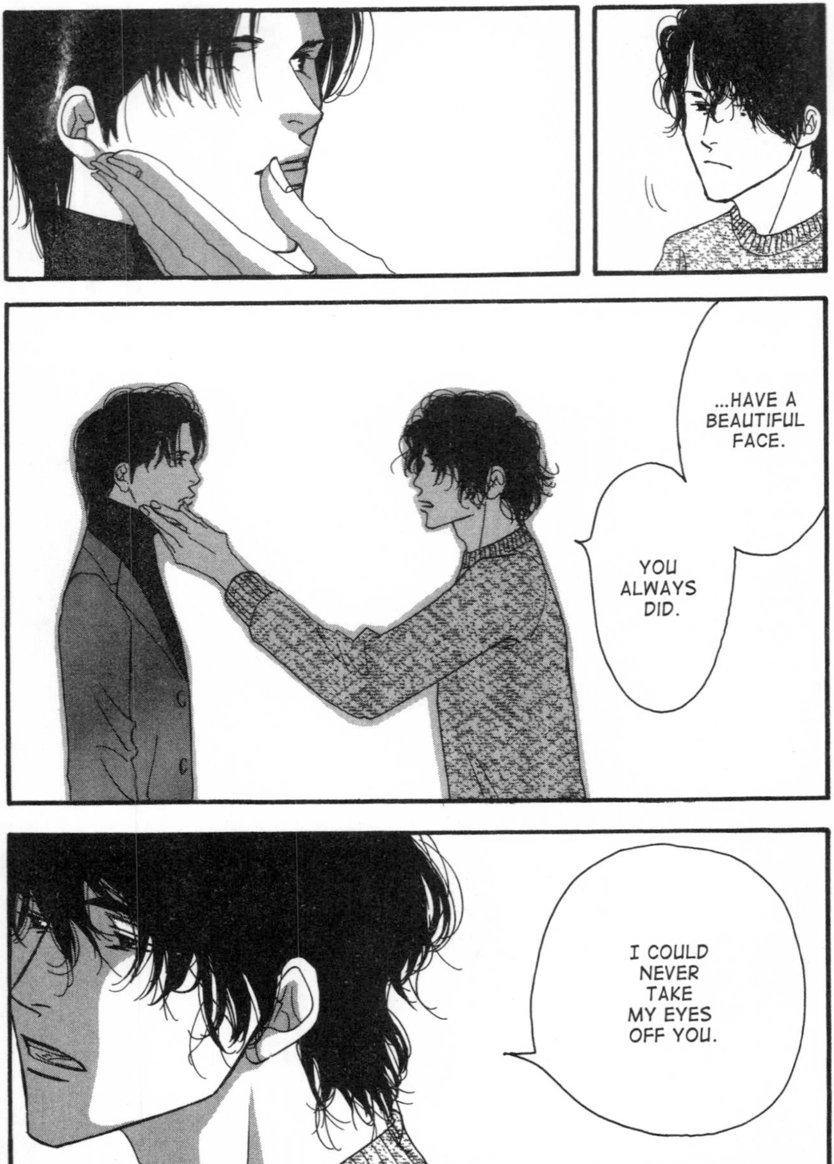
...HAVE A BEAUTIFUL FACE.
YOU ALWAYS DID.
I COULD NEVER TAKE MY EYES OFF YOU.

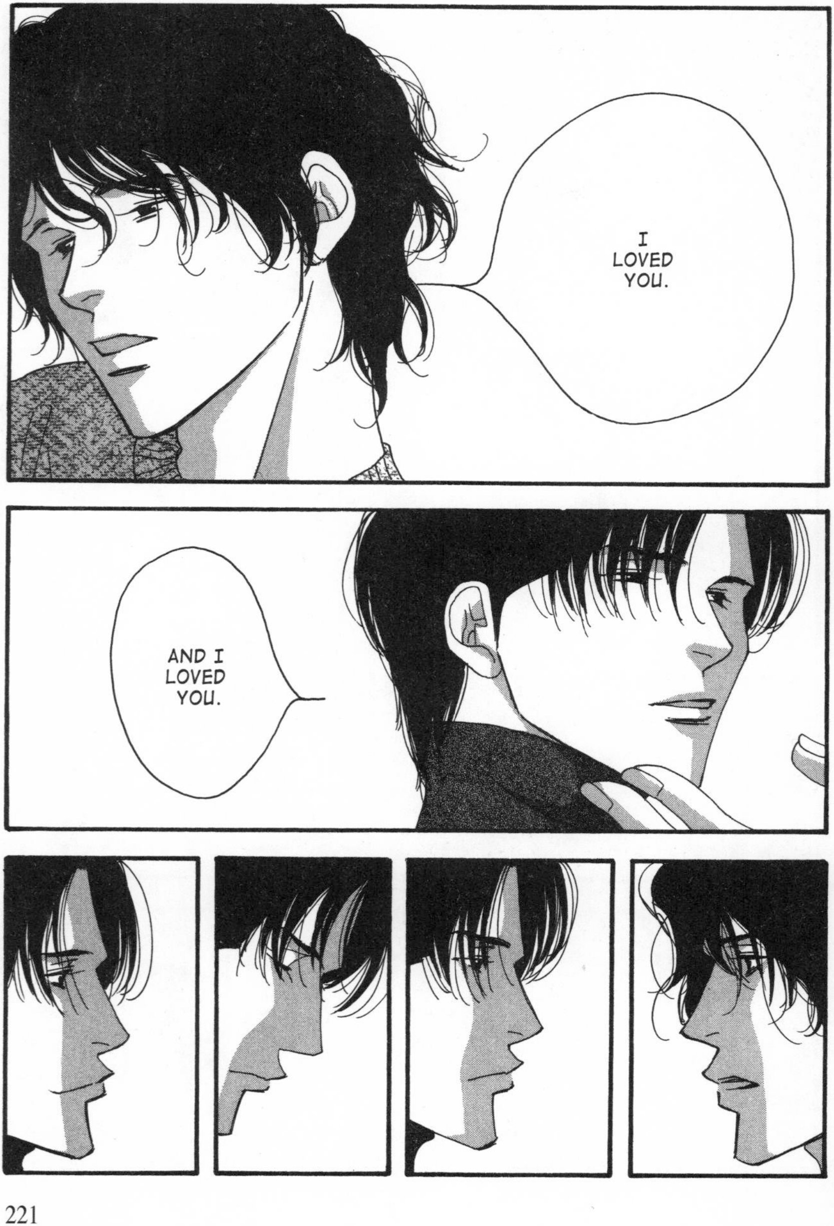
I LOVED YOU.
AND I LOVED YOU.

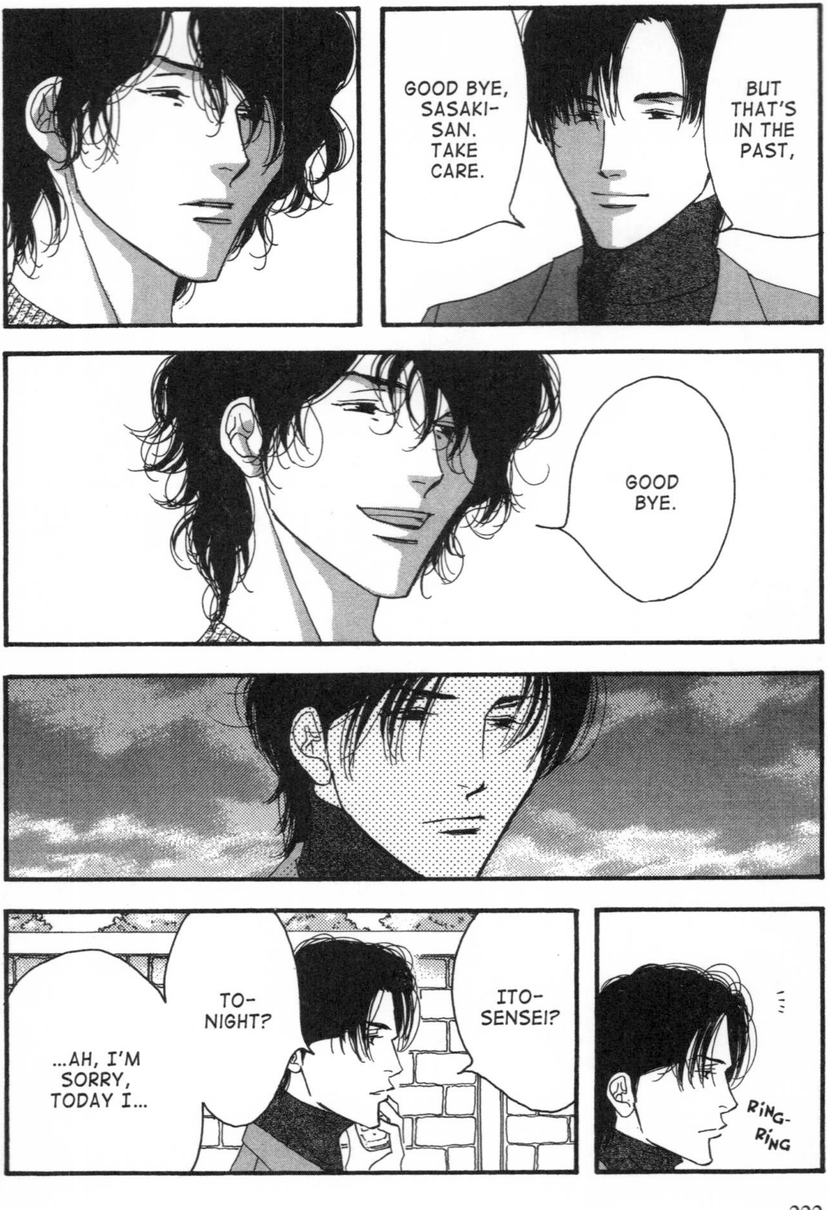
BUT THAT'S IN THE PAST,
GOOD BYE, SASAKI-SAN. TAKE CARE.
GOOD BYE.
...
RING-RING
ITO-SENSEI?
TO-NIGHT?
...AH, I'M SORRY, TODAY I...

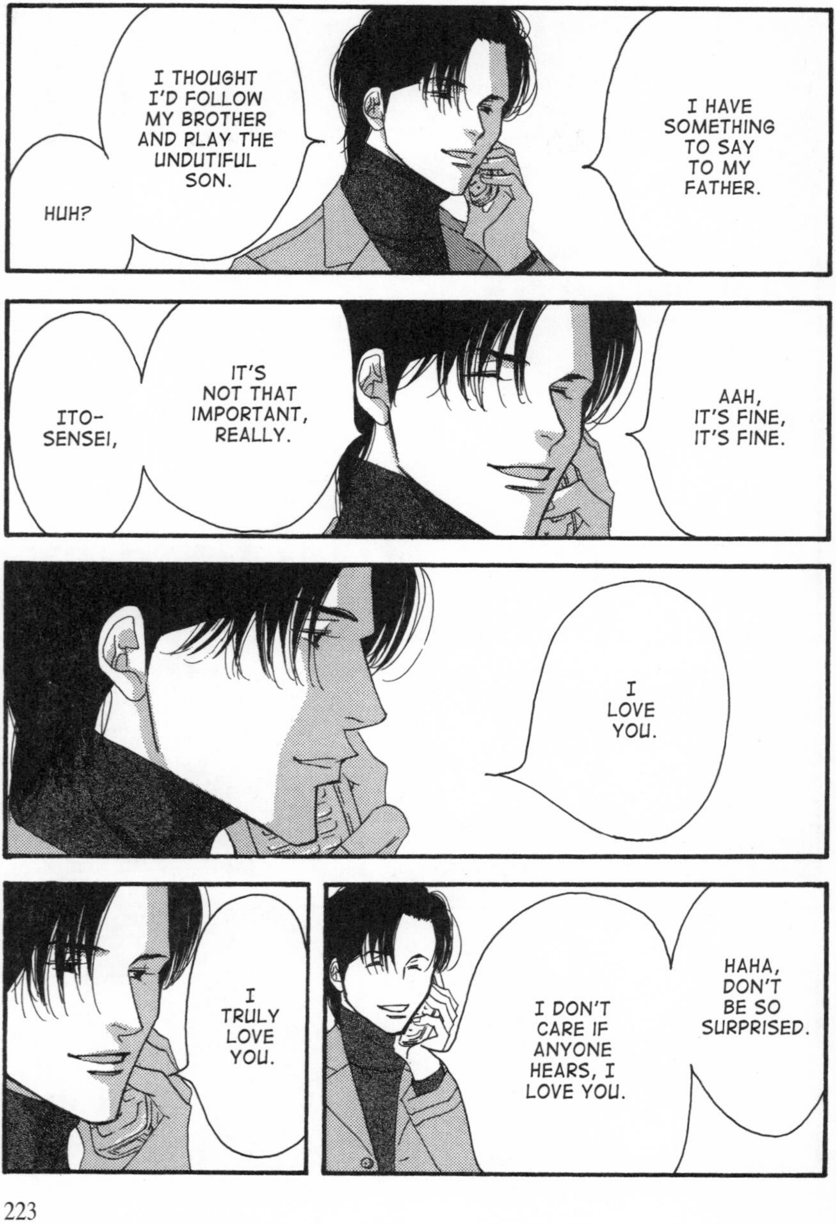
I HAVE SOMETHING TO SAY TO MY FATHER.
I THOUGHT I'D FOLLOW MY BROTHER AND PLAY THE UNDUTIFUL SON.
HUH?
AAH, IT'S FINE, IT'S FINE.
IT'S NOT THAT IMPORTANT, REALLY.
ITO-SENSEI,
I LOVE YOU.
HAHA, DON'T BE SO SURPRISED.
I DON'T CARE IF ANYONE HEARS, I LOVE YOU.
I TRULY LOVE YOU.

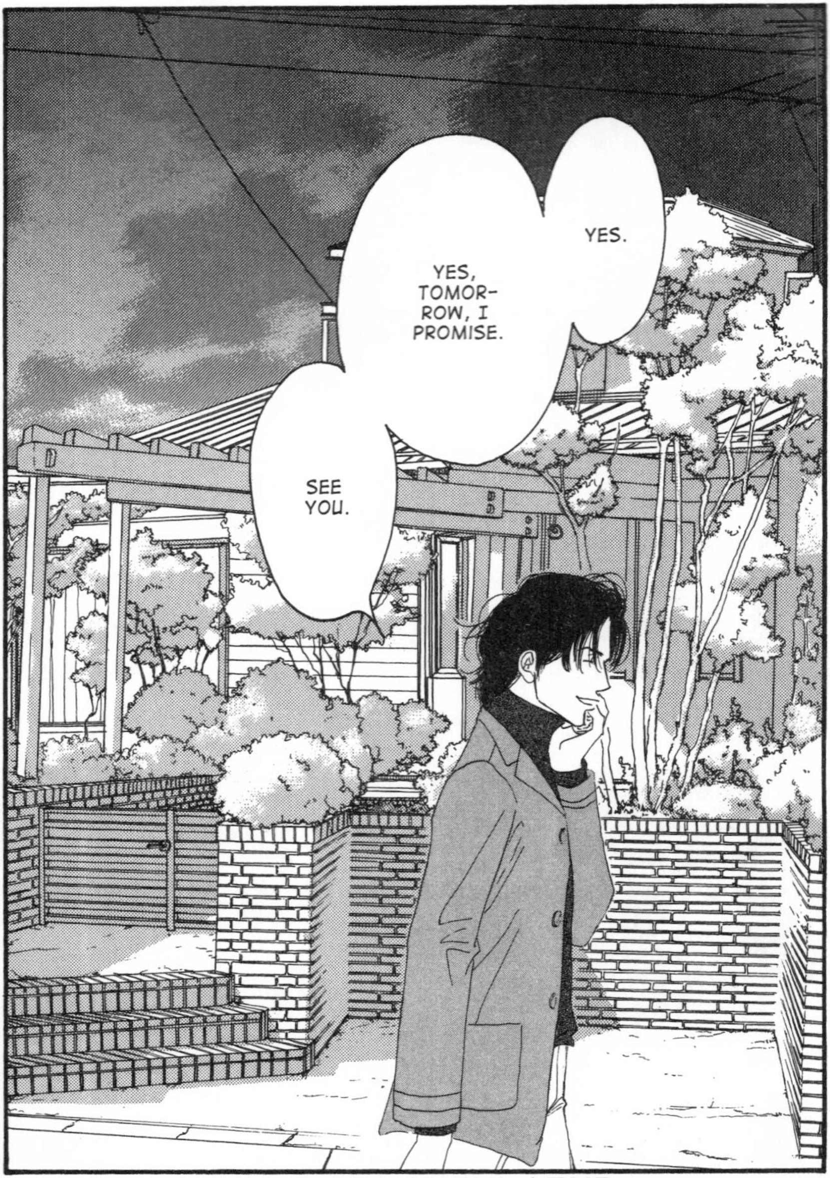
YES.
YES, TOMOR-ROW, I PROMISE.
SEE YOU.

HE WAS BEAUTIFUL / END

The Moon and Sandals Vol. 1

月 と サ ン ダ ル

SEE ME AFTER CLASS!

ISBN# 978-1-56970-802-9   SRP $12.95

june
by DMP

As a newly appointed high school teacher, Ida has yet to gain confidence in his abilities. His insecurity grows worse when he feels someone staring intensely at him during class. The piercing eyes belong to a tall, intimidating student – Koichi Kobayashi. What exactly should Ida do about it? Is it discontent that fuels Kobayashi's sultry gaze… or could it be something else?

Written and Illustrated by:
Fumi Yoshinaga

junemanga.com

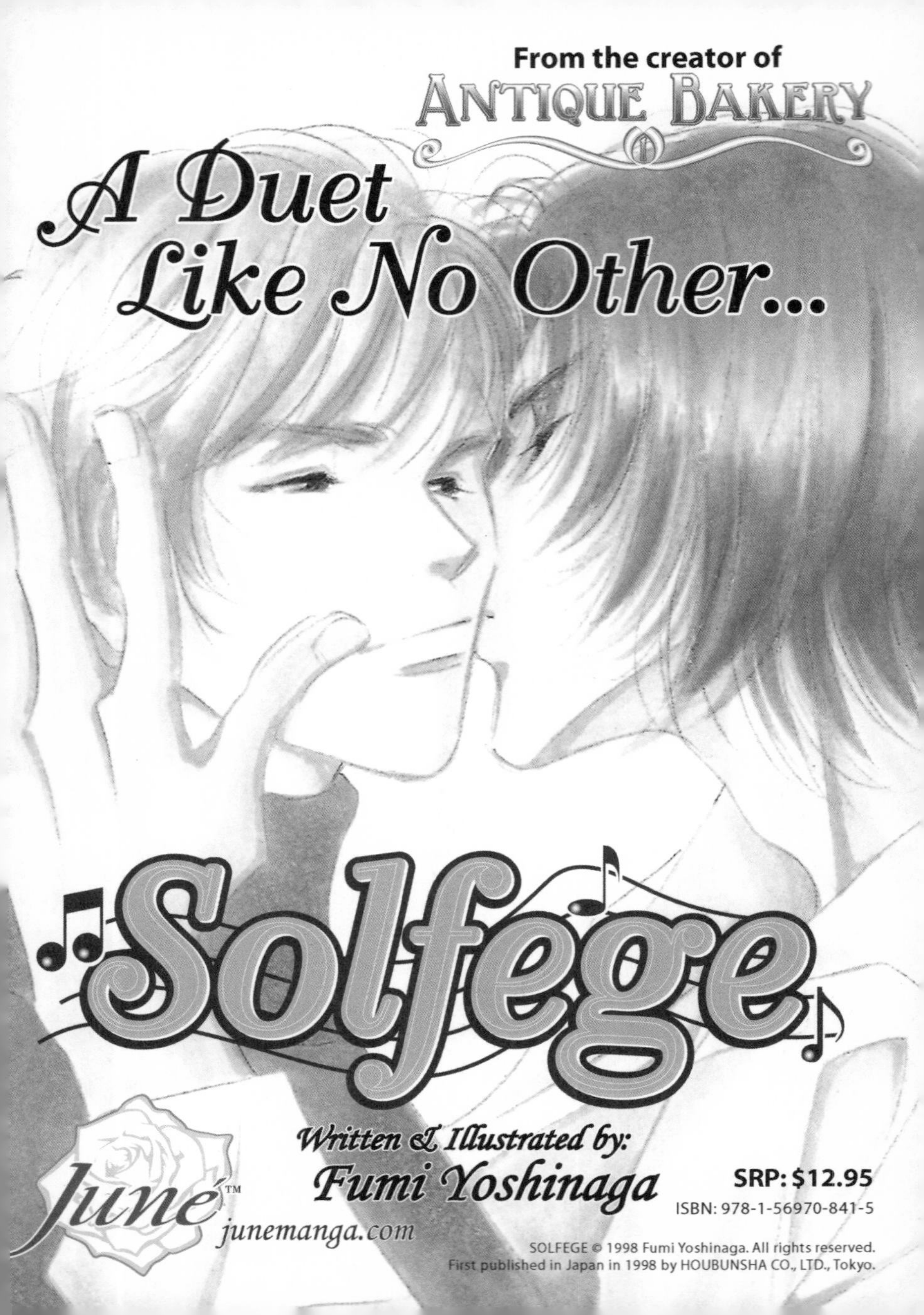
From the creator of
ANTIQUE BAKERY
A Duet Like No Other...
Solfege
Written & Illustrated by:
Fumi Yoshinaga
June™
junemanga.com
SRP: $12.95
ISBN: 978-1-56970-841-5
SOLFEGE © 1998 Fumi Yoshinaga. All rights reserved.
First published in Japan in 1998 by HOUBUNSHA CO., LTD., Tokyo.

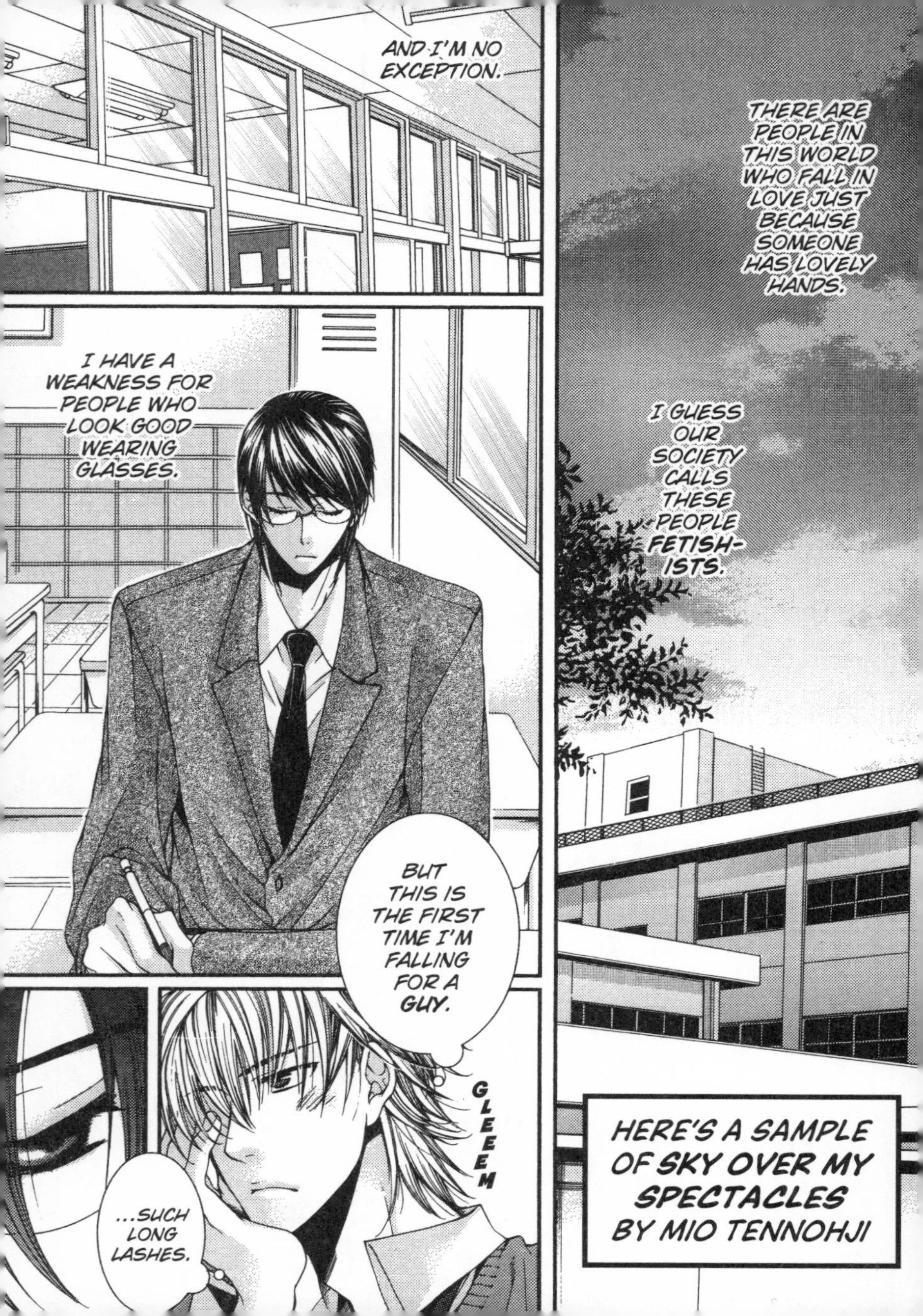
THERE ARE PEOPLE IN THIS WORLD WHO FALL IN LOVE JUST BECAUSE SOMEONE HAS LOVELY HANDS.
I GUESS OUR SOCIETY CALLS THESE PEOPLE FETISH-ISTS.
HERE'S A SAMPLE OF SKY OVER MY SPECTACLES BY MIO TENNOHJI
AND I'M NO EXCEPTION.
I HAVE A WEAKNESS FOR PEOPLE WHO LOOK GOOD WEARING GLASSES.
BUT THIS IS THE FIRST TIME I'M FALLING FOR A GUY.
GLEEEEM
...SUCH LONG LASHES.

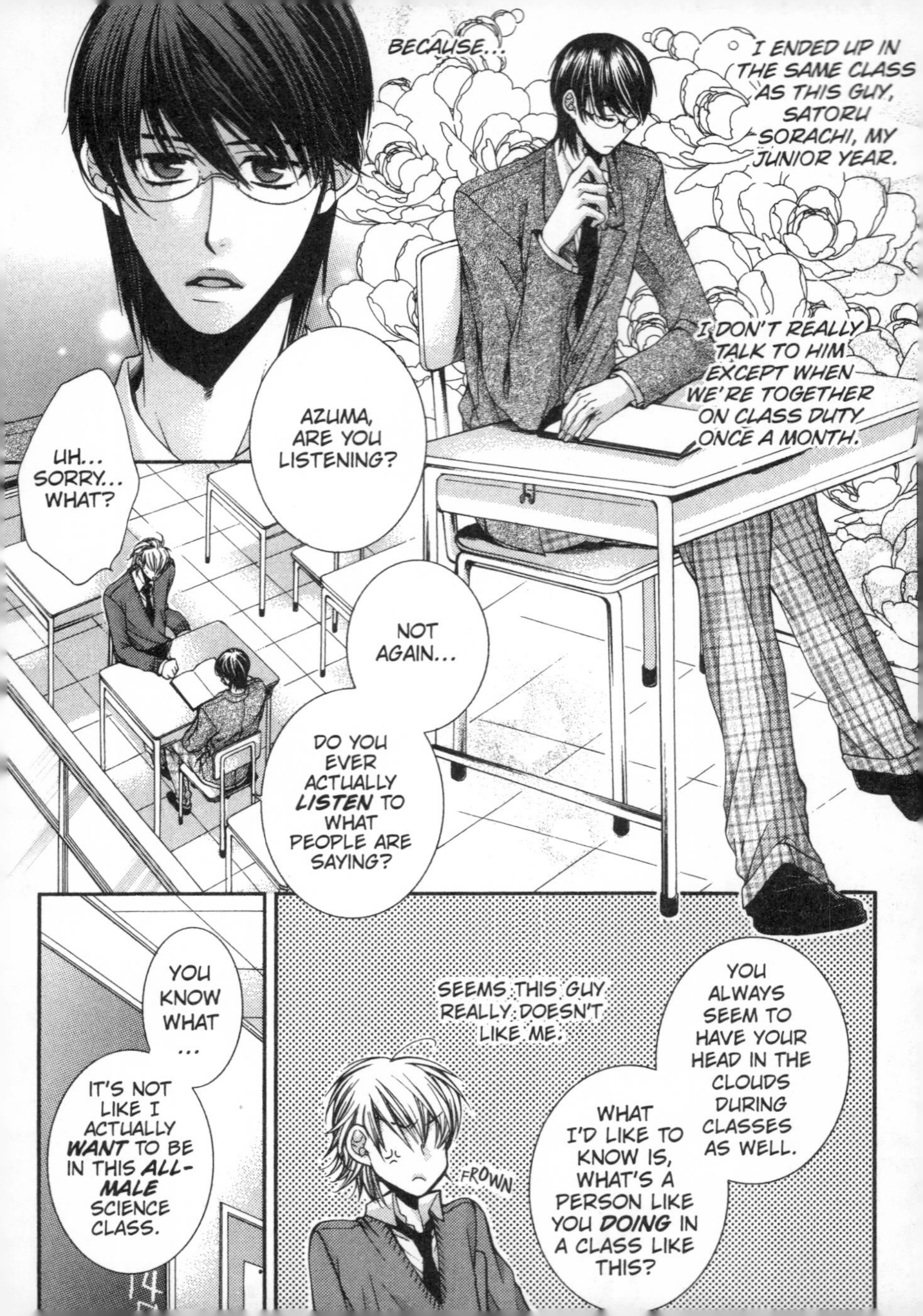
BECAUSE...
I ENDED UP IN THE SAME CLASS AS THIS GUY, SATORU SORACHI, MY JUNIOR YEAR.
I DON'T REALLY TALK TO HIM EXCEPT WHEN WE'RE TOGETHER ON CLASS DUTY ONCE A MONTH.
AZUMA, ARE YOU LISTENING?
UH... SORRY... WHAT?
NOT AGAIN...
DO YOU EVER ACTUALLY *LISTEN* TO WHAT PEOPLE ARE SAYING?
YOU ALWAYS SEEM TO HAVE YOUR HEAD IN THE CLOUDS DURING CLASSES AS WELL.
WHAT I'D LIKE TO KNOW IS, WHAT'S A PERSON LIKE YOU *DOING* IN A CLASS LIKE THIS?
SEEMS THIS GUY REALLY DOESN'T LIKE ME.
FROWN
YOU KNOW WHAT ...
IT'S NOT LIKE I ACTUALLY *WANT* TO BE IN THIS *ALL-MALE* SCIENCE CLASS.

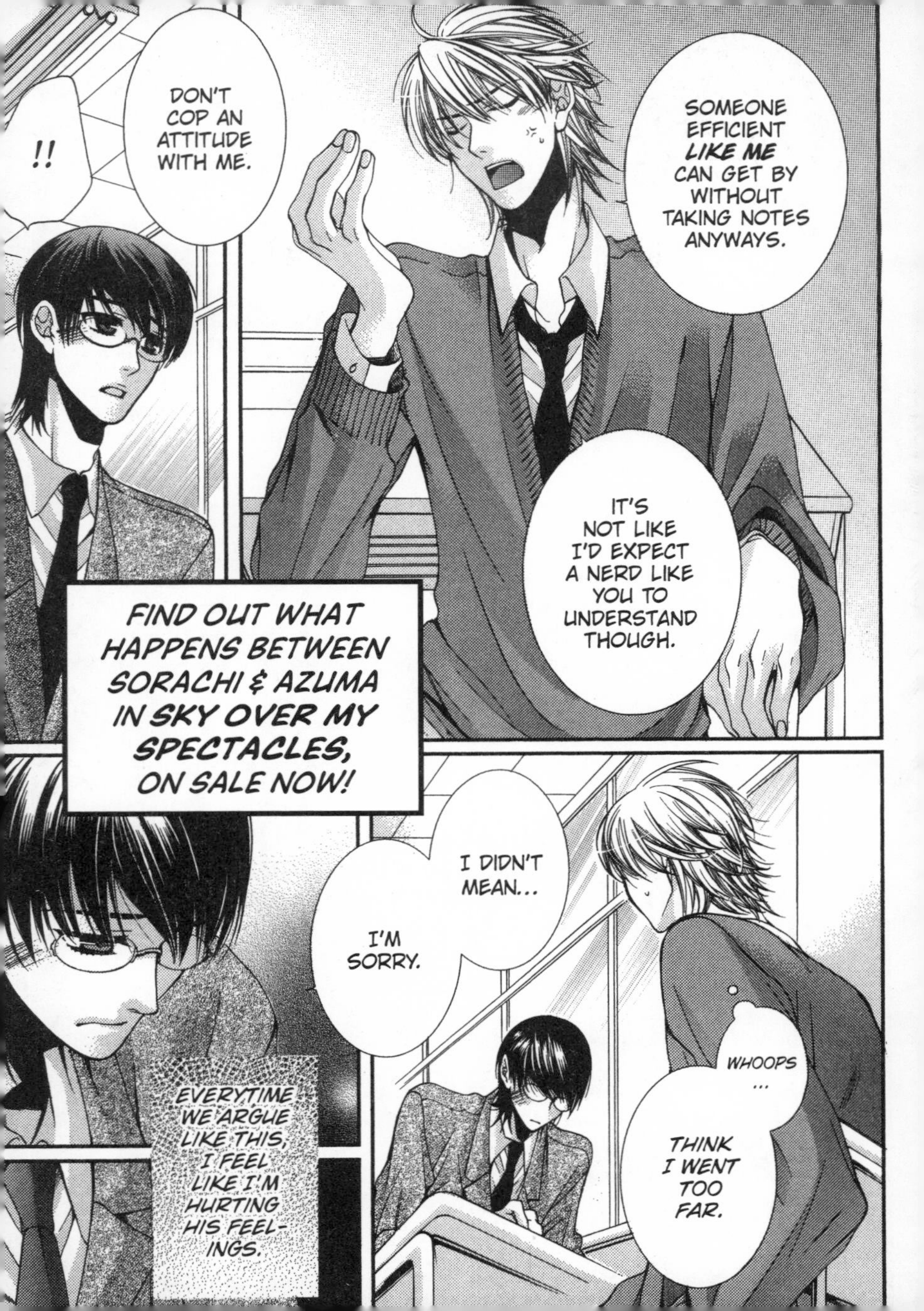
SOMEONE EFFICIENT LIKE ME CAN GET BY WITHOUT TAKING NOTES ANYWAYS.
IT'S NOT LIKE I'D EXPECT A NERD LIKE YOU TO UNDERSTAND THOUGH.
DON'T COP AN ATTITUDE WITH ME.
!!
FIND OUT WHAT HAPPENS BETWEEN SORACHI & AZUMA IN SKY OVER MY SPECTACLES, ON SALE NOW!
I DIDN'T MEAN...
I'M SORRY.
WHOOPS ...
THINK I WENT TOO FAR.
EVERYTIME WE ARGUE LIKE THIS, I FEEL LIKE I'M HURTING HIS FEEL-INGS.

Presents...

Childhood friends and now high school seniors, Hokuto and Yukito will both be living in Yukito's family's house. Hokuto is actually Yukito's first love, and because of that, Yukito's been avoiding him since middle school... Upon meeting again after such a long time, Yukito's heart throbs at Hokuto's now very handsome appearance.

Gifted with intelligence and looks, student council president Azuma confessed his love to Mizuki, and with a little push, they "successfully" started dating. The entire school has even officially recognized their relationship. So you would expect things to be progressing smoothly...

Being with an older lover is hot on just sooo many levels...
Seiji-kun is a novice manga artist. He's also completely addicted to the body of the incredibly beautiful Sono-san, despite the fact that Sono-san is a guy. Is this love?

Sakai Kazuya is a man in love. Unfortunately, the object of his affection is a woman who is only interested in well educated men. Sakai never finished high school, so he enlists the help of her younger brother, Ezumi, to help him pass the entrance exam. Ezumi is happy to help, but his services come with a very steep fee.

801 Media

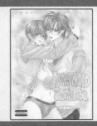

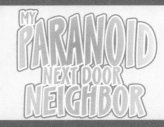

My Paranoid Next Door Neighbor

My Paranoid Next Door Neighbor

by Kazuka Minami

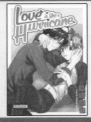

Love is Like a Hurricane

Love is Like a Hurricane

Volume 2

by Tokiya Shimazaki

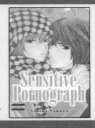

Sensitive Pornograph
Ashika Sakura

Sensitive Pornograph

by Ashika Sakura

SHIUKO KANO

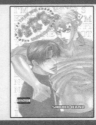

I'M NOT YOUR STEPPIN' STONE

by Shiuko Kano

Liberté! Egalité! Fraternité!...and Love!

Become enraptured by a thrilling and erotic tale of an unlikely pair of lovers during the tumultuous French Revolution. Freed from a high-class brothel, noble-born Jacques becomes a servant in Gerard's house. First seduced by his new master's library, Jacques begins to find himself falling for the man as well... but can their love last in the face of the chaos around them?

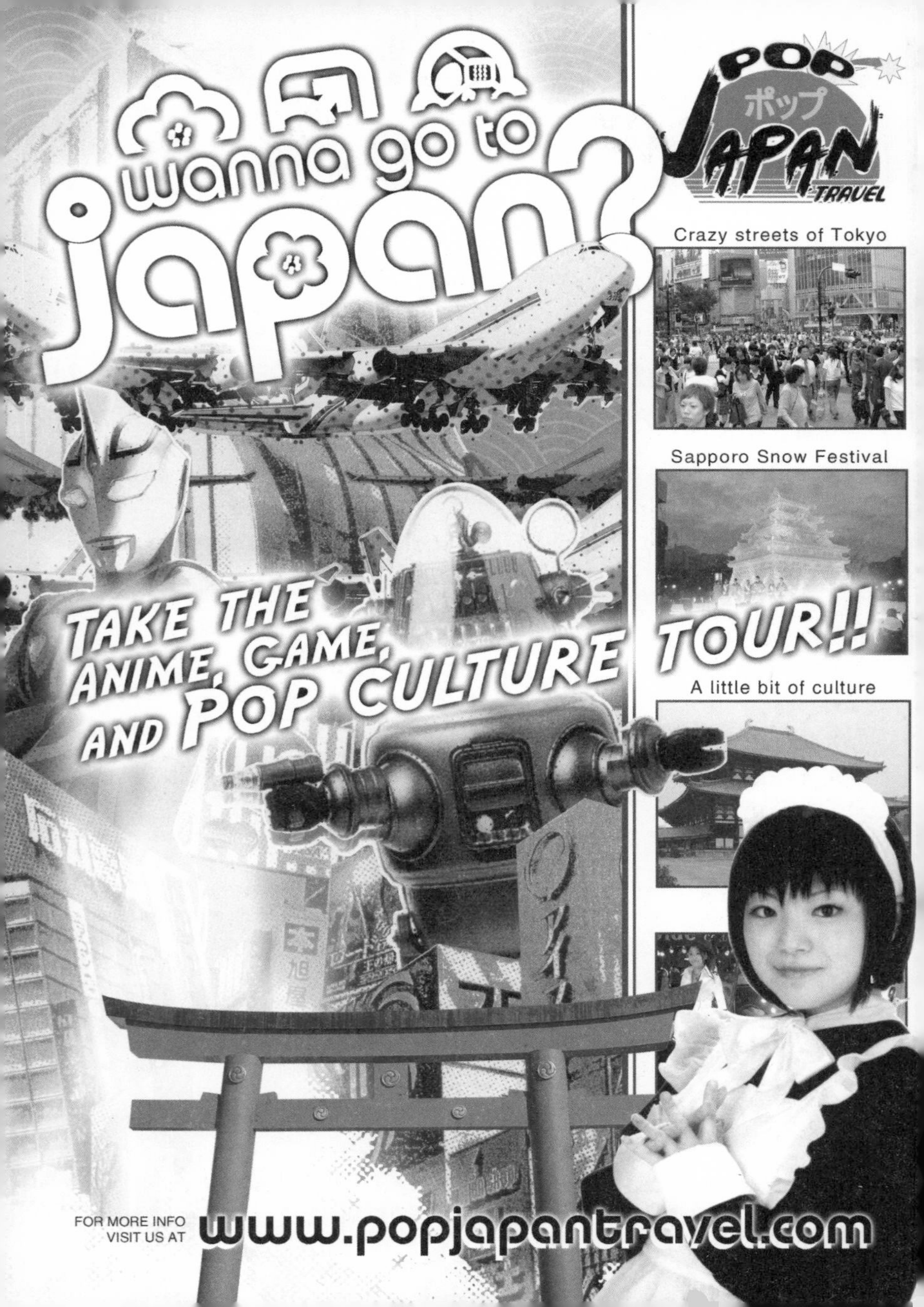
wanna go to
JAPAN?
POP
ポップ
JAPAN
TRAVEL
Crazy streets of Tokyo
Sapporo Snow Festival
A little bit of culture
TAKE THE
ANIME, GAME,
AND POP CULTURE TOUR!!
FOR MORE INFO
VISIT US AT
www.popjapantravel.com

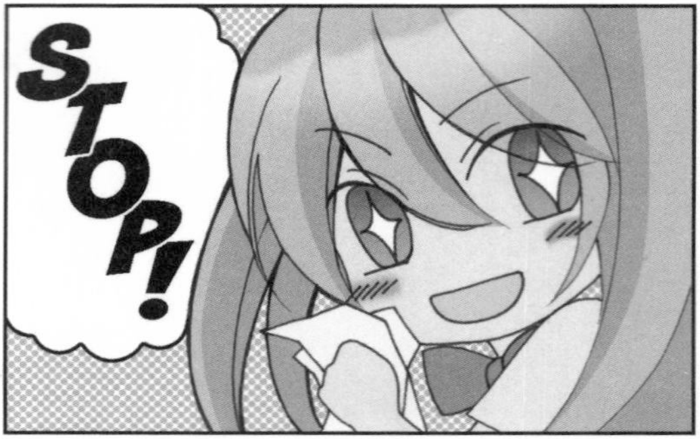
STOP!

801-chan Says!

"Manga reads from right to left, not the usual left to right you may be familar with.

So unless you want to spoil the ending, flip me over and start from the other side!"

TRANSLATION AND EDITOR'S NOTES

SHOUKADO (P.49)
SHOUKADO IS THE TRADITIONAL BLACK-LACQUERED BENTO BOX.

ONIGIRI (P.51)
ONIGIRI IS A RICE BALL USUALLY WRAPPED IN SEAWEED AND STUFFED WITH VARIOUS FILLINGS. IN THIS CASE IT HAS LEEKS AND MISO.

JURIST (P.83)
JURIST IS THE LEADING LAW JOURNAL IN JAPAN.

ONIICHAMA (P.107)
A TERM OF ENDEARMENT THAT REFERS TO AN OLDER BROTHER. CAN ALSO BE USED TO REFER TO AN OLDER MAN THAT THE SPEAKER IS FRIENDLY WITH. A CUTE VERSION OF "ONIISAMA" THAT OUR CHARACTERS USE (SINCE THEY'RE GAY!).

SALTED KOMBU (P. 140)
SALTED KOMBU IS KOMBU SEAWEED MARINATED IN SOY SAUCE WITH ROASTED SESAME SEEDS.

MITSURU HIRATA, LEO MORIMOTO, YASUNORI DANTA, ISAO HASHIZUME, MASAHIKO NISHIUMRA AND UTAMARU KATSURA (P.146)
FAMOUS JAPANESE ACTORS IN THEIR 40S-50S. UTAMARU KATSURA WAS A RAKUGO PERFORMER.

KAISEKI (P.155)
A VERY TRADITIONAL JAPANESE MEAL OFTEN SERVED DURING THE TEA CEREMONY.

GINZA (P.155)
GINZA IS AN EXPENSIVE, UP-SCALE SHOPPING AND BUSINESS DISTRICT IN TOKYO.

DAIGINJOU (P.181)
TOP CLASS SAKE WHERE THE RICE USED IS POLISHED TO LESS THAN 50% OF ITS WEIGHT TO IMPROVE THE PURITY AND FLAVOR.

NAUSICAA (P.218)
THE FAMOUS HAYAO MIYAZAKI FILM ABOUT A PRINCESS, NAUSICAA, WHO DESPERATELY STRUGGLES TO PREVENT TWO WARRING COUNTRIES FROM DESTROYING THEIR DYING PLANET.

Thanks for reading with us!

• 801-chan